Summer 1997 | Volume 17, no. 2 | ISSN: 0276-0045 | ISBN: 1-56478-161-5

THE REVIEW OF CONTEMPORARY FICTION

D1714678

Cover Photos: Margaret Harris (Wilson Harris),
Sue Kylonnen (Alan Burns)

The Review of Contemporary Fiction is published three times a year (February, June, October) by The Review of Contemporary Fiction, Inc., a nonprofit organization located at ISU Campus Box 4241, Normal, IL 61790-4241. ISSN 0276-0045. Subscription prices are as follows:

Single volume (three issues):
    Individuals: $17.00; foreign, add $3.50;
    Institutions: $26.00; foreign, add $3.50.

DISTRIBUTION. Bookstores should send orders to:

University of Chicago Press Distribution Center, 11030 S. Langley Ave., Chicago, IL 60628. Phone 800-621-2736; fax 800-621-8476.

This issue is partially supported by grants from the Illinois Arts Council, a state agency.

Indexed in *American Humanities Index, International Bibliography of Periodical Literature, International Bibliography of Book Reviews, MLA Bibliography,* and *Book Review Index.* Abstracted in *Abstracts of English Studies.*

The Review of Contemporary Fiction is also available in 16mm microfilm, 35mm microfilm, and 105mm microfiche from University Microfilms International, 300 North Zeeb Road, Ann Arbor, MI 48106-1346.

THE REVIEW OF CONTEMPORARY FICTION

FUTURE ISSUES DEVOTED TO: Rikki Ducornet, Raymond Queneau, Carole Maso, Curtis White, Milorad Pavić, Richard Powers, Alexander Trocchi, Ed Sanders, and postmodern Japanese fiction.

BACK ISSUES

Back issues are still available for the following numbers of the *Review of Contemporary Fiction* ($8 each unless otherwise noted):

DOUGLAS WOOLF / WALLACE MARKFIELD
WILLIAM EASTLAKE / AIDAN HIGGINS
ALEXANDER THEROUX / PAUL WEST
CAMILO JOSÉ CELA
CLAUDE SIMON ($15)
CHANDLER BROSSARD
SAMUEL BECKETT
CLAUDE OLLIER / CARLOS FUENTES
JOHN BARTH / DAVID MARKSON
DONALD BARTHELME / TOBY OLSON
BRIGID BROPHY / ROBERT CREELEY / OSMAN LINS
WILLIAM T. VOLLMANN / SUSAN DAITCH / DAVID FOSTER WALLACE

WILLIAM H. GASS / MANUEL PUIG
ROBERT WALSER
JOSÉ DONOSO / JEROME CHARYN
GEORGES PEREC / FELIPE ALFAU
JOSEPH MCELROY
DJUNA BARNES
ANGELA CARTER / TADEUSZ KONWICKI
STANLEY ELKIN / ALASDAIR GRAY
EDMUND WHITE / SAMUEL R. DELANY
MARIO VARGAS LLOSA / JOSEF SKVORECKY

SPECIAL FICTION ISSUE: Fiction by Pinget, Bowles, Mathews, Markfield, Rower, Ríos, Tindall, Sorrentino, Goytisolo, McGonigle, Dukore, Dowell, McManus, Mosley, and Acker
NOVELIST AS CRITIC: Essays by Garrett, Barth, Sorrentino, Wallace, Ollier, Brooke-Rose, Creeley, Mathews, Kelly, Abbott, West, McCourt, McGonigle, and McCarthy
NEW FINNISH FICTION: Fiction by Eskelinen, Jäntti, Kontio, Krohn, Paltto, Sairanen, Selo, Siekkinen, Sund, Valkeapää
NEW ITALIAN FICTION: Interviews and fiction by Malerba, Tabucchi, Zanotto, Ferrucci, Busi, Corti, Rasy, Cherchi, Balduino, Ceresa, Capriolo, Carrera, Valesio, and Gramigna
GROVE PRESS NUMBER: Contributions by Allen, Beckett, Corso, Ferlinghetti, Jordan, McClure, Rechy, Rosset, Selby, Sorrentino, and others
NEW DANISH FICTION: Fiction by Brøgger, Høeg, Andersen, Grøndahl, Holst, Jensen, Thorup, Michael, Sibast, Ryum, Lynggaard, Grønfeldt, Willumsen, and Holm
THE FUTURE OF FICTION: Essays by Birkerts, Caponegro, Franzen, Galloway, Maso, Morrow, Vollmann, White, and others

Individuals receive a 10% discount on orders of one issue and a 20% discount on any order of two or more issues. Postage for domestic shipments is $3.50 for the first issue and 75¢ for each additional issue. For foreign shipments, postage is $4.50 for the first issue and $1.00 for each additional issue. All orders must be paid in U.S. dollars. Send payment to:

Review of Contemporary Fiction, ISU Campus Box 4241,
Normal, IL 61790-4241, *tel* 309 438 7555, *fax* 309 438 7422

Contents

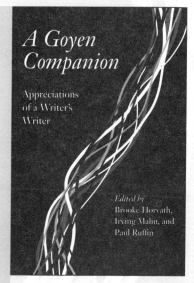

Wilson Harris

photograph by Richard Marshall

Wilson Harris: An Introduction

Joyce Sparer Adler

> Harris has done so much to unblock the Western mind-set. But even now genius is not totally inhibited by all the counter-forces of the world in crisis. Harris may be one sign of a changing wind.
>
> —Kathleen Raine

> All generations are blended: and heaven and earth of one kin . . . the nations and families, flocks and folds of the earth. . . . . All things form one whole.
>
> —Herman Melville, *Mardi*

> The whole crew was one spiritual family living and dying together in a common grave out of which they had sprung again from the same soul and womb as it were. . . .
>
> —Wilson Harris, *Palace of the Peacock*

Wilson Harris is usually described as a Caribbean writer. He should also be thought of as a South American writer. His early years leading government surveys in the interior of Guyana and his contact with the Amerindians—their culture, myths, and condition of being forgotten by the dominant culture—deepened his imagination and concern about all those nameless people in South America who, since the period of the conquistadores, have remained lost in written history. But, above all, Harris has to be thought of as a universal writer, not only because of his concern for all women and men of all times and places but because his imagination plunges into the depths of the earth and also out into the universe. His implied question is: Why must we build bridges between cultures, times, places, earth, and space? Our day is filled with potentialities for a totally destructive human future or a truly creative one. His Christ figures may be of pre-Christian times or non-Christian cultures of any time or land. He speaks of the pagan past from which we all have come. His novels may be set in places other than Guyana, but wherever they are set, Harris has all of us in mind. He has hope that humanity will begin to change and re-create itself. Humanity in his fiction is "at the crossroads."

Although Harris's work gives evidence of enormous reading of the work of others, it is fundamentally unlike that of anyone else. Awakening the imagination of his readers beyond its usual limits, he challenges us to think in entirely new ways. His style—if we can consider anything so honest a "style"—is sometimes breathtaking, uniting all the arts and senses, sometimes bare or scientific. At times there are abrupt and, for a while, puzzling narrative switches. His recent works contain many "analytical dialogues," as Hena Maes-Jelinek calls them. This is true of the passage from *Jonestown*, his new novel, included in this issue. Harris conceives of his novels as epics, a form he believes need not be lost in a remote past. Some critics have divided Harris's work into periods. To me it has always seemed to be one continuing and growing work, never possible to complete. Other critics today think so as well, although Harris's style has changed and his philosophy has become more probing. The reader of Harris's work cannot drift tranquilly along with the narrative. Every word is necessary, almost all are resonant in their suggestiveness. Symbols, charged with new or enriched meanings, reappear. Since each character represents the potentialities of humanity, we who read are participants in the narrative and the thought/feeling of the work.

So Harris's novels need to be read with utter attention. His is an integrated imagery of the arts and sciences. The appeal is to the whole person—inner, outer, mind, heart, "soul"—and to aspects of ourselves of which we are unaware. That is why the novels take the form of dreams, dreams being freer than conventional thinking and feeling. Harris's sense of time—of the past alive in the present and of the seeds of the future in both—is central. Most of his characters have names from the past or are symbolic—e.g., Penelope, Amaryllis, Poseidon, Faust, Bone, Hope, Abram—but their nature has changed to show the negative and positive potentialities of humanity. The implied question is: Which of these will we develop for a changed future? The creative or the destructive? Harris calls his opus a comedy. Although he does have an irrepressible sense of humor, his use of comedy resembles Dante's in *The Divine Comedy*. All the characters, representing humanity, are dead. When they are "resurrected," how will they (we) think, feel, act? None of the characters represents a static extreme of good or evil. In the unforeseeable future things may be different. For example, a representative character, the female Emma, may become archbishop. If there are no true changes, the human race will end—all possibility of resurrection gone. But Harris retains his hope that we will fundamentally change in time, that the "soul," by which he means the hidden unity of humanity, will prevail.

Harris's introduction to literature began when, as a small child, he found books in his dead father's trunk and his mother taught him to read from them. (His introduction to the *Odyssey* came at that early age.) He was later to read them anew and reinterpret them in his own revisionary imagination, investing them with new significance for our crucial time. To help us see differently, unusual things happen: there are marriages between people not only of different places but of different times; people other than he are the writers of the novels—or are they other people within him?

Experiences in life that impressed him deeply have given his novels their startling titles and symbolism, as exemplified by *Palace of the Peacock*, *The Four Banks of the River of Space*, and *Resurrection at Sorrow Hill*. His sensitivity to the oneness of human life, past and present, and to our environment stems from the years in the rain forests and his dialogues with nature. He questions the rocks whose markings tell of their past, mountain ranges that give evidence of the time when they were under oceans, rivers that relate where they have been and why their paths have changed—all giving answers presenting new mysteries. At the center of it all is "the frail heartbeat" of humankind.

At the age of thirty-eight, Harris left what was at that time British Guyana to go to London. He has lived for more than thirty years in the United Kingdom. He and his poet and playwright wife Margaret, born in Scotland, live in Essex. They have traveled extensively since his first novel, *Palace of the Peacock,* was published in the sixties. Besides his twenty novels, all put out by Faber and Faber, he has written much poetry, one short play, numerous critical essays, the texts of talks abroad, and a long book of criticism published by Greenwood Press, *The Womb of Space: The Cross-Cultural Imagination*. (Note: the word *cross-cultural* implying bridges between cultures; the word *multicultural* often implies treating cultures as unbridged islands.) This theme is the main emphasis in his work. He has been invited to speak and has taught briefly in many parts of the world. In 1992 he received Italy's Mondello Prize for Fiction. He has been awarded Guyana's main literature prize. In the U.S. he has lectured at Yale, the Universities of Buffalo, Texas, and Iowa, among others, and has been a California Regents Professor.

Wilson Harris, like Melville, can be viewed from apparently endlessly different angles. The essays here are different and yet enrich each other. They are part of the ongoing project of opening up the work of this most universal and most human of authors.

Quetzalcoatl and the Smoking Mirror
(Reflections on Originality and Tradition)

Wilson Harris

There are conflicting legends about the parentage of Quetzalcoatl. One is inclined to say he was an orphan. And the legend of the "orphan song of ancient Mexico"—upon which I shall comment later—may well confirm this.

Some of his putative ancestors wore the mask of Light and of the Sky. The feathers of the quetzal bird signified the Sky. Others wore the mask of the Earth. The scales of the wise serpent signified the Earth.

Quetzalcoatl was revered by his people as a god. But on looking into the Smoking Mirror he was confounded by a prophecy of the death of gods. Strange prophecy. For it was as if gods constituted a succession of densities or veils between humanity and an everlasting, unfathomable creator.

The Smoking Mirror symbolized those veils that lay between oneself and the creator. The veils were everywhere, in a tree one took for granted as passive or lifeless furniture, in landscapes, riverscapes, creatures, natures, one took for granted.

Quetzalcoatl was stricken by a kind of cosmic terror. It wasn't only the veils in the Smoking Mirror. It was a sudden upsurge of guilt. He had contemplated—if not actually performed—incest with his royal sister.

Incest, in this context, was not necessarily a physical act but a symbolic, protective, kith and kin cloak over a privileged family whom an immortal god seeks to embrace absolutely as his property. The chosen sister, or representative of the family, becomes a pawn of immortality.

What does one mean by a "pawn of immortality"? Does not immortality imply true freedom? A pawn is unfree. If immortality does not imply a true freedom then the soul of freedom may need to rid itself of the net of one-sided immortality, so one-sided, so reserved for those who are chosen or elected to receive it, that it serves as a weapon to extinguish others who are foreign or outside of the chosen family.

Let me put it this way: when Quetzalcoatl looked into the Smoking Mirror, and into the densities or veils that lay between himself and an unfathomable creator, he felt a wholly different compassion for the world than entertained by incestuous love. He touched his sister and she became less of a pawn. Or let me put it differently. As a pawn of immortality she had overlooked the ruses of Lord Death and how subject she was to such a commander of human and animal destiny. Was Lord Death an immortal? The plaster of vanity and incestuous love slipped from her eyes. Lord Death was the commander of all things and species and yet a very strange, unpredictable thing happened. Death appeared to break into plural masks to reveal an enigma of Soul.

Here is an important seed of epic. Eurydice was a pawn of the Lord of the Under World, Lord Death. Orpheus sought to bring her back into the life of consciousness . . . I shall come back to this later. It is an important strand. But now let us return to plural masks and to the enigma of the Soul.

The Soul is a solitary wanderer yet steeped in plural masks it may pluck from the fractured body of Death itself into curiously living sculptures, curiously living paintings, curiously living Word or ventriloquism of Spirit.

This incredible humour (the Soul has a profound sense of humour), this incredible grace, in which the Soul leans upon fractured Death for its plural masks, is pertinent to the paradoxical life of the Soul as it wanders everywhere. For then the Soul implies what a vocation in the imaginative arts should mean. Such vocation should wrestle with distinctions between conquest, absolute conquest, privileged by Death, and a breakage of Death's commandments through the mystery of living arts.

Any attempt within ourselves to gain enlightenment from the Smoking Mirror must take the Soul's humour, the Soul's unique comedy, into account. The Smoking Mirror brings through and beyond cosmic terror a sensation of being plural, of a capacity within ourselves to wear many masks, each mask possessing its *partial* eye that glances into a core of mystery at the heart of complex traditions. Singular bias structures us to bypass the rhythms of plurality. Singular bias is *not* the solitariness of the dreaming Soul in space . . .

Let us imagine a fall-out from the Smoking Mirror across two thousand years into solitariness of Soul, solitariness in our bewildering universe . . . How would that fall-out clothe the Cartesian ego that underpins the mindset of Europe? The Cartesian dictum runs *I think therefore I am.* It sounds familiar as though a brooding solitariness of Soul is to be equated with the biased ego!

But when I contemplate brooding solitariness I have in mind neither the Freudian Ego nor the Cartesian Ego but a gnostic concept in which one is, as it were, lifted above one's age, upon an imaginary constellation (such as I visualize in my novel *Resurrection at Sorrow Hill*) in order to steep oneself in a theatre, so to speak, of plural masks that bear on the travail of humanity—in an orchestration of ancient and modern histories and characterisations and imageries as well revolving, so to speak, around a transitive principle or musical chord.

Plural masks are *not* the same as Cartesian dualism. Plural masks imply a living cosmos in all its grain and particularity that may appear to sleep, to be dormant, but is susceptible to riddling proportions of eruptive life. Unity then is paradox, the core of paradox. Unity appears dormant, passive, but may be fired into rhythms of differentiation that make us aware of inequalities, jealousies, passions, that may bedevil our world absolutely unless—by stages as it were—a transfiguration of appearances occurs, appearances we take for granted.

I mention this in order to bring into play a glimpsed goal, a glimpse—little more do we have—of the enormous potential to be realised in the rebirth of original epic within the suppressed fire of the Smoking Mirror, suppressed rhythms and music as well.

Resurrection at Sorrow Hill drew me back to *Palace of the Peacock* and to the music-maker Carroll who reappears at the end of the book within a corridor in ancient El Dorado. He whistles through a window in the palace, *a window that becomes a medium of transitive density.* I emphasize *density* and *transitive*, as though a *chord* exists within the window—within the density of the window (let us say)—the window becomes a medium of *transitive density* as the chord fires, so to speak, and Carroll's whistle is transformed as it passes through the window. It is transformed into an eruption of majestic music within the text of reality. The transitive chord within the window, within a body of density, fires—as I said before—and thus, coincident with the music, appears the lightning bark of a tree.

Music in the text is simultaneous with the incandescent imagination. I am told that this kind of simultaneity, in which density is a transitive medium into music and the incandescent imagination, is consistent with quantum mechanics, but *Palace* was written in 1959 (published in 1960) and I knew nothing of quantum mechanics at the time.

Indeed though I have read *Quantum Reality* by the physicist Nick Herbert, and have been excited by it, and what I discern as validating premises to certain things I have been doing in my fiction, the truth is that I did not see, in Nick Herbert's thesis, the role of densities as transitive media planted in nature. The matter truly came home to me on the publication of *Resurrection at Sorrow Hill* at the end of 1993. At the core of *Resurrection at Sorrow Hill* one finds the eruption of music in the text simultaneous with the incandescent imagination. It was this that suddenly enabled me to return to *Palace* and speak of it now as I have done.

I find now that I could give many examples of this phenomenon in the work I have written within the past four decades. With hindsight they are abundantly clear to me. Densities are not uniform. They vary, they vary with multiple strands, multiple transitive chords within them. I could give many examples but I trust the essential point is made. One thing that I should add is this: transitive densities may instil themselves in fiction that is shaped in "the mind of the imaginative writer who has been deeply affected by the life of primordial landscapes, tall rapids, burning savannahs, rainforest rocks imprinted with the markings of ancient cultures, markings that resemble extra-human messages from the gods who write in fire and wind and water."

In earthquake-prone regions buildings are now being constructed that seek to incorporate in themselves rhythms that may respond to, and thereby withstand, the shock of a quake that may last only thirty seconds but is able to do immense damage to conventional architectures. The daring architectures that are beginning to come into play have a long way to go. I tend to visualize such architecture, however new, as hinged, let us say, to a primordial cradle as the earth moves and the ground shakes. The moving earth, the shaking ground, is akin to a primordial cradle that takes us back to riverscapes and the geology of landscapes, the genesis of the architecture of the earth itself as it turns in space.

Through the eyes of my own fiction I see transitive chords, implicit music, instilled or orchestrated into a building. When the earthquake comes, the building releases its transitive chords, there is hidden music in the cells of the building, a concert is created between the mind of architecture and the primordial instinct in the quake, the sailing plates in the earth.

For an instant, while the quake lasts, a new space or dimension in the mind of architecture is realized that unravels and absorbs the energies in the living earth.

It is no doubt unusual to suggest that modern architecture needs to conceive of itself as hinged to a primordial cradle; I do so now to indicate a link between architecture and the multi-dimensionalities of epic; epic—unlike conventional fiction—is steeped in upper worlds, under worlds, and in a theatre of plural masks plucked from apparent catastrophe and from histories around the globe.

In the light of all I have said it is interesting to note Iris Murdoch's statement—or that of the narrator in her book *Under the Net*—that "the present age was not one in which it was possible to write an epic."

Needless to say I do not agree with this but it tells us something of the state of mind amongst leading intellectuals and writers.

Obviously epic is a misunderstood term; it is misinterpreted by the mass media which judge any large-scale Hollywood performance to be epic. Epic is *not* Hollywood *Ben-Hur* or Hollywood *Moses*.

Epic is an *arrival* in an architecture of space that is *original* to our age, an *arrival* in multi-dimensionality that alerts us to some kind of transfiguration of appearances—in parallel with science and architecture—that implies energies akin to extra-human faculties inserted into the fabric of history.

I say "arrival in" to make a distinction from academic *descriptions* of epic as something that belongs to the past and is now a museum-text to be imitated in the theatre or in performances of virtuosity . . .

To arrive in a tradition that appears to have died is complex renewal and re-visionary momentum *sprung from originality and the activation of primordial resources within a living language.* We arrive backwards even as we voyage forwards. This is the phenomenon of simultaneity in the imagination of times past and future, a future that renews time in its imaginary response to gestating resources in *the womb of the present and the past.* It is unlike the linear biases that prevail in conventional fiction.

To arrive in a place where we are not brings into play transitive chords within densities, transitive dimensionalities that unlock doors within the body of language itself. Arrival then differs from photographic description.

Arrival then is a concert between unfathomable psyche and place-in-depth, place displaced, recovered in the living Word.

Photographic descriptions of places, like academic descriptions of past traditions relegated to the museum, are useful, needless to say. But they do not offer us the criteria we need when we are challenged by the rhythms of creative work that give a re-visionary sensation of the life of epic, the transitive chords of epic that bear on many activities.

The impossibility of writing epic in our age—innermost epic as distinct from virtuoso performance, epic that alters the surfaces of language—may *not* be an impossibility at all . . . Rather claims of impossibility may suggest difficulty in assessing—with an open mind—the emergence of such epic, difficulty in arriving within the medium of a new criticism that does not take the genesis of fiction for granted, the genesis of science for granted.

True there is a vested interest in the novel-form of the eighteenth and nineteenth centuries, a novel-form that was a response to social patterns and classes one associates with the Industrial Revolution.

Indisputably that novel-form has exercised considerable dominance around the globe within the expansion of European empires. But such an expansion involves many cultures and began long before the eighteenth century. It is not linked solely to the Industrial Revolution; its contours and horizons may be traced much farther back than the eighteenth century through the inception of the Middle Passage into ancient Rome, Macedonia, Persia, ancient Greece and India. The Caribbean poet Kamau Brathwaite writes in his long and remarkable poem *X/Self:*

Rome burns
and our slavery begins.

Such an expansion may need, does need, I think, to be considered and reconsidered for different clues it offers us about alternative fictions and latent cross-culturalities between diverse ages, past and present, that bear on imaginative truth.

Carnival, in its most subversive and regenerative essence, gained new ground within South America, Central America, and Caribbean cultures that suffered abysmally at the hand of the conquistadores who came into the Americas on the heels of Christopher Columbus.

The gestation of New World epic arguably began in a peculiar and terrifying way. We *arrive* in New World epic when we experience or re-imagine the earthquake of conquest as if conquest is native to our very bones.

The Spanish conquistadores came to the ancient Americas under the banner of Christ, Christ the law-giver and saviour of Mankind. And then—despite ruling assumptions of law and salvation—they engineered the massacre and the decimation of the American Indians to acquire land and gold, a process of decimation that continued under wave after wave of settlers and colonisers. Conquest is native when our bones begin to question every skeleton gateway into the New World.

The life of the Carnival skeleton introduces us, in surprising and surprised ways, to ourselves. Our antecedents were the victims of conquest, our antecedents were paradoxically also victors who gobbled up land and gold. We are all, in that sense, dialectially mixed and impure. And this blend of victor and victim arouses us to the meaning of Death within Carnival, Death which wears the mask of global commander, global conquistador, Death—on the other hand—which is sensitive to the terror of the crushed, the victimized, Death which brings merciful release from pain.

It is logical to assume that the tenderness, originality, compassion that seeps through—almost subconsciously—the blood-stained fabric of history into the margins, the corners, of South American and Central American arts (as I witnessed these when I visited Mexico, Easter 1972) would have been a total impossibility (Christ would have been totally negated) had Death, the conquistador, triumphed absolutely.

The ancient animal riddles that bear on messengers of Soul within pre-Columbian traditions opened the body of conquest, touched on the mystery of Christ the tiger which springs in the New Year (if I may adapt a line from T. S. Eliot), as much as on the mystery of Quetzalcoatl, the winged serpent which flies in space, to release at the heart of a cruel masquerade of power, a disturbing, unsuspected heresy that I read as one of the cornerstones of recovered epic that bears on our age.

A word about animal riddles. Animal beings associated with divinities or divine heroes or god-men is a crossing of frontiers that seem absolute in their own right. The animal state seems absolute in its own right. The divine state seems absolute in its own right. When absolute frontiers, enshrined into absolute separation of animal being and divine being, are broken, a revisionary momentum is set up within the depth resources of language to question the surfaces of language and the reification of conquest in the name of the divine. When we perceive an animal ingredient in the divine, we find ourselves steeped in plural masks that break an addiction to power, that break a hubris or proclivity to enslave others whom we deem inferior creatures. In breaking the hubris, so to speak, of the ruling or commanding state we break a commandment, we commit a heresy.

The crossing of frontiers, or heresy I have in mind, in this instance, is *sacramentalized adultery* between the creaturely spouse, or wife of the conquistador Lord Death, and a fractured epic hero in the extremities of Western civilisation in South America. In *Resurrection at Sorrow Hill* I call the fractured hero Hope and I name the wife of the commander Death (Death spelt with an apostrophe D'eath) Butterfly. *Butterfly*—the spouse or wife of Mr. Universe with a gun (another title for commander Death or D'eath)— *is, as her creaturely name implies, a vessel of all species. She is human and creature, animal and soul, angel and naive maiden. A drop of her angelic blood gives oceanic value to the voyages of Christ the tiger and Quetzalcoatl the winged serpent.*

To put it as simply as I can: we are involved in an orchestration of imageries divine and human, creator and creature, Death and complex liberation from death-dealing regimes that embrace humanity in many areas of the globe. This desire for liberation is instinctive to ancient epic but it needs to be grasped differently, realized differently, it needs re-visionary capacities in our own age.

Let us recall that, in an ancient epic, Eurydice—the wife of the music-player Orpheus—is plucked away from him by Death, the Lord of the Under World. Orpheus is given a chance, it seems, to recover Eurydice but disobeys a command *not* to look back. Eurydice is snatched back into the Under World. In this I see a prime motif of the unfinished genesis of the imagination, of a necessity written into the collective unconscious to return to, and take up, the theme of Orpheus differently from the way it is enshrined as a museum text in the humanities. *Orpheus disobeys a command.* Intuitively, subconsciously—I would venture to say—he glimmeringly perceived, when he looked back, that Eurydice would remain a pawn of the Under World if her apparent release had been sanctioned or sealed by Lord Death himself or itself. Something more radical and disturbing within death-dealing and conquistadorial regimes was gestating within layers of the unconscious.

In *Resurrection at Sorrow Hill* Butterfly is *not* Hope's wife. Eurydice was Orpheus' wife. Butterfly is Death's (or D'eath's) wife. Butterfly is a spouse that has been cruelly used by a death-dealing establishment, by the Lord of the quake and the Under World. Hope's adulterous affair with her is conducted in fear and trembling. Even when he outwits D'eath and brings Butterfly back to life, after he dreams they have both been shot and killed by the jealous commander, he knows that Death is still at his heels. Interwoven with his fear of D'eath or Lord Death runs a multi-layered perception that the surfaces of the language, the commanding surfaces of the language, are creatively fractured to expose an ambivalence in Death that is *not* apparent in the traditional frame of the Orpheus/Eurydice legend.

In the sacramentalized adultery between Hope and Butterfly, Death or D'eath is exposed, the seal is partially broken into ambivalence, ambivalent majesty, ambivalent despair, and an orchestration of histories and imageries around the globe erupts, as a consequence, into other figures and other characters.

There is Christopher D'eath for example. The mystery of the resurrection of Christ is implicit in the Christopher faculty in D'eath or Death. Thus D'eath breaks into two and grows capable of remorse. He desires that his abused spouse should be lifted into another realm and tenderly embraced by Hope. But that desire cannot be forced in the fiction, in the evolving life and language of the fiction, it is too far-reaching to be forced, for force after all is the faculty of conquest. The desire to release his spouse is unmistakably active but it cannot be forced. Let us say it gestates and looms as a significant element that bears on the future . . .

What emerges I find is that D'eath (or Death) is broken into a series of plural masks. His command over all species is questioned very deeply in fictionalisations of the heart of nature within the unfinished genesis of the Imagination. As a consequence D'eath succumbs to despair. He seeks to extinguish himself, he seeks to commit suicide, but fails and is left with bullet marks—the stigmata of the bullet on his face. Those markings have the imprint of a creaturely Spider.

One of the issues that the fiction raises—in my attempt to raise to your attention provisional criteria that may help us into an appreciation of the re-birth of original epic—is that the resurrection of Christ has been fallaciously aligned to the *conquest* of Death or to a structured immortality replete with one-sided bias.

There is an apparently commonsense equation between resurrection and the conquest of Death, conquering Death, to conquer Death.

But *uncommon sense* surely tells us that to stress *conquest* is to succumb to the very monster we fear; *Death's vocabulary is rooted in a predatory coherence,* in ruthless competition, in cannibalistic plans of living and of industry that may promote the downfall of others. Such, we are told, is the real world.

To conquer Death involves us in a cruel irony, it involves us in crusades, in inquisitions that burn men's bodies, kill heretics and infidels, in order to save their souls (a wholly mistaken notion of the solitariness of the Soul which is intent—when it paints constellations in the heavens to endorse remoteness and solitariness (as has been the practice in ancient cultures from times immemorial)—on steeping itself even as it appears to levitate in space, in a rich diversity in theatres of the enigma of truth on planet Earth).

That the conquest of Death, the conquering of Death, is equated with the resurrection of Christ tells us much about ruling premises civilisation plasters on the surfaces of language; such ruling premises upon language, such predatory coherence, tell us much—when we reflect upon it deeply—of the closed mind of the conquistadores who raped a continent under the banner of Christ.

Original epic in our age, I would hope, begins to move the enigma of the resurrection into new dimensions that we need to nurse within the complex life of the Imagination; original epic may help us to take up afresh the burden of an uncertain but far-reaching rescue of the universal spouse (animal spouse, creaturely spouse, human spouse in all its pigmentations and differences) that death-dealing ideologies and regimes marry and imprison around the globe . . .

The work of writers such as Juan Rulfo and Octavio Paz, both Mexican, may carry indirect thresholds into the re-birth of original epic. The seed of epic, however buried or remote, may also reside in some of the fictions of Angela Carter with their animal messengers from other worlds. I think the possibility also exists in the work of two Guyanese-born writers, by whom I am considerably impressed, namely Pauline Melville and Fred D'Aguiar.

One has to wait and see. There are other imaginative writers whose work you may begin to approach through recent critical studies such as Vera Kutzinski's *Against the American Grain* (published by Johns Hopkins University Press), Nathaniel Mackey's *Discrepant Engagement: Dissonance, Cross-Culturality and Experimental Writing* (published by Cambridge University Press), and *The Repeating Island* by the Cuban writer Antonio Benitez Rojo (published by Duke University Press).

Space does not permit me to go into these and I must emphasize that these studies are not engaged with a direct approach to the issues I have raised about epic, but in going against the grain—as they all do—they heighten our attention to masking and musicality and cross-culturality.

For instance Nathaniel Mackey, a very gifted, imaginative writer, and a scrupulous scholar, discusses in illuminating ways what he calls "the genius of black music" as it has affected various texts by twentieth-century American writers.

Let me quote what he says of the "orphan song of ancient Mexico." He writes—"In divergence and dissent one hears the voice of the orphan, the outsider, the excluded. Music and the writing that embraces it are something like the *icno-cuicatl* or orphan song of ancient Mexico which, as Gordon Brotherson explains, 'explores feelings of cosmic abandonment and the precariousness of mortal life before the unknown.' "

Let me tease a clue from this that may fruitfully bear on epic.

I am thinking of the orphaned state—if I may so put it—of the Soul of tradition, the way tradition is enshrined in museum-texts, the way the orphaned Soul of tradition may open our minds to a state of cosmic abandonment that humanity experiences despite technologies of progress. Also the promises of tradition, whether in scriptures or elsewhere, remain unfulfilled. The disciples of Christ may have been promised the end of the world, and the descent of the kingdom of heaven, in their lifetime. The promise remains unfulfilled. And yet the potency of such a promise seems to imply a hidden kingdom committed to universal compassion and justice: a hidden kingdom unable to disclose itself to a divided humanity plagued by closed minds that continue to disfigure the body of civilisation in their pursuit of fundamental causes enshrined into terrorising absolutes.

I repeat: the promises of ancient epic, like ancient scriptures, remain unfulfilled. I have already commented on Eurydice in ancient Orphic legend. I suggested that Orpheus' disobedience may be re-read or re-interpreted afresh as unconscious or subconscious insight into Eurydice's fate as a *continuing pawn* of sovereign Death if her release is sanctioned within a frame of absolute rules and commandments issued by the identical regime that promises to liberate her. Is such liberation a genuine liberation? When Orpheus looks back he disobeys. And my interpretation of that is that *subconsciously* he knows that Eurydice's liberation would have been a hypocrisy, a fraud. She would not have been free . . .

In other words the absolute commandment issued by a sovereign death-dealing regime is partial (when seen in another context or light) and that partiality is threaded into inequalities, into injustices, harboured by one-sided traditions. You may recall how Virgil—who had laboured for Dante in guiding him through the inferno and the purgatorio—was unjustly excluded from the paradiso. He was deemed a pagan because his address lay in a pre-Christian age. How one-sided is such a paradiso? Does it not need a profound, re-visionary momentum of the frame of language in which it is cast?

Once such deep-seated inequalities remain within traditions, the Soul of tradition itself is orphaned, it suffers cosmic abandonment in that it *appears* to nurture absolutes which polarise humanity irreconcilably. Unless such absolutes can yield their partialities within plural masks that question themselves, the Soul is cut adrift and may lose its potency to arbitrate, with profoundest creativity, between divisions in humanity. The Soul then appears to endorse a state of affairs in which cultures languish between worlds. Sometimes they are seized or cajoled or bribed with promises that can never be fulfilled.

Perhaps this throws some light on the fate of the Mesopotamian giant Gilgamesh who was promised immortality. He secured the plant of immortality but fell asleep upon the bank of a river. A chthonic or Under World god arose and consumed the plant.

Let us venture to re-interpret what happened. I would suggest that an obscure feud, obscure rage, inserted itself into the inequalities of Mesopotamian epic and this cancelled the promise of an immortality inevitably and tragically steeped with bias. Gilgamesh does have a peculiar limbo immortality nevertheless that may throw some light on the anguish of genius, the orphaned state of the Soul as it confronts a demiurge in the feuding depths and in the feuding heights of creation, a demiurge that may claim to be its parent, a parent that may be its enemy.

A deeply troubling and important question now arises. Let us look at it through the eyes of a gnostic Christian. For gnosis, or inner knowledge—the knowledge of the solitary (of whom I spoke earlier)—is said to pre-date Christianity and to be as old as epic. For the gnostic (the gnostic Christian or the gnostic pagan who dreams of extra-human parents interwoven with cosmic enmity and abandonment in Orphic song as much as in the song of ancient Mexico) the consent of a parent-creator (who may reconcile the vagaries and contradictions of parentage) is an invaluable quest within the language of time. Indeed it is essential if the Soul of tradition is to resume its voyage out of the past and into the unknown future.

All well and good to take the future for granted in a purely materialistic way in which one day's greed is another day's greed but when the future opens itself to the Soul of traditions it cannot be taken for granted.

Each day is a voyage into forbidden realms, a conversation with messengers of deity, with angels, in the Blakean sense. Each day is a reckoning with veils or densities that lie between us and a God with whom we have at times a sensation of inner rapport, or of whom we may have some inner gnosis or knowledge, but who remains unfathomable and beyond description; who seems to imply at times our orphaned predicament.

Gnosis then is steeped in densities and bodies of knowledge through which we hope to pass—changed in heart and conscience and mind—into unknown, parenting futures that may bring justice at last.

Here we touch the core of the problem. What is the distinction between consent (the consent of a parent-creator, consent to adventure into the genius of the future in concert with the re-opening of the deepest, gravest, unfulfilled promises to Mankind, implicit in ancient traditions) *and* commandments one associates with jealous gods of Upper Worlds and Under Worlds who have become prey to traumatic inequalities in the womb of tradition?

Such jealousies and rages remain as pertinent to us, as they were to the fate of Gilgamesh, when the chthonic or Under World serpent cancelled the promise of immortality issued presumably by some other oceanic or rival commander of rivers and tides.

Look around our world. Catholics rage at Protestants; equally a high-ranking Protestant minister—I won't give his name—recently claimed that the Catholic Pope was the anti-Christ. A year or two ago Hindus were intent on killing Muslims in order to secure the site of an ancient temple in India. Christians and Muslims are at war in Bosnia . . . One could go on and on. Each group has—it would seem—no misgiving in issuing its commandments to its followers . . .

By and large civilisation remains in pawn to savage commandments, ruthless creeds and ideologies. Within the re-birth of original epic the consent of a living creator for the voyaging artist or scientist to trespass across forbidden frontiers would seem to imply a radical shift in such premises of feud built into commandments. Not that diverse faiths and religions should be conquered and unified. Such conquest, as we know, deepens the pressures of rage and a longing for revenge within the defeated who bide their time in Under Worlds.

Rather—to put it as simply as I can—the radical shift in premises of commandment, that claim to be absolute when they are partial, invites an approach to the spouse of death-dealing regimes through a descent into inequalities all over again but with a difference.

That difference rests on diverse cultures, a capacity within diverse cultures to create and re-create windows into the enigma of truth. Each window's susceptibility to rigidity, rigid commandment, breaks, turns, I am suggesting, into a transitive architecture, a transitive medium into other dimensions within the unfinished genesis of the Imagination. Diversity then sponsors the liberation of the orphaned Soul within re-visionary and plural masks. The Soul is heightened even as the capacity of humanity to nourish itself in new perspectives of imaginative truth is deepened . . .

What promise then—may I ask—does the re-birth of epic offer?

It offers a renewed scrutiny—as I have already implied—of the unfulfilled promises of tradition and of descent and ascent all over again into inequalities, unequal cultures. *It offers in stages a conversion of such inequalities into numinous inexactitudes.*

Such numinous inexactitudes breach the role of dogmatic exactitude or fanatical ideology and creed *not* by conquest but by civilisation's arrival upon bridges from one closed mind to the other, from one closed world to the other. Within such subtly and complexly breached closure the orphaned Imagination, orphaned from its creator, is imbued with an inner immensity, an inner dynamic, that learns through all its carnival manifestations and masks. Does such inner immensity imply a new and evolving role for the Soul of traditions? This question, this implicit promise, moves us into a future into which we arrive with hope, yet fear and trembling.

For a breakthrough from conquest-driven imperatives is a task for which a fallible humanity is scarcely equipped. Let us remember however that epic sustains an engagement with extra-human parents who may resemble feuding and warring commanders but are intrinsically sponsors of diversity that may assist us to free ourselves from apparently incorrigible bias.

Address to Temenos Academy, London, 7 February 1994

From Jonestown

Wilson Harris

The Longman *Chronicle of America* tells of the "tragedy of Jonestown" and of the scene of "indescribable horror" which met the eyes of reporters from every corner of the globe when they arrived in stricken Jonestown after the self-inflicted holocaust engineered by a charismatic cult leader, the Reverend Jim Jones.

It happened in late November 1978 in a remote forest in Guyana.

In my archetypal fiction I call Jim Jones Jonah Jones.

All the characters in Francisco Bone's Dream-book are fictional.

Deacon was born in the Courantyne savannahs where he was exposed as an infant child and adopted by peasant farmers and rearers of cattle and horses. Legend also adopted him as "an angel fallen from the stars." Deacon became Jonah Jones's right-hand "angel" in his Church of Eternity in Jonestown.

Francisco Bone was born in Albuoystown and is a descendant of a French landowner of the late eighteenth century and his African mistress.

Bone is the only survivor of the Jonestown holocaust. He wanders in the Bush for seven years before arriving in New Amsterdam on the Guyana coastlands where he begins his Dream-book.

He builds a Virgin Ship in his Dream-book upon which he sails back into the past. The ancient Maya conceived of "twin-ships" on which pasts and futures were blended.

Francisco Bone's fragmented memories become pieces of an epic jigsaw which portray the emotionalities and passions and self-questionings and roots of trauma resulting from the Jonestown catastrophe. All this brings into play the bonds of a curious, antagonistic friendship that developed between Bone and Deacon and Jonah Jones at San Francisco College where they first met in the early 1940s. Francisco and Deacon were scholarship boys from British Guiana.

In the extract that follows one is provided with a series of insights and staggered episodes, so to speak, that bear on Bone's memory theatre in the dreadful wake and aftermath of Jonestown. Such theatre is inhabited by living ghosts whose activity deepens one's apprehensions of potential capacity yet dangers in the cross-cultural fabric of American society to which Jonestown belongs. Mr Mageye, for instance, was Francisco's teacher in Albuoystown. He returns as the magus-jester of history in the Dream-book and a cinematic guide as well into legends of the betrothal of Deacon, the fallen angel, and Marie, the Virgin of Port Mourant.

A word about the element of Jest which runs through the extract that follows. I associate Jest with Oracle as one wrestled with its utterances in the ancient world. Maya Oracle was as enigmatic as ancient Greek Oracle. Its responses to those who sought enlightenment from it in times of crisis in ancient Greece as in ancient America possessed at times a measure of numinous Jest in order to tap the mystery of truth. As a consequence therefore the strange comedy of Oracle enlightened and deceived (at times enlightenment and deception were simultaneous).

In *Jonestown* (as in the extract that follows) the role of "deception" is qualified in a peculiar way. The characters, Bone, Deacon, Mr Mageye, Jones, address each other but at times one of the participants in the conversation may speak or respond from within a medium of silence. Another participant therefore seems to read the mind of the silent speaker or gain telepathic intelligence from it. *This is the nature of the Jest in the fiction.* Jest, in this context, suggests that the framed Word is always partial.

The reverie of Silence becomes curiously active to imply a background which encompasses everything even as it subtly unframes through numinous absurdities of speech what it encompasses. Thus it is that the mystery of truth edges itself into the one-sided, biased conversations which take place.

The role of humour in fiction may be radically deepened and transformed I think within insights into sacred Jest. Such insights may seem riddling but paradoxically they break the alarming polarizations between cultures that are visible today in the mind-set of civilisation.

Three days had passed since the Day of the Dead when I lay on a pillow of stone at the edge of the Clearing in Jonestown.

I had made my way to the Cave of the Moon at nightfall.

The shock of events had been so great that I remained hidden in the cave above a Waterfall descending into the Jonestown river.

This was three miles or so above the Mission. I lay hidden but my privacy was soon to be breached. I heard the bell of the Church of Eternity tolling a requiem mass for the dead with the arrival of the grave-digger and his crew. They were accompanied by Mr Mageye (the magus-Jester of history), a Doctor (the magus-medicine man and God of poor people's hospitals), and an Inspector of police (the magus-clown of the Law).

These were my three magi who were associated with the creation of a Dream-book or the cradle of Bone (as Mr Mageye called it).

The tolling of the bell may have been caused by my phantom-Lazarus arm when I sneaked into the Church the day they arrived but quickly withdrew back to my Cave. I was to discover later from Mr Mageye that no one knew who had actually rung the bell. There was talk of a high wind blowing the stench of dead bodies into the sky and invoking a chorus of bells or lighthouse messages. Some—who those were I do not know—swore they saw the great-great-grandmothers of the dead rise from the brothel of the grave to declare themselves nurses of infinity . . .

"A sacred jest," said Mr Mageye. "Slaves break every brothel in a sky of cloud, polluted cloud, in the teeth of their ancient masters to declare their love—despite everything—for their tragic, illegitimate progeny . . . Such is the vocation of a nurse in a poor man's graveyard or hospital."

My choice of Mr Mageye as magus-Jester of history was crucial to the creation of my Dream-book (or cradle of Bone) in the years that followed the catastrophe of Jonestown.

He gave apparitional weight and comedy, for instance, to the way I dressed, the wretched Nemesis Bag that I wore over my head.

"Do you know Mr Mageye," I said, "you were at my mother's funeral (her coffin was borne sky high by beggars) when three threads sprang from the Nemesis Bag and sprouted into three blades of grass, the colour of velvet, on my mother's grave? It was a relief, it was as if a ton had lifted from my head . . .

"When I arrived in New Amsterdam, took up my abode in Trinity Street and began to write I was virtually in rags. But I felt light as a feather. The year was 1985."

"Yes," said Mr Mageye, "your mother's death in Albuoystown caused quite a sensation. I have a yellowing newspaper with me. *Carnival Argosy* dated 1939." He pointed to a headline which ran as follows: WOMEN OF THE BROTHEL AND BEGGARS IN PROCESSION TO GRAVE OF THE VIRGIN OF ALBUOYSTOWN.

"I wandered in a state of limbo for seven years before I began to write," I said to Mr Mageye. "But all the time I was being written into the Dream-book with each thread that fell from the Bag on my head and from the garments that I wore. These became the substance with which to dress innermost Bone into the composite populace in my book. Is it my book? It's as much yours, Mr Mageye. I am not even sure of the Day or the year I began to write. The Maya speak of Dateless Days that become a medium of living Shadows in which history retrieves an emotionality, a Passion, to unveil the facts and go deeper into processions into the body of the womb. Think of the Virgin of the ancient city of Palenque. She died resisting a Tiger to save the life of her son. One of her arms was torn from her body. It gestated in space. It gestates still in forgotten traditions of fiction and grief in Beauty. There are many languages of the Imagination that affect us in the fibre of dismembered cultures that remain mysteriously whole in their resistance to the predatory coherence of fact that masquerades as eternity. The true fact is Love's intervention in blended times within dreadful circumstances I grant. The true fact is the undying originality of such interventions. Without this art is dead. IMAGINATION DEAD IMAGINE."

Mr Mageye applauded my wild outburst.

Emotionality and passion gave substance to his apparition in the Dream-book. It was as if one fed him with one's blood and flesh to make him live. And an irony, a paradox, flashed into my mind. Tigers seek to live on the flesh of women. No wonder Jones had been addicted to brothels in San Francisco when Deacon and I met him there for the first time in 1942.

Deacon and I had both been the recipients of scholarship prizes that took us to San Francisco College, where we met the young American. Our prizes had come out of the Fund that the ghost-Frenchman (my ancestral father) had left when he returned to Napoleonic France in 1800. Jonah was two or three years older than we were. But he seemed even older. He intrigued us with fictions of whales, Moby Dick, whales that swallowed civilisations and threatened the Virgin Ship.

His sense of humour was broad, sometimes Whitmanesque, but threaded with anger and despair.

"Survivor Ishmael," he said, "hangs on Aeneas's ship, on Jason's *Argo* as well. He hangs in dread of a brothel of history. Is Medea a whore or a Virgin Queen? Aeneas betrays Queen Dido. He had promised her fortune and then he abandoned her. He was a hero and a monster. Yes, Aeneas betrayed her," Jones said and smacked his lips with a curious satisfaction.

A silence fell over us like a beam from the brothel of history. I nailed it nevertheless into the deck of the Virgin Ship.

Deacon was pensive. We listened to the young American with a sense of foreboding. Deacon was of Indian descent. His grandparents had arrived as indentured servants from South India.

"Mind you," I said to Mr Mageye, "I am speaking of his adoptive parents who were rice farmers and rearers of cattle and horses. No one fathoms Deacon's ancestry. He fell from the stars as an infant child. War in heaven, rebellion in heaven, it is said, in accordance with savannah folklore."

Deacon was pensive. He had been affianced—in keeping with East Indian indenture custom—to the maiden Marie of his own age when he left British Guiana to take up his scholarship. Would he betray her? Would he betray the young Marie of Port Mourant, the maiden, the Virgin Marie of Port Mourant?

"Three Maries," I said to Mr Mageye, "appear in the Dream-book. Marie—this Marie—is destined to be Deacon's bride. When I saw her myself on visits to the Courantyne I fell head over heels in love with her. I would have married her like a shot. I hated Deacon. I was jealous of him. Hate is too strong a word. But the truth is we were antagonistic to each other. Racial antagonism? Racial antagonisms between East Indians and Blacks and people of mixed descent? It's rife in British Guiana. It's rife in the Guianas—Dutch and French as well. Surinam. Devil's Isle. Guyana."

"Will he betray her?" asked Mr Mageye.

Deacon caught the drift of my silent conversation with Mr Mageye.

"Never, Never," said Deacon. He bared his arm. On it was tattooed the

Constellation of the Scorpion. "This gives me immunity to pain," he said. "Why should I inflict pain on my bride?"

"All the more reason why you may," I protested. I bared my arm. On it was tattooed an imprint of Lazarus.

Deacon glared at me. "Heroes are saviours of the people," he said. "They build strong gaols and fortresses and coffins. But in the end they save the people, don't they? As for you, Francisco, fuck you! Lazarus eh? You are a ghost's ill-begotten son. I shall take you under my wing. I shall adopt you as brother and son. I shall even give you my Mask to wear in times of Carnival. Then everyone will think you are me and you shall be honoured."

I shrank from him. I had not a word to say. But I pitied poor Marie. She was the adopted daughter of the Doctor-God of the poor people's hospital of Port Mourant. Her parents had died in a car crash on the busy road between New Amsterdam and Port Mourant.

"The Doctor is your magus-medicine man," said Mr Mageye.

"Deacon has taken him in," I said. "Deacon has persuaded him that Marie and he will give birth to a true Lazarus . . ."

"But you," said Mr Mageye, "you . . ."

"I may have magi within my book but I am a surrogate of the cradle of the Bone that will flesh all races into genuine brothers and sisters . . ."

Deacon may have overheard my silent conversation with Mr Mageye. He bit his lips savagely until blood came. Heroes eat the flesh of monsters in themselves to fuel life, to strengthen life.

The friendship, the curious enemy friendship between Deacon and Jones and me, was a phenomenon of the modern age, indeed of many past ages.

Jones's terrible moods of anger fuelled our resolution to face the world, to withstand insults, racial insults in America.

"All who aren't white are black," said Jones. "I shall protect you. You are all one to me."

"Are Alexander and Genghis Khan one to you, Jonah? Would you have recruited them to sail on the *Pequod?* They were sons of gods, they were fallen angels like me. Brace yourself Jonah for a new peasant uprising across the Americas. All you need is one man who contains millions . . ."

"God help that one man," I said, "when he opens the door of the cell in which the Old God resides . . ."

"What Old God?" Deacon cried. But Mr Mageye put his hand to my lips. His face became grave as an Enigma or the Sphinx. And I said nothing. Indeed I was plagued by uncertainties and my allusion to a Prisoner upon Devil's Isle, or Old God, was rash in all the circumstances. Jonah was angry. Old Gods were useless unless they could bring time itself to a standstill.

Phenomenal, as it seemed, peculiar in the light of common sense, a strange aspect of the fuel that drove us into forging a treaty or a pact—a pact between the white American Jonah Jones and racially mixed and uncertain ancestries within Deacon and myself—was anger.

Though I had said nothing when Deacon taunted me as a "ghost's ill-begotten son" I was angry as much with him as with myself, angry with Jones as well in some classic, elemental way. Jones's antecedents had owned slaves, they had decimated the peoples of ancient America from the sixteenth century onwards. An astonishing factor in all this was that Jones appeared to be the most angry one of us. No wonder he revered Herman Melville's *Moby Dick* and Edgar Allan Poe's *Arthur Gordon Pym*. Such classics of anger seemed rooted in the cosmos itself.

Jones—in the Mask of the Whale into which he descended at times—raged at the prejudices, the biases, the hypocrisy, that were visible everywhere. *His anger therefore appealed to us.* But it left me with a bitter taste in my mouth. I did not like the way he savoured anger as if it were the sweetest dish in the restaurants of San Francisco. Anger became the seed of his charismatic pursuit of eternity, eternity's closure of time.

I feared the gross enlargement of emotion, the enlargement or complex pregnancy of the male charismatic priest. He hunted women in brothels everywhere. He sought to fuck them, to fuck himself, and to become a pregnant decoy in a pulpit for the annihilation of his age through mounting apparitional populations, mounting apparitional numbers to be weighed on the scales of time, blended pasts and futures.

Anger at injustice everywhere could turn nasty and become an involuntary ape of imperial hubris rooted in the despoliation of the law of conquered peoples. Involuntary apes are the "ill-begotten bridegrooms" of deprived peoples led to the altar within military coups or rigged elections.

What was deeply alarming to me—in my crossing a chasm of years from dateless day in Trinity Street, New Amsterdam, back to San Francisco, United States, when the Japanese bombed Pearl Harbour—was that such Jonesian anger, such common-or-garden apehood of hubris, *appealed to us, fascinated us, fascinated both Deacon and me.*

True, it also aroused a sensation of foreboding and Nemesis. But the fascination remained. A fascination rooted in an addiction to holocaustic sacrifice and rivalry that ran deep in antagonistic cultures around the globe. Jones, poor Jones, was as much their pawn as they were his.

When the first nuclear Bomb exploded and sent its dread beauty, its fantastic mushroom, into the sky above an American desert, long-sunken ships and coffins of the dead arose from their sea-bed.

A fleet arose to greet the constellation of the *Argo* encrusted on Jason's head in the stars.

Mr Mageye held a Camera in his hand which he—as magus-Jester of history—had brought from the future as much as from the technologies in the past: a Camera stored with paradoxical archetypes, new-born yet old as the mysterious anatomy of time.

His apparitional figure stood on the deck of the Virgin Ship with the futuristic, ancient Camera in his hand.

He drew my eye to peer into the depths of archetypal oceans and skies.

"Do you see Francisco?" he asked.

At first I saw nothing but Chaos. I saw floating planks from the forests of King Midas, I saw floating cargoes of South American rubber bound for the Golden Man in the kingdom of El Dorado, I saw the mastheads upon broken slave-ships, I saw frail residue like the beard of Titans, I saw celestial mathematics written into rockets and sails upon space stations. An air of wreckage hung over them in the degree that civilisations had foundered but the fleet was now half-afloat upon ocean and sky.

"The Virgin Ship," said Mr Mageye, "transforms the fleet, converts the fleet, into a cradle of Bone fleshed by resurrectionary mathematics.

"Bone is our innermost Cross that we scarcely countenance or understand.

"It is as old as time.

"On it hangs not only our flesh but the ragged flesh of populations and failed captaincies and heroes who are illumined nevertheless by the promise of a divine huntsman who hangs on the Cross in our flesh, our ragged flesh, to hold the Predator at bay when humanity is in the greatest danger.

"The Cross in the mirror of celestial mathematics is sometimes a net that salvages all wreckages of time in which to build the Virgin Ship anew.

"Remember Francisco there is a curious fragility to your Dream-book, the log-book of the fleet. But its true spiritual capacity lies therein. It wreathes itself in the collapse of high-sounding garments and punishments and glories to illumine Bone or Cross.

"Celestial mathematics of space! That is how I see the evolution of the divine huntsman in our ragged flesh. That is how I see a procession of brothels and wrecked architectures and wrecked fleets and marketplace cathedrals backwards into the stark Womb of the Virgin—shorn of intercourse with violence—from which the true, compassionate huntsman may yet evolve and arise . . . Remember all this Francisco."

Deacon had caught the drift of Mr Mageye's conversation with me. He seized upon "celestial mathematics" as a platform for his own ambitions, his own perverse longing for glory.

"Celestial ambition," he said to me and to the apparition of Mr Mageye, "fires a peasant like me to perform great deeds, to fight unimaginable duels, to frame arenas for impossible (yet I believe possible) duels in space. Think of the Moon! What an arena for duels and commerce and sport. We shall fight on other planets, believe me! Buy yourself a ringside seat now, Francisco, before the price soars. Shall I—a mere peasant—dwarf Alexander the Great and Genghis Khan? Why not? I am born from the obscurity of the stars as they were! Poor Jonah believes in eternity. And that is why I have forged a pact with him. He will bring me the chance to duel with eternity. And if I fail then celestial mathematics will provide me with a ladder to climb back into heaven, to wrestle all over again with the Titans, the Tricksters of heaven. Yes—remember Francisco—civilisations fail and perish and begin all over again in some remote forest . . . As for you Francisco I shall give you a taste of my fallen angel's blood when or if I fail. I shall clamp my Mask into your head. I—and an Old God you shall meet (you love epic theatre, don't you?)—shall imbue it with conviction and life-like appearance. Carnival's great Francisco." He was laughing uproariously.

I said nothing. I was familiar with his taunts. I was familiar with his mockery of others and his self-mockery. Self-mockery was a moral fable, a moral truth, that fuelled peculiar underground sympathies between us though at another level we scorned or hated each other. Such self-mockery illumined hypocritical patriotisms, hypocritical loyalties, and it strengthened the pact between us and Jonah Jones. We seemed to eat our own mutual flesh in order to expose salutary lighthouse or Bone or Cross.

Mr Mageye eyed me with the oddest approval, the approval of self-questioning conscience, self-questioning imagination. He relished Deacon's joke—if joke it was—about Tricksters of heaven. Sacred Jest! It appealed to him as a nourishing resource of comic flesh-and-blood: comic, yes, but curiously divine in flesh-and-blood's ambition to equate itself with Gods.

Such comic divine equation enlivened the apparition that he was in my Dream-book. He had died in Albuoystown the very year that I left for San Francisco to take up my scholarship. I recalled standing over his grave on the eve of my departure. He was my beloved school teacher, the wisest, strangest man I had ever known. He saw all his pupils as potential tyrants, potential liberators, potential monsters, potential saints. He roamed all texts, all worlds, all ages to help them see themselves as stripped of everything yet whole and majestic and comical (all at the same time). I visualized myself sailing with him into futures and pasts. I visualized the Nemesis Bag on my head. Three more threads fell from it and took root on his grave. This had happened on my mother's grave as well.

"I am no ill-begotten son of a French Catholic ghost," I cried. "I am Mr Mageye's South American pupil. He is my magus. I wish he were my father. But I—a nameless orphan really—must respect the wishes of my poor mother who saw herself on the Cross as the bride of a slave-owning, masquerading, divine imperialist."

Having nourished itself on comic divine flesh-and-blood the apparition of Mr Mageye was able to feed my imagination in turn.

He stepped from his coffin into a classroom in San Francisco College and looked across the water to the famous prison of Alcatraz.

Why are prisons famous? What secrets do they keep?

Are they the abode of apparitions across the ages, legendary kings of crime, legendary Napoleons, Bastilles, legendary pirates knighted by queens?

My eye flicked into Mr Mageye's Camera and I saw the prison of Devil's Isle, French Guiana. A prisoner or Old God was housed there. He was as old as Quetzalcoatl (the most ancient king of the Americas), he was as young as the French Revolution.

"Kingship is a sphere within us," said Mr Mageye, "that dazzles and tricks our senses again and again. We hunger for romance, or chivalry, or knights in shining armour, or Scandal (with a capital S), or pageantry (with a common p as processions line the streets).

"But all this is an evasion of the complex necessity for kingship. At the core of kingship resides a true embattled reality that we forfeit or lose sight of at our peril. Kingship witnesses to the agonizing problematic of freedom, the gift of freedom to ourselves within ourselves yet bestowed upon us by some incalculable design in heaven and upon earth . . ."

I raised my hand, but Mr Mageye rushed on, a rush yet a peculiar deliberation—"I know, I know . . . Freedom is seen as the achievement of the common people . . ."

"Is it not?" I demanded.

"At the heart of the common people exists an invisible fortress in which a Prisoner or Old God or King is held as a guarantee, a half-compulsive, half-spiritual guarantee that some principle lives in the Primitive mind (surviving Primitive archetype) to sift the problematic resources of freedom."

"I do not follow," I said. But in myself I knew or thought I knew.

"The Prisoner or Old God places a question-mark against the extravagant gift of freedom. Is freedom anarchy? Is freedom reserved for the strong, does freedom nurture crime, does it come when we are not ready for it? At what age are we equipped to bear the burden of freedom? Do we need to cultivate wholly different philosophies of the Imagination to bring us on a wave of the future from which to discern how free or unfree we were in the past and still are in the present, how just or unjust to others we remain, how prone to exploit ourselves and others in the name of high-sounding lies?"

I could not help voicing a protest—"Kings need to be forced, do they not, into granting freedom to their subjects?"

"And they pay a terrible price," said Mr Mageye, "their heads roll. Force—in such a context—may be an explosion of conscience in the King or Old God himself. He knows without quite knowing (he knows in the collective subconscious and unconscious) that he has failed in the problematic authority that he exercises. He is as much condemned as self-condemned. And without that tension of visionary, interior condemnation and trial by others at the heart of composite epic, epic populace, epic king, art dies, philosophy dies, faith in truth perishes. Freedom needs to weigh, examine, reexamine its far-flung proportions which radiate from a core of the Imagination, it needs to promote a variety of cautions in the body politic, freedom is not a gross or even a subtle indulgence of public appetite; or else it deteriorates into cynical diplomacy, it becomes a tool, a machine, a gravy train, a sponsor of a rat-race."

I was appalled and aghast at all this. I felt as if I had been dealt a blow by an apparition, a solid apparition arisen from a coffin, the coffin of ancient kings that empowered the magus-philosopher-jester of history that Mr Mageye was.

"Where does it all start?" I demanded. "If Old Gods and Prisoners are a sphere within ourselves, acting and running more deeply than the mechanics of political sovereignty, where does it start?"

"Deacon would say it starts with wars in Heaven," said Mr Mageye. He was jesting but his face seemed straight as a bat in the hands of a weirdly gifted cricketer of genius. He had umpired many a game in Albuoystown. His apparitional nose seemed to have flattened itself. But then it grew again, it straightened itself into the colour of sculpted soil in Deacon's Courantyne savannahs.

"Let us," he said, "prepare the ground of theatre, the ground of folklore in the ancient savannahs. First the infant Deacon falls from the baggage train of routed angels. He falls to earth and is given a home by the savannah folk."

I was angry. I was jealous.

"Is Deacon a bloody king?" I demanded.

"He is an adversary of Old Gods. He sustains on Earth an age-old quarrel in Heaven. When is the gift of fire to be exercised and bestowed upon humanity? When is the gift of freedom to be exercised and bestowed upon humanity? That is in large part the substance of the quarrel. Should humanity claim freedom? Perhaps it has with detrimental consquences on every hand! Should humanity claim freedom in the teeth of obstinate and uncertain regimes? Where does authority truly reside? We may think these questions are old-hat but they are not. They are more savagely pertinent to human affairs than we care to admit. Should we pursue our adversaries, should they turn on us at every opportunity? Should we perpetuate forms of punitive logic to punish those who punished us when we rebelled? I tell you all this, Francisco, for it is pertinent to your visitation of the childhood of Deacon in the folklore, archetypal theatre of the Courantyne savannahs."

The scales of blended times had changed in the half-apparitional, half-concrete fabric of my Dream-book and arrival on the Virgin Ship in the Courantyne River from which we made our way into the savannahs.

"Deacon had been affianced to Marie of Port Mourant before he left to take up his scholarship in San Francisco," said Mr Mageye.

"Yes I know. He told us so."

"But he met her for the first overwhelmingly intimate yet expansive time (that fires both love of art and science, and greed for fame) at the age of nine," said Mr Mageye peering into his Camera as if it were a computer of chasms in creation and visionary years. "That meeting was the fulfillment of an age-old prophecy for the savannah folk. An infant child would fall from the stars in 1930. Carnival has its calendric humour, has it not, Francisco? The child—in his tenth year, 1939—would encounter a wonderful maid, a dangerous maid, a Virgin, in the savannahs at the end of a drought season when the first, torrential rains broke the walls of heaven.

"This would confirm the adversarial destiny of the angel fallen from the baggage train of the stars. It would confirm the venom of the Scorpion in his veins. The mark of a great hero . . ."

"Monster," I cried.

"You need to see it happening all over again in your Dream-book. It is pertinent, believe me Francisco, to a discovery and re-discovery of the depth of your own passion and emotion which you may have eclipsed or hidden from yourself until the tragedy of Jonestown brought you face to face with the accumulated spectres of years, the dread spectre of the twentieth century as it addresses the psyche of ageless childhood."

I adjusted the Nemesis Bag on my head even as I looked into Mr Mageye's Camera.

"Deacon ran into the maid in the torrential rain. She seemed utterly changed from a child he knew! Had he not seen her before at school? Human magic dazzles the eyes of a fallen angel when destiny declares itself. Such is the precocity of love, the precocity of feud as well. Marie was known to be the adopted daughter of the Doctor at the Port Mourant hospital. Doctors are Gods to peasant folk in poor people's hospitals. But there was an ominous side to Marie's parentage. One report claimed that her parents had been killed in a car crash and that—above the debris of the car—an Old God, or escaped Prisoner, materialized. Escaped from Devil's Isle. The Inspector of Police seized him. Escaped prisoners from French Guiana were an occasional feature on the British Guiana coast. Carnival fastened on the event. *The Old God claimed that he was Marie's father and that the Doctor was not to be trusted.*" Mr Mageye was smiling.

"No laughing matter," I said. "Carnival is no laughing matter."

"Indeed not," said Mr Mageye. "In the reaches of great wind-swept, rain-swept, sun-swept savannahs, the most ancient feuds between heaven and earth are revived in villages and upon roads that may seem jam-packed at times but are insubstantial and frail against an immensity of sky and land and sea that borders the coastlands. The peasantry and the people are native to, yet tormented by, such extremity. They long for a saviour, for authority, for truth. Where does authority reside? Does it reside in European empires whose presence they feel? Does it reside in the new power-hungry politicians? Does it reside in upper worlds, nether worlds? Tell me Francisco. *Feed my apparition in your book.*"

I hesitated for a long while and then I found the confidence to speak.

"I would say," I began hesitantly, pulling a loose thread from my Nemesis Bag and letting it fall to the ground, "that all the ingredients of uncertainty that you stress Mr Mageye are woven into a car crash—as into the wreck of the *Argo*—into . . ." I hesitated . . . "into wars and rumours of war across the sea, into submarines and the shadow of fleets patrolling the Atlantic seaboard of South America.

"No wonder the Old God hovers in space only to be seized by the inspector and placed in a cell." I stopped, but then it occurred to me to lay bare my heart to Mr Mageye. "That Prisoner or Old God wrestles with the Doctor and the Inspector to claim Marie as his Virgin daughter . . ."

There was much more that I wished to say, my desire for Marie even

before I met her, my jealousy of Deacon, but Mr Mageye interrupted—
"Look! there they are."

It suddenly occurred to me—as in a Jest of Dream—that my jealousy of
Deacon had helped to flesh out the occasion, to give content to both Deacon
and Marie in the backward sweep of years since I began to write. There they
were indeed, large as life, within the raining, mist-filled savannahs in which
Mr Mageye and I stood invisible to them.

We were I calculated half-way between Crabwood Creek and Port
Mourant.

Deacon was naked. The tattooed Scorpion Constellation shone darkly on
his child's arm. On the other monstrous, heroic arm stood the double star
Aldebaran associated with Taurus, but the Bull had been overturned into
Horses on the Moon. I was able to draw close to him with Mr Mageye's
assistance and to read every pore in his body.

Deacon had abandoned his school uniform to come into his own as the
masterful child-bridegroom who secures the Virgin of the Wild on her
appearance at the end of every long, searing drought when the rains com-
mence.

Deacon had paused as if locked into the thread of my glance. But he shot
forward again in my Dream-book. Mr Mageye (Camera in hand) was out of
sight—as on a film set—and I (in my Nemesis Hat) kept in touch (though I
was invisible to him). Such are the wonders of technology and science
within futuristic strategies of the Imagination.

He ran with a miraculous stride. Amazing to maintain his stride on the
slippery path that he had taken. But the long drought had hardened the
ground. The water table was low and it would take a day or two at least for
the soil to change into an ankle-deep rich overflowing sponge.

The rain swept all around as if sky and cloud had been broken in cosmic
theatre to provide a Waterfalling shower in the eye of the Camera down
which Deacon had floated and come when he fell as an infant in space. Now
he was in his tenth cosmic year and destiny was to equip him with a lasso to
seize the Horses of the Moon and bring them showering and hoofing their
way to Earth.

I saw the affianced child-bride in the corner of my eye. The rain swung
into an encircling perimeter around her, the rain lessened, the ground acquired the look of a mirroring, flat wave as if a portion of the sky had fallen
to the ground.

Deacon saw her now clearly. She was naked as he was. She too had abandoned her uniform, a child's nurse's uniform which the Doctor, her adoptive
father, had given her to wear when she assisted him in the Port Mourant
hospital after school.

Deacon stopped upon the perimeter. Carven into momentary astonish-
ment. He had not seen her naked before. He knew her from school but she
was not the same child that he took for granted when the Doctor-God and
his savannah parents met to seal the promise of selves (savannah-self,

Godself) in marriage.

His lithe body responded to hers by sheathing itself all at once in wings that blew around him as if a bird, an eagle, a fluid eagle, perched on his head in a fountain of mist as the rain appeared to boil around his ankles in the rising heat of the soil.

Marie began to dance on the mirror. She danced upon a portion of sky, skin of the shining rain on the ground. Her feet were suddenly and lightly and mysteriously laced with three threads that fell from my Nemesis Hat. They were the colour of velvet. Yet the springing grass or slenderest blades of rain were silver. The blades of grass from my mother's grave levitated and fell from the sky. The blades of grass from Mr Mageye's grave levitated and fell from the sky. Despite such beauty I was stricken by heart-rending grief. I felt the strangest foreboding. And I would have fired a bullet—if I had possessed one—at Deacon and swept his affianced bride into my arms.

Deacon moved and edged his wings into the mirror on which the Virgin of the Wild was dancing. A long plait of loose hair fell down her back from the nape of her neck to her waist. It was the colour of the mane of a Moon-horse that shook itself and encircled my head. Why me? How was I tied to her? By what fate, or trial of spirit, or torment of freedom?

Deacon seemed to glide and reach for her hair upon the fantastic mirror. He swept it from my brow even as—with a mocking glance—he seemed to nail it into the space where I stood invisible to him. The nail pierced me to the Bone. I cried for immunity to pain such as Deacon appeared to possess.

Marie swirled and the nail fell from my head into Deacon's wing. He may have felt no pain in the Shadow of the Scorpion but he stumbled and was unable to bind her to him in this instant of a doubling of stars in the sky or mirror on the ground, Aldebaran's twin stars in which I played an invisible role, twinned to a fallen angel.

The lessening rain and slightly clearing sky brought the pool of the Moon onto the ground. Deacon darted forward as if he flew or danced on water—his wing free again—and he held the Virgin's hair at last. But when he sought to draw her to him, in the theatre of the Moon, she dazzled him and thrust him away. They encircled each other, sometimes upon the perimeter within which they danced, sometimes upon an upright Wheel as though the flat circle or perimeter inclined itself into a vertical dimension, a wheeling dimension.

Step by step the Horses of the Moon materialized as a turbulent extension of the Passion of the dance. A haunch grafted itself into the archetypal momentum of cavalry of fate. Such apparently insoluble archetypes were native to ancient and modern civilisations and they drew Marie's Wheel in the dance.

Horses akin to Cortéz's troop fleshed themselves into a scale of grafts within apparitions on the Moon.

Horses akin to Genghis Khan's hillsides rose into shoulders and necks around the edges of the Moon.

Eyes of flashing, poisoned gold sprang from the bodies of Alexander's infantry upon Darius's wheeling chariots beneath Marie's fleet foot.

From every corner of legend and history arose an assembly of the parts of engines of flesh, jigsaw cavalries, ribs, equine muscularities, bunched muscles, grapelike memories of blood, tanned, leathern proportions, giving substance to the terrible Horses of the Moon within which Deacon and Marie pursued each other in their dance.

No horses in Chichén Itzá but the dreaded Chac Mool possessed the countenance of a Chimera, half-human, half-horse. Chac Mool was a signal of militaristic atrocity in the Maya world and it foretold the decline of a civilisation.

Who were the riders, who were the giants of Chaos upon such Horses? Were they Deacon's kith and kin in heaven and upon earth? Were they Marie's dangerous host and accompaniment of furies? Furies are omens, signatures of uncanny foreboding, and they tend to arrive hand in hand with Virgins of the Wilderness whose untameable spirituality in nature is misconceived for brute violence.

Were the riders princes of Carnival Lord Death's regime in theatres of history, were they dictators in South America, were they solid, stable, riggers of elections in Nigeria and elsewhere, were they Amens or Amins, were they gagged priests, gagged popes, gagged bishops, bankers, statesmen, scientists, crusaders, evangelists?

Or were they shepherds from times immemorial, poor labouring folk in the savannahs of Guyana since El Dorado fashioned its whip to encircle the slaves who dug the earth, rode the earth from cradle to grave with an eye on the stars for the coming of a saviour, a saviour susceptible to miscasting in the theatres of Church and State, miscast as warrior-crusader-priest?

The poor, labouring, awkward folk seemed to Mr Mageye and to me to combine dictatorship and feudal features in themselves as they rode the Horses. They were also uncanny judges of themselves and others. They were submissive to Deacon now as they rode the Horses, rode the lotteries on the Moon, rode expectations of fortune on the Moon, but I felt—as though I were on trial—that they were capable of breaking themselves, melting themselves, re-shaping themselves, in order to judge him in themselves, bring him before them on the Moon.

"Why the Moon?" I asked Mr Mageye, "why not the Earth?"

"In a Universe that quarrels with itself in Carnival sciences, the Moon is a ripe theatre, the Moon drifts to Earth, drifts into a sphere of incredible theatre and gravity, a space-station, if you like, within a quarrel of dimensions that plague us . . ."

Marie was now under the hooves of the Horses ridden by controversial, pathetic, victimized, victimizing, paradoxical self-judges and giants of chaos. She slipped through them unhurt but saw the danger to humanity in the triumph of the warrior-angel that Deacon was. She was now betrothed to him as the dance confirmed. It was too late to turn back. She was destined—

according to folk legends—to bear him a child, the people's promised child that would herald his departure from her, in dread circumstances, to build a new Rome in South America in alliance with an American warrior-priest from San Francisco and left-handed Bone from Albuoystown.

It was a prophecy that was unclear to her. Unclear to me. I should have remembered the past in coming from the future but the trauma that I suffered in Jonestown had wiped a page or pages from my mind and those blank spaces or chapters filled my Dream-book with renewed foreboding.

"Am I left-handed Bone?" I cried. I should have known better than to indulge in self-pity. Mr Mageye did not reply. A Sphinx-like look came upon his face, a gentle hand on my brow . . .

Marie slipped through the Horses' hooves even as she saw the danger. She saw—within her untameable beauty—the grief in the Womb of Space (when space quarrels with itself and becomes a potential series of battle-fields).

I drew close to her and succeeded in helping her secure a triangular seat within the Wheel even as it spun. *I swore she saw me.* She turned her mysterious and wonderful and grateful eyes upon me. *She knew me.* But then I wondered. Did she mistake me for Deacon whose shadowy Mask fell upon her? Winged, Shadowy Mask? Black? Yet pale and silvery as the feathers around his Beak?

I placed my shoulders to the Wheel and gave it an additional push. It flashed. It flashed through the limbs of the great Horses and their riders. And she was gone in a flash. Back to her nurse's uniform in Port Mourant Hospital.

Deacon's venom rose with Marie's flight and helped to harden his heart for an enterprise that lay before him: the capture of the Horses of the Moon and their riders . . .

He had secured a long thread of hair from Marie's head. The rain had ceased and he would need to take full advantage of the respite to perfect the task on which he was engaged and the lassoing of the Horses.

Their necks gleamed as he lifted the glancing hair from the bride of the wilderness. That hair was curiously part of the topography of the landscape. It had been plucked as much from the map of his Brain as from the Virgin's body.

It glanced and stood before him as upon a draughtsman's sliding scale of uprooted contours and tributaries, the slenderest, coiling fabric of recalled rain coursing alive after the long drought through the savannahs.

Coursing alive along Crabwood Creek in the moonlight pouring through broken clouds.

"I read in the *Carnival Argosy* in 1939," said Mr Mageye, "that engineers were contemplating diverting the tributary to the Courantyne River known as Crabwood Creek into an enclosure, or giant spatial lasso, so to speak, for horses and cattle to prevent them straying onto and grazing upon the rice fields."

As he spoke to me I saw the extraordinary congruence of apparition and concreteness in the Camera of the mind within the Jester of history.

Deacon held the wilderness hair and lasso in his hand as if it were the sliding uplifted creek itself coiling upon its fragile, serpent's tail.

He whipped the serpent in the air with an engineer's bark, a peasant boy's ambitious dream and cry and prayer for the marvels of technology.

The wilderness lasso fell around the Horses' steaming necks in the moonlight. They shuddered and bundled themselves together uneasily but on the whole they were content to be mastered by an angel from the stars.

Mr Mageye studied—as upon a platform of invisibility separating him from the action of a rolling film—the amorphous, magical roles a child plays within the hidden uniform of a man already shaping itself into existence within him and around him. The amorphous magic in the psyche of a child is the sponge of growing pains, trauma, the trauma of deprivation, the trauma of acute longing for power, the power to rule, to execute gigantic projects that may symbolize glory or ashes in one's mouth unless one learns to see deeply into the cinematic theatre of cells and blood in mind and heart.

"Such a beautiful—however grief-stricken—theorem is the psyche of a child! Capsuled into childhood is the latent marriage of Brain and myth, feud and grace, terror and dance. Deacon's obsession (which may also be yours Francisco) surely was plain to you as a lucid dream when he studied engineering and politics in San Francisco College."

Horses and Giants of Chaos came towards Deacon now. He lengthened his tributary lasso, he pulled hard.

It seemed as if it would snap into Virgin blood on the Moon but it held.

He relaxed his grip into a wide angling—almost gentle—invocation of space and drew animals and riders across the perimeter of the Moon into the river catchment of Earth and along the line of the creek. It was a remarkable procession that invested the heights of the Moon with the qualities of a watershed upon which distant falling rain escalated upon a mountainous cloud and then glided on both flanks into space.

Horseflesh flanking the Moon and the creek became the shadow of a wall, or a dam, as the procession advanced towards the Courantyne River.

The projected new polder, or diversion, materialized as a gift of passion inherent in his betrothal to Marie, reined-in animal passion, curbed and manifest in engineering, wilderness genius.

It was as if Deacon were intent upon converting the Wheel upon which Marie had fled into a simultaneous asset of culture, into gradients and stages down which he drew the Horses of the Moon.

Celestial mathematics!

He drew the Horses along the lassoing hair—*with or in* the lassoing hair—in the Virgin's body to the wide Courantyne River. He came upon a box koker or sluice at the point where the tributary entered the main body of the river. The wide estuary was vacant except for a schooner on the bar and the Virgin Ship which Deacon failed to see.

In his child's mathematical, engineering, mythical eye, infused with wars and baggage trains and advancing, retreating armies, the box koker or Dutch culvert assumed the proportions of a giant coffin. He stood against it and lifted the lid. Then with a tug he propelled each beast and rider into its depths. The colour of new taxes he would propose (if he were prime minister) shone on each flank, money-flesh, political/economic flesh, ballot-box flesh, everything that was pertinent to the betrothal of a hero or a monster to the Virgin of the Wild. They were content to recline in darkness and await the fulfillment of his promise. He inscribed on the lid of the coffin Heracles strangling serpents—unleashing serpents—in his cradle and Hermes herding cattle, outwitting his brother Apollo on the day he was born . . .

Mr Mageye and I—even as Deacon propelled Horses and riders into a coffin—let our platform with its filming futuristic yet ancient Eye levitate in space. Such verticality, such a sliding scale, was native to blended times, past futures, future pasts. We saw Deacon's procession along the creek in a new fictional, factual light of peculiar irony and folk indefatigability and deprivation. Conversion of folk deprivation into glorious cradles allied to coffins and taxation in the grave ran hand in hand with mundane, plodding existences. We saw Deacon's processional wall in the lassoing of space change into apathy yet dogged hope.

The empolderment of the savannahs had been shelved when the War in Europe began in 1939. Money was short in the colony. Posters advertising the Crabwood Creek Scheme (as it was called) began to loosen into tattered newspaper flags on the walls of buildings and in schools.

Deacon read the scraps and pieces nevertheless in his school. They flapped like wings of a noble scavenger or vulture or eagle that he attempted to draw within and around them into popular graffiti. One day he would come to power. One day his offspring would ensure an indefatigable cradle . . . Such were his larger-than-life thoughts as he led his plodding, smaller-than-life procession of horses from upriver Courantyne to downriver Crabwood Creek now that the drought was over.

Not giants in cradles to Mr Mageye and me on our platform and ladder in space but processions of hardy, ant-like creatures on the globe beneath us, as ant-like and enigmatic as the moving stars with feet in shadow above us.

Deacon's dwarf-like substance, the dwarf-like procession that he led—dwarf-like train of giants in the comedy of the wilderness—was nothing unusual in the life of the peasant folk. Peasants as young as Deacon were initiated into the savannahs virtually from the day they began to crawl. Mere lads—in the eyes of the Gods who contested the parentage of wilderness Marie—were skilled herders of cattle. It was a tough, dangerous life. As tough and as dangerous as it had been in ancient Palestine and ancient Greece where hardship was the name of the game.

Where were the new Biblical lands, the new Classical lands, but where exoduses and diasporas, and the threat of drought, of famine, prevailed in variable, unsuspected forms?

Where were the new ships, the new *Aeneid*, but in a web of ancient, conflicting cultures, modern Romes and Jonestowns overshadowing space even before they were built? Such overshadowing drove us forwards and backwards simultaneously into celestial mathematics. Deacon and Mr Mageye and Jonah Jones and Bone (myself) and the Prisoner and the Doctor and the Inspector and giants of chaos were witnesses to the diminutive composite epic that drove us into trial and error betrothal to fates and furies and dangerous maids, trial and error gestations in the Womb of space, infinite tragedy yet hope of divergence from absolute plot, absolute doom.

Deacon and his procession below us in the savannahs was a subconscious miniaturisation of collective mystery, miniaturisation of Classical Palestine, Classical Greece, Classical Maya in dwarf-like substance, true, unsuspected intercourse with complex, cross-cultural tradition . . .

Deacon had propelled himself upwards as he led his father's beaten horses, beaten by sun and drought, ribbed cages on which weak members of the family sat, from upriver Courantyne to downriver Crabwood Creek.

Propelled himself upwards into a Shadow beside Mr Mageye and me on the Platform of the Camera where we sat.

He was exhausted after the long journey. He seemed naked Shadow as I was naked Bone and Mr Mageye was naked, spiritual Jester. We pushed him down again as he had pushed his train into the darkness of a coffin. He was exhausted. He settled in sleep on the lid of the coffin. The sigh of the river against the bank resembled buried souls in the wood of the box koker on which his head lay. Then he arose at last and made his way home.

Discovering Wilson Harris

Kathleen Raine

It is the mark of the new that we never know what it will be until it arrives. Of one thing only we can be sure, that it is unpredictable and is never the outcome of existing "trends." The wind that bloweth where it listeth is unconstrained, blows round corners. Current ideologies determined by mechanistic and "evolutionary" premises are likely to see the future as the product of the past, whereas perhaps that past is the product of the future in a living—and therefore purposeful—universe. Teleology, rejected by Darwinian evolutionism returns. In Wilson Harris's world it is premises which are in question, the unknowable determinants. Thus the figure of Virgil and the meaning of his epic are changed by Dante, and Dante in turn resituated by what he becomes for Wilson Harris. The past is living and continually changing because of the future which changes it. Or perhaps there is only one time, one place, one total being in which every human life, every creature and every particle, has its eternal presence within a whole participated by all. Throw away our preconceptions and all becomes very simple—but it is precisely our preconceptions of which we are least aware.

If Harris's work and his world are difficult to come to terms with (as I have gradually discovered), it is not because they are more complex but because they are simpler, closer to the reality of actual experience, than the way of seeing that our highly complex Western civilization has imposed on us, as if it were an unquestionable norm. In reality that "norm" is fragmented and incoherent. We live, for example, as if our waking and our sleeping selves were different persons; our past and our present were separate worlds, as if our dead are no longer with us when they no longer share our present. More and more we have come to live in the immediately sensibly perceptible space circumscribed by our bodily senses at a given moment. Wilson Harris, by contrast, sees clearly that there are really no such boundaries and frontiers to the universe we inhabit. The final imaginative realization to which he leads us is an unbounded unity, of which every part has access to the whole, and that living whole includes every part. He gives us access to ourselves in a way that does not destroy but restores an original simplicity, the simplicity of our original Edenic state, which we have lost and to which we are forever seeking to return—and which in reality we have never left, otherwise than by thinking ourselves into the unnoticed complexity of the modern world.

We find ourselves in a simpler, but also a very much larger world than the restricted universe of Western materialism. Wilson Harris restores us to the world of soul, as it rightly belongs to us; however we may have struggled to accomodate ourselves to the lifeless universe of a materialist ideology for which not consciousness, but "matter" is the ground of what we have chosen to call reality. In that lifeless world we ourselves are mortal, and meanings and values have all but vanished into an ultimate *nihil*. In Harris's world our "carnival masks" are worn by the ever-living; they are at once our human guises, which we present to the world, and the "windows" through which the ever-living may look into world's carnival—as Lear imagined "God's spies." The masks change, come and go, sometimes we do not know if the guiser is the same or another, whether the mask is the same or another, for the law of this old-new world Harris opens for us is metamorphosis, continuous and subtle and liberating. Indeed, liberation is the final meaning, the shedding and assuming of selves in an open universe. It is, as it seems, a Christian universe, whose work and end is redemptive— indeed, Harris uses the word *resurrection* in his title *Resurrection at Sorrow Hill*. The Cross and the Two Thieves—the two Brothers enacting the parts of Good and Evil—move through the great Epic of Redemption—Christo is the name of another epic masquer.

The impression of characters who come and go, disappear only to reappear elsewhere, is at first reading bewildering but we come to accept the truth of this interweaving of unbroken continuities flowing like water mingling in the one river. No one and nothing can be pinned down—Wilson Harris's intent is at the opposite extreme from the depiction of clear-cut and unique identity of "characters" in a nineteenth-century novel, created by their authors, participants in a world where individuation seemed more significant (and in a certain tradition of the novel this is still so) than epic universality. Harris writes of a quantum world—by *quantum* so applied to persons I take him to mean the property of a particle which is at the same time a wave, simultaneously located and unlocated. We are all increasingly aware of such a world, as measurable matter converges with immeasurable mind, aware of the space-time universe itself continually traversed by waves and particles, coming and going on their invisible trajectories to which we are continually but for the most part unconsciously exposed—if indeed these quanta are not ourselves. This is a most modern paradigm and also most ancient, the world soul traversed by angelic and elemental spirits, its aspect at once novel and deeply familiar. To read his novels is to experience a new strangeness that yet comes to us like a memory of something already and forever known. "Originality," in the sense of something never previously thought of and quite different from the already known, is incomprehensibly nowadays deemed an academic virtue and encouraged even among students of philosophy. Yet what *is* can only be itself, and its recognition leads not into outer space but is always a homecoming—"so it is true after all"—a building, not a dismantling, of what we term reality.

This recognition and assent belong not to reason but to the Imagination, which is a totality, is, according to William Blake, "the human existence itself," perhaps the Self of Vedant with its triple aspect, being-consciousness-bliss (*sat-ohitananda*). Reason, so far as I know, has no means of making a value judgment of a work of imagination. But this unscholarly account of a personal response to the world of a new great writer's vision would be incomplete without making reference to the power of Imagination, which for Harris himself is central. The first is too simple for the professional critics of today, though well known to the writers of the Jewish Bible: the response of the body, when the hairs of the head rise up in response to the presence of the Spirit. My gray hairs stir red in response to a quality in the writings of Wilson Harris that I would venture to call beauty—a word which has lost all meaning, one might be tempted to believe, for modern secular criticism and for a great deal of the work criticized also. Beauty has come to be deemed a falsification of reality, whose presently accepted image is closer to that powerful nihilist painter Francis Bacon's rotting yet protesting corpses than to Dante's "perfect human body." Yet for Plato, as for all traditional thought, beauty is the very aspect of the real, announces its presence in a numinous manner (the body's response of the hair stirring at the roots), the sense of deep recognition of what we are and what our universe, that we know also as the Good and the True. Of which indeed we have no knowledge other than this instantaneous assent of the Imagination.

Wilson Harris has written poems of great beauty—for poetry is normally the use of language in the service of this imaginative vision—but as it seems the poet has chosen to speak in the guise of the novelist, or, as it might be truer to say, of the epic, "The Infinite Rehearsal," as Harris himself calls that mystery we enact. What distinguishes the epic narrative above all from the narrative of the novel is that the latter is concerned with events in the life of the empirical daily self, without regard to that level signified in earlier epics by the participation in human affairs of the gods. Or should I rather say the participation of human life in the mysteries of higher worlds? Are the gods returning, of late, to participate in our lives? One thinks of certain novels from Latin America or Africa. It is this dimension which is, to my mind, the proper theme of poetry, and the narrative works of all great epics, not to mention the world's fairy tales. *The Mahabharata,* Homer, Virgil, Dante, the Arthurian Cycle. Proust described himself as a poet, and so, curiously enough, did Balzac. Under no circumstances could the word be applied to Dickens or to George Eliot. Poetry is the language of the soul—sometimes we may be inclined to believe it is a dead language, so far as our own Western civilization is concerned. But then one reads some new work—I think of my own first reading of David Jones's *In Parenthesis* or at an even earlier time the novels of Thomas Hardy—and the vision unexpectedly returns. In the novels of Wilson Harris a new and fresh beauty announces the sacred presence. Amazingly beautiful descriptions of the natural world, river and waterfall, tropical forests, tropical flowers, human participation in something cosmic, in a great mystery, the Great Battle, in resurrection and metamorphosis. And we know ourselves back on familiar-unfamiliar ground, the lost country, back where we belong. Yet all is simple, the people who wear the carnival masks are almost anonymous, and for all the marvelous exotic scenery of *The Guyana Trilogy* and elsewhere, the author deals with simple central human issues of the one human story in which we are all involved. No other writer known to me at this time writes from the imaginative depth and truth communicated by Wilson Harris.

Lines Composed after Reading
The Guyana Quartet

Zulfikar Ghose

A garden and below it a forest sloping away down a valley comprise the landscape beyond my window, a world populated—naturally enough, because there can be no intermediate state—by the living and the dead. One ought to be able to affirm that the intensity of the present is all there is: the light this November afternoon, sharply picking out the migrating monarch butterflies dawdling at the garden's edge where clusters of milkweed flourish, is so punctiliously revelatory that even the summer's last flowers on the abelia bush fifty feet away, their tiny white bell-shaped flower-heads like bits of ivory in the jade-green leaves, are as distinctly outlined as the image of a constellation of squares in a framed etching on the wall across from where I sit, looking out and in. Some brown-edged leaves have fallen on the lawn, a squirrel hops among the acorns scattered in front of the garden bench below an oak tree. And oh, there's a blue sky above it all, no doubt about it!

But truly, there is only the intermediate state, the one in which we are not yet dead but no longer wholly among the living either: premonitions are projected before our startled eyes of a future already envisioned as a fossil embedded in ancient rocks; or there is a curious after-image which glows at the back of one's brain as if one saw the dying embers among the ashes of one's own cremation; and of birth the images are of a catastrophe yet to be endured in the *ritual of waste and the purest consolation of being*. I look away from the window and am possessed by *the mesmerism of shadow and flickering illumination*. A breeze shifts the limbs of an oak, momentarily a beam of light splits the shadow, or it could be that, book in hand, I have dozed off and the air-conditioning just coming on with a sudden cool current has awakened within my sleep, deep within the shadow of my consciousness, a cinematic flickering of images which were only now mysterious and perplexing words. The black-winged carrion crow drops down to the beach where the corpse of Abram, which is no longer his body—for a tiger has eaten his identifiable flesh—wears the clothes of the living Cristo who is compelled to be a fugitive from the habitat of the living and must wear the tiger's skin upon his back.

Spitting out an angry tuck-tuck-tuck-tuck from the back of its throat, a squirrel expresses its irritation and defiance, staring down from an upper limb of a chinaberry at the cat on the ground looking up at it with an ambiguous intent; the squirrel's loud threats draw my eyes up from the page— with its camouflage of language that vividly paints the unmistakable design on the tiger's skin and yet alerts the mind to the *extravagant deceptions* of exegetical pretension—to the scene outside the window. But there is no squirrel there; and the cat, I remember, lies buried under the mound of rocks I piled to mark his grave—oh, a year ago—in the forest of junipers and oaks on the sloping land below my garden. Far down in the forest, I suddenly perceive the source of the sound I took for the squirrel's quarrel with the cat. For now it has stopped and the air is pierced by the deep-throated call of a Carolina wren.

But there is no wren there either. This has been the land of the Apaches for some centuries. I cannot believe this silence. The world has gone empty, its creatures withdrawn, sucked back in some universal regression as if time took a deep breath and held it within its blackhole gullet. My eyes stare at the etching—an explosion of little squares, lit up at the center as if reflecting some distant sun or moon, darkening into nothingness in the outer illusion of black space—and *execute a picture of the void in themselves,* my suddenly shocked eyes *surrendering to the open violence of time.* From my dumbstruck mouth come daSilva's words—*Everything Ah tell you dreaming long before the creation I know of begin. Everything turning different, changing into everything else Ah tell you.*

I look down at the hallucinatory forest of junipers and oaks. No, I have wandered far into it, this primeval forest of serpentine roots and choking vines, as when, for this time is always that time, in the small craft with its outboard chug-chug-chug motor I entered the mouth of the great river, my whole being but a bubble in the swift flow of the river's blood, and was ferried as if to the source, the dark, throbbing heart, in the equatorial interior. Who could have dreamed of birth in that masquerade of the rainforest with its thick canopy through which filtered a vague recollection of light *in the half-shadow and the half-world?* Only the dead, surely, of whom I was one, who can doubt that, not I, surely, in my marvelous *stumbling intuition of self.* The world had to be accorded a speculative body, creation was a what-if/what-if-not thought to be entertained, or else *the difficulty in overcoming the context of appearance* would be insuperable. I was prepared to believe that I heard birds singing and that in sudden openings in the roof of the rainforest when the wind tore open gaps there were caught in the quickly passing penetration of light the gaudy colored wings of parrots and araras and that my passage was not *in the shadow of pure nothingness.* It was a persuasion of will, as if mine were the turkey buzzard's vision from above the crown of the forest which must seek matter, an anxiety really for sustenance, that forced reflective surfaces to sparkle back from the coal-black facets of that substantial shadow to feed the soul's hunger for light. A *wild visionary prospect* leaped from that darkness, presenting to my now perfectly receptive and undoubting perception *the lucid design which demolished all dimensions.*

An Apache stands in the shade of a juniper on the stony bank of the dry creek where the forest slopes to the valley floor and when he hears the squirrel's tuck-tuck-tuck-tuck he cups his hands in front of his mouth and produces the Carolina wren's deep-throated call. Then all is silent in the forest, or there is the semblance of the absence of speech, and that time when there is no sound becomes fragmented and I find myself staring at the Apache as if *he was myself standing outside of me while I stood inside of him.* Time is scattered about me like bits of broken glass around a wrecked automobile and catches unexpected points of light that shoot up as arrows. From my resurrected Apache self I aim an arrow at my own *immateriality and mysterious substantiality,* and see from his envisioned future this moment of our common delusional history; it is as when the eye is drawn into the revolving vortex of colored lines on the video monitor showing a computer-generated representation of a picture transmitted from space where no human has been, one is not at all surprised by the design. Constructivist artists invented that geometrical representation of the universe a century ago. Arrows of time flying off in all directions intersect here and there in a million places and at one point the image within the mirrors of the Hubble telescope is of a garden in Staffordshire where a manuscript page is fallen on the grass showing a schematic drawing of the forking paths of an ancient maze. Oh, but I have a longing *to see the indestructible nucleus and redemption of creation,* a longing like Prufrock's to hold and squeeze the universe into a ball, a longing that all time become *one serial fused moment,* which it is, which it is, but oh there is no doubt about it. Abram, Cristo. The one consumed, the other consuming, dressed in the lustful animal's skin, the one dead, the other mourned as dead though living. And Donne and Fenwick, the one who journeys towards *the palace of the universe,* the other who has arrived at the still core of darkness, the lip of the abyss or *the prison of the void* whence originated time, in a boat that bears the name of the same palace, the one who must see himself inwardly melting into nothingness, the other who coming to the end has arrived at the beginning and awakens to witness the seventh day dawn. And Beti, *the bride of spiritual fantasy,* and Magda, whore and mother with *the heresy of truth locked in her bosom,* women of biblical dimension. And Mohammed, Kaiser, Rajah, Ram, with their land and money preoccupations to distract them from their shadow existence so far from ancestral India it is as if they found themselves in some underworld, whose fault is it, they ask, *if the only language we got is a breaking-up or a making-up language?* These are also the inhabitants of my forest, my Apache eye follows their comings and goings, for long ago *they had passed the door of inner perception like a bird of spirit breaking the shell of the sky which had been the only conscious world,* almost as if reading the fiction now I merely affirm the empirical force of a cognition essentially mystical. But if this time is that time, there is another still in the succession of days on each of which awakens the resolutely rational self determined not to be deluded, when I have come out of the equatorial interior, risen out of the great river and out of the jungle's *vision of buried fertility,* and come to the blinding desert, so much light that there is a reversal of the properties of perception, come so far from under the shadow of the rainforest where wildly the waters ran past the fork in the river and tumbled in frothy white cascades and leaping falls into dark valleys, come to this *border of mystery and blind apprehension.* Nothing but sand dunes and barren rocks now ochre and now nearly white and now orange as the sun rises, stops for its eternal noon, and sets. This is a land of *strangeness and catastrophe in a destitute world,* so far from any dream of earthly fertility it is known in all recorded accounts as the Valley of the Moon. Though my feet sink in the sand, I experience an airy levitation, for there is not a drop of moisture between the blue ceiling and the white floor, no reason for being in this nothingness, I am overcome by *the unfeeling heresy in the sceptical weight of existence.* But between this sand at my feet and the barren mountain on the horizon there is, invisible now but I shall soon come to it, a depression in the land, a deep canyon in fact, where an underground river springs out of the lifeless sand and for two miles there is a strip of green land where, unplanted and untended, wild flowers grow, proving that the deathly shadow in the Valley of the Moon is but *a cruel ambush of soul,* or the soul's apprehension of finding no release from the body's leaden weight where it sinks in the sand. And yet there is this sudden contradiction in the desert, where the flowering is aggressively fertile, which creates an unbearable, but curiously pleasant, itching on one's shoulders, as if wings were beginning to grow there.

NOTE

The phrases printed in italics are quotations from *The Guyana Quartet* (London: Faber and Faber, 1985) and, in order of appearance, are taken from the following pages: 450, 279, 396, 462, 457, 87, 277, 206, 169, 459, 28, 348, 26, 82, 101, 305, 112, 464, 228, 268, 155, 76, 311, 145, 116, 414, 33.

Wilson Harris
"In the Forests of the Night"

Pauline Melville

For those of us who are following Wilson Harris in the tradition of Guyanese literature, there is no doubt that he has transformed the literary landscape of the region, and we would be unwise (as would the rest of the world) to ignore his blazing signposts as we try to chart our way forward.

As a writer of fiction and as a fellow Guyanese, there are certain lessons that it has been my privilege to learn from this extraordinary writer. Like Wilson, I have spent many years out of Guyana. But from him I have learned that nationalism is not necessarily important for the creative artist. He gave me confidence in the idea that my imagination can be my homeland and that it can be fed from many sources.

Each of Wilson Harris's novels is a dense nexus of dream, myth, archetype, and prophecy that cuts clearly across the conventions of much Caribbean literature—a literature which mainly focuses on the purely historical features of slavery, colonialism, or indentured labor and which surrenders to an overwhelmingly materialist view of the post-Columbian period. I can think of no other English-speaking writer who deals with pre-Columbian myth and history reaching back through time to the Aztec and Mayan civilizations and who weaves threads from other civilizations as well, Greco-Roman for example, into a complex picture of the present. His work is courageous and visionary. It is revolutionary both in content and form, a melting-pot of the material and spiritual history, not just of the region but of the deepest levels of all humanity. He is not afraid to draw on whatever tradition—European, South American, Asian, or Judeo-Christian—that will give form to his ideas. In that sense his writing is a benison and a living example of redemption through integration.

There is no doubt that we experience, when reading his novels, the sense of a writer who is at some level possessed. This tradition, the tradition of Dante, Milton, and Blake, has mainly deserted modern European literature. The Amerindian shaman who was also in touch with spirits and was able to time travel, communicating his insights in the poetic, oral tradition is similarly an increasingly rare phenomenon on our continent. In modern times the sacred is dangerously under attack from the profane. Science and rationalism, for all their benefits, are hunting down and destroying other sorts of wisdom. Imagination is on the run. Much contemporary writing throughout the world has eagerly and exclusively embraced the profane surface of daily life and deals with the face of things. Wilson Harris deals with the archaeology of human experience and knowledge. The mysterious links and structures that so often remain hidden from us are revealed and shown to have a beautiful and cohesive pattern. The work is a rare repository of the sacred and the visionary. He is the man who can see the mask behind the face and write about it.

It seems to me that Wilson is the most Dionysian of writers. And in some ways this is terrifying to many people. We should not underestimate the terror that can be produced by his work. The books speak to us in tongues. Many people in this secular age do not have the framework in which to receive them. Dionysus is a god of rapture as well as a deliverer and a healer. All these qualities are present in Wilson Harris's work. He understands ecstasy too—a rare gift these days and a dangerous one. For the writer who only seeks commercial success or tabloid popularity, these extremes of inspiration and this rigorous integrity are things to be avoided. For the writer who addresses his fellow human beings from a certain tragic consciousness and who knows that if his audience does not listen they run the risk of being destroyed, these qualities possess a poignant risk. Here we have a writer of great intellect as well as passion who pits his imagination against certain titanic forces of emptiness, tyranny, and death that are at work in today's world.

Dionysus is a god who will overwhelm those who ignore or deny him. We cannot say we have not been warned.

It is no reflection on the man himself, whose gentleness and grace is known to many, if I say that his work is like a leopard loose among us. Everyone regards it with awe and no one quite knows what to do about it. But admire it, we do. And it is no coincidence that the leopard, or tiger/jaguar as we call it in Guyana, is both the sacred animal of our region and, according to classical tradition, the favorite animal of Dionysus. The creature is astonishingly beautiful, exceedingly graceful, untameable, powerful, elegant, and highly dangerous. In the Rupununi district of Guyana where I spend much of my time, stories of this beast are legendary. It makes no compromises. It does not negotiate. The danger as far as the reader is concerned is that the illumination from the burning bright tiger of Harris's work is too dazzling after the shadowy world of half-lies, sentiment, and complacency that is the province of much modern fiction and most modern politics.

I should not like this essay to concentrate so much on the power of the work that it neglects to mention Wilson Harris's sense of humor and the delicate irony he uses in playing, for instance, with the fictional autobiographers who frequently dictate their work to him. There is a great deal of delight in this playfulness.

However, it is the power and originality of the work that is most impressive. It is groundbreaking work. And in some ways I imagine that he must suffer from the isolation that all true innovators have to bear. Those in the vanguard are often way ahead of their time. When I talk of the danger in his work, it is not to say that the work is harmful but that the author takes death-defying risks with form. Such pioneering work invites attack from the forces of reaction and others are initially too timid to follow where such a writer leads. That is the challenge for the generations of Guyanese writers who follow in his footsteps. Who will dare to pick up such a mantle?

Few modern writers possess the qualities of the prophet and seer in addition to possessing an inspired gift for fiction. Wilson Harris has such gifts. What many of us feel about his genius is, perhaps, best expressed in the words of Coleridge:

> Weave a circle round him thrice
> And close your eyes with holy dread
> For he on honey-dew hath fed
> And drunk the milk of Paradise.

Postcoloniality/Modernity: Wilson Harris and Postcolonial Theory

Stuart Murray

The continuing theoretical debate over the shape and size, the resonances and the responsibilities, of postcolonialism grows daily more complex. Questions of what might be termed—generalizing—the "local" (an adversarial nationalism, an essentialized concentration on the subject body within postcoloniality, the relationship between the term *postcolonial* and the praxis of localized politics) are set against the "interstitial" (Homi Bhabha's concept of the "in-between," the rejection of binary oppositions, a genealogical spectrum for the fracturing and flawed nature of colonial discourse and postcolonial articulation). And this example of the local/interstitial is itself an instance (and only one among many that could have been chosen) of the ways in which presentation of fluid issues finds itself funneling into dualities even as it tries to question the validity of such a model.[1]

I will hang on to the framework articulated above, even though it encompasses gross oversimplifications, and though through his work he reconfigures it, because it seems to me to be a useful starting point for a discussion of Wilson Harris's continuing problematic relationship with postcolonial theory and its developing methodologies.

Hena Maes-Jelinek has provided the most comprehensive and articulate description of Harris's ambivalent relationship with the orthodoxies of postcolonial theory (as well as modern critical theories in general). In " 'Numinous Proportions': Wilson Harris's Alternative to All 'Posts' " Maes-Jelinek outlines the forcefulness of Harris's vision and the incapacity of modern theories to account for his working method, in particular the creative disruption of Harris's configuration of the imagination, the drama of consciousness, and the "living fossil strata" (Harris, "Validation") that ties the past to the postcolonial present through a bridge of cross-cultural communication. Maes-Jelinek is interested primarily in a discussion of Harris within the framework of a debate between postmodernism and postcolonialism, but her stress on Harris's connection between art and life, his conception of the moral nature of literature, and his view of language as an enabling device toward a nonessential truth, places him outside standard poststructuralist theories of writing.

The force of Maes-Jelinek's critique is formidable, yet what seems interesting is that a writer who is so successful at effacing narrative authority (from the vanishing of the narrator in *Palace of the Peacock* to the constant revisions and modifications of Hope's "asylum book" in *Resurrection at Sorrow Hill*) is discussed so continually in terms of the primacy of authorial intent. The alternative that Maes-Jelinek identifies, and what I want to discuss in terms of a relationship between postcoloniality and modernity, is constantly located within the locutionary position occupied by Wilson Harris as creative, individual artist.

I shall return to this primacy of Harris as author in a moment, but first it will be useful to stress the ways in which his work intersects and challenges the dominant dynamics of contemporary postcolonial theory. Both Linda Hutcheon and Stephen Slemon have been at pains recently to point out the potential crisis in postcolonial criticism, one where the broadly agreed emancipatory and anti-imperialist project of such criticism runs a risk of descending into an institutionalized squabble over methodologies. Harris, in both his fiction and his criticism, has always sought to stress the necessity for postcolonial articulation, a writing back that claims the locutionary (local) position for the decolonized. But he does so with a parallel call to redress what he terms "a form of self-righteous deprivation" in the mechanics of postcolonial study (Interview with Riach 37). Harris is no anti-essentialist set against the varied essentialist discourses—whether they be a concentration on the physicality of the body to produce a radical subjectivity or an aggressive adversarial nationalism/regionalism creating a decolonized collective—that postcolonial theory utilizes. He has no wish to be involved within the terms of that debate. In his concentration on the "multi-faceted, partial images" (Interview with Riach 33) that he seeks to express in his work and the necessity to take on "the burden of the double" ("Literacy" 20), Harris positions himself firmly against the arguments within postcolonial theory that function through binary oppositions. He does not set the local and interstitial natures of colonial and postcolonial discursive practices against each other, but reconfigures them as a flexible continuum.

In this sense Harris comes close to points of postcolonial theory articulated by both Homi Bhabha and Gayatri Spivak. In his articulation of the constructions of identity through colonial discourse, Bhabha returns to re-read Frantz Fanon and emerges with a view of the perversion of the space between colonizer and colonized:

The representative figure of such a perversion, I want to suggest, is the image of post-Enlightenment man tethered to, *not* confronted by, his dark reflection, the shadow of colonized man, that splits his presence, distorts his outline, breaches his boundaries, repeats his actions at a distance, disturbs and divides the very time of his being. (ix)

In *Resurrection at Sorrow Hill* Harris presents the inmates of the postcolonial asylum *who are also* their historical doubles from a time when that space was a colonial prison. Thus Caribbean personal identity, the local characters of the novel, are at one and the same time Leonardo, Marx, Socrates, Montezuma, Judas, and the mother of Akhenaton, in a display of cross-culturalism that is an example of the tethering (and the lack of confrontation) of which Bhabha speaks. Similarly, Harris's method in his latest novel is the kind of technique that, to quote Spivak, "pluralizes the grid" in a fashion that maintains the "adequate narratives of the concept-metaphors" (17) of decolonization within the space of the decolonized and not through the catachrestic maneuvers of the colonizers. In Spivak's articulation of the current debate, Harris's refusal to engage with the orthodox postcolonial formulations of community, identity, citizenship, or sovereignty means he is also outside a number of neocolonial institutionalized instruments of control.

And yet, it is too easy to argue a generalized pluralism that situates Harris within a framework articulated by Bhabha and Spivak. A concentration on pluralism or multiculturalism without adequate interrogation of these terms is simply another essentialism. It is in his conception of the imagination, of intuition, of the formulation that Maes-Jelinek terms a "mysterious reality" (58) that Harris sets himself outside the theories of Bhabha and Spivak. The inevitability of the unknowable, the untranslatable, the ungraspable, underpins much of Harris's fiction—the pre-Columbian past that feeds into the Guyanese present—and it is these ideas that produce a cleavage between his theories of the postcolonial and those emanating from poststructuralist or deconstructive practices.

Here it is useful to return to the question of Harris as author. I would suggest that a method for the exploration of this question is to understand that, for Harris, the postcolonial is situated necessarily within the framework of a wider, global, modernity. The fact that this modernity—organizing around voyages of exploration, the consolidation of capital, and the formation of the social and the individual in modern political terms—emanates from Europe is in no way to devalue twentieth-century Caribbean political independence and the force of contemporary postcolonial articulation. Much of this modernity was articulated in the eighteenth century by writers in Scotland whose position could be interrogated within questions of colonial discourse or by writers in France who expressed strong anticolonial opinions. In detailing the postcolonial present, Harris argues for firm links with a number of pasts, not just the precolonized literal and figurative spaces of South America but also the heritages of writing from Europe that accompany the colonial project. (In a 1980 interview with Daryl Cumber Dance, Harris talked of the "valuable" nature of "the European imagination with its obsession with the significance and the importance of art" [86]). In this formulation the local becomes destabilized, radicalized, while the interstitial becomes a matrix of connections, a numerous multivoiced conversation of differing geographical, institutional, psychic, and formal origins.

The implications of this modernity for the concept of Harris as creative artist, as creative author, can, I think, be read usefully through Foucault's idea of the author effect at the cusp of the modern. As Foucault shows in *The Order of Things,* the emergence of the concept of man as an object of scientific study and as the focus of modern knowledge at the end of the eighteenth century creates the category of History that posits a lack in man and then charts a teleology of progress of consciousness centered around ideas of the will that mesh with the new modern focus on temporality. Harris does not see either history or humanity in these terms. The way he charts representation (a key concept to Foucault's arguments), the concentration on the doubling and partial images, is characterized by the kind of emphasis on subjectivity and its ability to represent the object that is traced by both Foucault and Heidegger in their analyses of the origins of the modern.

As C. L. R. James and others have pointed out, Harris studied Heidegger and positioned the implications of Heidegger's concept of *Vorstellung* within a postcolonial context. For Heidegger, the "freedom" produced when man becomes the subject of man is the unique formation of modern power. Implicit here is the ability to construct the Other, but Harris is wary of such a duality. His fiction retains a common ground between Science and Art and refuses to allow the kind of polarization that Heidegger sees as one of the defining criteria of the modern. In this sense Harris resists what Foucault would term the modern obsession with life, where knowledge is channeled into a series of sciences that aim to explain and codify man's relationship with the world. I would suggest that Harris's work is more in keeping with Foucault's definition of the classical episteme, where language functions in terms of multiple representations which are not fixed to the world within set material or historical codes.

In a sense this is to argue that elements of Harris's attitudes toward the expression of his postcolonial vision could be labeled premodern. In his desire to retain the resonances of both colonizer and colonized within the imaginative fabric of his fiction, Harris returns to an authorial and epistemological position that precedes the codifying practices of early modernity. (This premodern sense of the author could be argued in terms of the loss of narrative authority in so many of his novels.) In "What Is an Author?" Foucault sees the authorial ownership of discourse—the creation of the author—as a process codified by the move from the classical to the modern episteme. I would argue that Harris produces fiction that seeks to bypass this coding process. When Foucault writes of writing "creating an opening where the writing subject endlessly disappears" (116), we can see how Harris as an *author function* creates a complex locutionary position that attaches itself to the polyvalent notion of postcoloniality we find in his fiction. Harris's notion of "alchemy," the creative response to the deprivations inherent in much postcolonial praxis, is set explicitly against the kind of centralization formed around the genesis of the modern project. As the word itself suggests, an alchemic response reaches back toward a less codified series of representations.

This is the outline of a wider thesis. There are a number of key points—revolving around questions of language, logic, morality, value, modernism, and tradition—that I have not been able to address in depth here. And this is no attempt to force Harris into a particular form of categorization; his writing defies this. But precisely because of the problematic labeling of Harris's work, it has become all too easy to resort to a general celebration of pluralism when reading his fiction. I feel that an investigation through the inchoate cultural formations of an early modernity offers new insights on Harris's postcolonialism.

NOTE

[1]Of course the validity of this model is under continual interrogation from postcolonial theorists and critics. Gayatri Spivak's articulation of "strategic" interventions is perhaps the most forceful theory to address this.

WORKS CITED

Bhabha, Homi. "Remembering Fanon: Self, Psyche and the Colonial Condition." Foreword to *Black Skin, White Masks,* by Frantz Fanon. London: Pluto, 1986. vii-xxvi.

Foucault, Michel. *The Order of Things: An Archaeology of the Human Sciences.* New York: Vintage, 1970.

————. "What Is an Author?" Trans. Donald F. Bouchard and Sherry Simon. *Language, Counter-Memory, Practice: Selected Essays and Interviews.* Ed. Donald F. Bouchard. Oxford: Basil Blackwell, 1977. 113-38.

Harris, Wilson. *Palace of the Peacock.* London: Faber and Faber, 1960.

————. "Literacy and the Imagination." *The Literate Imagination: Essays on the Novels of Wilson Harris.* Ed. Michael Gilkes. London: Macmillan, 1989. 13-30.

————. "Validation of Fiction: A Personal View of Imaginative Truth." *Tibisiri, Caribbean Writers and Critics.* Ed. Maggie Butcher. Aarhus: Dangaroo Press, 1989. 40-51.

————. Interview by Daryl Cumber Dance. *New World Adams: Conversations with Contemporary West Indian Writers.* Leeds: Peepal Tree, 1992. 80-95.

————. Interview by Alan Riach. *The Radical Imagination: Lectures and Talks.* Ed. Alan Riach and Mark Williams. Liege: Université de Liege, 1992. 33-65.

————. *Resurrection at Sorrow Hill.* London: Faber and Faber, 1993.

Hutcheon, Linda. "Complexities Abounding." *PMLA* 110 (1995): 7-16.

James, C. L. R. "On Wilson Harris." *Spheres of Existence.* London: Allison and Busby, 1980. 157-72.

Maes-Jelinek, Hena. " 'Numinous Proportions': Wilson Harris's Alternative to All 'Posts.' " *Past the Last Post: Theorizing Post-Colonialism and Post-Modernism.* Ed. Ian Adam and Helen Tiffin. New York: Harvester,

1991. 47-64.

Slemon, Stephen. "The Scramble for Post-Colonialism." *De-Scribing Empire: Post-Colonialism and Textuality.* Ed. Chris Tiffin and Alan Lawson. London: Routledge, 1994. 15-32.

Spivak, Gayatri Chakravorty. "In a Word." Interview by Ellen Rooney. *Outside in the Teaching Machine.* New York: Routledge, 1993. 1-23.

Toward the Reading of Wilson Harris

Timothy J. Cribb

This essay sketches an approach to the nature of narrative in Wilson Harris's writing. I have chosen a passage ending book 2 of *Palace of the Peacock*, running between pages 26 and 31 of the one-volume edition of *The Guyana Quartet* (Faber and Faber, 1985). The text is identical with that on pages 24 to 31 of the single volume paperback edition first published in 1968. My choice is guided by the fact that in this passage the ordinary narrative of events is readily ascertainable; yet even so, a reader is likely to feel a degree of uncertainty. In Harris's later works that degree is much increased. By attending to the sources of the uncertainty here, one can obtain some guidelines for reading the later writing.

But first for the relative certainties. Tutored by four centuries of narrative tradition from Sir Walter Raleigh to Sir William Golding, a Western reader immediately recognizes the situation as a typical moment in a narrative of exploration: the portage of an expedition's boat and equipment around rapids on a venture to the interior. This recognition is itself instructive for reading later Harris, since typical situations derived from traditions, whether of exploration or domesticity, still function beneath the surface. The reader is thus well advised to read quickly, without preconceptions, trusting the text to trigger recognitions which, once realized, lend orientation for a much slower rereading. Anyone who has had the experience of reading *Finnegans Wake* or parts of *Ulysses* will know how to do this.

Orientation, however, is precisely not what the writing seeks to impart. Compare the passage chosen with three other moments of fear within the tradition of novels of exploration: Robinson Crusoe's discovery of the footprint on his island, Conrad's Marlow, perturbed by an eerie cry coming out of the mist in *Heart of Darkness*, or Forster's Mrs. Moore in the Marabar Caves in *A Passage to India*. After his initial panic, Crusoe analyzes the event in the light of reason, recovers self-control, and sets about extending that control over the new situation. Marlow, situated within Conrad's play of irony as he is, nonetheless preserves his stoic calm, which is instrumental to the operational success of his mission, however hollow the success. Forster's Mrs. Moore, after peering into her own heart of darkness, emerges to find that the experience of the echo gathers force within her, draining life of meaning, leaving her in an irritably posthumous state, playing patience, waiting for actual death. These three moments mark the stages of a traditional movment from confidence through crisis to exhaustion. The moment of fear is like a test, which all in varying ways survive. Were they to have failed the test, the story line would not have been able to continue and that is what makes them the heroes of their stories.

Harris's narrator is both the heir of this heroic tradition and a departure from it, and as such is closest to Mrs. Moore. One index of this is gender, normatively masculine in the tradition of exploration. Here, at the beginning of the passage, the male crew toil to thrust the prow of their boat deeper into the interior; by the end, the narrator has succumbed to his irrational panic and is explicitly unmanned.

Of itself this might make him no more than an anti-hero, coming late in the tradition, as in Graham Greene. But Harris's writing goes beyond this. With Defoe, Conrad, and Forster, the moment of fear is something that is overcome or, at the least, known and hence completed; the narrative can proceed through it and out the other side. The temporal horizon of the narration is concealed from the reader so that the events have the immediacy of experience, but this is really only a rhetorical device to achieve a reality effect, and the narrative is driving toward its horizon all the time. That is what keeps us reading.

Harris takes up the capacity of the first-person narration to immerse the reader in the immediacy of experience, but instead of leading the reader out the other side, leaving a completed incident behind, he lets it hang in the air in a curious state of undetermined suspense. True, in this instance the narrator appears to faint and appears to come round from his (or her) faint in the arms of old Schomburgh and young Carroll. But what actually happened? Old Schomburgh asks three times, but each time Carroll interposes an answer, and this can have only the status of a hypothesis, a possible interpretation. Carroll believes that the narrator saw something. A reader seeking to answer the question might observe that it seems more as if the narrator heard something. And, at the end of the section, when the narrator appears to be about to deny that he saw something, he represses the impulse to deny and instead leads us back over the narrative ground from which the incident sprang, multiplying its traces to the point where the exploring reader finds it impossible to determine whether the narrator dreamed the incident or the incident dreamed him.

The reader thus has to read like a common reader, with a naive openness to experience as it occurs, especially when Harris employs first-person narration, yet then question and revise the experience just had, not according to the lights of reason and doubt, but within the manifold of infinity. This process of revision is built into the writing. In a sense the act of interpretation, of speculative revision, has already been incorporated into it. In Harris's later writing that process is taken much further and consumes more of the ordinary narrative. The reader has accordingly more work to do in recognizing its vestiges and allowing their implications to expand in the mind.

What keeps us reading in Harris, then, is the experience of rereading, a constant recirculation of narrative event and sensory description. This is the pleasure of it. The originating experience is not annulled but liberated; the moment of fear becomes a moment of freedom, entered into, accepted. The driving quest of the original narrative is freed from necessity. The result is a rare and strange kind of comedy.

Take the case of this passage. The primary source of the narrator's experience is probably a complex of Amerindian beliefs. Harris would have encountered these during the fifteen years he worked as surveyor in the rain forest and had them confirmed later in his reading of local ethnographers, such as Walter Roth, or travel writers like Michael Swann. According to Roth, writing in the *Thirtieth Annual Report of the Bureau of American Ethnology* in 1908–9, a number of different tribes in the Guyanas believe an individual to be partly composed of spirits, belonging to different attributes or aspects of the individual, such as the head, heart, or even footprint, and after death, these migrate to various parts of the forest. Still proceeding synthetically, Roth observes common factors in Amerindian mythology grouped around the figure of Yurokon, Yolok, Iya-imi, etc., which resemble those of the Aztec Huracan. He speculates that these figures may be identical with the Arawak idea of the Shadow-spirit of the bush, met with suddenly after an often unrecognized premonitory sigh. Any Indian so visited in the bush returns home to die.

The ubiquitous sigh, the footprint, the moment of fear, the sense that experience comes from both inside and outside the narrator—the analogues in the passage from Harris are obvious enough. That this ethnography is probably the primary material is important, because it positions the writing on the colonized side of the historical line dividing the colonizer from the native Other. That is the source of its moral responsibility. But Harris is the last person to be caught up in the sterile and typically Western dichotomies of self and Other. The act of narrating a story of exploration superimposes on the primary material a number of narrative layers—Robinson Crusoe's footprint, Marlow's eerie cry, and Mrs. Moore's disconcerting echo—all part of a Western tradition. But Harris's writing is determined neither by the native nor the Western. As he writes in his meditations on Amerindian beliefs in *The Age of the Rainmakers*: "The story or stories circulated about Awakaipu . . . are largely bound up I feel . . . with projections of a formal pattern—an unfeeling heroic consensus, closed plot, consolidated function or character—upon the inner breakdown of tribal peoples long subject to conquest and catastrophe." These same terms could be turned equally on the Western tradition, save that it is one of subjecting rather than being subjected. Harris's writing frees itself from both alike. Here, for instance, his narrator does not return home to die, for he is not a character in the traditional Western sense: he has no home, and he is already, from the beginning of the story, dead. One sees the strangeness of the comedy.

Thus in Harris the nature of the narrative incident and hence of overall narrative is radically redefined. He leaves the company of Defoe and Conrad and Forster and Greene and aligns himself with the modernism of Joyce. But in *Ulysses* the realism of Dublin's streets and of Stephen, Bloom, and Molly's thoughts has a nineteenth-century fullness of detail, and the modernism consists partly in the imposition on that realism of a series of linguistic filters through which we discern it as best we can; in *Finnegans Wake* such distinctions become impossible to maintain and all that can be known is in and through the play of language.

Neither in *Palace of the Peacock* nor in later Harris does language become preeminent in that way. True, he shares with Joyce a sense of the relativity of our means of knowledge of the world, and that relativity inevitably includes language, but supervening on this is a more ontological concern with the world and its salvation. Harris describes *The Age of the Rainmakers* as a personal exploration of vestiges of legend, then adds: "In defining this exploration as an arch or horizon I have sought not to ring those vestiges round but to release them as part and parcel of the mind of history— the fertilization of compassion—the fertilization of imagination—whose original unity can only be paradoxically fulfilled now."

Harris is both a modernist and a visionary and in this last respect jumps the smooth tracks we lay down for the development of the novel and joins company not with any other novelist but with a poet, Blake. As with Blake, the best gift one can bring to a reading of Harris is a capacity for wonder.

Breaking Down Barriers as Genesis of a New Beginning in Wilson Harris's Palace of the Peacock

Fernanda Steele

Palace of the Peacock, Wilson Harris's first novel, tells us of a scientific expedition from the savannahs into the interior of the Guyana forest, which the head of the expedition, Donne, and his crew can reach only by river. I should like to point out some formal aspects of *Palace of the Peacock* that might puzzle the reader on a first reading because he is plunged immediately into a world where everything happens in a rapid flowing of images and sensations, where many of the usual "barriers" have been abolished: life and death; dream and nondream. Past, present, and future are not distinguishable and often result in images I would call transparent in the sense that they allow one to see other images, other realities—as, for example, is the case with the old Amerindian woman who reminds us of Mariella, who in turn brings us to a Mission also called Mariella. Spaces interpenetrate, so that when one thinks he is reading of the crew on the river, suddenly he becomes aware that he is following them while they climb some rocks to reach the palace of the peacock.

All these are not "technical devices" in the mechanical sense one often talks about "narrative techniques," but they are part of the design of the novel which proposes precisely to abolish barriers that fossilize thought in order to arrive at a more real vision of the world that it narrates and whose boundaries it continuously expands. The reader is involved in this process, and he has to abandon his own burden of preconceived ideas, of prejudices, of static, fixed things, and abandon himself, on the contrary, to the narrative. The reading of *Palace of the Peacock* could be an experience of magical frustration, but not of arcane difficulty.

Immersed in what might seem a particular geography and particular history, those of Guyana, the novel uses the myth of El Dorado in its duality to explore not only the meaning of the conquest of the New World—which includes all of South America and the Caribbean—but the very concept of conquest. In *Tradition, the Writer and Society* Wilson Harris himself points out the duality of El Dorado: "The religious and economic thirst for exploration was true of the Spanish conquistador, of the Portuguese, French, Dutch and English, of Raleigh, of Fawcett, as it is true of the black modern pork-knocker and pork-knockers of all races. An instinctive idealism associated with this adventure was overpowered within individual and collective by enormous greed, cruelty and exploitation" (35). This sense of "enormous greed, cruelty and exploitation" caused entire indigenous populations to be annihilated to be later replaced by slaves imported from Africa and by East Indian people "contracted" in India, when slavery as a system of labor was ending. It has also been a reason for so many individuals in the New World to feel alienated from a land to which they have been brought by force and to wish now to rediscover their history in order to recover a sense of community to which to belong. All this is reflected in much of the literature of the region. But this holding on to "ethnic roots" leads to the same divisions which colonialism itself had strengthened and on which it had based its power for centuries. And, in some areas of the Caribbean, it has also led to serious social and political consequences.

I think that against this background, a reading of *Palace of the Peacock* can be based. The novel tells of a search, of a journey where two forces confront each other: a cruel materialism and an idealism in search of a spiritual community, represented by Donne and "I" respectively.

I should like to focus my attention first on "I" and for a while break the rules of a "normal" reading by beginning from the last pages of the book, where one reads: "This was the inner music and voice of the peacock I suddenly encountered and echoed and sang as I had never heard myself sing before. I felt the faces before me begin to fade and part company from me and from themselves as if our need of one another was now fulfilled, and our distance from each other was the distance of a sacrament, the sacrament and embrace we knew in one muse and one undying soul" (116-17).

If I then trace that "I" a little farther back, I find that he is the narrator, in fact, of the last two chapters of the book, the first of which says in its second sentence, "And the creation of the windows of the universe was finished" (111), while the second begins with, "The windows of the palace were crowded with faces" (116), and in between these two sentences I read a strange story that takes me to savannahs, cliffs, and windows of a place made almost of air, filled with music, built, it seems to me, together with the "we" and described by the "I." And I understand now that this place, this palace, the palace of the peacock, is not a construction made of stone and mortar and whatever else engineers and architects use to build houses with, one of those palaces that can even be photographed and maybe sent to friends on a postcard duly stamped, but it is the visualization of that "I"'s imaginary construction—one that he could build only because of his relationship with others (the "we" to which he refers)—of an inner space which, remembering that I have in fact read the book, is the end of the quest, of the journey with which the novel began. And I also know that when I read that "In the rooms of the palace where we firmly stood—free from the chains of illusion we had made without—the sound that filled us was unlike the link of memory itself. It was the inseparable moment within ourselves of all fulfillment and understanding" (116). I also know that this palace, this inner space, not only is "I"'s possession but also can be mine when I free myself of the fetters of time, of space, of learned things, of taught things, of dates and history books, of frozen static images, of frozen static judgments, of memory that freezes all events into a static time frame, and allow all these elements to roam freely within myself and to open new ways of feeling, understanding, interpreting, seeing.

I have mentioned that *Palace of the Peacock* breaks barriers. The first barrier is that imposed by learned ways of reading, where the reader is required to engage his "reason" to find answers. *Palace of the Peacock* requires the reader to use this reason, yes, but it goes beyond that, in that it also compels him to use his imagination to fill gaps, to follow a sentence, to forget a given idea of time and space. *Palace of the Peacock* is always leading the reader to a threshold, only for him to discover that there will be another one, in other words, into "a universe that can never be taken for granted as dead matter."

Let us take, for example, the threshold between death and life. The novel begins with an image of sudden death—"A horseman appeared on the road coming at *breakneck* stride. A *shot* rang out suddenly. . . . The horseman *stiffened* . . . and the horse reared, grinning fiendishly and *snapping* at the reins. The horseman gave a bow to heaven like a hanging man to his executioner, and rolled from his saddle on to the ground" (19, my italics).

This image is immediately followed by one of life: "The shot had *pulled me up.* . . . I started walking . . . and *approached* the man. . . . Someone *was* watching. . . . *Watching* me as *I bent down and looked* . . ." (19, my italics). These images of death and life are followed by one in which, somehow, the terms are inverted, as the action of seeing seems now to be performed by the dead man "whose open eyes stared at the sky" (19). However, this reversal of terms does not produce new static spaces, one for the living "I" and one for the dead man, but rather a space in between, for a peculiar kind of relationship is established as both "I" and the dead man are actually looking at each other from one meeting point, which I have called a threshold, borrowing this word from much of Wilson Harris's work: "The sun blinded and ruled my living sight but the dead man's eye remained open and obstinate and clear" (19).

As one proceeds to read the novel, one becomes aware that somehow the ground is always shifting and one is not quite sure whether one is reading about living or dead people. One reads, for example, that the members of the crew whose journey one thinks one is following had already drowned in the rapids: "Everyone remembered that not so long ago this self-same crew had been drowned to a man in the rapids below the Mission" (37), that "The whole crew was one spiritual family living and dying together in a common grave out of which they had sprung again from the same soul and womb as it were" (39). And, furthermore, the names of the members of this crew were those of another crew that had perished before them: "The odd fact existed of course that their living names matched the names of a famous dead crew that had sunk in the rapids and been drowned to a man, leaving their names inscribed on Sorrow Hill which stood at the foot of the falls.

But this in no way interfered with their lifelike appearance and spirit and energy" (26). What the narrative proposes and, indeed achieves, is precisely to break down such barriers, to abolish such clear-cut divisions so as to reach a vision of unity in which all the elements that compose it are encompassed.

Similarly, the novel breaks down barriers between dream and non-dream, barriers of how time and space are perceived. Dream and non-dream are woven together in the narrative. Just as events, real or imaginary, produce dreams, dreams in *Palace of the Peacock* also give an insight into events, often bringing us into a past that is no longer frozen by memory, but made alive by its being in a dream, making it an existing present and therefore offering possibilities of new ways of interpreting the events. Consequently, time can no longer be measured as a sequence of chronological events because these are presented as taking place simultaneously in the human mind. In this way, any hierarchical order of importance is abolished and ways are cleared for different evaluations. Within this context, space is presented as continuously shifting, and when the reader asks himself whether the narrative has led him into the camp or the savannahs, whether the crew is still maneuvering the boat on the river or is climbing a cliff, the answer is often in all these places at once, just as one often is in more than one space in one's imagination, for space in *Palace of the Peacock* is not simply a backdrop against which events take place, but has a status of its own, a life of its own that affects the lives of others.

WORKS CITED

Harris, Wison. *The Guyana Quartet.* London: Faber and Faber, 1985.
————. *Tradition, the Writer and Society.* London: New Beacon, 1967.

The Leech-Gatherer and the Arawak Woman

Louis James

One of Wilson Harris's most extraordinary passages of writing comes not in his fiction, but in an essay published in 1973. Harris tells of two moments of danger surveying the Potaro river above the Tumatumari rapids at a time of high water. An anchor snagged and had to be cut loose. Three years later on the same river, the anchor again caught under the water, and, with the boat filling with water, the boatman was unable to cut it free. Just before disaster struck, the anchor came free and was brought up, interlinked with the anchor that had been lost three years before.

For Harris, the moment brought a moment of vision:

It is almost impossible to describe the kind of energy that rushed out of that constellation of images. I felt as if a canvas around my head was crowded with phantoms and figures. I had forgotten some of my own antecedents—the Amerindian/Arawak ones—but now their faces were on the canvas. One could see them in the long march into the twentieth century out of the pre-Columbian mists of time. One could also sense the lost expedition, the people who had gone down in these South American rivers. One could sense a whole range of things, all sorts of faces—angelic, terrifying, daemonic—all sorts of contrasting faces, all sorts of figures. There was a sudden eruption of consciousness, and what is fantastic is that it all came out of a constellation of two ordinary objects, two anchors.[1]

Harris emphasizes the ordinariness of the anchors to stress the extraordinary power of the imagination they evoked. But looking at Harris's account of the scene, one can see the context that contributed to the moment of vision. Waterfalls and rapids are dramatic features of the Guyanese interior, marking violent fissures in the vistas of intermeshed forest and dark, sluggish rivers. They are transformations in the landscape and terrifying tests of the human spirit. With a surveyor's eye, Harris notes, "at the foot of the Tumatumari rapids or falls the sand is like gold. Above, an abrupt change of textures occurs—it is white as snow. These startling juxtapositions seemed to me immensely significant in some curious and intuitive way that bore upon an expressionistic void of place and time."[2]

Significant, too, is the moment at which the vision came. In both scenes there was a flurry of activity, indeed of extreme danger ("I am sure I could not have swum to the river bank if the boat had gone down"), followed by a moment of release. The experience of the moment of vision is, of course, one familiar to other creative writers. Harris invokes Coleridge, Melville, and Conrad. But a closer parallel may be the romantic poet, William Wordsworth. Wordsworth also had visionary moments when seeing the most common objects, characteristically at a moment of suddenly changed attention. When seeing a beggar in a London street, "Caught with the spectacle my mind turned round/As with the might of waters. . . ." Other visions have more dramatic settings. Standing by a waterfall in the Alps, he experienced a moment when

> the light of sense
> goes out, but with a flash has revealed
> The invisible world . . .

As in Harris's vision, the revelation goes beyond time and place, giving a sense of all things coexistent in a transcendent reality.

> Tumult and peace, the darkness and the light—
> Were all like workings of one mind, the features
> Of the same face, blossoms on one tree;
> Characters of the great Apocalypse,
> The types and symbols of Eternity,
> Of first, and last and midst, and without end.[3]

Although the root experience may be similar, this only increases our sense of the difference and unique quality of Harris's writing. The experience by Tumatumari rapids was for him the beginning of a life-long process to transform it into words: as he declares, "it was a number of years before I found I could really work into narrative that kind of vision, if one may so describe it." And he continues by quoting and analyzing moments in *Palace of the Peacock* and *Tumatumari* where an experience in space and time is again implicated in the interaction between phases of history and culture, as intimated in his earlier vision by the rapids.

Harris's imagination emerges as extraordinarily *literal*. His fiction is continually rooted in factual places, dates, historical and geographic data. Wordsworth also wanted to bring imaginative and scientific reality together in his writing. In his well-known words, "Poetry is the breath and finer spirit of all knowledge; it is the impassioned expression which is the countenance of all science."[4] But his ambitious attempt to put this into practice did not get beyond writing *The Prelude* and *The Excursion*.

The extent to which Harris succeeds where Wordsworth fails rests in part on Harris's attitude toward *language*. Wordsworth sought to escape from false jargon to recover the plain "language of men." Harris goes beyond this to unlock the potential trapped by convention within the simplest words. This is partly stated in the passage Harris gives to the schoolmaster, Mr. Becks, in *Carnival:*

"Language is, or should be, as much an art as a tool or a medium of tools. We need to question, to say the least, the innermost resources of language through the creative imagination, in the creative conscience. Such questions sometimes evolve into profoundest answers to the plague of robot intelligence. A living language is a medium of imaginative death as well as imaginative rebirth and life. It is a medium of *creativity* in morality. Fiction as much as language dies otherwise."[5]

Harris fences this round with comic irony. Becks is a schoolmaster in "Brickdam" (Harris's schoolmaster, in New Amsterdam, Guyana, where he grew up?). And the colonial schools did *not* teach "creative" language. Becks is careful himself to "read nothing but mediocre novels and poetry. It is better to be on the safe side, to assume there is no hope."

The way the two approaches to language, by Wordsworth and Harris, change the experience they inscribe, may be seen by briefly comparing two well-known passages by each author. Wordsworth first. "Resolution and Independence" has as its inspiration a transformative vision that could well have been seen by Harris. It is framed in a morning of movement and activity: this is suddenly arrested by the sight of an old, gray-headed leech-gatherer standing "motionless as a cloud" before a pool of water. As he talks, the poet experiences a disturbing vision in which the still man paces "about the weary moors continually,/Wandering about alone and silently."[6] The moment passes, and the appended moral—that he should learn from the old man's fortitude—is curiously irrelevant to the communicated power of the vision. For a moment Wordsworth had penetrated to, in Harris's words "the substance of life," sensing his own place in a profound history of human endurance. But beyond describing the moment itself, he had no terms in which to understand or communicate this.

In a central passage of *Palace of the Peacock* the expedition crew also become aware of the "substance" of the Arawak woman they have taken on to be their guide. The passage is too well-known to require detailed analysis. But it is worth asserting first what is, at one level, its *realism:* "Her long black hair—with the faintest glimmer of silvery grey—hung in two plaints down to her waist. She sat still as a bowing statue, the stillness and surrender of the American Indian of Guyana in reflective pose. Her small eyes winked and blinked a little. It was an emotionless face."[7] The description will be immediately recognized as startlingly apt by those who have seen aged women in the Indian villages of the Guyanese interior. The vision is both subjective and an outpouring of self. At the midpoint of the novel, the narrator senses, as Wordsworth did in contemplating the old man, a still center of reality. Here "life had possessed and abandoned at the same time the apprehension of a facile beginning and ending. An unearthly pointlessness was her true manner, an all-inclusive manner . . ." (72). Yet we are also back with Harris's vision by Tumatumari rapids. He wrote there, "all this has a bearing on the nature of community." The anchor with the past has become contact with the roots of the Guyanese peoples. What for Wordsworth ends as alienation—he dismisses the man with a self-defensive laugh—for Donne's crew becomes something that profoundly disturbs their consciousness.

But Harris does not say "the crew was disturbed." He literally transforms the woman into a life-threatening rapid. The concept becomes an image. The words themselves become the alchemy, the magic. "Tiny embroideries resembling the handwork on the Arawak woman's kerchief and the wrinkles on her brow turned to incredible and fast soundless breakers of foam. Her crumpled bosom and river grew agitated with desire, bottling and shaking every fear and inhibition and outcry. The ruffles in the water were her dress rolling and rising to embrace the crew" (73). The interaction transforms both viewers and seen, the crew and the woman. The Arawak woman's soul and body engulf them like a wave, sexual and regenerating, "flowing back on them with silent streaming majesty and abnormal youth and in a wave of freedom and strength" (75). Then the vision is gone, leaving them with the consequences of what they have seen, swept dangerously through forbidden rapids, "keeping our bow silent and straight in the heart of an unforgiving and unforgiveable incestuous love" (74).

Harris's achievement has profound relevance to debates about literature in the modern world. In spite of his dalliance with the French Revolution, Wordsworth wrote within a rigid social framework. He remains trapped within a social consciousness that undermines the validity of his psychic sympathy with the old man and the humanity he represents. Harris, contemplating the Arawak woman, directly confronts such restrictions. Thus far, he deconstructs the colonial perspective. But, as Homi Bhabha has pointed out, postcolonialism in itself can imprison what it seeks to release. "What is profoundly unresolved, even erased, in the discourses of poststructuralism is that *perspective of depth* through which the authenticity of identity comes to be reflected in the glassy metaphorics of the mirror and its mimetic or realistic narratives."[8]

The passage could well have been written by Harris himself, and thirty years earlier. For it is not only in the recognition of the Other but the understanding that this act of recognition profoundly changes both perceiver and perceived, that Harris moves beyond postcolonialism and points to the future. This future is being always re-created. The final act of transformation is on his readers. Indeed, it is on *you*.

NOTES

[1]"A Talk on the Subjective Imagination," *New Letters* 40 (1973): 41.

[2]"A Talk on the Subjective Imagination," 39-40.

[3]William Wordsworth, *The Prelude*, book 7, 11. 643-4; book 6, 11. 601-03; book 7, 635-40.

[4]William Wordsworth, *Preface to "The Lyrical Ballads"* (1802).

[5]*Carnival* (London: Faber and Faber, 1985), 74.

[6]"Resolution and Independence," 11. 131-32.

[7]*Palace of the Peacock* (London: Faber and Faber, 1961), 71; hereafter

cited parenthetically.

[8]Homi Bhabha, *The Location of Culture* (London: Routledge, 1994), 48.

New Personalities: Race, Sexuality, and Gender in Wilson Harris's Recent Fiction

Vera M. Kutzinski

> In the virgin womb of the imagination the word was made flesh.
> —James Joyce, *A Portrait of an Artist as a Young Man*

In *Tradition, the Writer and Society*, his first collection of essays, Wilson Harris writes eloquently of "the series of subtle and nebulous links" that might provide "the latent ground of old and new personalities" (28). The retrieval of such obscure links, Harris argues, would make it possible to recover a "conception of the human person" from "the ideology of the 'broken' individual" (27). Harris effectively distinguishes between "the historical self-sufficient individual, as such, and a living open tradition which realizes itself in an enduring capacity associated with the obscure human person" (36). From these formulations emerges the notion of a literary text as a "drama of living consciousness" (34) that "begins to write itself" in the sense that it reveals to the author-as-reader "developments he had not intellectually ordered or arranged" (47). In challenging the concept of an individual consciousness in control of his or her own narrative, Harris implicitly reimagines narration as a process not of adversity but of intimate collaboration between two or more authorial figures.

I will comment on the dynamics of collaboration in Harris's *Carnival* and, more briefly, in *The Infinite Rehearsal* and *The Four Banks of the River of Space*, the other two volumes of *The Carnival Trilogy*.[1] I take these texts to be instances of fictional reversibility, which means that their characters do not function consistently in accordance with fixed allegorical positions, whatever interpretive clarity these positions may appear to promise. "A reversible fiction," explains the ghost of Everyman Masters in *Carnival,* "unsettles false clarities . . . reopens the profoundest human involvements and perspectives to illumine a truth," namely, that "Violence is *not* the corner-stone of a civilization" (90). Struggles for narrative control are part of such foundational violence in that they allegorize and aestheticize it. My main interest is in how such reversibility affects the reader's perception of narrators'/characters' identities and, relatedly, the construction of narrative voice and authority.

Carnival foregrounds collaboration, which usually occurs between characters designated as male, to a greater and different extent than do Harris's other novels. Here, Harris does not explicitly cast himself in the role of editor or scribe. *Carnival* lacks the editorial preface with which Harris's readers are quite familiar and which reappears in both *The Infinite Rehearsal* and *The Four Banks of the River of Space.* Unlike such characters as Anselm in *Resurrection at Sorrow Hill,* Everyman Masters does not deliver a manuscript into the trusting hands of his would-be biographer Jonathan Weyl. Rather, the situation in *Carnival* is one of *internal* collaboration externalized in the text as a series of remembered and imagined ("dreamed") conversations between Masters and Weyl, who are similar enough to function as doubles for one another: both are educated, racially-mixed Guyanese men. It is important that their relationship is not premised on the kinds of inequities that derive from race and class differences. Masters's "legal father was coloured, . . . his mother, was coloured, his biological father, whom he had never met, was white" (29). Similarly, Weyl's "mother was fair, perhaps white; my father was coloured; and I was of indeterminate origin or pigmentation" (94). Even white can refer to racially mixed descent in *Carnival,* which foils any racialized binarisms to which readers may be tempted to resort. To wit, "A black or brown divinity could wear a *white* mask and *red* lips and still reveal itself complexly, profoundly, as other than whiteness or redness" (9). Colors confer only partial identities, especially in conjunction with race, but they cannot represent personhood in all its "terrifying wholeness"—"Terrifying in an age that had settled for fragmentation, for polarization, as the basis of security" (46). Both Masters and Weyl levitate between races, colors, selves, and others as the literary text they jointly produce cheerfully blurs distinctions between fact and fiction.

Masters, who is, paradoxically perhaps, quite dead by the end of the novel's first chapter, specifically charges Weyl with writing his life. "Write a biography of spirit as the fiction of my life," he enjoins Weyl only hours before his death (15-16). The novel's first chapter, devoted to Master's ultimate sexual encounter in his London apartment—what Masters himself calls, not without a tinge of irony, "Our, or my, birthday performance" (12)—employs biography's conventional third-person narrative mode. In the second chapter, however, when Weyl steps forward as first-person narrator soon to be in conversation with his deceased mentor, it becomes evident that biography can no more be separated from autobiography than fact can be distinguished from fiction. It is as if the trauma of Masters's ritualized death, "the bliss of reciprocal penetration of masks" (9), occasions a blurring of boundaries between genres and personalities, indeed, between different modes of existence. Writing here is predicated upon a death, Master's "second" death, which is also a rebirth:

News of the death of Everyman Masters in the summer of 1982 was a great shock to me and to my wife Amaryllis. We were younger than Everyman by fifteen years but he had been a close friend for as long as I could remember. He and I sailed from New Forest in 1957 on a converted French troopship that offered us economic berths to Marseilles from where we made our way to London. . . . I began that very year to compile notes of his life. In the wake of the news of his death in 1982, I was possessed by lucid dreams that intermingled fact with imaginative truth. (15)

In stating that he will "endeavor to paraphrase" these profuse notes (42), Weyl implies that his concern is not with sociological accuracy but with acts of the historical imagination.

Weyl's book returns to "the stages of [Masters's] 'first death,' " a process during which the latter's ghost assumes the role of "intuitive Virgilian guide" for Harris's updated Dante figure (*Carnival* 16; *Resurrection* vii). At the same time that Masters is Weyl's "principal guide," indeed his "foster-father," he is also the one "who bestowed upon me [Weyl] the privileged mask of fiction-parent" (*Carnival* 121, 33). Weyl confesses that

> Soon I was to perceive in the complex loves and sorrows of Masters's life that I was as much a character (or character-mask) in Carnival as he was. Indeed in a real and unreal sense he and other character-masks were the joint authors of Carnival and I was their creation. They drew me to surrender myself to them.
>
> My hand was suffused as I wrote by their parallel hands. (31)

Weyl is dually positioned as both the narrator of and a character in his own fiction; symbolically, he is Masters's father, his son, as well as his erotic subject. As the narrative progresses, Weyl deliberately risks and eventually surrenders what might otherwise have been a contested position of writerly authority. In *Carnival* this surrender places in luminous relief the seams of collaboration that other novels would seek to erase. Harris's focus on risked and relinquished authority delivers a trenchant metafictional commentary on the limitations of certain allegorical relationships that haunt postcolonial Caribbean fiction, notably those drawn from Shakespeare's *The Tempest* (see Nixon). Unlike the majority of postcolonial Caribbean novels, *Carnival* employs differences in gender, sexuality, and race as provisional constructs only. As it revises these constructs, *Carnival* reimagines the very idea of literary conceptions. Such reimagining makes it possible for Harris to recast the agonistic and antagonistic relationship between colonizer and colonized as a tale of complicated mutuality and intellectual collaboration. In *Carnival* narrative authority is distinctly a function of collaboration that depends on the abdication of individualistic narrative control.

Joint authorship, or "parallel" writing, that is, writing by characters who inhabit alternative fictional universes and who catch occasional glimpses of each other, is at the core of Harris's "revisionary strategies" in *Carnival* and throughout the rest of this trilogy. In *The Infinite Rehearsal* Ghost, a revised version of Masters, patiently explains both to fictional autobiographer Robin Redbreast Glass and to the reader, "I say revisionary strategies to imply that as you write of other persons, of the dead or the unborn, bits of the world's turbulent, universal unconscious embed themselves in your book" (46). Harris's "cross-cultural imagination," then, is an interior "intuitive theatre" (47), a kind of Jungian collective unconscious filled with arche-types, or divinities in "animate costume." Within this theater of the mind, gender distinctions, much like racial differences, do exist, but they are conspicuously arbitrary. *The Infinite Rehearsal* calls attention to this in Glass's decision to gender Ghost:

"Thus it was that I welcomed Ghost, conquistadorial and victimized Ghost (was (s)he male/female? I could not tell) when IT appeared on a beach in Old New Forest . . . *I decided to accept IT as male persona* and trust that new fragile complications of divinity's blood would drive me to see the phenomenon I had encountered in the wholeness of a transformative light bearing on all genders, all animates and inanimates, all masks and vessels in which a spark of ultimate self-recognition flashed . . . faded . . . flashed again. (1-2, my italics)

Glass can relate to Ghost only by gendering "IT" as male, despite its feminine, or actually androgynous, appearance: "He (Ghost) wore a long, rich plait of hair on the back of his neck. . . . It was so long and marvelous it could have been the wonderful text of a woman's hair through which to read the mysterious birth of spirit" (2). An earlier version of this image of mediating femininity appears at an epiphanic moment in *Palace of the Peacock:* "The woman was dressed in a long sweeping garment belonging to a far and distant age . . . all threads of light and fabric from the thinnest strongest source of all beginning and undying end. . . . Her ancient dress was her hair after all" (138-40). In *The Infinite Rehearsal* this "threadbare" garment is further transfigured into the "seamless robe of eternity" placed on the shoulders of the priestess Emma who is charged with the "vocation" of making "the body of the resurrection beautiful to the woman in the man, the man in the woman" (73). This series of changing images exemplifies a "narrative fiction that revises itself inwardly" (*Four Banks* xi). No longer locked into intractable binary antagonism, femininity and masculinity can be embraced as separate aspects of the same personality. They are but different masks that the same person may wear.

Throughout *Carnival,* sexuality is as much of a changeable mask as are gender and color. In Jonathan and Amaryllis's marriage, for instance, Harris's fiction wears a heterosexual mask as a figure for spiritual wholeness. Yet *Carnival*'s overall textual politics reveal themselves as profoundly other than heterosexual: in its main relationships, the novel discloses a " 'latent homosexuality' or 'latent bisexuality' " (88). Consider that Weyl's erotic and visionary attachments are both, equally, to Masters and to Amaryllis. Similarly, "bisexual" Masters produces both literary and biological offspring: a text with Jonathan Weyl and a child with the second Jane Fisher. This is possible only because, here and elsewhere in Harris's writings, intellectual creativity, especially in a situation of male homoerotic collaboration, does not exact the price of sexual impotence and sterility. Nor, for that matter, is literary creation coded as procreative and hence as essentially feminine. Amaryllis, who ultimately takes Masters's place as Jonathan's "guide" and can thus be read as Masters's feminized double, does not herself bear a child. Instead, she and Jonathan choose to adopt the daughter Masters presumably conceived with Jane Fisher just prior to his death. The family that results from this adoption is a testimony and a tribute to multidirectional sexual, erotic, and emotional attachments among Masters, Weyl, and Amaryllis and their understudies. *Carnival*'s revisionary logic invites readers to recognize the limiting partiality of familiar analytical and social categories such as gender, sexuality, and race, and to imagine truths and personalities beyond their bounds.

NOTE

[1] A longer version of this essay, titled "The Cult of Caliban: Collaboration and Revisionism in Contemporary Caribbean Narrative," is forthcoming in *ICLA History of Literature in the Caribbean,* vol. 3, *Cross-Cultural Studies,* ed. A. James Arnold (Amsterdam: John Benjamin).

WORKS CITED

Harris, Wilson. *Carnival.* London: Faber and Faber, 1985.
————. *The Four Banks of the River of Space.* London: Faber and Faber, 1990.
————. *The Infinite Rehearsal.* London: Faber and Faber, 1987.
————. *Palace of the Peacock.* London: Faber and Faber, 1961.
————. *Tradition, the Writer and Society: Critical Essays.* London: New Beacon, 1967.
Nixon, Rob. "Caribbean and African Appropriations of *The Tempest.*" *Critical Inquiry* 13 (1987): 557-78.

Creative Bridges: Some Aspects of Myth in "Couvade" and The Four Banks of the River of Space

Patricia Murray

The multidimensional nature of myths, their oral transmission and constant transformation, makes it impossible for them to be known in their entirety. In the contemporary context Wilson Harris perceives further complication in the inevitable postcolonial hybridity of myth: "when you go into the so-called Third World, the archetypes, if I may use that word . . . those archetypes, which they call 'native' archetypes are all overlaid by European skeletons and archetypes as well. You will never activate them unless you activate the so-called 'European' as well. They are locked together and there is no way around that."[1] This sense of the layers of myth is characteristic of Harris's writing where no single myth or mythology prevails but where the various ways in which myth is used give the work a mythical character. As Harris goes on to say, this focus on the *layers* of myth engenders a *creative* cross-culturalism in which the dynamic resources that lie at the heart of myth can be visualized as a response to the dilemmas of the present. It is in this way that myth appears in Harris's "Couvade" and *The Four Banks of the River of Space* as both a creative bridge between cultures and as a resource through which stases of oppression can be revised.

The idea of a creative bridge or arch of community is particularly appropriate to the story of "Couvade," in which Harris re-creates a ritual dream of the Caribs to suggest an archetypal image of spiritual progress and renewal. The first of a Carib trilogy entitled *The Sleepers of Roraima,* "Couvade" is based on the vestiges of a Carib myth and we are told in the author's note: "The purpose of *Couvade* was to hand on the legacy of the tribe—courage and fasting—to every newborn child. All ancestors were involved in this dream—animal as well as human, bird as well as fish. The dust of every thing, cassava bread (the Carib's staple diet), the paint of war, the cave of memories, were turned into a fable of history—the dream of *Couvade.*"[2] In rewriting this dream of Couvade, Harris is challenging the conventional view that the Caribs have disappeared without trace. For while, at the level of content, the story tells of the imminent extinction of the Carib race, the creative potential of their legacy is explored ("relived") through its mythical form. It is significant that the dream is described as: "some strange dream of history in which his grandfather's people feared they would vanish from the face of the earth" (18). Although the historical perspective defines the Caribs as extinct, myth tilts the boundaries of such perspective to reveal the reflections and circularities that continue to connect us with that past age.

The first line tells us that the name *Couvade* here means "sleeper of the tribe" and this immediately signals the journey into the unconscious which is about to be undertaken. Rather than the polarity of a conscious/unconscious life, however, the multilevels of dreaming/waking in the text enact a drama of consciousness akin to Jung's process of individuation in which the individual, having unlocked the personal unconscious to reintegrate the self, becomes aware of how that self is connected to all other selves in a much larger collective consciousness. In order to begin this journey Couvade must listen to "the ancestral voices of waterfall and forest" (16) and learn the intuitive perspective of the guacharo bird whose "uncanny reflexes (piercing vision and echoing wings) guided it through the darkest underground caves" (16). Although Couvade is ostensibly guided by the figure of his grandfather, that figure takes a variety of forms, benevolent ancestral lizard as well as ancient trickster, so that Couvade is forced to negotiate the shifting reality of his dream through a variety of means. Having entered the cave of ancestors, which is described as a return to the womb, he wears the two disguises of half-bird, half-fish in an attempt to swim across to the spectre of his lost parents. When both of these fail, Couvade realizes that he must go to them in his own form and so removes the disguises: "He carefully restored the head-dress, spectacles, feathers to the ground of the cave, the scales and eyes of the fish to the wall where they shone now like stars and constellations" (19-20). Only when he exposes himself to his ancestors, becomes susceptible to them, does the bridge of souls appear to carry him across to the other bank of the stream. That this has been a symbolic, an imaginative bridge, is made clear in the obvious reflection of this other bank: "No one was there to greet him but he saw that they had left their sunglasses suspended from a branch. Their head-dress too and the scales and eyes of a fish like a starry cloak which shone in the water against the trees. Couvade was glad. It was as if they wished to surrender to him all their disguises as he had surrendered his to them on his side of the cave" (21). It is not that Couvade has crossed physically to another bank but that we (through him) have *altered* perspective. Through these journeys, these changes in perspective, Couvade becomes a part of the cycle which deconstructs, through connecting, polarities of hunter and hunted, friend and enemy.

The story is structured around various polarities which it becomes the function of the myth to mediate. The struggle between hunter and hunted reflects the history of the Caribs, their fierce reputation, and eventual conquest by another people. This is connected to, and contained within, images of male and female. The Carib practice of taking wives from the tribes they conquered engenders a cross-culturalism in the child (Couvade) who embodies both self and enemy. Chapter 3 tells us that the head-dress of feathers belonged to the father (huntsmen of night) and the scales and eyes of the fish to the mother (fishermen of night), revealing that the disguises Couvade had tried to inhabit had failed because both were necessarily partial. Although Couvade is initiated into the motherhood of the tribe, one of the most poetically rendered scenes of the journey tells us, "He shook himself now—the dust of stars—as if he too danced to the music of the river. In fact his feet began to move and spin. Ballet of the fish. Dance of the fish. Song of the river. Net of the river. He said to his grandfather in an ecstasy of happiness, 'I have caught her. My mother. She sings and dances in my net, in my heart. Song and dance of the fish painted on the wall of the cave' " (27). It is in the complementarity of male and female energies that the journey reaches its climax: "The fish-net of his mother, which was no other than the bird-cloak of his father, whirled and danced in the sky, then settled itself into the bridge of dawn. Couvade felt the presence of both his lost parents crossing and re-crossing the shimmering bridge" (31).

Chapter 3 is the longest section of the story and the one in which Couvade, having unlocked the personal unconscious to reintegrate the self, begins to connect to a larger collective consciousness; this is surrounded by two shorter, and then two yet shorter chapters or sections. As Mark McWatt has noted, the story is thus structured to suggest three concentric circles, each deeper and more complex as you move toward the center, suggesting images of the whirlpool or vortex, and in attempting a linear progression of the story, the reader experiences a cross section of the whirlpool.[3] The final chapter, in which Couvade discovers the riddle of his name and identity, thus enacts the emergence from the whirlpool: "At long last the retreat began. Was it retreat of enemy or retreat of friend? The idol of the moon fell from the sky. The idol of the stars began to fade. The long ghostly armies crept across the blanket of tribes, the blanket of Couvade sound asleep in his hammock. And in the mouth of the cave where he dreamt he lay since the night his parents ran from the tribe, he too seemed to be passing into the light of freedom—a new sobering reflection—bridge of relationships" (34). The historical moment when the Caribs are invaded is transfigured through myth to illuminate the freedom and evolution also present in that cross-cultural encounter as Couvade, the ritual dream of the Caribs, crosses the "bridge of relationships" to become an imaginative resource for the future Caribbean. Though Harris emphasizes the need to activate such resources, such latent spaces in the cross-cultural psyche, he does not underestimate the task: "Uncertain of the figures coming alive on the wall of the cave. Uncertain there was not a long hard way to go before the idols and paintings would truly melt, truly live, birth of compassion, birth of love" (35).

The usurping of the victor/victim stasis forms the first stage in Harris's quantum journey through *The Four Banks of the River of Space*. The journey takes place in the rainforests of Guyana, which are, for Anselm, "the heartland of the twentieth century."[4] In crossing the rivers of the living and the dead,[5] Anselm's task is to move into hidden spaces, to inhabit a variety of half-real, half-mythical identities that will challenge static archetypes of twentieth-century history. As he declares on The First Bank: "We may only heal the wounded archetype when we *live* the divide at the heart of language and place its enormity on many shoulders . . ." (30). The king of thieves whom Anselm inhabits in this first chapter is a multidimensional historical and psychological character—a Guyanese miner called Black Pizarro with antecedents in Christian and colonial history, who also signals an aspect of self. As Harris makes explicit: "He is the thief who mocked Christ and turned his face away from paradise's door. Such a thief lives in us all and in a door that haunts us in every century" (14). A composite figure of this king of thieves emerges at the end of the chapter to lead a procession for the victim and make an offering in his honor: "It was as if in so doing he released for an instant the heavy burden of gold he had stolen across the centuries, the heavy obsession that tormented him and his fellow miners whom he led. He became the last tormented thief in the world in that miraculous instant" (40). In illuminating the contiguity that exists between "those who bury and those who are buried" (40), Anselm breaks the absoluteness of the archetype (The King of Thieves) and transcends the stasis of victor and victim. In recognizing this "quantum stranger" (6) as also a part of himself, he is able to cross to The Second Bank where he becomes the Carnival Heir of Civilizations.

As the above title indicates, Anselm proceeds on his journey through a variety of masks and personae. Like Odysseus, "he has become plural and is borne upon the shoulders—re-born within the flesh—of many cultures." *The Four Banks of the River of Space* is a cross-cultural rewriting of the *Odyssey,* but one in which the characters of Ulysses and Penelope are fragmented throughout the text, both as partial aspects of the self and as complex revisions of the myth that frames them. In transporting the classical epic to the Guyana rainforests, Harris also elicits parallels with Christian and Amerindian myths to reflect the cross-cultural hybridity of the Americas and to demonstrate bridges of myth that connect apparently distinct cultures throughout the world. In the same way as Jung regarded dreams as communications from the unconscious and identified recurrent images (archetypes) that could be found in all epochs and which served to connect the individual with the totality of his or her psyche—"they bring into our ephemeral consciousness an unknown psychic life belonging to a remote past. It is the mind of our unknown ancestors, their way of thinking and feeling, their way of experiencing life and the world, gods and men"[6]—so Anselm is the "living dreamer" who is able to reintegrate his own and the collective American psyche through seizing the unexpected correspondences that appear on his journey through the cross-cultural imagination.

Anselm's meeting with Penelope on The Second Bank is typical of the way in which Harris writes such multitudinous significance into a single encounter. Penelope is an English missionary who, with her second husband Ross George, worked in South America from 1948 to 1966. The preface tells us that they both died in Kent, England, in the early 1980s. Penelope carries with her the shadow of her dead husband, Simon, a British officer who died in the Second World War. Together, these three represent the colonizing powers of the army and the Christian church. Anselm meets them on The Second Bank where he travels back into his own past in the Guyana rainforest: "Penelope and Ross re-emerged from the margins of nothingness into which they had almost vanished. The depletion of spiritual memory, the curious fast of memory which I endured, strengthened in a paradoxical way the open, broken yet flowering seed of visualized presences within me, before me" (52). These presences are described as "unsuspected and piercing ironies of spirit that nailed one into the congregation of all one's characters and even into the shoes of the king of thieves" (52). They are thus a part of the community of being each of us carries within and with whom, Harris urges, we must become acquainted. Language and imagery—"congregation," "the king of thieves"—signal a Christian framework, although the reference to "the king of thieves" is already multilayered in echoing the archetype confronted on The First Bank. The focus on "the shoes" reflects Harris's method of sudden, concrete visualization to hinge a complex psychological concept. The oblique reference to the spectre of Christ in the use of the verb *nailed* is picked up in the next movement: "One bears the wounds of the past into the future and the present. One is oneself and other than oneself . . . it was thus that I limped, as though nailed upon an Imaginary walking tree in stained glass window that I painted, into the presence of the last missionaries on earth . . ." (53). The use of the capital *Imaginary* draws attention to the multiple connotations that are being exploited in the linguistic structure. Anselm is both subject and object here, experiencing a connection while at the same time painting/imagining the tableau of that connection. It is significant that Anselm is walking "into the presence" of Penelope for she, as feminine Wisdom, draws him into *her* canvas, as well as the other way around.

Penelope speaks at this point and informs Anselm of her relationship to Simon and to Ross. Simon is the "epic soldier" (53), a Ulyssean figure whose heroism is challenged by an emerging female voice: "she whispered almost under her breath—'I shall tell you later about some of the terrible things he did to me despite the many decorations he wore on his chest' " (53). Ross—"who was no base suitor at Penelope's court" (25)—is the husband with whom she lives the sacramental marriage. Since his death in 1981 and her own in 1982, she tells Anselm, she has been weaving a coat: "I have been slaving at a coat for many a month, many a year, in this day or century. A coat that is woven of the fabric of sunset, the stillness, the transience of flame. A coat that is as much a tapestry of the world, as of fire and water, to fit the shoulder of a hill, or the body of rock in a Waterfall" (34). The coat that never fits Ross or Simon is also "the coat of tradition that never quite seems to fit the globe" (58) or Anselm's narrative, which is constantly disrupted by Penelope: "Did you really put that key there, Penelope, in the loom of tradition without knowing you had done so . . . ?" (58).

The image of Penelope as feminine Wisdom and the importance of her perspective in guiding Anselm along his Journey are constant themes throughout the novel. In this meeting it is Penelope who illuminates the nature of their dynamic interplay: "*You* painted me into the Day of my age, the cathedral of stained-glass window sunset, as if the needle with which I work and sew were a match. The match of sunset. And because of the impermanence of darkness and light the match of sunrise as well" (54). The cyclical way in which Penelope appears and reappears is reflected in her unraveling of the garment that is never complete: " 'Yes,' she continued, 'always a discrepancy. And as a consequence I unravel the work I have done, unstitch everything, and start all over again from the very beginning whenever that was. I unravel my Day and start all over again' " (54). Penelope is involved in the revisionary cycle, the revision of tradition and of static archetypes, and her next words make explicit the echoes of sunset and sunrise that have linked her with the Aztec myth of Venus/Quetzalcoatl: "I shall be emancipated woman in heaven. Ageless sunset and sunrise woman for all I know. A status of Wisdom, a status of elemental Wisdom, not easily achievable on earth! The perfect fit, the perfect marriage between light and darkness, Night and Day" (54-55).

In an example of just three pages, then, we can trace threads of Christian, ancient Greek, and ancient pre-Columbian imagery as Harris invests in the figure of Penelope a variety of cross-cultural associations, which serve to connect overlapping cycles of history and myth. As Anselm says: "—in drawing you out of the margins of nothingness into visualized being—I needed to bridge the centuries-long Night, the Night of ancient Greece into North African desert Night where Simon, your first and jealous husband, fought in Montgomery's army, the Night of Spain into the Night of South America where the reincarnated thief ransacked the gold of the Incas" (57). As the twentieth century draws to a close and Anselm unravels cycles of oppression to reveal "a theatre of interchangeable masks," it is the spectre of Penelope that appears to spin the cycle of a new day:

This rain of night seemed to glimmer in the stars. Captors and captives began to loom in the new darkness of the Dream, the new guardian rocks, the new guardianship of sky and cloud at the heart of the Waterfall of space, a theatre of interchangeable masks and fates and elements upon savages and civilizations. The rain that fell upon us was so fine-spun and delicate that it seemed an impossibility when within it we discerned the burden and mystery of the rising sun. (161)

NOTES

[1]Harris in interview with Alan Riach in *The Radical Imagination: Lectures and Talks,* ed. Alan Riach and Mark Williams (Liege: Université de Liege, 1992), 40-41.
    [2]*The Sleepers of Roraima* (London: Faber and Faber, 1970); hereafter cited parenthetically.

[3]Mark McWatt, "Form and Originality: The Amerindian Fables of Wilson Harris," *Journal of West Indian Literature* 1.2 (1987): 38.

[4]*The Four Banks of the River of Space* (London: Faber and Faber, 1990); hereafter cited parenthetically.

[5]The visible river of the living and the invisible river of the dead form the four banks of the river of space.

[6]Jung, *Selected Writings,* 223.

Renewal in a Far More Resonant Key: Reflections on the Mad, Sin-Eating Relics of Fire in *Resurrection at Sorrow Hill*

Desmond Hamlet

Kenneth Ramchand's virtually prophetic observation in 1968 that *"Palace of the Peacock* contains all Harris's basic themes, and anticipates his later designs" resounds as late as 1993 with an uncanny accuracy. For in *Resurrection at Sorrow Hill* we witness once again the fundamental validity of Ramchand's perception, as Harris escorts us through an elaborate and complex dramatization of one of the important themes of *Palace of the Peacock*: nothing less than the crucial and determinative *resurrection* that takes place *at Sorrow Hill* in the "rounded poetic vision" (as Ramchand puts it)[1] of Harris's first novel.

Most students of Harris's fiction will remember Sorrow Hill from *Palace of the Peacock* not only as the small community in Guyana's hinterland "where Schomburgh lived,"[2] but far more significantly as the location where "a famous dead crew" had left their names "inscribed." As Harris puts the matter in this introduction to Sorrow Hill, "The odd fact existed of course that their living names matched the names of a famous dead crew that had sunk in the rapids and been drowned to a man, leaving their names inscribed on Sorrow Hill which stood at the foot of the falls. *But this in no way interfered with their lifelike appearance and spirit and energy*" (23, my italics). Clearly, the almost cryptic, final sentence here is meant to hint at the astounding possibility that the current crew may well be the famous dead crew *resurrected.* Indeed, as the narrator immediately adds, "Such a dreaming coincidence we were beginning to learn to take in our stride" (23-24), a perception that is obviously meant to reinforce the implication of an extraordinary occurrence such as a *resurrection.*

This, as a matter of fact, is exactly the narrator's meaning in his next two references (in chapters 4 and 5) to the matter of a possible *resurrection,* and a resurrection that would have taken place *at Sorrow Hill*—in both of which the "dreaming coincidence" is communicated to us, even if obliquely, as perfectly plausible within the symbolic world of the novel. In chapter 4 the narrator informs us:

> We had barely succeeded in tying our boat securely to the bank than they had left us alone. . . .
> The young children playing and scrambling near the cocerite houses had vanished with the entire population, and the Mission now looked abandoned.
> "We sleeping in a funny-funny place tonight," Wishrop said wonderingly.

"Them Buck folk scare of dead people bad-bad," Cameron laughed, chewing a sweet blade of grass. *"They done know all-you rise bodily from the grave.* Big frauds! that is what all you is." He spoke with affection. (39, my italics)

And in chapter 5, he tells us:

Schomburgh gave one of his hoarse brief chuckles. "They bound to vanish. They don't *see* [Harris's italics] dead people really, do they? Nor dead people seeing them for long."
"I ain't dead," Cameron cried. "I can prove it any day." He sniffed the air in which had risen the delightful smell of cooking fish.
"Uncle thinking of his epitaph," daSilva said with his slow heavy brand of humour, " *'pon Sorrow hill.* You must be seen you own epitaph sometimes in your dreams, Cammy? Don't lie." He winked at Cameron impressing upon him a con-spiracy to humour the old man. Schomburgh intercepted the wink like a man who saw with the back of his head.
"I see you, daSilva," he croaked out of an intuitive omniscience. (51-52, my ital-ics)

Though partly cloaked in humor and innuendo, both passages convey the serious sense of an extraordinary rebirth, a *resurrection at Sorrow Hill*, which indeed lies at the very heart of the narrative. For it is, in the final analysis, precisely through this second birth, that the crew (to a man) is given a second chance to experience the necessary cleansing and liberation that their second death provides, a second death that, in effect, becomes the prerequisite for and gateway to the kind of regeneration and apotheosis which the novelist dramatizes in the concluding scenes of the narrative.[3]

Notwithstanding his almost preternatural perception of *Palace of the Pea-cock* as a seminal source of Harris's later themes and strategies, even Ramchand could hardly have imagined in 1968 how deftly Harris would later reinforce, amplify, and enrich the essential themes and devices of that first novel, published some thirty-six years ago. But that, of course, is ex-actly what Harris has done during the past three and a half decades, when-ever he has chosen to return to *Palace of the Peacock* for a theme or for a technique of some sort, invariably providing (to our good fortune) a new depth of insight or a fascinating variation on a particular theme or strat-egy—within the fundamentally cohesive context of his oeuvre. And that is exactly what he has done, once again, in *Resurrection at Sorrow Hill.*
Harris deliberately reminds us on the very first two pages of the narrative that Sorrow Hill was not merely a local settlement and harbor at the confluence of three of Guyana's rivers but also "an epitaph and a cradle," indeed "a place of myth," "an embodiment of legend."[4] This much we al-ready knew of Sorrow Hill, of course, from *Palace of the Peacock.* What is engagingly new in Harris's characterization of Sorrow Hill in 1993 are the inferences and the reverberations of the novelist's perception of Sorrow Hill

as a place of myth and of legend. Harris, in fact, goes on—through those inferences and reverberations—to characterize the nature and the function of the mythic and legendary Sorrow Hill in pointedly *global* and *cross-cultural* terms and in terms as well of a significant fluidity of consciousness among the inhabitants of Sorrow Hill, "as if they traversed a border-line between madness and genius," as if, in effect, they pursued an "involuntary association between all states of mind and imagination that were native to them" (3).

Given such fluid, universal, and intercultural dimensions of the mythic and legendary Sorrow Hill, one is not surprised to learn that Hope, whose "asylum book" ("his Dream-book") Harris has characteristically undertaken to edit, is himself a product of a somewhat "disparate and discredited genealogy," a remarkably cross-cultural lineage which included European, American Indian, African, Chinese, Pakistani, and Indian antecedents, but a fact which, in our crass and narrow-minded age of "political purges and ethnic cleansings," was seen as "scandalous and discreditable" (141). It is exactly the redefinition and rectification of such pathology and bias (of what the narrator calls "the world's paranoia, the world's racism")—by means of "transfigured oppositions" prompted by a "transfigurative conscience"—which Hope's fiction, entitled *Resurrection at Sorrow Hill*, is meant to dramatize and to communicate to the alert reader. Doctor Daemon explains the matter (in his instructive speech toward the end of book 4) with compelling precision and clarity:

Hope's peculiar neurosis drives him to create fictions in which transfigured oppositions are necessary if the incorporation of one culture by another is to become an evolving source of re-visionary healing within diverse bodies and cultures that do relate to each other yet are at war with each other everywhere . . . What is occurring here . . . in Hope's asylum book . . . is the wholly unexpected, transfigurative conscience that addresses an entire civilization, it seems to me, from within the broken fabric of the family that becomes a numinous resource . . . (162-63)

Clearly, the primary focus in Harris's *Resurrection at Sorrow Hill* "addresses an entire civilization," which is to say, the entire global community—and addresses that community in terms that seek to discover, even within the habitual and universal clash of cultures (with its persistent conflicts and fragmentations), a "numinous resource," a "re-visionary healing," through an innovative and creative "transfiguration" of those very conflicts and fragmentations. It is precisely in such terms that we are meant, I suggest, to read the story of the "illegitimate" Hope, the unlawful and unwarranted product of an obviously dysfunctional family, with a renegade father and an overburdened but determined mother, but a family in which, paradoxically, a deep, new core of *wholeness*, an inverse wholeness, resides within the very recesses of the various fragments of the broken family. In Hope's intriguing perceptions, that "inverse wholeness associated with fragmentation is real, utterly real, but we need to approach it in all humility *through what he* [Hope] *calls inexactitudes or profiles of myth*" (160, my italics). It is, as a matter of fact, Hope's pursuit of such inexactitudes or profiles of myth that transforms the simple, rational tale of his personal experiences, within his own dysfunctional family, into a universal metaphor of passionate and persistent hope, nurtured and sustained by a deep-seated, inverse wholeness within the very fragmentations of the equally broken global family, an extraordinary, paradoxical community of "diverse bodies and cultures that do relate to each other yet are at war with each other everywhere."

"And the resurrection at Sorrow Hill?" Doctor Daemon asks, as he comes to the end of his incisive speech in book 4. The answer, which he confidently offers at the end of the very paragraph that begins with his provocative question, is as astounding as it is novel and distinctive: "the resurrection breaks open all incorporations . . . and thereby gives profoundest numinosity to an Imagination that recovers, in a variety of guises, those we appear to have lost" (166). What an extraordinarily expansive and altruistic resurrection this is, compared, especially, to the regeneration (or recovery, or revitalization, if you prefer) of the *individual* psyche, which we are shown at the end of *Palace of the Peacock,* after the re-creative, seven-day journey of expiation by Donne and the members of his crew. Here, in the 1993 narrative, the resurrection, which appropriately manifests itself "in a variety of guises," is principally, indeed exclusively, for the essential rescue and rehabilitation of the *community*, the global and obviously dysfunctional family to which we all belong.

Significantly, the *inverse* (as Harris would say) of our smugness and our self-centeredness, which drives the urgency to reclaim the essential wholeness of our broken global family and so ensure, at least, the survival of the universal community of nations and of cultures, is, quite simply, the reality of a genuine concern and love for others. This is clearly the central focus of Doctor Daemon's remarks toward the end of book 4, in which he deliberately ties the fact of the illness of all the inmates in the Asylum for the Greats to a definite lack of love from which they have all suffered as "victims of broken families" (166). As Doctor Daemon observes in connection with Hope, the chief inmate (so to speak), whose asylum book *Resurrection at Sorrow Hill*, in fact, is, "I trust that anything I may say will throw light on his book which you may read on your stay here. Hope's madness bears on the nature of love and our capacity to evolve into creatures who may bear the enormity of compassion and love that we need if we are to solve the crises in our civilization and the heartbreaking misery of humanity" (158).

Thus the essential capacity to love and the fundamental need to be loved become, in the final analysis, not only the moral imperative for solving "the crises in our civilization and the heart-breaking misery of humanity," but the inescapable cause as well of the state of so-called madness in all the inmates of the Asylum for the Greats. Paradoxically enough, it is precisely this state of "madness," brought on by the simple human need to love and to be loved, which, in turn, opens up for Hope and his fellow inmates in the asylum the most extraordinary insights into the subtle psychological processes which enable them to *eat* (which is to say, to *bear*) the sins of others and to perceive of themselves as *relics* (that is to say, as *potent survivors*) of a re-creative, resurrectionary fire.

At the heart of these insights and perceptions, of course, lies the central fact of the *resurrection* of the inmates in the Asylum for the Greats, which the novelist virtually goes out of his way to "prove." Harris is, for example, almost solicitous in calling our attention again and again to the significant fact that Christopher D'eath (a subtle reference to the ironic relationship between the profile of *Christ* and that of *Death* in the makeup of this particular character—"the spectre of Christ within Death," as Harris puts it early in the narrative [14]) had systematically occupied in consecutive years each of the seven cells in the former prison during his seven-year term in the old Mazaruni gaol. Quite apart from the implied idea of creation and creativity which the number *seven* suggests (*seven* cells, *seven* years, and even the *seven* books into which the narrative is divided), the fact that Monty the Venezuelan, Len the Brazilian, Mark, Nameless, Ruth, Captain Diss, and Archie or Archangel, especially in their perceived dual personalities, now occupied the very cells in which D'eath once dwelt is the most dramatic evidence in the novel of the displacement of *death* by *life*, and life lived, as a matter of fact, on an extraordinarily ecstatic and visionary level.

Thrown, as it were, into a world of ecstasy and exceptional vision, precisely because of their state of "madness," the inmates of the Asylum for the Greats obviously live their lives beyond the so-called normal scheme of things. But it is, ultimately, the nature of their peculiar neurosis, brought on by their traumatic lack of love within the dysfunctional families from which they come (as Doctor Daemon observes: "They are all the victims of broken families. They have all suffered from lack of love" [166]), which determines the character of the particular insights and perceptions they share. Not surprisingly, all of their insights and perceptions seek, within the context of their individual experiences, to redress both the dysfunction of the family by rediscovering the essential wholeness of the family and their desperate need to love and be loved—be it in the form of "dialectic" and "shamanic" sin-eaters (130) who willingly acknowledge and readily bear the sins of their earlier life or who sacrificially shoulder the burden of the sins of historic others, or in the guise of relics of fire, the potent survivors of the complex challenges of history, "living relics of the *transfiguration* of the terror of death" (236), who pave the way for us all to share in the re-creative possibilities of the resurrection at Sorrow Hill.

In the end, those re-creative possibilities may best actualize themselves, Harris makes clear, in the resolute reclamation of the revitalizing wholeness and efficacy of the global family—through the simple fact, however seemingly hazardous, of a selfless and restorative love. The alternative, far too depressing even to contemplate, is the sterile dead end of life without a future—in effect, as Doctor Daemon's grandmother eloquently observes quite early in the narrative, "to surrender to death's fortress" (9). The liberating alternative to such a disastrous end, on the other hand, is—as the wise, eighty-seven-year-old grandmother perceptively declares—to visualize the Shadow, the effect, the impact of resurrection "as a numinous embodiment of potential creativity in the *community*" (9, my italics).

NOTES

[1] "Preface" to *Palace of the Peacock* (London: Faber and Faber, 1968), 6.

[2] Wilson Harris, *Palace of the Peacock* (London: Faber and Faber, 1968), 77; hereafter cited parenthetically.

[3] Interestingly enough, in Harris's *The Eye of the Scarecrow*, where Sorrow Hill is also mentioned, the narrator significantly juxtaposes Sorrow Hill, the place of the dead, with the idea of *conception* (and by extension, the idea of *birth)*—and, in fact, virtually identifies Sorrow Hill as the locality and context of *life* rather than *death,* as the focal point within "the lost womb of a mining town," within "the jungle of conception." See *The Eye of the Scarecrow* (London: Faber and Faber, 1974), 48.

[4] Wilson Harris, *Resurrection at Sorrow Hill* (London: Faber and Faber, 1993), 3-4; hereafter cited parenthetically.

Charting the Uncapturable in Wilson Harris's Writing[1]

Hena Maes-Jelinek

> He saw the complexities yet simplicities of a fiction one may in-
> voluntarily write which involves a broken family with an entire
> humanity though its seed lies in obscure provinces, obscure sor-
> row hills.
> —Wilson Harris, *Resurrection at Sorrow Hill*

> May it not be that God continually writes the world, the world
> and all that is in it?
> —J. M. Coetzee, *Foe*

In his recent writing, both self-reflexive analytical fiction and imaginative
criticism, Wilson Harris has returned emphatically to the Amerindian presence in Central America, as part of "the womb of space," at once actual
territory pregnant with physical and psychical resources, "largely submerged territory of the imagination," and primordial seat of life and of a
creativity that can never be fully apprehended nor given final expression:
"No art of total capture or subordination of originality within formula exists
despite appearances,"[2] originality evoking here both origins and significant
innovation. Harris pretends neither to a complete recovery of Caribbean
origins nor to absolute originality but rather concentrates on the way creativeness can operate, particularly in a postcolonial context. In this respect
his exploratory narratives form a unique matrix of new cartography, both
geographical and metaphorical, which reconceptualizes the Caribbean and
its creative potentiality.

Though a highly sophisticated technology now makes possible perfectly
accurate topographical surveys, cartography is still influenced by self-cen-
tered and hegemonic nationalism, and in spite of pretensions to the contrary, such persisting subjectivity and domineering self-assertion find their
equivalent in all disciplines of the humanities directly influenced or not by
geopolitical perceptions of the world. The process by which Europeans ap-
propriated not only the geographical but also the mental and psychological
territory of the conquered peoples has by now been elucidated.[3] But
whether the victims of conquest recovered their original imaginative space
together with political independence, whether they even *can* or should do
so, remains a much debated question, particularly in postcolonial post-
structuralist criticism, though, inevitably, the debate is conducted in, and
therefore limited to, the intellectual epistemological terminology of the
colonizing West. Moreover, although much postcolonial criticism chal-

lenges the claim to accuracy of the mimetic representation of actual territories with its political and cultural consequences, comparatively little attention is given to the similar conception of mapping of the human experience and psyche in literary texts. For example, Edward Said in *Culture and Imperialism* argues that the rise of the English novel is inextricably linked with the growth of imperialism which underpins and supports the image of society presented in English fiction. Yet while questioning the "consolidated vision" of the "central authorizing subject," he doesn't say a word on the subject's chosen mode of representation, which certainly contributed to the consolidation of the imperialistic vision, but merely states that "the 'what' and 'how' in the representation of 'things' . . . are circumscribed and socially regulated," while "allowing for considerable individual freedom."[4]

Wilson Harris, who emphasized the link between imperialism and the rise of the novel nearly thirty years ago, claimed, on the contrary, that "this freedom . . . however liberal [it] may appear—is an illusion,"[5] and he has since repeatedly shown that realism both as a way of perceiving and acting upon the world and as a mode of writing is arbitrary in its failure to acknowledge whole areas of experience, while the concomitant growing influence of rationalism reduced the earth itself to a "passive creature" cut off from its roots. The difference with Said's analysis is that, for Harris, undermining a consolidated vision is not exclusively or mainly a matter of political change, though ultimately it includes that too, but first requires a renewed grasp of the human psyche and of a profound reality at once phenomenal and cultural.

In a well-documented article entitled "T. W. Harris—Sworn Surveyor," Tim Cribb demonstrates in the light of geographical surveys he consulted in Georgetown that Harris's response to the Guyanese landscape together with the epistemological mutation it entailed in his worldview and writing has a solid base in his experience as a professional surveyor.[6] His analysis of Harris's surveys throws light on what was indeed a neglected source of exegesis of his conception of art, though I would say that Cribb's emphasis on its pragmatic origins complements rather than corrects other interpretations that privilege a conceptual genesis of Harris's fiction. His own article testifies to the correlation between the two approaches. I would even take one step farther his assertion of the scientific verifiability and correspondence of Harris's vision and suggest that both the practice and the concept of "infinite rehearsal" Harris has evolved through his twenty-one novels run parallel with a similar process in science. For in its attempt to understand the universe, science continually challenges its own discoveries and is involved in an "infinite rehearsal" of its own, an endless revisioning and revising of earlier, sometimes partial misconceptions, or, in Harris's words, "consuming [its] own biases," also called "sin eating" in *Resurrection at Sorrow Hill*.[7] And if man has made tremendous progress in knowledge and understanding, he doesn't seem any closer to answering ultimate questions about the mystery of creation, the origins of life, and what is, apparently at least, the finality of death, whether of individuals or whole societies. *Resurrection* does not claim to give conclusive answers to these questions; that would run counter to Harris's rejection of finality whether in ontological or epistemological concepts. But the territory it charts opens onto dimensions suggesting an increasingly deep perception of sources of renewal both of man's endless capacity for development and of art, particularly in the Caribbean.

Harris's spatial narratives were always conceived in terms of mapping, itself a preliminary to a renewed apprehension, and therefore rebirth, of neglected areas, people(s), and their psychological motivations. The dreaming narrator's vision in *Palace of the Peacock* already fashioned the geopsychic setting, the equation between self and space, to be found in all Harris's fictions. The majority of the crew were then also from Sorrow Hill, an actual small settlement in Guyana, a country mostly ignored in our highly mediatized, globalized world. Putting it on the map, however, involves far more than filling the blanks of colonial cartography or exposing its distortions. Sorrow Hill in the later novel is both "native and universal . . . born of a precipitation from voyages and movements of peoples descending from ancient America, from Renaissance Europe, from the Siberian straits, from Africa, from India, from Asia . . . equally it sprang from the soil of written and unwritten histories at a confluence of three rivers and three civilizations, pre-Columbian civilization, post-Columbian civilization, and a civilization that dwells in spaces still unplumbed . . ." (4). By locating his narrative in an obscure heartland territory, Harris reiterates his belief that a solution to the present crisis of civilization could emerge from the margins. "The future of Guyana lies here" (24), says Hope, the gauge-reader protagonist who writes the novel as "a book of space" (17). When he and his mistress Butterfly, the beautiful and vulnerable queen of ruined El Dorado, are killed by her husband, the ambivalent Christopher D'eath, Hope nevertheless survives to re-create the history of the inmates of the Sorrow Hill Asylum for the Greats, a former prison under colonial rule. Like other Harris characters who partake of several dimensions of being, the inmates are both dead and alive, ordinary men yet dual personalities, who in their schizophrenic dividedness impersonate famous historical figures like Montezuma, Leonardo, or Socrates. They harbor the tension between destruction and survival, annihilation and the pull toward resurrection, between despair and faith, the crucial choice men face in the "Age of Sorrows," miniaturized in their asylum. Hope, too, the "visionary madman" (240), suffers from an acute breakdown and is split between fear of extinction and a saving love, while Dr Daemon, ambivalent genius and doctor of souls, goes through bouts of despair after his bride's death.

Resurrection at Sorrow Hill is an all-embracing epic in Harris's revised sense of the word, in a setting that bears marks of modern invasions, but, as suggested, it is pregnant with the neglected resources of a still primordial world. As a "confluence of spaces" (6), Sorrow Hill is at once a theater of collapsed cultures and a "theatre of psyche," whose complexities Hope charts on a scale that registers the eruption from the unconscious of extra-human faculties personified in animal creatures but also gods or semigods, like Quetzalcoatl or the androgynous Tiresian seer, now maimed judge, now Daemon's grandmother, who recalls the old Arawak woman of ancestral wisdom who keeps surfacing in Harris's fiction. Ancient myth co-exists with the invasion of science and technology. Hope's gauging is computer-ized, while Dr Daemon's sophisticated telescope enables him to scan the primitive landscape under his eyes, mythical and actual constellations, and the wider cosmos with its intimations of other parallel worlds. The fall of Montezuma's empire and his personal tragedy are echoed by the fall of the Ptolemaic universe and Giordano Bruno's burning at the stake, though it is Montezuma who bears the burden of these falls. And the historical disasters of the Renaissance reverberate in present-day conflicts. But above all, the intense individual emotions that fire such conflicts prove major sources of violence, and the inmates' split personality and impersonations of famous past figures are symptoms of frustration generated by these undigested overwhelming emotions. Monty, for example, imprisoned for a crime he has not committed, is obsessed with the same desire for revenge as Montezuma, the fallen emperor. The mute cry of a child for whose murder Brazilian feels responsible pursues him in Sorrow Hill. Len takes himself for Leonardo da Vinci and sees the murdered child on da Vinci's *Virgin of the Rocks*. A strik-ing metaphorical web unfolds from the painting, first misused by a fascist league in Brazil as emblem of the ethnically pure virgin state they want to establish, then revealing the possible transubstantiation of the murdered child into the eucharist.

This is just one example of the inmates' capacity to transfigure their catastrophic experiences into a creative potential, a major theme in Harris's art, which repeatedly points to the creativeness and possibility of renewal inherent in the disruptive wounds of history. In their present condition the inmates share the silence and voicelessness into which the ghosts of the past they impersonate have fallen as well as the eclipsed state of the Amer-indians who haunt the narrative and take part with them in the carnival procession of funeral masks awaiting resurrection (228). Their role offers another instance of the correlation between historic trauma and possible re-birth, between what Hope calls "the substance of the voice of the dumb" (75) and "a multi-dimensional creator or god" (29). One is reminded of *The Secret Ladder* when Poseidon, the god-like leader of the runaway slaves, soundlessly addresses the surveyor Fenwick in "the silent accents of an age-less dumb spirit."[8] In the new novel this has developed into a "ventrilo-quism of spirit" (78), which animates the "originality in the ramifications of apparently passive psyche in nature to break the hubris of one-sided human discourse" (78-79). This "ventriloquism of spirit," also "speech prior to speech" (75), informs various expressions of creativity (language, music, sculpture, creative fire) that Hope can only partially apprehend.

Indeed, if resurrection is creation and vice versa, "there is no second coming which is absolute and singular" (193). Rather Hope's nonlinear charting narrative progresses through myriad images of breaking and partial re-memberments, through an alternation of sensuously evoked landscapes, sexual desire and ecstasy, and a perception of the more abstract "compositional reality" (112) of existence, a mosaic of its oppositional elements across ages and cultures. Analytical dialogues are succeeded by the resurgence of Amerindian gods in nature out of their postconquest silence. The *Timehri* hand of god, for instance, is everywhere perceptible on the canvas of nature, and the mask of the Aztec monkey-god advises Montezuma to acknowledge he was partly responsible for his fall. The major metaphor running through the novel is the ceaselessly arriving, splintering ship of space (31, 36) re-enacting different catastrophes *in conjunction*, however, with the reconstitution of "the composition of the vessel" (68). The multiple variations on the structural metaphors of breaking and reconstitution are so many manifestations of the resurrection as process of transformation or conversion, translation from one mode of being into another,[9] on which Harris has commented: "Christian ideology invests . . . in the resurrection as the conquest of Death. And I would suggest that to do so is to forfeit a revisionary momentum within resources of language. The resurrection may imply *not conquest at all* but a transition from one dimension or universe of sensibility to another."[10] In keeping with the complete absence of monistic absolutes in Harris's narratives, the resurrectionary process combines with alternations both in Hope's perceptions and the configuration of the territories he charts. Subject to spells of insight and deception, Hope advances through unplumbed and resurrected spaces, through opacities or densities which alternate or run parallel with transparencies (174), sometimes gripped by "congealed yet eruptive energies of flight" (64) until, unpredictably, in a split second of illumination, he hits on the possibility of creation:

He was involved from the beginning of time and space in the composition of the vessel . . . Above all . . . he was involved in the possibility of originating dimension that gave a new intensity to every splinter . . . in the bristling orchestra of BIG BANG. Big Bang drum of the rapids.
    Was such inchoate origin or unfinished capacity an inimitable progression in its own right in parallel with the crumbling progression of the end-game world, the end-game vessel of the globe within the rapids? (68)

As "space attendant" (26) and "resurrection guide" (28), Hope is in search of "a truth that lies behind the ruins of adventure, colonization, that infest the face of the globe" (55), but he discovers that he can gain only intermittent access to windows into a reality out of reach in its totality yet partly perceptible through a growing "phenomenal literacy" (10, 12, 18, 28), another meaningful Harris coinage, conveying a capacity to read terrifying yet exalting depths and heights of landscape and history and translate them into art. And just as his mapping thrusts him nearer the unseizable "composition of wholeness" (110), so his fictional charting allows him to apprehend a voiceless spirit that had surrendered its voicelessness "to sounding rocks and waters and fires and soil" (35).

The victimized dumb intermittently reappear in Harris's fiction in a character called Nameless. Significantly an Archangel in this novel, he throws further light both on Hope's writing process and on the nature of the resurrection. He questions Hope's claims to single authorship and says that he writes himself into the pages of Hope's book (171). Indeed, the narrative, initiated by Daemon's grandmother, not only unfolds through Hope's dialogues with the "mad" but is also frequently taken over by those who guide, inspire or point to the self-deceptions of his charting. He is in no way a self-sufficient author; rather, the narrative shapes itself through him, though as Harris was careful to point out some years ago, this kind of effacement does not mean "the death of the author" in Barthes's sense or postmodernist practice, which, in his view, can lead to language games in the absence of referential meaning. The relativization of authorship in his fiction is inherent in creativity as process of reciprocity: "linkages between characters and authors, linkages between a painted world that paints the painter even as the painter paints . . . a written world that writes the writer as the writer writes . . ." (147); "In such mutuality of living text, living fiction, it was possible to bear the shock of becoming a tool of an elemental God . . ." (155).

The resurrection too evolves from such reciprocity between, on the one hand, altering, extended, or keener perceptions and, on the other, active presences and phenomena erupting from Hope's unconscious. So, like fiction writing, the resurrection is endless process or, to use another Harris expression, "unfinished genesis." It is above all latent survival and possible resurgence of an essential component in the make-up of men and cultures. When Nameless explains to Hope the way he may envisage it, he concludes "We are relics of fire" (242); in that fire and the rhythmical harmony perceived on and off in the narrative lies the secret of the resurrection, a multifaceted phenomenon, revival of unmapped dimensions, of the spirit in man and nature, of consciousness and conscience, of love and of meaning. It issues from a fracture in what Nameless sees as "the paralysis of materialism" (241). Daemon had earlier encouraged Hope to a "spiritual subversion . . . instinct with creative insight" (84). This can be read as a concise summing up of a religious strand in Harris's writing, which also involves breaking prior to transfiguration. We saw that the mad, broken by life, were associated with the dumb victims of conquest, themselves ghosts partaking of an elusive creator. The mad ones too, one character says, "know that a vulnerable humanity may strike a concert with Shadows of divine element that are alive" (156). Though never idealized, madness can nevertheless be "involuntary genius" (53), a spur to its own transfiguration into "creative schizophrenia," as Michael Gilkes called what he also sees as a major source of creativeness in the Caribbean. In Harris's fiction the Caribbean predicament extends its creative potential to the resolution of similar world-wide crises: "Hope's peculiar neurosis drives him to create fictions in which transfigured oppositions are necessary if the incorporation of one culture by another is to become an evolving source of re-visionary healing within diverse bodies and cultures that do relate to each other yet are at war with each other everywhere . . ." (162-63). At the end of the novel Hope hears a kind of music synonymous with creation and finds in all ruptures the origin of an art opening onto what can only be a ceaseless renewed charting:

A trinity of pens [Hope's, Daemon's, Archangel's] lay now within the breach of catastrophe, eloquent, cool flame, charcoal burn and splinter, and archangelic hand of the Clock.
    Hope seized them all with ecstatic gratitude as if he stood upon the very threshold of his book and a chorus of griefs arose within which an unseen orchestra moved and reassembled singing, dancing pillars where flame had stood around the ageless Mask of the seer. (244)

"And the response in the book?" the reader could then ask with one of the characters. "There is no dogmatic response [says Dr Daemon]. . . . The ship of the church, the ship of the state, the ship of a civilization, are weathered, weathering masks of a broken family (and its outcasts, as well as its survivors) through which the resurrection breaks open all incorporations . . . and thereby gives profoundest numinosity to an Imagination that recovers, in a variety of guises, those we appear to have lost" (166).

NOTES

[1]This is a shortened version of a paper read at a conference on "New Cartographies" which took place at the University of Oxford on 5 and 6 March 1995.
    [2]Wilson Harris, *The Womb of Space: The Cross-Cultural Imagination* (Westport: Greenwood, 1983), xix, xvii.
    [3]See, among others, Peter Hulme, *Colonial Encounters: Europe and the Native Caribbean 1492-1797* (1986; rpt. London: Routledge, 1992).
    [4]*Culture and Imperialism* (1993; rpt. London: Vintage, 1994), 84, 95.
    [5]*Tradition, the Writer and Society* (London: New Beacon Books, 1967), 29. In this essay Harris had also anticipated the connection between empire and the rise of the novel suggested later by Said: "the rise of the novel in its conventional and historical mould coincides in Europe with states of society which were involved in consolidating their class and other vested interests" (29).
    [6]"T.W. Harris—Sworn Surveyor," *Journal of Commonwealth Literature* 28.1 (1993): 33-46.
    [7]*Resurrection at Sorrow Hill* (London: Faber and Faber, 1993); hereafter cited parenthetically.

[8]Wilson Harris, *The Whole Armour and The Secret Ladder* (London: Faber and Faber, 1973), 156.

[9]On this subject, see Hena Maes-Jelinek, "Faces on the Canvas: The Resurrection Theme in *The Tree of the Sun*," *WLWE* 22.1 (1983): 88-89; and "Altering Boundaries: The Art of Translation in *The Angel at the Gate* and *The Twyborn Affair*," *WLWE* 23.1 (1984): 165-74.

[10]Charles Rowell, "An Interview with Wilson Harris," *Callaloo* 18.1 (1995): 194.

"*Space* Sounds" *in Wilson Harris's Recent Fiction*

Mary Lou Emery

> "We may carve or sculpt or paint with a hand that falters even as it seeks the true, exact hand it can never capture, *Timehri*, hand of God. . . .
> "I have dreamt, Judge, of writing a manifesto of the ship of the globe. . . ."
> —spoken by Hope in *Resurrection at Sorrow Hill*

As readers of Wilson Harris's writing, we are drawn into the fictions, drawn almost literally, as his characters "carve, sculpt, or paint" themselves onto the pages that become simultaneously canvases, galleries, and theaters of a reimagined globe. The dynamics of visual creativity figured in Harris's novels engage a conversion of verbal art into visual art, an apparent crossing from the sign system of words to that of visual images. Drawn into this illusionary transfiguration, we see vision itself refigured through and beyond the "imperial eye"[1] of conquest, extending the senses and body of the text-reader relation in a dialogue of and about creation where "space *sounds.*" As Canaima, twin of Anselm in *The Four Banks of the River of Space,* expresses it: "Extending our senses, Anselm. We cannot solve the world's terrifying problems otherwise" (9).

One of the most significant metaphors through which the crossing of verbal into visual art occurs is that of the Timehri or Arawak rock paintings of Guyana. A number of Harris's novels evoke the Timehri as visual signs of ancient cross-cultural myths, imprinted by a divine hand. In his most recent novels the Timehri appear as the visual scripts for the narrative action of the novels themselves.

For example, in *Resurrection at Sorrow Hill,* the characters voyage in ships or "vessels" that are also "crafts" and "temples," images converging in the sacred glyphs of the Timehri, which visibly portray the narrative action of their voyages. As rocks in the rapids above the Guyanese waterfalls, the Timehri cause the ships to crash, a narrative action also presumably carved or painted on their (thus, breaking) surfaces. The legends figured on the rocks find, in turn, visual shape in the constellations through which diverse creatures, in states of metamorphosis, are lifted into the sky by the blind seer and ambiguously gendered narrator of the book, Tiresias.

These verbal illusions of visuality and transformation are, to me, enchanting. To a certain extent, they are the illusions of the classical rhetorical device of *ekphrasis,* the representation in literature of a visual work of art.

In its most famous example, the description of Achilles's shield in the eighteenth book of the *Iliad*, *ekphrasis* creates an illusion which is, in Murray Krieger's words, both "mirage" and "miracle": the illusion of visual art appearing before us, yet in words; the mirage of narrative action suspended by the representation of a spatialized, yet nevertheless narrated, visual object; and the miracle of gaining access to a reality beyond language, yet represented within it. In the *Iliad* the reality beyond language is that of the god Hephaestus, creator of the shield on which is represented all of the cosmos and thus of creation itself. In Harris's writing the mirage and miracle extend into a dynamic, mutable, expanding whole of creation, which remains partial and incomplete, as they draw us all the more intensely into their palimpsestic visual frames. Reading these scenes, we experience vision as a dangerous liberation, an excess of mimesis that evokes the ecstasies of spiritual witness to "the hand it can never capture, *Timehri*, hand of God."

These scenes of dynamic visuality in Harris's writing counter the colonizing gaze and its reduction of the visible to that which can be observed, measured, classified, and acquired. If we accept an analysis of the expansion of European commercial interests in the New World as bound inextricably to the rise of natural science and its empiricizing, classifying, commodifying gaze,[2] we can well understand why contemporary writers of the Caribbean must address the "dead seeing material eye" of colonizing figures such as Donne in *Palace of the Peacock*. However, Harris's writing does not homogenize the imperial European eye but finds within its failures and in its encounters with African and Amerindian worldviews the potential for renewed vision expressed in the ongoing epiphanies of his prose. The opportunity to experience that renewed vision has long seemed to me the gift offered by Harris's writing. Yet reading Harris's more recent fiction, I have become increasingly aware of the ways that the expanded *ekphrases* of his writing, expanded to the very shaping of the novels, take us as readers through the politics of vision to a threshold and translation of sight coextensive with the breaking up of social and narrative patterns of sexual violence.

Repeatedly in *Resurrection at Sorrow Hill*, the "crafts" in which the characters voyage break, and in the image of the rocks breaking (visual images shattering/vessels crashing) appears a link with the tapestry coat that Penelope, the El Dorado missionary, weaves, unravels, and reweaves following the death of her husband in *The Four Banks of the River of Space*. She describes the cloak to Anselm, the narrator of the novel, as "A coat that is as much tapestry of the world, as of fire and water, to fit the shoulder of a hill, or the body of rock in a Waterfall" (54). "The body of rock in a Waterfall" joins with the crashing vessels of the Timehri in alluding to the Guyanese legend of Chief Kaie who, though badly crippled, climbed to the top of the Kaieteur Falls to descend, crashing, and thus to unite in spirit with the God Makonaima who dwelled in the "huge mountain rock" in "the swift black waters."[3] Not only does "the body of rock" appear in Penelope's description of her tapestry coat but also the body's breaking, both literally and figuratively. As Penelope states, "the coat never quite fits. Always a sleeve of element or a fluid stitch that's out of joint." Saying this, she lifts her arm to reveal "the faint but indelible colour of bruises on the soft, bright flesh" (54). The coat which may fit "the body of rock," activated and breaking up, is made of fabric breaking with itself, "out of joint," which she must unravel every day with her hands and arms, the bruised and broken fabric of her flesh.

In both novels the broken social code of marriage underpins the characters' conflicts and transfigurations. Penelope in *The Four Banks of the River of Space* and Butterfly in *Resurrection at Sorrow Hill* have married militaristic or mechanistic and (at least partially) tyrannous figures in sacred contracts that each violates. These broken bonds motivate the breakthrough transformations undergone by the characters in stories inscribed and also ruptured on the crashing painted rocks.

The vessel/images of the Timehri fracture when Butterfly and her lover Hope, en route to the Camaria Falls, undergo a metamorphosis in a vastly expanded *ekphrastic* passage. As their ship, composed of images from "Timehri Arawak craft," breaks up, it also comes alive and is transformed: "The boat became a constellation in the nightsky of the river. The planks of wood came alive, murmuring tongues were heard erupting from the shell of ancient trees. . . . [T]he mast-head was alive, they were the blind/seeing eyes, deaf/hearing ears, from the tree-gender of Tiresias, the cosmic tree of stake from which the serpent had sprung" (19). Is it the breaking of wooden laws and structures that makes their passage through and into these multiple visual frames of the cosmos possible? Not only do readers experience a visual vertigo reading this passage but we are dizzied by the "murmuring tongues" as the passage seems to erupt from itself through sight to sound and movement. The petroglyph is speaking; it breaks out into voice as it also re-creates the "tree-gender of Tiresias."

As postcolonial critics have questioned the dominance of the visual in their critiques of the "commanding gaze" of colonialism, so to similar purposes have feminist critics inquired into the dynamics of sexual power through the "masculine gaze." Jacqueline Rose, addressing projects of contemporary art, has argued further that visual space itself is not sexually neutral. In Freudian theory the space of visual experience becomes "troubled" or disturbing due to a perceived difference of the feminine.

Perhaps one of the most important things that Harris's extended *ekphrases* do is to set the eye, and thus the sovereign "I" of identity, in motion, refracting its view and shifting its identificatory positions. The objects of the gaze must shift too in a great leap of subject into object of sight: "how could Timehri rock canvas live unless the viewer, the viewed, were prepared to leap into each other, to engage with a mutual spark that ran through every line, every crack, every mad detail of the composition?" (*Resurrection* 69). This leap of self into Other seems to require a profound disturbance of the field of visual/sexual politics. In the breaking of social codes of sexual possession in marriage and visual art, does the representation of vision also break form? Does this suggest that gender has transformed, too, from an apparently indelible opposition upon which violence plays ("the indelible colour of bruises") to a creative, transfigurative force, a fantastic metamorphosis and metamorphosis of fantasy?

"The tree-gender of Tiresias, the cosmic tree of stake from which the serpent has sprung" recalls several mythologies, including the transformation of Tiresias from male to female and the mutably gendered rainbow serpent Damballa, associated here with broken laws of sexual possession in a cracked visual composition. Hope's narrative directs us to "See through (rather *hear* through, prize open) what is an *involuntary* storage until one lifts sound, the caveats of stored sound into consciousness and space *sounds*" (*Resurrection* 45). It seems to me that in these broken "vessels" of sex/gender laws, Harris's writing prizes open visual space so that we see and hear through vision to a space where "space *sounds*." It is an Orphic leap outside the plot whereby the masculine gaze sentences both man and woman, subject and object. The narrative voice of Tiresias thus wavers in blind visionary gestures from "I" to "she" to that of a "ventriloquist of spirit" and muses, "It was odd that I should speak of myself in the third person" (*Resurrection* 9), while the bruised skin of Penelope's arm shadows the broken masculine body of Chief Kaie. Here "in a theatre of mediations [that] bridges distances between the singing Orphic head (that man in pride—proud dismemberment—is) and the electric hummingbird streaking the air with its rainbow wings webbed into vibration" (*Resurrection* 105), characters make another resounding leap, or a leap of revised sounds, into the dynamics of creation: " 'Leap into the masses!' said Marx. 'Descend BIG BANG SPIDER Christ!' " (69).

Ekphrasis has been translated as meaning "to speak out in full." In this reading of the device, it frames within the narrative a visual image that, by virtue of the framing, speaks out in resistance to the dominant narrative action to tell another story. Returning to Penelope's tapestry, I notice phrases such as "the thread of her song" and am reminded of another weaver in Greek mythology, Philomela. In Ovid's version of the story the husband of her sister, Procne, rapes Philomela and cuts out her tongue. Prevented from speaking about the crimes against her, Philomela weaves the story into a tapestry sent to Procne. The sisters enact a bloody revenge which ends in their metamorphoses, Procne into a swallow and Philomela into a nightingale so that the threads of Philomela's weaving, result of a silenced tongue, turn to song that forever haunts the woods.

The murmuring tongues erupting from the shells of trees in the breakup of Hope and Butterfly's boat also speak a silenced story of "ancestral tongues . . . that have been eclipsed." Penelope's tapestry coat "which may fit the body of rock" speaks, too, and now for me they sound together in a counterpoint of readings from one novel to another. Both breaking rock/vessel and flawed woven coat speak through the break traditional *ekphrasis* makes with narrative action and through a simultaneous break in Harris's expanded *ekphrases* away from the visual, a miraculous extension of sight beyond words and an ecstatic, terrifying bridge into sound.

With its flawed fit and "out-of-joint" pattern, Penelope's weaving represents a violation. However, unlike Philomela's weaving and the tapestry finally completed by Homer's Penelope, Penelope's cloak in *The Four Banks* resists silent conformity "to a convenient climax with a potent ghost or with a dutiful, conscientious suitor," which in Harris's view, would repeat formulaic epic cycles of conquest, revenge, and, in my reading of the novels, of sexual violence coextensive with visual order. Its pattern resembles instead those described by Robert Farris Thompson as typical of some African weavings, "rhythmized textiles" of the Mande, who create patterns of "rich and vivid suspensions of the expected placement of the weft-blocks." Since it "never fits," Penelope's weaving suspends placement also, of "a convenient climax" to Harris's epic. Its broken pattern, like those of the Mande weavings, creates a counter-rhythm, in "designs virtually to be scanned metrically, in visual resonance with the famed off-beat phrasing of melodic accents in African and Afro-American music" (207). Thompson reports that the off-beat and pattern-breaking figurations in the cloth "symbolize passing through two worlds, the quest for superior insights and power of the ancestors" (qtd. in Lippard 74). In Harris's evocation of such visual rhythms as incomplete, undone in their making, is threaded also the possibility for refiguring the epic narrative of repeated conquest and violence.

"We may carve or sculpt or paint with a hand that falters even as it seeks the true, exact hand it can never capture, *Timehri*, hand of God. . . .
  "I have dreamt, Judge, of writing a manifesto of the ship of the globe. . . ."

Rereading this passage, which I quoted as epigraph to this essay, I can almost hear the beat, like a wing, of the "hand that falters." Is it in the *faltering* of mimesis (the limping of Legba, crippled Hephaestus, and old Chief Kaie; the wavering of blind Tiresias) that we hear the off-beat and glimpse, through its "numinous inexactitude . . . the incredible exactitude of eternity's solitaries beyond our reach" (71)? Nathaniel Mackey has written of a "fugitive spirit" in the musicality of Harris's writing. In these two recent novels the faltering of the hand cracking the vessel sounds also the breakthrough of fugitive sexual identities and thus of epic plots altered through cross-cultural, cross-sensory passages—"sensational realities," as Harris has written—in "the ship of the globe."

NOTES

[1] I am borrowing this term from Mary Louise Pratt's *Imperial Eyes:*

Travel Writing and Transculturation.

[2]See, for examples, Mary Louise Pratt, *Imperial Eyes,* and David Spurr, *The Rhetoric of Empire: Colonial Discourse in Journalism, Travel Writing, and Imperial Administration.*

[3]These phrases are from A. J. Seymour's poem "The Legend of Kaieteur." See also Grace Nichols, "I Will Enter," *I Is a Long Memoried Woman.*

WORKS CITED

Harris, Wilson. *The Four Banks of the River of Space.* London: Faber and Faber, 1990.

—————. *Resurrection at Sorrow Hill.* London: Faber and Faber, 1993.

Krieger, Murray. *Ekphrasis: The Illusion of the Natural Sign.* Baltimore: Johns Hopkins Univ. Press, 1992.

Lippard, Lucy. *Mixed Blessings: New Art in a Multicultural America.* New York: Pantheon, 1990.

Mackey, Nathaniel. *Discrepant Engagement: Dissonance, Cross-Culturality, and Experimental Writing.* Cambridge: Cambridge Univ. Press, 1993.

Nichols, Grace. *I Is a Long Memoried Woman.* London: Karnak House, 1990.

Pratt, Mary Louise. *Imperial Eyes: Travel Writing and Transculturation.* London: Routledge, 1992.

Rose, Jacqueline. *Sexuality in the Field of Vision.* London: Verso, 1986.

Seymour, A. J., ed. *A Treasury of Guyanese Poetry.* Georgetown: Guyana National Lithographic, 1980.

Spurr, David. *The Rhetoric of Empire: Colonial Discourse in Journalism, Travel Writing, and Imperial Administration.* Durham: Duke Univ. Press, 1993.

Thompson, Robert Farris. *Flash of the Spirit: African and Afro-American Art and Philosophy.* New York: Vintage, 1983.

Wilson Harris at Faber and Faber

Frank Pike

When I was asked to contribute to this issue of the *Review of Contemporary Fiction,* I felt a strange mixture of exhilaration and apprehension. Here was the chance to record my feelings about one of the most rewarding relationships in my personal and professional life—how could I possibly refuse? But how could I possibly do it justice? It ought to be the kind of piece which would forever after be spoken of as "the stuff of publishing legend." But the editor who plucked *Palace of the Peacock* off the slush pile in 1959 wasn't me, it was Charles Monteith, who had done the same thing for *Lord of the Flies* a few years earlier (in those days slush piles were slush piles). I can't even remember the first time I read *Palace:* it certainly wasn't the first work of Wilson's I read. Nor can I remember the first time we met. Some legend this was going to be.

Memory told me my involvement with Wilson and his work covered my entire publishing life, but I knew I couldn't have been involved with *Palace of the Peacock,* because it appeared in 1960, and I only joined the firm in the autumn of 1959. My first job was largely administrative and I only gradually became involved in editorial matters over a period of years. Initially that involvement consisted mainly of reporting on the occasional manuscript and writing the occasional blurb, and not exclusively for Charles Monteith. It would seem that it was in this fashion that I came to read my first Harris manuscript: as it turns out, *The Secret Ladder.* So, until I checked the record, I didn't realize that my acquaintance with the *Quartet* began with the last volume. No doubt that accounts for the fact that, when asked by readers intimidated by Wilson's reputation for "obscurity" for advice on what to start with, I've been for years recommending that particular work. This is no doubt a tribute to the impression it made on me, but also a demonstration of the kind of solipsism which makes publishers unreliable critics (in the sense readers of the *Review of Contemporary Fiction* would understand the term) of their authors—this in addition (no doubt frustratingly for those readers) to the discretion surrounding any professional relationship. This was in 1962, by which time *Palace* and *The Far Journey of Oudin* had already appeared and *The Whole Armour* was "in the press." Wilson and Margaret came to a seasonal authors' party at Fabers in October, and I suppose I could have met them then, but embarrassingly I simply can't remember. From then on I seem at least peripherally to have had something to do with the succeeding books as they came in—*Heartland, Eye of the Scarecrow, The Waiting Room, Tumatumari, Ascent to Omai*—over the rest of the decade.

Although Charles Monteith had handled all our dealings with Wilson, by April 1968, he evidently thought my involvement was sufficient to entitle me to join them for lunch, and it seems to have gone well enough for us to be invited to Addison Road later in the year before Wilson's departure for Cuba in December. There was another lunch the following January, and it was on our walk back to the office that Charles and I found ourselves spontaneously remarking to each other on Wilson's special brand of personal charm.

(By this time readers will have realized that Charles was the crucial editorial figure throughout the most critical phase of Wilson's career, and as far as Fabers is concerned probably the most appropriate contributor to the *Review.* Sadly he died before I had a chance to explore with him his own sense of the sequence of events just described. But if Charles was crucial, his fellow directors were just as important in initiating and sustaining the relationship between author and publisher. This was the body—the whole firm in editorial mode—which decided to publish *Palace of the Peacock.* The initiative was Charles's, but the decision was collective, as were the succeeding decisions to publish the rest of the *Quartet.*)

From then on, and particularly after Fabers moved offices from Russell Square to Queen Square, Charles's increasing responsibilities, first as vice chairman and then as chairman, meant he saw Wilson less and less and I more and more, as often as not as a dinner guest at the flat in Addison Road, to be brought up to date on the increasingly extensive travels which were by then the by-product of Wilson's increasing status in the world of letters. I can't be alone in noting that the increasing status made not the slightest difference to the way Wilson behaved toward me or anyone else. It's impossible to be a friend of his without becoming an admirer and—once you've met him—vice versa. What we admire, of course, is the work: its integrity and the austerity of commitment to an artistic vision and its means of expression over the years, the undemonstrative refusal to join coteries or to conform to literary or intellectual fashion. What we admire if anything even more is the fact that all this is combined with personal openness and warmth and a complete lack of affectation. If there's a scintilla of self-importance in Wilson's character, however justified, it needs someone more acute than me to spot it.

"Retirement" to Essex has meant that accepting the hospitality dispensed by the Harris household means a trip more demanding than the previous few stops on the Central Line, but it has given that hospitality a new dimension, with its excursions to country pubs and walks which become living expressions of Wilson's feeling for landscape and sense of place. There is still elevated conversation taking in Dante, Aeschylus, or Eliot, but I've known it to cover the distinctive qualities of various brands of Caribbean rum and the technique of off-spin bowling. Often one leaves for home with a small but memorable present—a miniature Aztec bird for the mantelpiece or a jar of Margaret's homemade whisky marmalade. But this is starting to take on the self-indulgently proprietorial tone I abominate in the reminiscences of certain of my professional colleagues. A publisher is an effective intermediary between writer and reader or he's nothing. There are writers, from Jeffrey Archer downwards (or upwards?), who demand or require editorial intervention which can amount to collaboration, and often it is expedient that this should be so, but the extent to which it happens is obscured by the professional confidentiality already referred to. However, it's my conviction that the books worth publishing are those written by authors to whose work "editing" (as distinct from "preparing for the press") is, in the strict sense, an impertinence. There are no prizes for guessing what kind of writer Wilson Harris is. The personal relationship I and my Faber colleagues have with him is a privilege and not a right, and we value it as such.

A Wilson Harris Checklist

Joyce Sparer Adler

Novels

Palace of the Peacock (London: Faber and Faber, 1961).
The Far Journey of Oudin (London: Faber and Faber, 1961).
The Whole Armour (London: Faber and Faber, 1962).
The Secret Ladder (London: Faber and Faber, 1963).
Heartland (London: Faber and Faber, 1964).
The Eye of the Scarecrow (London: Faber and Faber, 1965).
The Waiting Room (London: Faber and Faber, 1967).
Tumatumari (London: Faber and Faber, 1968).
Ascent to Omai (London: Faber and Faber, 1970).
The Sleepers of Roraima, A Carib Trilogy (London: Faber and Faber, 1970).
The Age of the Rainmakers (London: Faber and Faber, 1971).
Black Marsden (London: Faber and Faber, 1972).
Companions of the Day and Night (London: Faber and Faber, 1975).
Da Silva da Silva's Cultivated Wilderness and *Genesis of the Clowns* (London: Faber and Faber, 1977).
The Tree of the Sun (London: Faber and Faber, 1978).
The Angel at the Gate (London: Faber and Faber, 1982).
Carnival (London: Faber and Faber, 1985).
The Infinite Rehearsal (London: Faber and Faber, 1987).
The Four Banks of the River of Space (London: Faber and Faber, 1990).
Resurrection at Sorrow Hill (London: Faber and Faber, 1993).
Jonestown (London: Faber and Faber, 1996).

Nonfiction

History, Fable and Myth in the Caribbean and Guianas (Georgetown: National History and Arts Council, 1970).
Tradition, the Writer and Society (London: New Beacon Books, 1967; rpt. 1973).
Fossil and Psyche (Austin: Univ. of Texas Press, 1974).
Explorations (Aarhus: Dangaroo Press, 1978).
The Womb of Space: The Cross-Cultural Imagination (Westport: Greenwood Press, 1983).

Alan Burns in 1981

Alan Burns: An Introduction

David W. Madden

I first came to Alan Burns's fiction accidentally. Professor Jay Halio, who was editing a section of the *Dictionary of Literary Biography* on contemporary British novelists, invited me to contribute an article. Searching through a list of thirty-five or so names, I came across Burns and began reading *Europe after the Rain*. I had recently been reading such American writers as John Hawkes, John Barth, Jerzy Kosinski, and Donald Barthleme; Burns struck me as a British writer working from a similar aesthetic sensibility, and I was immediately drawn to the world of this novel. I quickly read his other works and established a correspondence that has now lasted fifteen years.

In the introduction to *The Imagination on Trial* Charles Sugnet remarks on a prevailing American attitude about modern British fiction: "that it remains traditional, nostalgic, even stodgy. If you are an American undergraduate interested in 'serious' or 'experimental' fiction, your instructors will direct you to French works . . . and certain North Americans . . . and the Latin Americans. . . ."[1] Burns has never been one of these so-called "stodgy," predictable, traditional British novelists. In fact, when asked if he saw himself as an English novelist in the tradition of the English novel, Burns responded, "I'm more interested certainly in the European novel and in the Russian novel, insofar as those terms have any meaning. . . ."[2] In fact in a letter to me he cited as important influences Tolstoy, Neruda, Brecht, Pasternak, Woolf, Ionesco, Shaw, and Arthur Miller.

Since the publication of his first novel, Burns has been regarded as among British fiction's most avant-garde writers with the likes of B. S. Johnson, Eva Figes, Ann Quin, Wilson Harris, Christine Brooke-Rose, and Michael Moorcock. However, Burns did not burst on the London literary scene immediately after emerging from the university, nor did his education suggest a later career as a writer. By his own account his education was "average middle class. . . . I was quite bright but also eccentric, called by some 'Batty Burns.' I went to a middle-range public school, Merchant Taylors' School," where he first studied science and then at "15 switched to Classics, not Greek, but Latin, plus History and English."[3] At this time he made a few contributions to student magazines but wrote little, slowly, with difficulty. From 1949 to 1951 he served in the Royal Army Education Corps. After working as a clerk and traveling through Europe, his father persuaded him to study law, and he became a barrister in 1956. He did courtroom work for a while but gave this up in favor of acting as a libel lawyer for *Reynolds News*. In 1959 he spent a year as a researcher at the

London School of Economics and then became a libel lawyer at Beaver-brook Newspapers.

A signal incident in his development as a writer occurred one day when Burns was walking down Carey Street on a lunch break and he saw

a silver frame for sale [in a jeweler's window] and in the frame a photograph of a youngish couple kissing, embracing. It was a sweet photo, rather old-fashioned, probably from the 'thirties, and it rang a bell because I'd seen a similar photo in the family album, of my father and mother kissing on their honeymoon in Monte Carlo, with orange trees in the background. I had long wanted to write about my parents and the love between them and the not-love between them but I didn't know where to start. At that moment I realized I needn't tackle their psychology or their histories, I could start with a picture. I discovered the power of the image. . . . And that became a starting point for my first book, *Buster*. (*Imagination on Trial* 161, 163)

The incident was significant for providing not only a subject and theme (the dynamics of familial relations) but a personal approach for the creation of fiction. Although later novels would not evolve so clearly from a single event or image, the power of an image does figure in all of his works, and the element of serendipitous discovery becomes increasingly important.

When compared with his later novels, *Buster* (1961) seems rather straightforward. The narrative advances through a series of incidents in the life of protagonist Dan Graveson who loses his mother and beloved older brother at a young age (as had Burns as well). Although a bright young man full of promise, Graveson cannot find his way in the world and fails at each new undertaking until he is homeless and penniless. The novel has all the attributes of the Angry Young Man literature of its era; however, it also acts as a precursor to later Burns novels. Besides the domestic theme, the novel is constructed around an episodic plot that is propelled by a mad rush of incidents that capture, with often minute precision, the fine details of situation, scene, or emotion. One curious incident involves an eccentric essay the protagonist composes about Samuel Johnson which provokes the ire of his teachers. The piece is a foreshadowing of the surreal effects Burns would develop more fully later; however, the Johnson essay actually springs from an unexpectedly early incident. " 'Johnson in the Modern Eye,' the essay on p. 90 of *Buster* (in the US edition) was originally written by me aged 16 and published in the school magazine! You can see how early I was playing about with words and styles."[4]

At this point there was little to suggest the startling direction that his fiction would take with the publication of *Europe after the Rain*, a novel that may remind one of Hawkes's *The Cannibal* though there was no line of influence between the two. Taking its title from a Max Ernst painting, the novel attempts to take fiction in the direction of a surrealist painting. The narrative is enveloped in ambiguity—the setting is vague though universal, the characters are unnamed, the motives underlying behavior are often opaque, and the temporal period could be anytime. The reader travels with the narrator-protagonist on an initially undefined journey through a war-ravaged landscape as he tries to penetrate behind the lines of combat to the camp of the insurgents. The reasons for the conflict remain obscure as is his mission, though he represents the conscience of the narrative and is the one character who appears above the fray, until he decides that the aging commander must be assassinated.

An air of illogic pervades all actions and much of the dialogue. Ardent patriots are double agents, macho commanders are actually feeble old men, and police control revolutionaries—in short, the usual expectations do not pertain, and the reader is constantly forced to redefine characters and the fictional universe until all frames of reference have been dissolved. The narrator warns the reader that he has discovered "the new human mind,"[5] a vicious sensibility given to endless suspicion and ruthless vengeance.

Europe after the Rain is furthermore important for the way it continues Burns's fascination with history as a source for fiction. In an interview years ago he remarked that he had made the novel "out of the concentration camps"[6]; however, when I asked where the camps were in the novel, he corrected himself:

I did not read (don't think I could have found it possible to read) books on Polish concentration camps. The "Polish" source was a journalist's book on post-war Poland. The nearest I got to the "truth" was the Nuremburg transcript [I had found] . . . I was going for—or was drawn into—another form of ambiguity. I did not want, was not capable of, journalistic accuracy, I was interested in something a lot hazier, yet composed of razor sharp details, splinters of fact. I've talked elsewhere of the landscape painter not staring but wrinkling his eyes and squinting at the landscape. "Hazy" is probably not quite right, because I was going for the precise imagery of Kafka which produces a floating sensation and suggests a kind of universality along with its specificity. It is of course that precious "quality of dream."[7]

The effect is a landscape of the imagination that has all the appearance and texture of nearly any war-ravaged place the audience may have witnessed. The "razor sharp details" give the otherwise elliptical situation a staggering palpability, and the reader is forced to balance the haziness of a hallucination with the hard particularities of a lived experience.

Celebrations (1967), on the surface, appears to be a return to the subject matter of *Buster*. Burns turns away from an exploration of history to examine a family that has slipped its moorings. One is introduced to a group of men who all work at the family business, a factory. Williams, the father, is employer and supervisor of his sons' lives—professional, emotional, and psychic—son Phillip dies early in the plot, and the other son, the more crafty and capable Michael, pursues Phillip's none-too-bereaved wife, Jacqueline. Family solidarity and support give way to predatory competition. Michael may have arranged Phillip's accident, and Williams quickly regards Michael as an annoying obstacle in his own pursuit of Jacqueline.

For all its surface similarities to *Buster,* the novel is actually a perfect bridge between the subject matter of the first work and the style of the second. The narrative progresses in a consistent fashion from the death of Phillip, to the competitive courtship of Jacqueline, Michael's marriage to her, her infidelity with Williams, Michael's rise in influence at the factory, Williams's decline in stature and death, and Michael's sudden death on a street. However, the steady progression of family chronicle is punctuated by surreal interruptions of the placid or predictable. "Whatever he was made of fell to pieces. He felt cold. The end of the life was the sound of yellow, rattling across the floor." "The judges retired to consider their verdict. The two drank the thin white wine, the green and tasty stomachs stood on the polished table, their wigs and hats on the convenient shelf, each day a brandy in a balloon."[8] Passages like these, of course, startle the reader, but they also convey emphatically a mood or atmosphere that is precise and supportive of the plot and characterizations.

The novel is significant as well for presaging the risks Burns would take with his "cut-up" method of composition. He has evolved his own form of Burroughs's technique in that he will gather odd fragments of material, cut and divide these, and then reassemble them into new and original verbal arrangements. *Celebrations* reveals the oscillations between Burns's desire to tell a story and to disrupt and undermine those traditional methods to accentuate the hidden relationships and unrealized possibilities in the narrative. As he commented, the novel "grew from a mosaic of fragments written with no concern for the ultimate plot connections. . . . In a succession of rewrites I pulled the pieces together."[9]

Emboldened by the critical success of *Celebrations* and wishing to push his cut-up method further, Burns published *Babel* in 1969, a novel that is his most experimental and, not surprisingly, least popular. In a letter Burns described his mosaic method as similar to Baudelaire's "Ragpicker" and to Schwitters's tram tickets and explained that " 'any old junk' can form the raw material, in which I find the words, phrases and images that build into the novel."[10] He included in that letter a section from a nonfictional work in progress, "Art by Accident," which analyzes the methods and effects of aleatoric art; in that study he quotes at length the techniques of Baudelaire and Schwitters:

Baudelaire's "Ragpicker": "Everything that the big city threw away, everything it lost, everything it despised, everything it crushed underfoot, he catalogues and collects. . . . He sorts things out and makes a wise choice; he collects, like a miser guarding a treasure, the refuse which will assume the shape of useful or gratifying objects between the jaws of the goddess of Industry." And Schwitters who declared: "I don't see why one shouldn't use in a picture, just as one uses colours made by paint merchants, things like old tram tickets, scraps of driftwood, cloak-room tickets, ends of string, bicycle wheel spokes—in a word, all the old rubbish you find in dustbins or refuse dumps."[11]

The notion of a free-ranging assemblage of all manner of materials is certainly obvious in the mosaic of subjects treated in Burns's narrative.

However, Burns was also searching to discover new stylistic possibilities for his fiction. Sentences no longer merely contain surreal images that convey a spirit of illogic or add a sense of texture to an incident. *Babel* abounds with sentences that not only challenge perception but that disrupt the expectations of syntax. "After a time he knifed her in the kitchen, between the counter and the machine, as the fork water turned dreadful, the noise from the machine as from eight women, trays of dregs of purplish colour full of the whirring fan continually in fever."[12] He has explained that "the quality I wanted was that not only the narrative but also the sentences were fragmented. I used the cut-up method to join the subject from one sentence to the object from another, with the verb hovering uncertainly between" ("Essay" 66).

As the title suggests, the novel is a panoply of voices and characters, all demanding their place in the narrative, struggling to enunciate their uniqueness, yet together overwhelming the reader and leading to a sense of cacophony and confusion. The Duke of Windsor, bolsheviks, the Queen, a Scottish sexologist, Billy Graham, General Westmoreland, Dylan Thomas, and a host of others crowd one another and fulfill Andy Warhol's dictum that each will have his or her fifteen minutes of significance. Yet in spite of the confusion and conflicting demands on the reader's attention, the novel does have a thematic center, and once again the concern with the coercive abuses of power is foremost: "it was about the power of the State. How in every street, every room, every shop, every workplace, every school, every institution, and particularly in every family, the essential pattern of power relations is dictated by the underlying rules, assumptions and moral principles of the State" ("Essay" 66).

In the same year Burns wrote his play, *Palach* (1974), as a result of a challenge by producer Charles Marowitz, and it can be seen as a perfect complement to *Babel* in subject and technique. It concerns the self-immolation of a Czech university student, Jan Palach, who protested the Soviet invasion of his country in 1969. Once again the theme of authority destroying freedom and individuality is foremost in the play, though in this case Palach has some limited choice in his own destruction. He and fellow students decide to draw straws to determine who among them will make their protest, and Palach, of course, loses. The idea of a young person being sacrificed for the sins of adults is furthermore consistent with incidents in Burns's other works.

Perhaps because he was not an experienced dramatist, Burns felt free to invent his method of exposition as he saw fit. To that end the play used a unique setting, with four separate stages on which actions took place simultaneously. The four stages, which surrounded the audience, were connected by planks that emptied into a central platform, and actors wandered among these areas throughout the performance. At the same time large speakers were placed throughout the theater to project voices, sounds, sometimes blaring noises that engulfed the audience and the performance. Once again the idea of a cacophony of sounds that compete with one another dominated the production.

The cut-up method continues in Burns's fifth novel, *Dreamerika!* (1972). Stung by the harsh critical reactions to *Babel* and seeking a new narrative technique, Burns sought to write a different kind of novel. "*Babel* had gone to unrepeatable extremes in the fragmentation of narrative, now I latched on to the story of the Kennedys whose characters and activities gave the reader easy reference points to help him through a sea of disparate images. I played hell with the documented facts, made crazy distortions of the alleged truth, in order to get some humour out of it, and also to raise questions about the nature of documentary realism" ("Essay" 67).

Once again the theme of power, corruption, and the tensions of family life are foregrounded. The Kennedys are presented as paradigmatic examples of modern coercion and corruption, as the narrative traces their rise to prominence from Joseph P.'s financial manipulations to JFK's presidency and assassination, the 1967 march on the Pentagon, RFK's rise and fall, Ted's collapse, Jackie's marriage to Onassis, and finally the children who inherit a destructive legacy. As he charts the varying fortunes of the family, Burns surveys the topography of postwar America to find a landscape as battered and torn as that in *Europe after the Rain*.

Arranged in chapters, which *Babel* was not, the narrative still relies on abrupt transitions and odd shifts in subject. To announce more dramatically the cut-up technique, the novel employs offset litho printing that highlights the wild assemblage of clippings that comprise the chapter and section headings—"Do you Hunt?," "The Day a Judge Was Duped," "Odd farrago of ritual and allegory." Arranged in different fonts and typesets, these cuttings have the look and feel of the British tabloids that scream their headlines and titillate the reader with hints of sensational stories.

However, on the sentence level, the narrative is far more straightforward than *Babel*. The effect is much closer to that of *Celebrations*, whereby the patriarch, for instance, is referred to as a man who "grew richer than himself. . . . He bought Boston for his children. He spread his name all over. . . . He offered to buy America for seventeen billion dollars and received assurances that the government would move out as their leases expired. . . . In adding to his millions Joe started selling members of his family. . . . He discovered that blood was cheap: he sold the heart and the head."[13] The subtitle—"A Surrealist Fantasy"—is as much a preemptive protection against a possible libel suit as it is a terse explanation of the novel's sensibility. The reaction of reviewers, as had been the case with *Babel*, was impatient and dismissive, with complaints of heavy-handedness, bitter satire, and cruelty.

With his next novel, *The Angry Brigade* (1973), Burns returned to history for his subject, but the work otherwise bears little resemblance to its predecessors. Responding to the reactions to his last efforts, Burns "gave up writing from the subconscious, making a mosaic of found pieces. I had written four books that way and the fun had gone out of it" ("Essay" 67). Instead of cuttings and combing through newspapers and magazines for fragments, Burns turned to a tape recorder to gather the raw material for this novel.

Like *Babel* it is a collection of voices, not a random and compendious assemblage but a collection of six narrators who alternate in the telling of their individual and collective tales. The six are imagined members of an actual small-scale guerilla movement responsible for some bombings which was labeled the Angry Brigade by Scotland Yard. Burns did interview some far-left radicals and a number of his friends, but he did not contact the members of the so-called Angry Brigade. While he had experimented with a subjective narrator in *Europe after the Rain*, this is the first of his novels to explore the possibilities of multiple narrators. The six are depicted as profoundly different people, with varying ethnic, educational, political, and emotional backgrounds. Their political motives are likewise often personal and highly individual, some acting for craven and others quite pure and noble motives. Reviewers and critics either criticized the novel or praised it for revealing the limitations of these political neophytes; however, Burns has admitted to a far different objective: "I had a natural sympathy with the group's aims, and even, though to a lesser extent, with their methods. They were, inevitably, portrayed in the press as psychopaths and hoodlums. I wanted to correct this version of red-baiting, by showing the true process of radicalization, or, to put it more punchily, what drove them to it."[14]

The collage effect is maintained by the frequent shifts between voices; however, the method of those reflections is the most syntactically traditional since *Buster*. Burns does a masterful job of creating a sense of immediacy between the reader and the individual speakers who offer their reflections in a conversational manner. In an interview conducted a short time after the publication of *Babel* Burns commented on his extreme technique at that time: "With cut-up techniques, it is possible to achieve an immediacy which was not possible under the tyranny of syntax. . . . This is a way of achieving simultaneity—to have one sentence implying many things, pointing in all sorts of directions."[15] With *The Angry Brigade* and the multiple narrators, however, he managed to maintain the sense of immediacy and simultaneity while moving away from the kinds of grammatical experiments he now found unworkable.

Up to this point Burns had been living in London and existing on the proceeds from books and a succession of Arts Council grants and fellowships at the University of East Anglia, Norwich, and the Woodberry Down School in London. In 1975 he left England to become a senior tutor in creative writing at the Western Australia Institute of Technology in South Bentley, Australia. There he taught fiction writing and oversaw a production of *Palach*, and he intended to remain, until he was lured back to London the next year with an Arts Council Fellowship at the City Literary Institute. In 1977 he accepted a professorship at the University of Minnesota, where he met and married his second wife, and they had a daughter, his third child. He remained there until 1990, when he returned to England and became head of the Department of Creative Writing at the University of Lancaster. Asked why he left the States after remaining so long, he responded:

my connection with the States was never solid and uninterrupted. I also had very strong reservations about the US political setup. Great country to have a good job in, hell if not. On the buses I saw Dickensian poverty, faces and bodies mutilated by bad diet and living conditions. . . . I was appalled by the desecration of that beautiful land. (Air-conditioned nightmare.) And so on. Your questions also make me ponder what are the things that make an environment, that distinguish one country from another . . . voices come first, I think, those unfamiliar accents got on my nerves . . . more the timbre than the accent maybe. Finally just to say that it was those years of kinda exile that made me discover how English I felt, my delight at being here, the greens, the way folks are with each other—not to idealise, the same lousy Tory lot in power, think the English upper classes are even more obnoxious than your rotten gang, but there it is, stop there.[16]

With *The Day Daddy Died* (1981) Burns returned to the domestic theme, this time in the figure of Norah, an indomitable working-class woman whose life is one long fight against forces that would exploit or just as soon annihilate her. She is orphaned early in her life and in adulthood seeks a surrogate father in a succession of men. In spite of her poverty she manages to raise five children in the first of Burns's fictional families to achieve some sense of cohesiveness and mutual affection. The story evolves in a fairly linear fashion, moving from Norah's childhood to adulthood; however, Burns returns to his surrealist practices in a pair of ways. Whenever Norah is overwhelmed by especially traumatic events in her life, the narrative shifts to the type of surrealist imagery found in *Celebrations*. "His daughter in his room was slender, miniature, soft, long skin, marked neck, her little cat-show smile. Her thick lashes were in the room and could not get out. Her poor father was ready for the archives now. He finished hot when she looked at him, he glanced as the kitten showed her claw."[17] Just as quickly as the narrative moves into these surrealistic passages, it shifts back to a realist mode of sharp details and carefully delineated characters.

The collage method reappears in a series of highly evocative photo montages by Ian Breakwell. The first of these, which introduces chapter 1, is the picture of a man in a suit whose face has been replaced by a large fist. A group of three others are fragments of a single photo of a little girl with a man standing behind her, his large, muscular hands resting on her shoulders. First the reader sees the left shoulder and hand, next the right shoulder and other hand, and finally the full shot with the child's face obscured by a third hand superimposed over her features. The effect is a perfect complement to the feelings of enclosure and suffocation Norah experiences over her absent father. The fifteen other collages further provide an emotional context for the action or startling counterpoints to events.

Although the novel is related in the terse, truncated style of earlier fictions, the experiment with multiple narrators surfaces again in a series of brief letters of those closest to Norah, which awkwardly grope their way toward communication, though their evasions and half-truths speak more tellingly than their declarations. This use of the epistolary allows the narrator to fill in gaps created by the highly selective presentation of details and thus to join often disparate elements into a cohesive pattern of exposition.

The same year, Burns also published *The Imagination on Trial* (1982), co-authored with University of Minnesota colleague Charles Sugnet. The work is a collection of interviews with eight British (J. G. Ballard, Eva Figes, Wilson Harris, B. S. Johnson, Tom Mallin, Michael Moorcock, Alan Sillitoe, and Burns himself) and four American novelists (John Gardner, John Hawkes, Grace Paley, and Ishmael Reed). The discussions, conducted between 1973 and 1979, center on the fictional methods and concerns of the writers, with special attention given to defining the ways in which ideas are implanted and then germinate in the artist's mind. The collection offers the rare opportunity to read interviews with writers conducted by a writer himself, and Burns reveals himself to be keenly aware of the variety of impulses, influences, and techniques that lead to a finished work. He has the ability often to ask exactly the right question of each person. He is by turns encouraging with cooperative subjects and persistent with reluctant ones, with the results being insightful and often quite forthright. Each interview is preceded by a photograph and a brief bio-bibliographical sketch, and despite occasional evasions and bits of humbug, nearly all the figures offer many cogent remarks about their own work and the state of contemporary fiction in general. Discussions range over a host of subjects—working methods, inspirations for individual books, attitudes about audience and reviewers, and individual methods of composition—however, a repeated inquiry involves the role of dreams and dreaming in fictional creation. In Sugnet's interview with Burns, he admits that the unconscious and dreams play major roles in his work, but the exact importance these have in his fiction he explains in a manual he distributes to students in his creative writing classes.

The major part of the writer's raw material comes not from the conscious but from the unconscious mind. That's the treasure-trove. There we find our deepest feelings, and images of particular originality and power. Writers in touch with their unconscious minds are onto a good thing. But how to do that? There are many ways, but Freud's "royal road to the unconscious" is through dreams. . . . In considering dreams, we are getting close to that movement in the arts called "surrealism." I have always thought that the key bit of that word is "realism." The content of dreams illustrates this nicely. They are generally made up of everyday objects: tables, chairs, boats, trees, rivers, recognizable people . . . solid, real, made of flesh or wood. Yet there is a deep contradiction between their apparent solidity, and the sense of precariousness, of uncertainty, that pervades them. . . . And that is a marvelous effect for the fiction writer to aim at. We must deal with the real life around us. But we should also share our awareness that the ordinary always carries with it the potential for the extraordinary. . . . There does appear to be a common language in dreams. If we can tap into that language, evoke it, speak it, we should be able to touch our readers at a deep, unconscious level—the more intriguing and powerful because it is only half understood by them and by us.[18]

The possibilities for the unconscious, dreams, and surrealism are clearly manifested in his next novel, *Revolutions of the Night*, another novel that takes its title from an Ernst painting. In fact the last chapter, which is highly surreal and confusing, is actually a tribute to Ernst.

The ruined town was like a continent after the flood. Masses of masonry and metal towered over rivers of bones and boulders, the trunks of trees, broken pipes and pylons, drains, poles, pillars, ladders, scaffolding, monumental gravestones, rusted machinery, worn-out engines, the rotting skins of animals and shreds of cloth, the skull of a buffalo, the skull of a horse, a siege of herons, a clamour of rooks, statues of princes mounted or on foot, an abandoned gantry, skeletal remains of old canoes, antlers, bedsteads, rafters, flowering heaps of rotten fruit, collections of corsets, an avalanche of carcasses, burning docks, a fairground, a forest, a quarry, an open-cast mine, an ocean bed, a lone pinnacle of bone. . . . A man in skins, with the head of an emu, turned towards an armless girl, wisps of hair beneath her hat.[19]

A close look at Ernst's *Europe after the Rain* reveals that this is a rather specific, detailed description of that painting, and throughout the novel Burns provides verbal renderings of other Ernst paintings. Thus his most recent novel comes full circle with one of his earliest and asserts a renewed commitment to the vision that has informed his entire career.

Once again the theme of family is prominent as another mother dies and is replaced by her husband's paramour. The children, Hazel and Harry, are emotionally cast adrift, first into an incestuous relationship, then Hazel off to an older capitalist named Bob, whom she throws from a hot air balloon, and Harry to a cocktail waitress named Louise. Eventually the siblings light out for the territory and enjoy a brief pastoral idyll in a cabin on the edges of civilization. However, pastoral calm is ultimately disrupted when invaders murder Hazel and threaten Harry's life.

In his closing description of Ernst's *Europe after the Rain* Burns notes that "caught between two pillars was a youth, blindfolded and gagged" (*Revolutions* 163). This image of a young person caught between implacable forces is a perfect leitmotif for all of Burns's fictions. In each of his works the young are sacrificed for the idiocy and obsessions of their elders, yet they yearn, even battle for, a freedom that is rarely achieved. The connection among dreams, surrealism, and the yearning for freedom Burns explains in this way: "we are free in our dreams. Not only free, but we are expressing those deep impulses that, if unleashed, are upsetting to the social order. And anything that expresses the essence of our free selves is itself subversive and dangerous to the hierarchy and the settled order. That's what my books are about. I hope to share that, to push it."[20]

Currently Burns is at work on four separate nonfictional projects. "Art by Accident" is nearly completed and ready for publication. This is a study of aleatoric art, where the creator, by design or chance, has allowed the forces of hazard to determine the end of the artistic process. The book is amazing for its wide range of references and for its multidisciplinary approach; novelists, poets, painters, composers, etc., are all represented and together the work shows a spirit of mutual dependence and influence among these media.

A second work, a fragment of which appears in this issue, is a biography of close friend and colleague, novelist B. S. Johnson, who committed suicide in 1973. In "Human Like the Rest of Us" Burns tries to capture the diversity of Johnson's personality, moods, and effects on others through a host of sources, assembled in a fashion that reminds one of Burns's fictional dependance on fragments, a method that is always deeply personal for him. "The fragmentation in my work seems absolutely grounded in my own experience of the world. One sees fragmentation duplicated and reduplicated: for example, in the fragmentation of the modern family, . . . the fragmentation of the personality, schizophrenia being the fashionable disease; the blessed fragmentation of empires; and, beneath, around, and above it all the fragmentation of the atom which is the basis of our physical world" (Gillen 11).

A second biography, provisionally entitled "Gangster," examines the experiences of a convict named Frank Cook who has spent most of his adult life in prison. At age thirty-eight Cook began sculpting in prison and showed such promise that two of his works have been exhibited at the Metropolitan Gallery in New York. Burns's approach is not an attempt at an apologia for Cook's offenses; both convict and biographer are quick to reveal the scope of his vicious past, but Cook is nevertheless humanized by the close inspection of his life and motives.

The fourth work, "Imaginary Dictionary," a portion of which is also presented in this issue, Burns sent me with the explanation that it "is my *real* voice, the one I have fun with . . . it creates a truer picture of the kind of writer I am."[21] As the extract printed here reveals, Burns devised a dictionary of whimsy, wherein words come alive, take on characteristics of their own, unhinged from the uses and expectations of readers. Definitions appear as verse, suggesting perhaps that poetry is the natural medium of words, and many of these poems are concrete presentations, such as the evocative "Ocean." This method underscores his stated objective that "it's poetry I'm after, and the vision that is a poet's rather than the extremely interesting and intelligent ideas of intelligent men, as Orwell and Huxley were. But neither of them was a poet. And neither of them had the real vision" (Firchow 53). Burns is also at work on a novel tentatively entitled "Brothers," which involves the brothers Wright, Grimm, Karamazov,

Kennedy, and Marx and which is born in part from his being one of three brothers.

All the emphasis on fragmentation, the cut-up method, surreal disruptions, and wild juxtapositions may suggest rather inhospitable reading for many audiences. After all, Burns has admitted that he wants "to shock readers into a new awareness" (Gillen 12) and that he wants "to work more like a painter than a writer; place images side by side and let them say something uncertain and fluctuating. This work will not be literary and will not lead to discussion or redefinition, but simply exist—like a Magritte painting" (Kitchen 21). Remarks such as these may give the impression of a chaotic, undisciplined art, but nothing could be further from the truth. Burns has long resisted traditional notions of the novel and certainly rejects any idea of the genre as being a rigid genre with fixed conventions. "The great attraction of the novel," he has said, "lies in its search for form. The secret may lie in the word *novel* itself. If it's new, then it's novel" (Firchow 61). In other words, he sees the genre as an infinitely adaptable medium, one that can change and accommodate the changing nature of a writer and the audience's perception. Burns has even nodded enthusiastically at John Hawkes's now famous dictum that plot, characterization, and the usual tools of the novelist's trade are passé; however, his long-standing insistence that fiction catch up with painting suggests a common area of concern. Burns has admitted that he strives for "a picture in every line—I want to get a physical picture" (Firchow 59). Thus in his novels sentences often achieve a separate, independent existence one might expect of an individual scene or whole chapters, and nowhere is this more evident than in the highly concentrated method of *Babel*.

Burns is also a writer of strong ideological convictions who has remarked that he favors a "libertarian or anarchist state with a small 'a.' . . . [I]f you ask me what kind of society would I write for, then I could only envisage the kind of stateless society that the anarchists envisage, but, quite frankly, I don't see that as a practical possibility in my lifetime" (Firchow 56). While these convictions are deeply held and extend back into his adolescence, Burns has never been didactic or hortatory. In fact, his political beliefs and aesthetic predilections inform a deeply humanist perspective found in each of his works. "It sounds pathetic—this avant-garde novelist wanting to change the world—but I do, I simply want to leave it a little bit better."[22] Burns insists that readers look unflinchingly at the ways that individuals are destroyed to satisfy greed, competition, and authoritarian control. When he asks us to view the humanity of the Angry Brigade, the senseless violence of *Europe after the Rain*, the megalomania of the Kennedys, or the hysteria of a society lost in a welter of the conflicting voices in *Babel*, Burns is not simply immersing the reader in gratuitous horrors but raising a voice of caution and pleading for an implicit alternative. As he explained over twenty-five years ago, "art has a certain function in befriending man, showing him that it is possible to venture into the empty spaces, as Beckett ventures, to chart one's journey to the most terrifying, imaginative limits, and after going to these ultimate places, to retain, still, one's essential humanity" (Hall 10).

NOTES

[1]Alan Burns and Charles Sugnet, eds., *The Imagination on Trial* (London: Allison and Busby, 1981), 2; hereafter cited parenthetically.

[2]Peter Firchow, "Alan Burns," in *The Writer's Place: Interviews on the Literary Situation in Contemporary Britain*, ed. Peter Firchow (Minneapolis: Univ. of Minnesota Press, 1974), 50; hereafter cited parenthetically.

[3]Alan Burns to David Madden, 5 June 1994.

[4]Alan Burns to David Madden, 5 June 1994.

[5]Alan Burns, *Europe after the Rain* (London: Calder and Boyers, 1965), 37.

[6]Paddy Kitchen, "Surrealism and Sculpture in Words," *Times Educational Supplement*, 8 Sept. 1970, 21; hereafter cited parenthetically.

[7]Alan Burns to David Madden, 6 June 1994.

[8]Alan Burns, *Celebrations* (London: Calder and Boyers, 1967), 17, 26.

9 Alan Burns, "Essay," in *Beyond the Words*, ed. Giles Gordon (London: Hutchinson, 1975), 66; hereafter cited parenthetically.

[10]Alan Burns to David Madden, 12 July 1994.

[11]Alan Burns, "Art by Accident," ts., unnumbered.

[12]Alan Burns, *Babel* (London: Calder and Boyers, 1969), 7.

[13]Alan Burns, *Dreamerika!* (London: Calder and Boyers, 1972), 11, 13.

[14]Alan Burns to David Madden, 18 July 1994.

[15]John Hall, "Novels from the Unconscious," *Guardian*, 30 April 1970, 10; hereafter cited parenthetically.

[16]Alan Burns to David Madden, 6 June 1994.

[17]Alan Burns, *The Day Daddy Died* (London: Allison and Busby, 1981), 10.

[18]Alan Burns, untitled manual on fiction writing (undated), 6, 8, 9.

[19]Alan Burns, *Revolutions of the Night* (London: Allison and Busby, 1986), 162; hereafter cited parenthetically.

[20]Shawn Gillen, "Slash and Burns," *Minnesota Daily*, 11 November 1988, 12; hereafter cited parenthetically.

[21]Alan Burns to David Madden, 21 June 1994.

[22]"Alan Burns," *Minnesota*, July-August 1989, 22.

An Interview with Alan Burns

David W. Madden

This interview was conducted entirely through the mail from May to September 1994. As I finished rereading each of his eight novels, I would send a group of questions to Burns and he would respond. Often our letters crossed in the mail, and wherever possible I have eliminated redundancies with one significant exception—the issue of his working methods. In rereading the essay he wrote about the evolution of his career in Giles Gordon's *Beyond the Words*, I found Burns delineating a steady pattern of development and change as he moved from one novel to another. However in responding to these questions here, Burns repeatedly invokes Picasso's dictum that "I do not seek, I find." I have left these redundancies in the interview because they emphatically reveal a reigning principle of his aesthetic. I want to interject that Alan Burns is a delightful correspondent—prompt, anecdotal, and delightfully witty, and this interview, despite its trans-Atlantic nature, was a genuine pleasure. To Alan I send my thanks for all his time and patience.

DAVID MADDEN: Was James Joyce much of an influence on or inspiration for you?

ALAN BURNS: Joyce changed everything, made everything possible. Master of all styles, all genres, all languages, all cultures . . . beyond that mere puffery, I'm wary of commenting on Joyce, overwhelmed not only by him as poet and novelist but by his mighty intellect. However, his influence on me was not intellectual but instinctive, which is to say, his achievement seemed to give me permission to follow my instinct wherever it lead. Word-coinage is an obvious example, but it goes beyond that to, say, the structure of *Babel*, and much more.

DM: I ask because of the opening scene in *Buster* in which adults are looking down on the reclining child and talking to and above him.

AB: No, the opening scene in *Buster* was not specifically influenced by Joyce—only in the general terms indicated above. The child, incidentally, is not intended to be "reclining," as you suggest, that's not in the text. I wanted the opening scene to contain the novel's essence and yet be credible in a naturalistic sense. "They stood over him" seemed to me then to do the job nicely. Now I think maybe it's too neat and makes the point too clearly. I still like the way I managed to introduce three generations at the start, the tensions between them, and the child's survival technique: "Who do you like best, your mother or your father?" "Both the same." Also the father's material and conventional ambitions for his son, sexuality, guilt, beauty, furniture, even the hint of war outside ("A soldier posted a letter").

DM: For many writers of your generation, World War II was obviously a major event, and the spectre of war figures prominently in your early novels. Can you talk about what it has meant to you and your imagination?

AB: I'm typing this letter on 5 June 1994 while D-Day is being recalled. It seems "a quarter million Germans" were killed in Normandy. How many more of them throughout the war, and Brits, Americans, impossible to list how many more, and 20,000,000 Russians . . . I know the grief attached the death of one young man, my brother Jerry. Can human consciousness begin to grapple with what all this means? Life is tough enough. We all die. But deliberately to smash another human being's skull in . . . why am I going about this, no point. Have dreamed since I was nine, off and on, of German paratroopers swinging through the night sky and landing in the garden. The lunacy of war is certainly at the heart of my politics and my writing.

DM: At the time you wrote *Buster* how would you describe your fictional approach? It strikes me that *Buster* is fundamentally a realist fiction, with strains of naturalism and surrealism filtering in.

AB: I had no "fictional approach"! I was grappling with the translation of experience into words. "Experience" includes dreams and lies and imaginings and fantasies as well as "what happened" (if it did). I also delighted in the words-in-themselves for their own sake. I think it's for critics and others to do the categorizing, but I think you've got it about right when you characterize *Buster* in the way you do.

DM: I would like to move to your second novel, *Europe after the Rain*, which works on the reader in strange and unexpected ways. For instance, the reader begins fearing for the girl and sympathizing with her concern over her lost father, only to discover their moral ambiguity. Were you seeking such an ambiguity?

AB: I don't *seek* a quality such as "moral ambiguity" in a character (I doubt that any novelist does). I follow a character and try to find out who she is. That of course is why it is necessary to *test* a character, compel her to make choices, so that she reveals who she is. (When Anna Karenina decides to leave her husband for her lover, Tolstoy has her go upstairs to her child's bedroom, see the child asleep (maybe for Anna the last time) and *still* go through with her flight. Thus Anna, and the reader, are put through hell: we don't merely know about, we suffer through the experience of her "moral ambiguity.") Needless to say I'm not making comparisons between the two novels, still less the two authors . . . Another source of "moral" and numerous other ambiguities in my characters generally is my awareness of *contradictions* within characters and between them. As soon as I become aware of a certain characteristic, I instinctively look for an opportunity to show its opposite. For the brave to show fear, the innocent guile, the timorous courage, and so on. An example of this is early in *Celebrations* where Williams is given one blue eye and one brown.

DM: Could you discuss your view of the connection between the novel and Max Ernst's painting of the same name?

AB: Some months after I'd started writing *Europe* (but before I'd found a title), I chanced upon a reproduction of the painting in a book on Ernst: I instantly recognized the very landscape I was—in my way—"painting." I knew I had a title—and a book jacket too! Beyond that, however, I can't say that I studied the painting particularly closely, though I think I always had it somewhere at the back of my mind. It was not until I was writing the last chapter of *Revolutions of the Night* that I did look intensely at the Ernst painting and made as precise and passionate a word picture of it as I could. Some years after *Europe* was published, I saw the original at an Ernst retrospective at the Tate in London, and was disappointed to see how small and seeming-not-so-powerful it was. In reproduction it makes the impact of a colossal work of art, not so in the original.

DM: A feature I've noticed in this and others of your novels is a slippery quality, even a vagueness about large issues of plot or character motivation (for instance, the reasons for the father's fall from grace) while details of appearance or descriptions are minutely and exactingly precise. Can you explain the idea or purpose behind this paradoxical method? Might this be explained in part by what you described in the essay in *Beyond the Words* as the "distanced technique of writing from the unconscious"?

AB: I like that phrase "slippery quality." Elusive, yes, it's yet another aspect of my wish to avoid any suggestion of an absolute, purportedly "accurate" statement as to what happened or where we are or what role a particular character plays in the novel. Look again, and—see, it ain't so—the opposite may as well be true. As soon as the reader is beginning to feel secure in the world I've made for him, it "slips," he slithers; me too. There's also a strong element of doubt; that's part of it too.[1] Some absurdist stuff as well, yet I temper that tendency with a genuine, even passionate, humanism. With nuclear bombs around, we must be careful not to get too far gone into the irrational—and when I yap about "instinct," I'm also aware, of the fascists' appeal to "gut feelings" and so on . . . so it ain't easy to get it right.

So, for example, and to get back from vague philosophizing to the novels, while I go for the "slippery," I'm concerned by your reference to vague character motivation. I'd want the father's fall from grace to be not arbitrary or author-driven but fully motivated in the traditional sense. In fact, I suggest that his "fall from grace" is largely accounted for by the simple notion that "power corrupts"—see the heavily ironic paragraph that starts, "The father received me in his spacious and magnificent apartment" and later the (probably too bare) statement that the father was "growing senile." Final word on "slippery"—it's close to the "precarious" dream—see my comments on Dali's *A Loaf of Bread about to Explode* in the attached material.[2]

DM: There are no names for any of the characters and thus pronoun references are sometimes vague. Why are identities so deliberately elusive?

AB: I could not find the "right" names . . . something connected with Kafka's "Joseph K." I regret pronoun uncertainties and would want to correct them, but there it is.

DM: Don't you think, though, that this nameless quality is exactly appropriate for this blasted place; it enhances the shadowy quality and the ambiguity that pervades so much of the book? Was this namelessness deliberate on your part?

AB: I think you put it perfectly, and I now adopt your formulation as my answer to your question (I particularly like "this blasted place"—with *Lear* nudging in there). "Namelessness" also reminds me of Wilson Harris—see p. 58 of *The Imagination*. My only quarrel is with your word *deliberate*, as you know. I feel the word is inappropriate, because it implies a degree of control I deliberately (!) eschew.

DM: Explain the narrator's presence in this world of military conflict. He has access to both commanders of the warring sides, yet he is seemingly outside the fray (though it appears he destroys the reconstructed bridge at the end of chapter 11). He talks of his job, but what is it? Is he a journalist, or is his "job" or purpose more subtle and perhaps even metaphysical?

AB: The narrator's uncertain role and status is vital in maintaining the novel's precariousness and ambiguity. Give him a job, and the novel becomes more reportage—everything would have been watertight, rational, the reader would demand it. But I have made a contract with the reader that allows me the freedom to slip in and out of the rational. That has to be established from the start and iterated and reiterated (implicitly, by conduct) consistently throughout. A key passage reads, "I changed my life. I went among the prisoners taken to the camp for labour purposes. I wanted to make certain, I wanted to get inside, I knew the language, I wanted to learn more, suddenly . . . My work was in that place. . . ." Remember, his work at that point is assassination.

DM: John Hall in the *Guardian* mentions Burroughs's cut-up technique as being yours also. Was *Europe* written as a series of fragments "synthesi[zed and] shuffle[ed] . . . so that they form new associations and build up fresh nuclei of meaning"?

AB: Yes, that quote applies to the writing of *Europe* and my other novels. I had not read Burroughs then, nor heard of his "cut-up" technique. I did not actually use scissors, but I folded pages, read across columns, and so on, discovering for myself many of the techniques Burroughs and Gysin describe in *The Third Mind* and elsewhere.

DM: Given Hall's quote and what I see as numerous echoes of Beckett in your work, have you or do you have affinities with existentialist thinking?

AB: I have only dipped into *Being and Nothingness*, but *Nausea* much impressed and maybe influenced me, along with Camus. As for Beckett, I delighted in *Murphy, Watt*, and a couple others, and *Godot, Endgame,* and more. However, *The Unnameable* I call *The Unreadable*. Like Joyce, Beckett extended the range of the possible. He is somewhere there in my mind when I'm working, but I don't quite know where.

DM: I'm always interested in tracing the development of a writer's career, and I think your essay in *Beyond the Words* is a superb articulation of your career up to *The Angry Brigade*. However, it all seems so clear, deliberate, and logical, and surely it didn't evolve that conveniently. Would you comment on how you see the development of your career?

AB: I've reread my bit in *Beyond the Words* and can see what you mean. It does indeed make the move from one book to another far more ordered and rational than it actually was. Having, in my dialogue with you, rejected the notion of deliberateness in my choice of this or that theme and so on, I in my "Essay" purported to discern just that element in my progression from book to book. So you've spotted a contradiction there, or, to put it more simply, I think I got it wrong in "Essay." But now I stop and ponder what was really going on, I'm stumped. I can and have, in my various answers to your questions, to some extent accounted for my attraction to the particular form and content of each book, but the overall structure of what I now concede can perfectly properly be called a "career"—that, mate, I leave to you . . . And the best of British luck!

DM: In the *FallOut* interview, which I'm sure many readers will have a difficult time finding, you mention your discovering "the value of the image" while writing *Buster*. Would you elaborate on the meanings and implications of this phrase for your prose.

AB: "Images think for me" (Paul Eluard, I think). I'll "find" an image, ponder on it, explore it, most importantly and usefully, *follow* it, and that means traverse terrain, "push on," and create the narrative structure of the novel. I'll give you one example to clarify my meaning. Take the bridge at the start of *Europe*. The novel's initial image. Explore and follow it. A bridge across a . . . river. Near-archetypal European feature—a river as a frontier, and there's tension between the river flowing one way, and the road across the bridge cutting across it and heading . . . where? Ah, there's a road. On the road a vehicle, what kind, not an isolating motor car but a socializing bus, and anyway, immediate postwar ravaged Europe—yes, a bus. Who is travelling on that bus? Whence came they? Whither go they? Find the answer to those key questions, not merely spatially or geographically, but in social and human terms. And of course, if these folks are travelling for a purpose (and only madmen would do otherwise), then we will wish to follow their pursuit of that purpose, and, needless to say, strew a few obstacles in their way. . . . Thus I, who would find "plotting" difficult or impossible, make, allow, the image to do the job for me.

DM: The style and plotting of *Celebrations* is quite different from *Europe after the Rain*. Were you consciously searching for or attempting a new style here?

AB: You will understand well enough by now that I do not search for or attempt new style for its own sake. The fundamental rule here must be: "content governs style (or form)." The only "progression" I'd see, from one novel to the other, is a certain growing confidence resulting from an admittedly mixed press but one that contained some thoroughly favourable reviews. They made me think I could "be myself" and "go for it." Thus *Celebrations* might loosely be called "more extreme" than *Europe*, getting further away from the traditional novel. Thus the leaps between the images are greater, the juxtapositions bolder, the risks crazier, and so on.

DM: While the plot is certainly more linear than *Europe*, it is not without its surreal aspects. These I see most obviously in the figurative tropes, the use of unexpected metaphors and similes—"the mouth hidden behind obscure houses," "the end of the life was the sound of yellow," and "he talked like a sickness," to cite just a few examples. Could you explain your use of these elements here?

AB: I see what you mean about the plot of the later novel being "more linear" than the earlier. I had not thought that was so, but you're right. The reason for this lies, paradoxically, in the very risks I was taking (see above) in all other areas. Thus I thought, if so much else is, or seems, haywire (not so though), then the basic story line must be clear and simple, to hold the thing together. Those phrases you quote, I love. The story line is just a peg to hang them on. The images and their juxtaposition result from that "I do not seek I find" cut-up method. I literally "found" (having carefully set up the conditions in which I could peer at and then find) those separate images: "mouth," "houses" "obscure" . . . and found a way to hurl them together. And so on, all the way through the book.

DM: At the end of chapter 7, after Williams learns that Jacqueline and Michael will wed, time collapses and Williams and Jacqueline have sex in his office. Is this an event taking place in chronological or dream time?

AB: Another example of those "reversals" you spotted early on. Once I'd pushed Jacqueline seemingly decisively in one direction (Michael), I felt the immediate need to drive her in the other (Williams). And the sooner after the wedding, the harsher the insult to Michael, and the more violent his response. Everything to hot up the tension. So you will see that this is intended to be "for real." As much as I go for the "quality of dream," I entirely eschew "real" dreams in novels. I feel that reader interest inevitably sags—the blood's not real, it's "only a dream." Also, it somehow spoils the overall dream effect, to have a "real dream" intrude, and invite comparison with the rest.

DM: I found your comments in the interview with Peter Firchow about sociology displacing fiction most interesting. Paul West commented to me that when preparing his novel *The Very Rich Hours of Count von Stauffenberg*, he read many histories on the Third Reich and found them wildly contradictory on the most elemental level. His response was that he refused to let historians appropriate the role of the novelist as a creator. Is something of the same impulse at work in your novels?

AB: What I think about historian *versus* novelist came up most acutely in connection with *The Angry Brigade*. The Brigade existed as a group which "did things" in London and elsewhere in the very early seventies. (I'll have more to say on this when I answer your questions on the book.) I cooked up a so-called documentary novel in which I purported to have interviewed six of them and the book consists of what are presented as interviews with them. The novel thus "tells their story." As the whole work is fiction, the story I tell differs from what actually happened. One vital detail: the novel has the Brigade leave a bomb which "blew a waitress into pieces"; whereas, the real Brigade did not, I believe, kill anyone. When the book came out, Stuart Christie, a well-known Anarchist who'd been jailed in Spain for his activities, wrote in strong protest to *Time Out* that I had defamed the members of the "real" Angry Brigade. I replied that the imaginative truths revealed by a novelist can be "truer" than the "facts" reported by a journalist. The darned thing is that I wrote the novel in protest against, and with the intention of off-setting, the demonizing of the members of the Angry Brigade in the press and other media. However, the book was pretty widely reviewed and generally seen as an attack on the "real" Brigade, satirizing them, depicting their petty squabbles, their male chauvinism, and so on. Those negatives were part of my intended subtle characterization of people I did not see as simple heroes and heroines, but with whom I had many sympathies. Finally I think I regret the novel's title. I now think I should have removed it more clearly from seeming-reportage.

DM: Could you explain the method in *Babel?*

AB: I start not with a method but a mood. The novel was published in 1969, written in 1967 and 1968. High days and holidays, it was a time to be alive! Events of Paris, and "things happening" in London too. The great antiwar (I always think it's wrong to say anti-Vietnam) demo outside the US embassy (there with my wife, met B. S. Johnson and others), and a so-called Assembly of Artists, met in a warehouse by the Thames, and so on. Writers Reading founded then also. Needless to say, I'm not putting such minor happenings on a par with Paris, but I had a feeling I was part of a general upsurge. I thought we were going to win! Add to that, I had two and a half books out. In *Celebrations* I had taken extraordinary risks with language and seemed to have got away with it, got through at least to some—Robert Nye's fantastic review, and B. S. Johnson's also, Angus Wilson's tribute[3] and the Arts Council support that followed from that (Wilson was Chair of the Literature Committee that allotted grants and prizes). You see, all this *has* to do with method. The mood in which the book was composed was almost exultant—in fact the tension between that and the grim events portrayed, notably the Vietnam war, is one of the strands that holds together a book that has an appropriately high explosive tendency to fly apart. Just as the reception of *Europe* gave me courage to go further in *Celebrations*, so the response to the second book made possible the third.

I've already written of "images think for me" and the "cut-up" and these continued to dominate my method—more so maybe. Just as the cut-up fragmented the sentence (you'll maybe have read elsewhere my description:

"the subject of one sentence drives in one direction, the object of another arrives from another, and the verb is left uncertainly alternating between the two"), I felt the same could be done with the novel's whole narrative structure. I also leaned on what became for me a familiar litany I cooked up that generalized out from the concept of fragmentation: the Empires were fragmenting, the concept of God also, the human personality (schizophrenia, Laing, and Cooper, et al.), the family (growing divorce), and matter itself (smashed atom). And frag-(let's fragment fragment)-mentation, needless to say, is at once a destructive process and one that liberates energy (follow it through: atom, empire, family, mind).

Finally, I attach a copy of a page from a marvelous book, *Kurt Schwitters in England*, by Stefan Themerson—you'll see by my asterisk, reference to the Merzists's ideas about introducing "symmetries and rhythms instead of principles"—that too says something about the way *Babel* evolved.[4]

DM: Method, I think, there definitely is. For instance, in the first twenty pages there is discussion of the bishop and other religious leaders, then of an unwed mother and her baby, and later there is a segment devoted to "the baby-sitting bishop [who] has a fur hat." The method seems deliberately fragmentary, only to have certain fragments united unexpectedly and abruptly. Comment?

AB: The above relates. Having abandoned solid, chronological narrative structure (i.e., storytelling), I knew I needed something else to give the book that essential unity properly required of any work of art. I knew I did not want a mere collection of aphorisms, which would have seemed elegant, dilettante, self-indulgent, and repellent. I insisted on the book being "of and about the world" and not simply clever. A network of recurrent images was the way, with, of course, not a mechanical, exact repetition, but a near-miss, a variation close enough to give the reader that satisfying sense of recognition, ah, yes, I have met something like that before, so that a discernible world slowly emerges, mapped out, always with surprises, but also with a growing sense of familiarity. And that progression to some extent provides a substitute for the traditional novel's narrative tension deriving from whodunnit or whatever. Again, as ever, this was not actively planned, but "found"—though of course that "finding" is not purely passive, there's a good deal of crafty organization and arrangement goes into it.

DM: The method also appears aphoristic; one of my favorite passages is, "Most people will claim to be people, usually." The circularity is hilarious, only to be outdone by the adverbial coda. How much were wit and humor concerns of yours here?

AB: Glad you like that quote. Me too. The "circularity" reminds me of Carver's *Will You Please Be Quiet Please*, which I also love. My favorite is "another month gone, you know" (11). As it happens, my desk is before a window that looks out onto "the forests' tall and bristly haircuts" (80). As to wit and humour generally being "concerns" of mine, Abso-bloody-lutely. In *Babel* and in each and every novel—*irony in every line*. In your excellent piece in the *Dictionary of Literary Biography* that was the only point you failed to make, though there were a few passing references. The tension between what is stated and what is implied goes or is intended to go spinning through from start to end. I could talk of text and subtext here, but not sure of my ground—you'll know better.

DM: In structure the novel reminds me a great deal of Beckett, especially *Watt* with the fragmentary, forking plot. Any comment?

AB: I love *Watt* (and have a slightly-battered-but-beautiful (aren't we all) Olympia edition, 1958—though I'm no kind of book collector). Though, like many books I love I've never read it right through, have dipped in many times, especially, "Here he stood. Here he sat. Here he knelt. . . ." and on and on for the next four pages. While I was not consciously influenced by *Watt* in any way, Beckett was certainly another of those writers who extended the range of the possible.

DM: I'm particularly interested in your intentions with the appendix of characters. Is this a salute to Beckett and his appendix or a parody of the nineteenth-century convention of providing a list of characters, usually as prefatory material, or was something else entirely on your mind (perhaps a guide to the lost or wayward reader)?

AB: As ever, no preplanning, stumbled into it—my fundamental creative method—trial and error—tried it out, scribbled down "A policeman called Lilian"—liked it—added more, yeah, fantastic *list*, funny, silly, readable, provocative, above all interesting—why not, try it. I remember puzzling for ages over whether the list should be at the start or the end of the book . . . This reminds me that B. S. Johnson and I say something about *lists* in *The Imagination on Trial*.

DM: You've commented that *Babel* "had gone to unrepeatable extremes in the fragmentation of narrative." Did you have that feeling of extremes as you wrote it or did that feeling come later?

AB: I think I pretty well knew what I was doing, except that I thought my few fans would go with the book. Not so. Even Robert Nye said I'd reached a dead end and so on. (He sent me a copy of one of his novels inscribed, "for Alan Burns—especially in gratitude for *Celebrations*"—which neatly makes the point.) And I did "retreat" from extreme fragmentation thereafter. *Dreamerika!* deliberately used the known Kennedy story to hold the thing together. And so on.

DM: In rereading *Babel*, I noticed the considerable number of segments devoted to the victimization of women and the young, and the novel now seems like a clear precursor to *The Day Daddy Died*. Was this theme of the exploitation and humiliation of women a conscious element in the novel's conception?

AB: I don't see *Babel* as about the exploitation and humiliation of women, except and insofar as that's one form of injustice and inequality among countless others. The humiliation of women in my work, as in others, contains an element of male chauvinist whatnot. The women I met in

Minnesota taught me to recognize that, and I've since then tried to reshape my writing to eliminate that strand, while still managing to say what I wish to say. (The powerful, sometimes heroic character of Hazel in *Revolutions of the Night* is an example of those women's influence on my work.) While we're on this, there's passages in *Babel* I would now write differently. An example is the term *queers* to denote homosexuals on the opening page, but there's no point in rewriting such stuff. (As, I believe, Auden did.) (My raising the point may sound like silly political correctness, but that's a term I loathe—it's a cleverer version of "knee-jerk liberal," an idiotic putdown designed to scare folks from stating Left views with conviction.)

DM: Could you comment on the novel's narrative point of view? In most places it is the voice of an anonymous, omniscient consciousness, with varying degrees of emotional engagement, and in others there is a first-person narrator, at times male and at other times female. What were you attempting with what appears to be a floating narrative point of view?

AB: Remember, as ever I was not consciously adopting a particular form; you could say I was not fully aware of what I was doing, and I'd reply that that is a necessary ignorance. I don't believe you can be creative writer and critic at the same time—rather, I can't, I know others can. So I'd happily settle for your perceptive and eloquent analysis, especially "floating"—like "slippery" earlier, you have a knack of hitting on out-of-the-way yet apt vocabulary.

DM: How would you explain your method in *Dreamerika!?* (For what it's worth, I see a distinct change from *Babel*. The fragmentation is on the level of the cut-up pieces that act as prompts or, for lack of a better term, "inter-narratives"; whereas, the narrative proper is far more linear than the last novel.) Why the Kennedys and why America?

AB: After *Babel* I felt I could go no further in the direction of fragmentation, without losing my readers altogether. I seized on the idea of referring to, using as a basis, some story line universally known—much like the Roman and Greek gods—part of the common language, common reference points, myth. I thought of Robin Hood, Bible stories, all sorts, and finally hit on the Kennedys as perfect to do the job I needed them to do. Only later did I realize that the Kennedys also repeated my family history, and my basic plot line, in their dominant father, and the double death of two young(ish) sons. The Kennedys' immersion in the media made my use of fragmented newspapers particularly apt. The fact that I could use a terrific "found" story line, and one universally recognized, made it possible for me to take the fragmentation of sentences even further than in *Babel* and I got a kick out of that. Finally, there's my constant fascination with the "look of the page"—almost literally painting with typography—that, *Dreamerika!* permitted, encouraged, delighted in.

DM: How much research did you do on the Kennedys before writing this? Some of the quotes seem entirely in keeping with Joe, Sr., for instance ("The newspapers say I'm worth five hundred million dollars. Why, if I had that kind of . . ."), and suggest more than a passing acquaintance with the Kennedy legend.

AB: Very little. I relied on my "common knowledge"—did not want to go in for esoteric research—wanted to be able to rely on tuning in to my readers' common knowledge. The quote you quote, would have been "found" by me, probably in the course of a cut-up, and I'd have seen instantly how it could be applied to Joe K. Another reason for eschewing research is that I wanted to be free of it—to allow as I've said elsewhere in connection with *The Angry Brigade*—to allow "some very undocumentary truths to emerge." So, finally, I've no idea whether Joe was "worth five hundred million dollars"—it's a good swinging phrase, and that's good enough for me.

DM: This was the first of your novels to have a subtitle ("A Surrealist Fantasy"). Why?

AB: "A Surrealist Fantasy" was not my idea and I don't like it. John Calder insisted, because of the risk of a libel suit, especially by Rose Kennedy. He thought that label would help show that anything in it should not be taken literally, and therefore we, if forced to defend such a suit would not be compelled to "justify," that is, prove that what we wrote was literally true. As a libel lawyer myself, I saw the force of his argument, but I dislike intensely the implication that surrealism is mere fantasy—on the contrary, it is supertrue, truer than mere "true"—but you know all that, at any rate you know that I think that.

DM: Was Kafka a conscious influence or were you deliberately invoking him with your title?

AB: Kafka's certainly an influence all through my work and my life. My title was not intended to invoke his *Amerika*, except and insofar as that spelling was in vogue and carried a political punch in the sixties. Also the fact that Kafka wrote his book without going there fits with my rejection of research, as per my response about research about the Kennedys.

DM: The novel was written well before the barrage of embarrassing personal disclosures about John Kennedy's personal life and the dystopian view of his presidency that replaced the "Camelot" myth. Was it the Panglossian view of his political and personal life that you were exploring?

AB: Nope, not really. I was intrigued, as ever, by a contradiction—my view of the US and their government as the quintessence of late capitalist evils at the same time there was their undeniable attractiveness, their Roosevelt-role in maybe tackling the most vicious and war-making elements, and so on, their being undeniably Big Money, yet opposed to certain deadly forces—the very fact that they were murdered, I presumed by the CIA (had or have since read the Garrison book) made them Goodies of a kind. Finally, those disclosures were not news to me, not in the sense that I had inside factual knowledge, but—as *Dreamerika!* I believe brilliantly (forgive me!) demonstrates—I had imagined all, long before the journalists dug up the dirt—back to my "undocumentary truths."

DM: I realize it is an unfair question to ask any writer what his or her own favorite book is, but barring that, do you have any special regard for *Dreamerika!?* Knowing that scissors and paste are as indispensable to you as a typewriter, this book seems to me to be the quintessential expression of your collage technique.

AB: Sure I love that "look of the page," but, for what it's worth, *Celebrations* IS MY FAVORITE—again it's happened—the Caps button took over—I tippexed it out but forgot to change the button, so heck let's leave it, it's trying to tell me something. And, yes, I like and adopt your characterization of *Dreamerika!* as "the quintessential expression of (my) collage technique"—or anyone's, I guess—show me another that compares . . .

DM: Where did the collage headings come from—found pieces or created ones or a mixture of both?

AB: In the text (as opposed to the headlines) it's almost always "both," i.e., you find something with potential, but you have to nudge and titivate it, to attain that potential. The headlines however, were mostly found as they appear in the book, though I may have altered one or two—would have been difficult, though, because I could not reproduce the typography—all I could do was cut bits out. I managed to "fit" the right headline in at the right place (insofar as I did) by collecting literally thousands of bits from newspapers and magazines (more the latter, as they're more varied and bold than papers). I lay them on big tabletops and then the floor—what fun it was! I remember spotting COME ON IN, EVERYBODY CAN FLOAT . . . and fitting it into the Chappaquiddick story with indescribable delight.

DM: Why is Robert Kennedy depicted as being gay?

AB: I don't know. When Angus Wilson, the book's dedicatee, came to the launching party, he (who of course was gay himself) grinned at me and said he'd always known that Bobby was gay. But I hadn't. I guess, as so often, I just stumbled into it—maybe wanted a bit of a change from Jack's aggressive heterosexuality, more likely, a mere "Why not?"—and also, possibly, another push in the direction of denying, sabotaging the documentary truths.

DM: Who is the novel's narrator; at one point (page 72 in the "Survive" chapter), the narrator uses the pronoun "I" ("I think you know what happened"). Is this an anonymous figure or someone in particular?

AB: I think you have spotted an error. Though it doesn't worry me too much, I think I'd delete it if there were a reprint. Don't want any intrusion of the first-person narrator—don't think the book could take it.

DM: The narrative moves along fairly smoothly until the last two chapters when the focus shifts to Robert Kennedy's son, Joe, living on a commune, and then to Charles Manson. In these sections and the last there is a sense of dissolution; comprehensible narrative gives way to fragments and discontinuity. Is the idea that the American dream is giving way to the American nightmare, a nightmare implicit in the history of the Kennedys all along?

AB: I'm not conscious of that change in the last two chapters, nor, I think, would I go along with "moves along fairly smoothly," though I know what you mean. Hold on a bit, I'm thinking as I type, maybe you are right, and I think I know why. Before the end of the novel (given that I was having a problem, as ever, in making it bulky enough to sell as a novel), I had, as it were, "run out of story line"—the notorious Kennedy story was told and I had to fill at least a few more pages, so yes, I think there is a change of gear, as I maybe rambled around in plot. That American dream/nightmare stuff is there alright, but I wouldn't make too much of it, if only because it's so obvious as to be trite (and was done so well in *Air-Conditioned Nightmare* and many others—now there's some real documentary truths worth telling). There's another clear change as from page 130, when I did want to give the whole story a wider perspective—something there of the Greek gods too.

DM: In the preface to *The Angry Brigade* there is a press report of bombings and a quote from someone at Special Branch blaming the Angry Brigade. Was this an actual press account that you clipped from the papers?

AB: As I recall, it was a real press account, though I may have edited it a little, to make it serve my purpose, which was of course to provide a documentary facade to my fiction.

DM: The preface also says that you met and interviewed two groups, but I recall your telling me years ago that all this was the product of your imagination. Which is it, or is there a blend of these methods?

AB: My reply is as per your *Dictionary of Literary Biography* piece, with one addition. While most of the material came from "friends," with that drastic rewriting I illustrated with my "dentist" story, I did talk to one or two genuine extreme anarcho-left guys and groups, and used those tapes more directly, though much cutting and shaping was still needed. I recall the name of one of those groups, but even now, so many years later, think it would be wrong to name them.

DM: This leads to my by now familiar question about your aims and methods. I suppose this question is becoming tedious, given your response about inspiration and the instinctual. However, I see development and change over the course of your career, and I'm trying to get your sense of that development (if, of course, you see it as such).

AB: Remember, I was "going popular," but not only for sheer commercial reasons. At around this time Heinrich Böll made a speech on receiving the Nobel Prize. It was about the need for novels especially to make—to be designed to make—a political impact—this in rather high falutin' terms— writers' political responsibility, etc.—and that the self-indulgent elitist "art" novel was intolerable. This hit home, and I resolved to write in a plain, accessible style, literally a "conversational" style, via the tape recorder. The recorder was a godsend to me. I cut out the cut-up and found this other way of creating the "ocean of raw material" I have always needed, so that I could "find" the good stuff among the debris—to mix my metaphors. I also discovered the wonderful music and subtlety of people's speech, and there was a bit of politics in that also. (I also found out what an exhausting method it was, with hundreds (?) of hours transcribing tapes, editing and rewriting them.)

DM: The technique of using multiple, first-person narrators is especially effective, but new for you. Did you do anything particular to capture the sound and feeling of voices speaking?

AB: Beyond what I've just said about taping, it was a matter of building a character out of multiple fragments, "seeing and hearing" the person—all the familiar stuff of the traditional novelist (because no one of my many interviewees turned out to "be" any one of my six characters—each was a collage of fragments).

DM: In your view who is the hero of the novel? I realize the idea is the montage of voices and personalities, but Jean and Dave strike me as particularly compelling for their generally humanist views of others, the struggle, and their eventual disaffection.

AB: I agree about Jean and Dave.

DM: I'm curious if any or all of your children have played important roles in your work—as creative provocateurs, models for characters, or whatever?

AB: Fascinating question. There's the old tag about a novelist putting all of himself into each sentence. Them kids are a vital part of me, maybe the best bit of me, I cannot go beyond that because I have so much to say about it. As for models for characters, bits of them for sure, here and there, and Danny and Sham were clear models (though not exclusively so) for Harry and Hazel in *Revolutions*. Maybe "models" is not quite right. I "had them in mind," "saw" them throughout.

DM: You mention in the "Slash and Burns" interview in the *Minnesota Daily* the method of buying old books and creating impromptu verbal collages with the pages. I'm afraid most readers won't have access to that piece, so could you revisit (I'm sorry) the inevitable interview question about your creative methods?

AB: Start with a word: browsing. Dictionary says it means "read desultorily." Desultorily means "going constantly from one subject to another, disconnected, unmethodical." The process begins with me browsing in a used bookshop. The state of mind is all: disconnected, unmethodical, unpurposeful, not hunting for good material, bumbling around, humming a bit (not really), glancing through pages, saying hm, from time to time, or not saying hm, saying mmm, or not, from book to book, maybe an hour or two, no hurry, never mind if nothing, but maybe piling up a few. Needless to say, what's happening is the subconscious taking over. I'm going on about the state of mind because the same is repeated more or less, at the next stage, glancing down at the pages of the books I've brought home. There's much more on this in chapter 5 of my book in progress, "Art by Accident," prefaced by Klee's incomparable: "Does inspiration have eyes, or does it sleepwalk?" "Sleepwalking" is maybe more apt than "browsing."

Sometimes I fold pages over, so I can read across, half of one page, half of another. I think I have never actually cut up pages, though in a couple of interviews I've said I have because it makes a good story. Then of course there follows the interminable process of peering (usually down, the cuttings or pages are on a table) and shuffling them around, by trial and error, finding a way in which they may go together, stretching my imagination and the reader's, to encompass a new, an unfamiliar aspect of each word or image, as it strains to hook up with its neighbor. The novel is plotted in the same way, as I see the possibility of one scene following another, again stretching my characters' potential—there, she's in a pub, but I have some good stuff on a mountain—how to get her from pub to mountain. Ah . . . I have used the analogy of the child's drawing book, where he joins up the dots—scrabble of dots at the foot of the page, a couple at the top, ah, it's a giraffe!

DM: Who is the narrator in *The Day Daddy Died?* In the first few paragraphs there are ellipses, to signify hesitancy, an almost stuttering quality to the narrative. Is this a case of narrative ventriloquism—a third-person narrator imitating perfectly the rhythms, intonations, dialectical idiosyncrasies of the main character, Norah?

AB: Again the way you phrase the question illustrates the difference between your approach and mine. It would not occur to me to ask myself, still less to answer, "Who is the narrator?" though I am now enjoying the analysis that follows. But to stay first with the general. I don't adopt a tactic in order to create a literary effect—"narrative ventriloquism" (great phrase) or whatever. I try to find the words that seem true to, that truly convey and share the bit of life experience I remember/imagine. Thus those ellipses arose from the subject matter—a man dying from some bronchial catastrophe that first hindered, then stopped his breathing. The man's choking to death. A few ellipses are the least I can allow him. There's another layer of hesitation too: the scene is being recalled by his adoring, grief-stricken (maybe overstates it) daughter. The words are closely based on one of the many tape recordings I made with the woman whose story forms the basis of the novel. Can't recall details now, but I would probably have edited it quite heavily, eliminating repetitions and all sorts, producing in the end a purity of language that's far from spoken speech, but yet retains some of that quality. In addition of course, Elsie (her real name) would have spoken in first person, and I transcribed into third. (I think all my novels are in third person, for the distancing.)

As well as the attempt to convey the experience, it occurs to me now that there's also the aesthetic qualities of the words themselves—their sound, the way they look on the page, and in relation to each other—I am particularly interested in that. Of course it's a cliché of commercial writing to avoid wedges of uninterrupted grey print—most obviously, use dialogue to break up the page, but I also have gone for more extreme methods—*Dreamerika!* for instance. And my other work in progress—"Imaginary

Dictionary"—goes for that in a big way. Finally, yes, your characterization of the third-person narrator, puts it nicely. (Though there are other voices in the book.) Oh, and I'm also "mapping my own mind," and there's other factors also. The result is an infinitely complex equation, more than my mind can grapple with, which partly accounts for my reliance on ill-defined aspects of (un)consciousness, like "instinct," and similar.

DM: In your interview with Charles Sugnet you talk about being "moved away" from the styles of *Babel* and *Dreamerika!;* did you feel you were abandoning a method you were deeply attached to or was the change in the order of a progression and new sense of artistic commitment (the latter one might assume from your remarks in the same interview about Heinrich Böll's Nobel Prize speech)?

AB: A bit of one and a bit of t'other. "Abandoning a method to which I was deeply attached" comes nearest, however. If my early novels had been commercial successes, if the film, for example, of *Europe* had been made (the option was sold, but it got no further), then a) I would have had the confidence to explore the surrealist possibilities further, and b) my royalties would have been enough to live on, giving me the time to write full-time . . . but that never happened. I had thought I could have the best of both worlds, artistic freedom and earn a living, but not so—Kafka: "To earn your living, or live your life, that is the question." On the other hand, that Heinrich Böll story also contains part of the truth.

DM: I'm curious about the use of the various letters; what were you trying to achieve with these? (Again from my point of view, these seem an extension of *The Angry Brigade*'s technique of getting a host of voices filling the narrative.)

AB: One critic made quite a thing about the so-called "epistolary" thread that runs through the book. For me, it fitted with my interest in junk and in found objects generally—an interest shared by many surrealist artists—Picasso, of course, and Schwitters and Miro's marvelous sculptures, i.e., each of the letters used was actually found by me and stuck in a cardboard box I keep for such things. And yes, I guess there was a kinda dawning that, yep, there's a "thread" developing here—after I'd used a couple, and then I would have, more deliberately, tried to build on that. The letters would have been ruthlessly cut, shaped and edited, to fit my story line. I remember the delight with which I found—in the street, the gutter I think—that sweet love letter to "Babe"—you see, I could never have written that but I don't feel I've cheated or stolen anything (though sometimes I say, as I think others have said, that a novelist needs to be a cheat, a liar, and a thief)—because I have a) recognized the potential of this "junk" material, and b) slotted it into a context in a way that enhances—maybe transforms—the found object and builds the novel. Again, remember that "child joins up the dots" notion—well those letters also stretch the plot by encouraging it to hook up with the content of the letters. (That letter demanding payment of a bill was based on one I received from my son's music teacher.) Finally, yes, a host of voices is right—another way of creating collages.

DM: I'm curious about your use of the surreal elements. I know the book originated from two sources—the Cockney woman you interviewed in London and the short story of a love affair between an older man and younger woman—and your desire to blend these two radically different stories and styles. However, the surreal elements are far more limited in this novel, and when they appear, they deal with inanimate things and lend to the novel's atmospherics. For instance, passages such as "music was the way the room said loud" (9), "Her thick lashes were in the room and could not get out" (10), "The sitting-down smile had been educated, taught to read and write" (57) illustrate what I'm suggesting. Could you comment on the change that indicates, as far as the surreal is concerned in this novel?

AB: My first response to your question is to relive the delight I had in those terrific images and phrases (though I sez it mesself). It confirms the fact that the "real me" is the author of that language. I would not dismiss the rest, but, for me, it is secondary, it is a compromise, a retreat, done for the commercial and other reasons I have already given. Interesting point you make about this voice dealing with "inanimate things." However, a key early scene between Norah and Dad used that heightened language in relation to them, as opposed to things. ("Key" because I think it's the first time I introduce the voice, and it's vital to get it right, so the reader takes it on board and allows you to use it throughout.)

DM: What led to your bringing Ian Breakwell into collaboration on the novel? Some of his images are truly sympathetic and harrowing complements to the narrative.

AB: I first met Ian very early on. He was running an Arts Centre in Bristol. Ian was/is a very versatile guy—writer, books and TV, films, happenings, painter, dedicated surrealist. (I've just invited him up to Lancaster U. as visiting speaker.) I think I was dipping into (as ever) *The Pickwick Papers,* illustrated by Phiz and others (watch it, Burns, are you making this up?), and I sez to mesself, I sez, maybe, why not? But I felt from the start there was no point in simply "illustrating," I wanted—and yes, this hooks up with your comments on "host of voices"—another voice. Ian seemed the right choice just because of his range of interests, literary and visual. I sent him early drafts of the novel, and he responded with early ideas for his collages. It was a neat additional interaction between his work and mine, that the text and the pictures together formed a collage, also the text and the pictures themselves were collages—a collage of collages.

DM: At one point Norah tells a companion that her favorite people are "those who live on the border-lines and edges, and burst into life from time to time" (52). This it seems to me could be said of most of the major characters in your novels. Would you care to comment?

AB: I'm fascinated by those moments when a writer unknowingly typifies himself in the course of a novel, and I think you have spotted one such—not that it's true of me, but of my characters, yes. Unless it's simply true of all novels' protagonists? Maybe it's only such protagonists who can generate the tensions that propel them through a novel?

DM: I'm interested in this and the other novels' sense of time. In each of your novels there is a telescoping of time—some events or scenes or descriptions will be rendered with great precision and detail yet other events will leap around with sometimes blinding speed. Could you comment on this temporal shifting?

AB: Your characterization is correct. All I would add is something parallel with the "velocity of the dream." That "quality of dream" I've written of before, partly, or even largely, derives from this way of handling time. The relation between the novel and the dream is dialectical, which is to say: the dream invades the novel, the novel inhabits the dream. More straightforwardly, I'd also say that the memory (and of course all fiction comes from memory) works in just that way—fits and starts, dwelling interminably in one place, with one image, one scene, one moment, only to zip and zoom away at astonishing speeds. So, it's not merely "right" and desirable, it is unavoidable and inevitable in a novel "written from the right point" (wherever that is, midway between the novel and the appendix, if you still have one, without one the question is more difficult to answer, maybe the place where it would still be if it were still there, anyway, it's somewhere in the guts).

DM: *Revolutions of the Night* begins enigmatically, with an anonymous pair of observers atop a tower looking down on the three generations of men in the protagonist's family. Who are these figures, if anyone, and was your intention here to create an atmosphere of foreboding that builds throughout the narrative? (For instance, the image of birds flying into dark clouds reappears surreally in the penultimate chapter, when babies come hurling out of the night sky to earth.)

AB: Those figures atop the tower are who they are. Where did they come from? From one of the hundreds of pictures, paintings, photographs I collected and assembled and from which grew the novel. I wanted to use the Ernst (cover/title) image early on, but not start with it—boring merely to repeat what the reader has just seen. Also needed to "place" the three figures from Ernst, and did so by placing them in a landscape suggested by another Ernst picture with a tower and a forest clearing. The three on the tower echoed the three on the ground. The two groups were connected by the young woman on the tower being Harry's sister, revealed in the penultimate line on page 10. Wanted her in the story from the start, but there's no female in the Ernst, so skewered her in this way. The atmosphere of foreboding—yes—I so much "wanted it," I searched for an image that contained it, and for reasons uncertain, sensed that it would make a good start. (Once you have "placed" your characters, the narrative obviously must move on, they can't stay there forever.) As for the "bookends" effect, I always think it's right (essentially it's sonata form, as described in "Art by Accident"), i.e., night sky image at the start and end, but I was not aware of it before you pointed it out. Maybe some instinct of which I was unaware headed me towards this, anyway, I'm glad it came out that way. Of course there's not an exact repetition, it's birds at the start and babes at the end. This is a chance to point out that the image of the "burning child flew into a tree. The tree became its funeral pyre" is my compressed version of precise, science-based information of the likely effect of nuclear war contained in a pamphlet I'd read.

DM: How would you describe your aims with this novel? I see a return to a more complex infusion of surreal techniques than those in *The Day Daddy Died*.

AB: As ever, my aims focused on content, not form or technique—their job needless to say was to serve, to express the content. However, I agree that they are more surreal than those in *Daddy*, though there is an extreme surrealist strand in *The Day Daddy Died*, but balanced, even outnumbered, by more pedestrian others. Not so in *Revolutions*. To that extent it's maybe "purer," but not as popular.

DM: Could you now comment on the role Max Ernst's painting played in the conception and execution of the novel (besides, of course, providing a title and jacket art)? I am also interested more generally in the influence of painting and the plastic arts on your aesthetics.

AB: The Ernst gave me license to go for it, as I suggest above. It also fit my father/son (and grandad for good measure). You'll have gathered that getting what seemed to me good usable stuff from Ernst, I launched into a wholesale raid on the mass of available works of European (mainly) art— all a bit quirky and chancy (all the better for that) in that the book was written on leave in England, and I had few books with me, a few more (reproductions of paintings and photos, that is) in the tiny village library. I'd have been swamped by "everything," so good that Chance did the initial selecting for me. This is the equivalent of hanging around secondhand bookstores for earlier novels. As to the general influence of painting—it's considerable. I have always thought, and on occasion argued, that the visual arts could teach writers a thing or two, in their multiplicity of schools, constant breaking ahead with the new—Picasso of course, the incomparable artist of our times—delete that horrible bundle of clichés—I get woolly when I enthuse. Also remember the visual/spatial/collage approach and method I use in assembling (itself a visual arts term) a novel on a tabletop, etc. Even the awareness of letters forming ideograms (is that the right term?) throughout but most extremely in, say, that dissection of the word *shack* in my "Imaginary Dictionary."

DM: The novel ends at a rural cottage after a flight from civilization. Were you consciously commenting on the failure of the pastoral ideal in modern life?

AB: The rural cottage stuff more likely came from where the book was written, a village in southeast England. I did much wandering around while writing it. I'll tell you (though you don't ask) an extraordinary coincidence that happened along the way. I'd got a character, Bob, stuck out there in the hills, miles from the city where the plot required him next to be. War-torn countryside, no gas, no transport, how does he make it? I went on a walk in the hills around and sat on a bench at a high point, guess what should swing towards me high in the sky—a hot air balloon! (There it is, on page 123 of the novel.)

DM: The tone of this novel reminds me very much of *Europe after the Rain*. The most outrageous events (Bob's being pushed out of a balloon to what appears certain death, the lion-man on the train who cuddles Hazel, a woman midwifing a fish giving birth, etc.) are narrated in the most cool, detached manner. Could you comment on this feature?

AB: Yep, that's true. In this I was aided by the technique of "copying" images from paintings. In other novels, especially those using the cut-up, I'd get the words themselves from my source materials; couldn't do that using pictures. So I was driven to use my own "natural" ability to put words together—an ability I thought had atrophied as a result of reliance on found materials. I was relieved and delighted to find I could put the words together—given the help of pictures. I'd place the book of reproductions or whatever by the side of my typewriter and simply swing into it—free fall—and found I could do it. There's another admission to make. The reason I need all these aids and tricks—cut-up, pictures, etc.—is that I find it so darned hard to write. I'm a page counter from page 1, so I seize on a picture, and an inexhaustible supply of such, with relief—I can complete the blasted book. Finally on coolness, note that certain passages, particularly towards the end, deal in ultimate catastrophe—nuclear war—what other style is there? I tell my students, "the hotter the content, the cooler the style"—when the content is the temperature of the sun, you'd better measure up to it, or cool it (man). By the way, the last chapter of *Revolutions* is a word picture of Ernst's *Europe after the Rain*.

DM: In many of the scenes in *Revolutions* there is a resonance or for me a vague quality of familiarity with many of the novel's scenes. Were there specific sources of inspiration in the novel, and if so, can you share some of these?

AB: That "vague quality of familiarity" you experienced while reading *Revolutions* may well derive from my use of countless paintings, mainly surrealist stuff, as the source of word pictures which I then sewed into the narrative—tried to make it seamless, invisible mending—though of course these set pieces not only thread into the narrative line, they also suggest extensions of it. (I've written before about kids' "dot" pictures, and the dot which tells you "it's a giraffe.") I've also written of having my kids somewhere in mind when drawing Harry and Hazel—it's just possible that your kids in your mind chimed with mine from time to time. Also perhaps your familiarity with those paintings or some of them, might have made you feel that you had seen that image somewhere before.

Needless to say, the whole range of sources that fed other novels, fed this one also—meaning, I suppose, my whole life experience. Thus the title image could not but suggest my experience as son and grandson and father.

DM: I'd like to turn to your only play, *Palach*, and ask you explain the reason for the self-reflexive introduction composed of correspondence between you and Charles Marowitz.

AB: You will know by now that I adopt a "grab-bag" approach to a book—in this case a play. Anything becomes usable once the central idea is truly launched. I "came across" my notes of those telephone conversations and simply found a place for them. I know now stuff about "self-reflexive" whatnot but at the time such notions were a million miles away. There's just one aspect that is down to earth and thought out, however, and it's not particularly admirable—the more reason for mentioning it. I've written elsewhere about what seemed to me Marowitz's self-aggrandizing manner, especially revealed in his later claiming co-authorship in the Penguin edition of the play. Therefore the inclusion of those notes of my conversations with him sought to establish, within the script, evidence of our writer/director relationship. If you read the lines again (sorry to put you through it), you'll see, I think, that my status as writer is, at least to some extent, confirmed. Finally, and more to the point, that "framing," I believe, is appropriate to such tragic and desperate subject matter. It intensifies the poignancy, to be shown how Jan Palach's ultimate act of despair is not only being commemorated, it is being exploited and turned into a play, a commodity, and coolly discussed as such.

DM: Is the failure of the play's voices to communicate with one another a verbal equivalent of the surreal that we find articulated in your novels?

AB: Not really! But maybe! I think it's mainly a straight political, even rather too obvious portrayal of what late capitalism has done to the human spirit. Late capitalism's problem of course is that it needs educated, skilled, even imaginative workers to produce sophisticated competitive products. Yet, those workers must not get ideas above their station. Hence brainwashing of myriad kinds, to keep those potentially revolutionary minds in check—advertising, media, all sorts. So "characters" mouthing advertising slogans at each other show the end result of that process, and given the primary subject of the play, it's clear that Stalinism is as guilty as so-called capitalism. The "maybe" above indicates that some of the scenes do create a dreamlike effect that could be labeled surreal.

DM: I'm curious about the play's comic elements. This feature is mentioned in the one of introductory comments (196), and I see it especially in the closing scene where each member of the family is locked into his or her private obsession—the mother with cooking a satisfactory pudding, the father with football, and the girl with her cosmetics. What were you trying to achieve with what I see as undeniably comic interludes? (For what it's worth I think they operate in the Shakespearean sense of lessening some of the grimness, but I'm sure you had other intentions in mind.)

AB: Lessen the grimness, sure. Also, the play deals centrally with utter despair (which precipitated Palach's suicide), and the comic is human being's ultimate weapon in dealing with such.

DM: Obviously this was your first play. What formal challenges did it present, especially for one whose career up to this point had been in fiction? How would you compare the two genres from your perspective?

AB: Terrific challenges: first the human element. As compared to the purity and isolation of myself at my desk, there was the messy, complex involvement of people . . . But I love collaboration on many grounds: political obviously—comradeship and all that, and a knowledge that "we are many and they are few." There's also an interesting connection with Chance, in that collaboration introduces the random element—obviously, I can't be sure what my collaborator will contribute, and vice versa—and that is stimulating, nerve-racking, precarious, all the things needed to cook up somethin' tasty. There was also the real and undeniable excitement of "seeing and hearing" my words made real. And when we got, among others, that sensational review by Harold Hobson (then the doyen—silly word—of the London theatre critics) then that was excitement and pleasure, all the better when shared with others. I was not much aware of the formal differences between writing a novel and a play—maybe I'd have done more and better if I had been clearer about what I was about—dunno. Remember, I was always dead keen on theatre, went often, even acted (in Shakespeare, with "traveling players") when younger, so I was familiar with its requirements.

DM: I've noticed in this play and in many of the novels sharp criticism of organized religion, especially the Roman Catholic Church. Could you comment on your feelings about the Catholic Church or religion in general?

AB: I think I'm instinctively a religious person, at least in the sense of having a deep need. But unhappily cannot begin to believe all that "God up there" stuff—and the intellectual versions, pantheistic and more—are simply pathetic. Did the Red Sea part for the fleeing Israelites? If so, great, except I don't believe it. If not, and it's symbolic of this or that, to hell with it, who cares. You'll note a kind of anger there, that's powerfully there in most of my references to churches or religions, and of course it's the anger of a jilted lover. One who longs to believe but cannot, has reason for fury. I simply loved the language of the Bible, Old Testament and New, adored Jesus as a man—the kind of leader who kneels and washes his disciples' feet is terrific. But the Church, especially the Catholic Church as an institution is of course another matter. My answer to your question should perhaps have begun with my saying I'm a Jew, but my Jewishness died with my mother, in 1944. My father remarried, a Catholic. I have always been wary of displaying my Jewishness, though I would not deny it, not only because I am and have for all my adult life been an atheist, but because I absolutely wish and intend to avoid any kind of labeling or stereotyping as a Jewish writer, which, in spite of my love for Kafka, I totally reject. One of the few traces of Jewishness in my writing may be seen in the intensity with which *Europe after the Rain* evokes aspects of the Holocaust. However, I always try to counter the notion that the Holocaust victims were all Jewish. Marx-ism, of course, provided all I needed in terms of religion—a reason for be-ing, a promised land, a complete understanding of human history, and my place in it. But if the promised land turns out to have been a nightmare—what then?

DM: In Chapter Five of "Art by Accident" you mention modern artists' disinclination to admit the force of inspiration in their works. Do you es-chew the phenomenon of inspiration in your work? Do you do anything to "feed the muse"? Your collecting pulp writing and journalistic clippings strike me as one way of—not creating—but provoking serendipity. Are there other ways you do this?

AB: I have just reread chapter 5 of "AbyA." I can tell you that each and every line was "true for me"—those (mainly) painters and composers and I, work(ed) in the same way. Yes, the religious associations and implications of the term *inspiration* put me off, but it can be a handy word and I use it occasionally, as in "AbyA." As to tactics, as opposed to the above, which could be called strategy: in addition to those cut-up tricks, I walk a lot, the pace of ambling seems to be just right, and the slow change of surroundings again seems "right" for the *reception* of thoughts, images, ideas—I don't even get active enough to "invite" ideas—just await them—and this is the active bit—I need to be able to recognize the good ones, meaning of course the useable ones, and even better, the ones that suggest, or in an odd sortofa way, bring others in tow . . . so—I say again—it's *the state of mind* that matters, it's the key. "Daydreaming" is a useful notion too. I also use bore-dom. I lie down and do nothing, think nothing, until I get so fed up, I jump up and start typing.

NOTES

[1]In response to an earlier question Burns added, "I know [in my writing] I am a willing accomplice . . . but . . . still at the heart of my heart is . . . DOUBT, which is why I put things next to each other (collage) and leave them [readers and critics] to work it out."

[2]The passage to which he refers reads: "The content of dreams illustrates this [the emphasis in the word *surrealism* on *realism*] nicely. Dreams are generally made up of everyday objects. . . . Yet there is a deep contradiction between their apparent solidity and the sense of precariousness, of uncer-tainty, that pervades them. . . . [Referring to Dali's *A Loaf of Bread about to Explode!*] Exactly! That is the precarious reality of the dream. And that is a marvelous effect for the fiction writer to aim at. We must deal with the real life around us. But we should also share our awareness that the ordinary always carries with it the potential for the extraordinary."

[3]This commendation, which has never appeared in its entirety in the US, reads, "Alan Burns, author of *Europe after the Rain* and *Celebrations*, is to

me one of the two or three most interesting new novelists working in England—and if this sounds cool, let me say that I mean that he is a very good novelist indeed. The exploration of the psycho/political/life/language/thought/action of our age in *Europe after the Rain* is as deadly accurate as it is exciting, frightening and also extremely moving. It is perhaps the more immediately impressive of his two books, yet I finally prefer *Celebrations* for it has a compelling sense of the composition of modern personality from the institutional (in this case industry), the cliché (this part is very funny), the instinctual (Mr. Burns can make poetry out of the language that describes this) and the small nugget of something which is ours alone that we hug so closely. It is a mysterious, rich and engrossing book."

[4]The passage Burns refers to is Themerson's explanation of the juxtaposition of unlikely elements playing havoc with "the classification system on which the regime is established." After citing a series of havoc producers, including Galileo, Einstein, Russell, and Schönberg, Themerson writes, "the Cubists with their funny ideas about shapes, or Dadaists or Merzists with their funny ideas about introducing symmetries or rhythms instead of principles."

IMAGINARY

DICTIONARY

Alan Burns

ESPLANADE   Stride along the promenade, all the way to Spain.
                   Iron legs in water, step across to Spain.

MUFFIN   ff are its doughy insides   mmmm

ANNA   consummate symmetry:
                   hint of dark in n and n
                   slight and oval a and a

shacks   a and c are kids tucked up, between high walls of h
                   and k, with s and s, bundles of firewood set aside
                   for winter, leant against the walls.

hut   is not so hot. hole in the roof. u lets in the rain.

workers, peas
ants

VOLVO   On a road in a region between Poland and Spain, a
                   big Volvo returns from a weekend by the sea. The
                   car contains four adults and a child.

perfect poem   L O N G
                   V E H I C L E

WHEELCLAMP   WHAT SQUAT POWER   CAR STOPPED   CLAMPED

Tolstoy and   T   O   L   S   T   O   Y   A   N   D
Dostoyevsky   D   O   S   T   O   Y   E   V   S   K   Y
                   doing the Lambeth Walk   O   Y   !

TYRANT   starts from highshelf T
                   slips down slimy Y
                   steadies with level R and A
                   shins up N
                   restored to the heights of T

BUM   UU

AMERICA   W H I T E   P I G   A S   W I D E   A S
                   A   M   E   R   I   C   A

LORRY   Lorry will hurry
                   but it lacks weight

TRUCK   Truck won't whizz
                         but it weighs

JENNIFER and   Jennifer is slender with N and N
MUM   Mum holds child in ample U
                         Hugged by M and M

JAPAN   J
                                                      a
                                                   p
                                                a
                                          n

KAMCHATKA   k
                                                      a
                                                    m
                                                  c
                                                h
                                              a
                                          t
                                        k
                                        a

RADIO   vowels hinged around big D
                         slipdip wavily
                         longitudinally

Bruce Chatwin   Bruce is clever Scottish doggie
                         Chatwin charm will wain notwin

BOOTS   BOOTS BOOTS BOOTS BOOTS
                         BOOTS BOOTS BOOTS BOOTS

handsome   Y
  andsome
                                                      T
Mussolini
notsolini   I

ALTAR   A   L   T   A   R   E
                 ┌──────────────────────────────┐
                 │ FLAT   TOPPED   BLOCK   │
                 │ FOR   OFFERINGS   TO   THE   │   D
                 └──────────────────────────────┘

THEATER	EAT HEAT AT THE THEATER

TOES

```
t   t   t   t   T       T   t   t   t   t
o                                       o
e   o   o   o   o       o   o   o   o   e
    e   e   e   e       e   e   e
```

OX	unamendable unchangeable untouchable invincible OX
CHRIST	IE'S
BRAIN	maggots
TIME	another month gone, you know
LIFE	what can we do
POLITICS	what is to be done
CLASS	war
FOREST	trees' tall and bristly haircuts
MARRIAGE	after eight years' marriage she discovered that her husband was a medium-sized man with a brown moustache
CONVERSATION	awful earthquake in Japan, Alan yearh
LAVA	tory
CH	aucer ick-pea ance
PING	CHONG

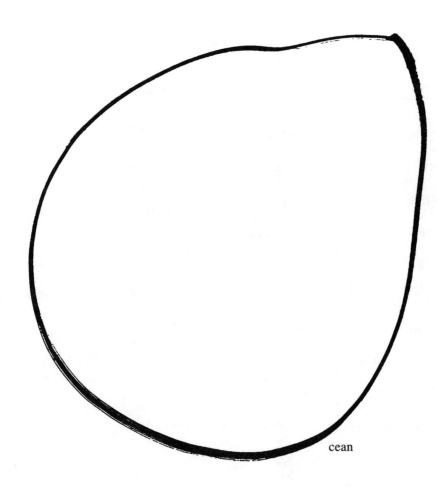

cean

BOUQUET

GOOSE	See MOOSE
MOOSE	See GOOSE

CORKAGE

Mehta: I organised a dance in the town hall. We brought our own drink, it was paid for, and we'd arranged that we wouldn't have to pay corkage or anything like that. We brought the stuff in and a guy comes up and says, 'You know you have to pay corkage?' We were just irritated. I said, 'What corkage?' So he says, 'Well, corkage is, when, you know, you . . .' I said, 'I don't want to know what corkage is. I said, "What corkage?"' So he said, 'Why don't you express yourself more clearly?' I blew up. I said, 'I can run verbal circles round you but that's not necessary. If you want to understand what I am saying, try to understand what I have said. Don't try to tell me to explain myself. Because if there's any lack of understanding it's on your part. I phrased myself correctly. What does it mean: "What corkage?" Did I say: "What *is* corkage?" *Then* you could have explained . . .' He was nonplussed by this sudden aggression and in fact we cleared it up in a few minutes because I kept quiet after a while, but I was determined to make the point that it is not that an Indian is not able to make himself understood, it is that there is a deliberate, or maybe not so deliberate conditioning of the Englishman's mind that makes *him* unable to understand, he is preparing his mind beforehand, so that he is not going to be able to understand.

KISS

Lipspush

PEOPLE

Most people will claim to be people, usually

BOMB

Man: We do have a cabin in Northern Minnesota, which is winterised, and we've talked about it, that if er a nuclear attack is come, that we run for the cabin. We've got it stocked with food. We have fish and poultry in the freezer. The canned goods are in a cupboard up there. It's enough to survive, well, a month or two.

Child: I would go outside and ride my bike. I

would put my raincoat on. I like to smell flowers, and I like to look at silver shells, ee ee ee ee!

PIES	LIES

JAM — it is the blackcurrant jam which makes a noise five feet wide, it is that which does this, with a little glass of laughter

POLAR ICE — A soldier with a pole placed packages on the ice.

DEATH — The sound of yellow rattling across the floor.

END

TEND
WEND
SPEND
LEND
DEPEND
DEFEND
UPEND
END
PERPENDICULAR

_____

_____

Has

The man on a horse has a stick
The woman he hits has no horse and no stick
The man on a horse has a helmet
The horse has hooves, hooves, hooves, hooves

This first edition is limited to 126 copies
of which 100 copies, numbered and signed
by the author, are for sale.
The remaining 26 copies, signed and
lettered A to Z, are for the author's use.

Inscription in B. S. Johnson's HOUSE MOTHER NORMAL (1971) which reads: "This one [unsure of this phrase] B is for Alan Burns—friend, comrade, exemplar Bryan 24/5/71"

Two chapters from a book
provisionally titled

"HUMAN LIKE THE REST OF US
a life of B. S. Johnson"

Alan Burns

October 22–25 1973

Chapter: *Fat Man on a Beach*

> VOICE: This is a film about a fat man on a beach.

> VOICE: Did you hear what I said? This is a film about a fat man on a beach.

> VOICE: Do you really want to sit there and watch it?

> VOICE: Well don't say I didn't warn you.

The voice is unmistakeably Johnson's. The mock-belligerent attention-grabber: "Oi! You!" The statement of fact is "true," yet undercut with self-doubt: "Do you really want to—?"

Johnson's last complete creative work was a thirty minute film for Harlech TV. Title: *Fat Man on a Beach*. Director: Michael Bakewell. In Bakewell's words, "The film managed to be, against all the odds, a complete summing up of Bryan's character and ideas. Given the events that followed, it's Bryan's buoyancy and cheerfulness that come across. It was an extraordinarily happy time."

Bakewell had sent "a two line idea" to Aled Vaughan, Harlech's controller of programs. The commission that followed was "pure Bryan." The writer who opened his novel *Trawl:*

I . . . always with I . . . one starts from and ends with I

was invited to dump himself down in a place of his choice, to play himself, to be writer, narrator, star. Vaughan had shrewdly perceived that Johnson would be inspired by the commission's arbitrary disciplines: "Take a film crew to a beach in North Wales. Make a film of a single day. (In real time it was to be shot in twenty hours spread over three days.) Bring nothing with you, take nothing away." Bakewell says there was some cheating, but not much: "The few things we did bring, essential supplies, were mostly worked into the film: a bunch of bananas, a few fireworks, some shells bought in a shop . . ."

The film's style was well caught by Elkan Allen in *The Sunday Times:*

A poet of forty wanders about the beach, changes his clothes when he feels like it, reads his poetry, reminisces engagingly, and reflects on life . . . Looking rather like Max Bygraves gone to seed, he keeps up a patter full of original jokes, interspersed with powerful verse about life and death.

Returning to the "El Dorado" of his first novel *Travelling People,* Johnson chose Porth Ceiriad Bay, near Abersoch, in Lleyn.

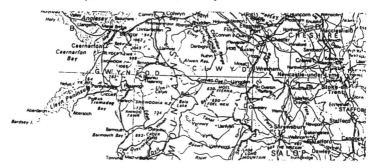

Harlech commissioned the film in late August and by October 22 Johnson and Bakewell were driving to North Wales to check out the locale. Leaving London at four in the morning, Johnson's mood was "exuberant" as the two old friends talked about the script all the way down in the car. They took a look at the Bay and worked out how they would get film crew and equipment into the inaccessible place.

Following the route taken by the characters in *Travelling People,* the two visited the country club where most of the novel is set. As in the novel, they drove to Bettws-y-Coed and stopped at the turn leading to the Club:

He took me as far as Bettws-y-Coed, and he said: "I am going down there" and I looked down there and it was a marvelously sunlit glacier valley. (from *Travelling People*)

When the novel's protagonist visits the Club later, it lives up to his expectations. He writes to a friend in London:

Sorry to disappoint you, mate, but this place turns out not to be the cesspool you hoped it would be: in fact it's all and more the brochure promised—the Garden of Gorgeous 'ydrangeas *is* lovely, there *is* marvellous scenery all round, and the Loggia *is* romantic . . . [ibid]

Bakewell says Lleyn had "romantic associations" for Johnson, and these are underlined by many poems quoted through the film:

Young fellow from Lleyn,
who's the girl of your heart,
You who wander so late in the
    evening apart.

The lyric mood is undermined by a number of elements, first the narrator's tragi-comic bulk. The film's most conspicuous feature, the fatness of Fat Man, has been rather overlooked by critics and viewers. This is partly due to its sheer obviousness, and is also the result of the film's camera technique. Johnson's big body is often lost in the landscape, dwarfed by sand, sea, cliffs, sky. Nevertheless the narrator's person is insistently *there* throughout the film, as this typical shot shows:

As late as September 24, a few days before shooting began, Harlech TV's correspondence referred to the working title, "The Lleyn Peninsular film." Johnson's last minute title "made" the film, it dictated its downright mood and tone. Whatever role Chance played in the film's writing and production, the title was deliberately chosen and deeply felt, the culmination of a lifetime's living with his own large body.

Three close friends and fellow writers give their impressions of the man and their sense of how he saw himself:

Peter Buckman recalls: "Bryan claimed it wasn't eating or drinking that made him fat, it was 'all in the genes.' We had a long discussion about the different types, big bones and little bones, long-headed and fat-headed. Bryan's excuse was that that was the way he was born, his size didn't matter because it was right for him."

As Barry Cole saw it, "Bryan's big worry was his weight. Naturally huge, he cossetted his grossness with a gourmet's self-indulgence. To his friends, Bryan's weight was normal, but to him it was a burden, usually borne with the stoicism he publicly maintained. But he was *huge*. By the end he must have been eighteen stone. He was a great trencherman, great beer drinker, wine drinker, spirit drinker, social drinker. He loved going to pubs, but drinking with Bryan could be difficult. There was me at ten and a half stone and Bryan at eighteen, and in a pub you buy each other drinks . . . He was not particularly tall, but he bulked large. He was broad, huge arms and thighs. Orson Welles had the same bulk, similar features, and the same intensity too."

Zulfikar Ghose writes: "When driving through France with Bryan, I noticed something about him that I had not remarked earlier. For some reason (e.g. going into different shops) we would part, and looking for him, I invariably found him in the *patisserie* devouring considerable quantities of cakes. Even in London, he had been a compulsive eater between meals. When we left pubs at closing time, he would make for a fish and chips shop or, when in Soho, the place in Great Windmill Street that sold salt beef sandwiches. But I had never seen him eat so many sweets before. And when I received news of his death, one of the images that came to my mind was seeing him in one of those *patisseries,* gluttonously thrusting a large quantity of cream, sugar and pastry into his mouth, almost as though his body were driving him to make up some obscure chemical deficiency, and I have often wondered whether, instead of some mental state, it was not some physical state, obscure but subtly malignant, the body constantly making its insatiable demand, that drove him to his terrible end."

The touch of cruelty in Ghose's description may be due to its being written in the aftermath of his friend's death, and the mix of grief and anger that greeted it. Johnson did not just guzzle his food, he enjoyed it, and shared his pleasure with his friends. Ghose had countless happy meals with Johnson, Peter Buckman also: "Bryan was always celebrating, always producing a bottle of wine. We would go out together and get very merry." Michael Bakewell and Diana Tyler were Johnson's trusted friends as well as his literary agents. When they speak of him, the word they use most often is "celebration." Another friend remembers "the physical bulk that did not prevent a lightness of touch, a nimbleness on his feet, as sprightly as Brendan Behan dancing an Irish jig, his body towering over his twinkling feet."

In his brilliant screenplay *Not Counting the Savages,* Johnson shows how well he understood the temptations and miseries of gluttony. The protagonist of this ferocious study of family hates is an "ugly, lumpish" fifty-year-old Husband. He opens the play "getting down to his food piggishly." He finishes his main course and follows it with a whole Camembert before a word is spoken. The play then explores the Husband's crapulence with pitiless ingenuity: feeding your face reverses the life-giving function of food. Sustenance becomes its opposite, a means of self-destruction. When he published the play in the Spring 1973 issue of *Transatlantic Review,* Johnson chose this drawing as its illustration:

And this is the cover of the notebook in which Johnson wrote the script of *Fat Man on a Beach:*

Johnson chose his stationery with unusual care:

I carry little notebooks, about three inches by five. I buy them in Paris actually . . .

It was no accident that *Fat Man* came to be inscribed in this particular pad. Johnson closely identified with his namesake, the more so since making the TV film *On Reflection: Sam Johnson* in 1971. Apart from the attraction of Dr. Johnson's personality and inimitable writing style, those Johnsonian jowls made B. S.'s own appearance more acceptable.

If Dr. Johnson ranked as exemplar and general inspiration, the other model for *Fat Man* was Jarry's *Père Ubu*, as this pair of portraits suggests:

"M. Hébert, prophaiseur de pfuisie." painted by Jarry while a pupil at the Rennes Lycée, a portrait of the teacher, nicknamed "Le Pere I be," who inspired the creation of Pa Ubu. *Coll. Jean Loize, Paris*

The two shared more than body weight.

FLUNKEY: Sir, there's a bloke out there who wants a word with you. He's pulled the bell out with his ringing, and he's broken three chairs trying to sit down. (from *Père Ubu*)

That could as well be Johnson as Ubu at the door.

He demonstrated that the beginning of wisdom lies where true stoicism meets profound epicureanism.

Said of Jarry, this applies equally to Johnson. If Jarry was a twentieth-century Rabelais, Johnson's identification was with Sam Johnson and Sterne.

Fat Man is as ego-centred as *Ubu*, but as ever "the opposite is also true." All films are to some extent collaborations, but *Fat Man* was the product of a peculiarly intimate interweaving of talents. First was that between Johnson and Michael Bakewell, his long-time co-worker and friend. The previous year, the two had worked together on *Hafod a Hendret,* a TV film also for Harlech. Its success had ensured the freewheeling commission for *Fat Man.* This time, Bakewell says, "I did far more directing, because Bryan was fully occupied with writing and acting."

The collaboration extended to the whole of *Fat Man*'s film crew. They dined together every night, and the film's ideas evolved around the table. Bakewell says, "The drinks bill was gigantic, expenses generally were monumental. At one stage we had to conceal them under 'Hire of boat.' "

Whatever others contributed, Johnson was the writer on the set. Bakewell says, "When everyone else had tumbled into bed, Bryan would take a huge bottle of wine up into his room, lock himself in, and steadily evolve the script. Next morning he was always last to arrive, but then he would use his notes from the night before to improvise that day's shooting . . . For myself, I found working with Bryan quite easy in a sense. I understood his mind, I knew his passions and had heard his stories. It was just a matter of finding ways to embody them."

Telling old tales and experiences he had carried with him for half a lifetime gave Johnson an ease and spontaneity before the camera that made Bakewell think "this is the way Bryan might well have developed, talking direct to the TV audience. He did it in his TV film on Dr. Johnson. Now the technique came into its own."

Johnson's engaging directness helped him get away with stories like the one about

the girl being taken to the pictures by a man and he said: "We are going to see a film about whales." And she said: "I am not terribly keen on Taffies as you know." He said: "No, not that kind of Wales. The film is called *Moby Dick.*" And she said, "I don't like sex films either."

Silly poems too:

Mary had a little lamb,
She put it in a bucket
And every time the lamb got out,
The bulldog tried to put it back again.

Followed by Johnson's characteristic "Ho, ho, ho, ho." This was all part of his high-spirited attempt to dismantle the conventions of the serious TV documentary. When the film was shown on the first anniversary of Johnson's death, *The Sunday Times* compared it to Peter Ustinov's *The*

Mighty Continent, three and a half years in the making. *Fat Man,* shot in less than a week, "will be remembered long after the other is forgotten."

If this had been all there was, *Fat Man* would have been no more than Goonery, or a souped-up *Running, Jumping, Standing Still Film.* Johnson's underlying seriousness is shown by his daring juxtaposition of these jollifications with poetry of a high order, among them *Porth Ceiriad Bay,* written years before on his first visit to Lleyn:

Descended to the shore, odd how we left
the young girl with us to herself, and went
straight to examine the stratified cliffs,
forgot her entirely in our interest.

You marvelled at the shapes the clockwork sea
had worn the stone, talking keenly, until
the pace of this random sculpture recalled
your age to you, and then its anodynes.

And so you turned, pretending youth, courting
the girl as if you were a boy again,
leaving the wry cliffs to their erosion
and me to my observant solitude.

[1964]

Those "stratified cliffs" are maybe a too obvious reminder of times past, but they underline the film's various levels of action and meaning. In *Travelling People*'s prose version of the scene described in the poem, the protagonist looks out to the sea that laps the Bay and calls it "the snotgreen gannetsbath (syzygy of *Ulysses* in mind)." Earlier in the film, Johnson says he is "besotted with Beckett and Joyce." So the girl observed on the beach surely recalls Gertie MacDowell "on the weedgrown rocks along Sandymount shore" in Joyce's *Ulysses.*

The film's basic "wanderer" theme also derives from Joyce. The day spent mooching around a beach is grounded in Bloom's day in and around Dublin. Starting with reminders of *Travelling People,* the "wanderer" appears in the film in many forms. Johnson's chance meeting with a friendly dog suggests Odysseus greeting his old friend. There are signs of Sinbad, Childe Harold also. Robinson Crusoe is there, complete with footprint in the sand. Fat Man is engaged on an "uncertain quest in search for peace" with a bunch of bananas in place of the Holy Grail. All through, Joshua Rifkin plays Scott Joplin, with a hint of stride piano, at an appropriate jog trot.

Porth Ceiriad Bay's last line leaves the narrator to his "observant solitude" and Johnson clings to that, as he wanders across the beach, whatever his excursions and distractions. He is amused and interested but undeterred by screaming seagulls, exploding light bulbs, a child's umbrella stuck in the sand, bunches of bananas, a broken altar candle, a dead sheep, footprints in the sand, changing weather, changing clothes, two blue toy inflatable rubber whales, frying sausages, shop-bought shells, exploding fireworks, breaking waves, skullcap, brass tack, an outsize paperclip, a Labrador dog, the remains of two sandals, a Schweik doll, a mirror found in the sand.

The succession of random events and lucky finds is not as haphazard as it seems. Johnson's constant changes of clothes, jump-cutting from brown sweater to green, pink-striped shirt to white, are not only designed to give away the tricks of the film maker's trade, they are fine sideswipes at those costume epics whose wardrobe budgets would have paid for *Fat Man* five times over. The sequence of constant shifts comments on time passing, role playing, the futility of everyday living.

For Johnson "art by accident" was a serious matter. Like Eisenstein leaving a door open on the set "for the unexpected to come in," or Flaherty letting the unaimed cameras run in *Man from Aran,* Johnson revelled in the paradox of "deliberate uncertainty." The whole film was a "found object," but the accident was just sufficiently contrived. Johnson and Bakewell set things up so things would happen.

Being able to trust their instincts and one another, produced in the two film makers an exhilaration that was shared by the camera crew. The collaboration already mentioned fed its own arbitrary element into the chance process. Cameraman Mike Reynolds had the idea of "treating the camera as if it were a dog." Johnson instantly knelt down, "patted it":

Come along. This way . . . Not so fast. Down boy. Down. That's a good boy. Sit. *Camera "sits."*

Spontaneity and Chance work together to disarm the writer. His unconscious acceptance of "anything that comes along" can lead him into dangerous waters. *Fat Man*'s plethora of death images—the more striking for their juxtaposition with moments of exuberance and celebration—are sadly prophetic.

Johnson relishes these morbid scenes:

At the foot of the cliff he finds a dead sheep. *Zoom in to close shot of its bloodied head.*

He recalls a road accident seen nearby years ago, remembered with utter clarity:

There had been a crash between two cars and a motor cycle . . . the rider of the motor cycle had been thrown across the road and had hit a wire fence . . . and the wires had gone through him like a cheese cutter through cheese . . .

Less gruesome but equally telling is the aimless violence: he throws stones at piles of stones, "stamps on a bunch of bananas," smashes a light bulb, explodes fireworks in a cave to scare the screaming gulls. These are the actions of a disturbed child. They bear out Michael Bakewell's prescient words: "Bryan could pass from incredible jollity to total belligerence to incredible pain within five minutes. We shared a room while making the earlier film *Hendret*, and Bryan was always moaning and shouting in his sleep. He was obviously deeply disturbed in his dreams. One got the impression of a terrible restless spirit going on inside."

In this context, visual jokes worthy of Buster Keaton or Beckett seem somehow grim, as when Johnson responds to the old philisophical questions:

I'll have to go away and think about it. *He paces back and forward . . . As he paces he wears a deep trench in the sand—and falls into it.*

Digging his own grave, but it is done with a chuckle. He explores his private dreads, but with lugubrious glee. Suicidal maybe, po-faced never. Each image has its other side. Building a column of stones then pelting it with stones is futile, but it is also a way of coping with the tedium of "a day by the sea," and it brings back those seaside holidays spent with Mum and Dad "before the war." Exploding fireworks are violent, but they make a lovely bang. (That the rockets produce their spermatozoic fizzle inside a womb-like cave only makes the equation more interesting.)

Johnson's "high spirits in hard times" were partly due to the delight he always felt at being back in Wales. After the trip that produced *Travelling People*, Johnson returned for the next three summers to work in Lleyn. In 1970 he had a wonderful six months as Gregynog Writing Fellow at the University of Wales, Aberystwyth.

In *Fat Man,* a "Welsh Voice" calls out: "What can an Englishman know about Wales?" Johnson replies with his fine translation from "the great Welsh poet David ap Gwilim." The first stanza of *Seagull:*

Gull all grace on the flood tide
Mailed hand of sea salt.
Moonlight white, reflected snow.
Perfect lily of the wave's valley.
Fish fattened, cork-like coaster,
shining piece of paper.

But the poem that most clearly, even tenderly, conveys Johnson's connection with Wales, is the one he wrote for his Welsh film *Hafod a Hendret* (Winter home, Summer home):

Once at Gregynog, not long after
arriving, we walked across a field
maculate with snow and lambing blood

and amongst the scattered
animals came upon a lamb so newly born
it had not yet laid eyes on its dam:

some instinct set it unsteadily
towards us as though we must have caused
the monstrous expulse it had suffered . . .
it parallels the raw helplessness

I feel in moving towards your so
much beniger and more properly
valued older civilisation:

a feeling I have hardly had since
bribing glass in hand outside a pub
I was a child waiting for parents.

Michael Bakewell describes how the two of them went about filming the
sequence that went with the poem: "It wasn't easy to find a new born lamb
actually staggering about. Bryan got to know an old shepherd by playing
cribbage with him in a pub, night after night, and eventually he led us to the
lamb . . ." Making the film was fun, but being in Wales brought back memories of Johnson's separation from his parents—for Johnson the seminal experience, even in the trivial context of waiting for them outside a pub.
Johnson's overwhelming love for his mother had recently been intensified
by his close attendance at her agonising death from cancer. To connect waiting for his mother with "moving towards" Wales was an indication of his
love for what had become his mother country.
    In *Fat Man*, the Welsh Mother Goddess appears to Johnson on "a moun-
tain called Carn Fadrun on Lleyn." He tells how he found himself one
morning "at dawn on top of that mountain, almost not of my own volition
and stripping off all my clothes and making what I can only think of as religious gestures—worshipping some sort of female deity."
    That surrender to impulse, that acceptance of the instinctive self, was in
line with the spirit and content of *Fat Man on a Beach*. The man's integrity
gives him dignity, as he alternately ambles about and skips around, playing
games, confiding secrets, being himself to the bitter end.
    The film's conclusion is prefigured by the couplet that ends "Young Fel-
low from Lleyn":

Dark, dark is my lover and dark-haired is she
And white shines her body like foam on the sea.

Only months before, Johnson's friend, the novelist Ann Quin, had walked
into the sea at Brighton, and drowned. Michael Bakewell describes the
film's final scene as "a reenactment of Ann Quin's death." The script states

simply:

BSJ walks determinedly towards the sea . . . He goes on walking until he is lost beneath the waves.

Bakewell says "Bryan was determined that he would not suffer from the simulated suicide, so we made enormous preparations for bringing him back from death, pouring brandy down his throat, rubbing him down with hot towels. As Bryan would only do it once, we had to get it right first time, so we rehearsed it over and over again."

October 26–November 13 1973

Chapter: *Home. Means Her.*

> Home. Means her. · · · · · · · · · · Good, for a start, that I think of her, Ginnie, in connection with home, home not in the sense of my home, I have no home: there are the flat I rent and my parents' home: but neither of these is truly my home. I can form the concept of my home, though, I can see the desirability of having a home. Which means her, in that home, making that home: with me. I'll rest there.
>
> (from *Trawl*)

Back home, Johnson tried to get to grips with the work that had piled up while he was in Wales. There was plenty to do. Michael Bakewell says, "Bryan was doing too much! *The Matrix Trilogy* was a full-time occupation in itself. To do that, and *Fat Man,* and edit two books, and to do the other teleplays, and the Writers' Union stuff, and everything else, meant he was incredibly fully extended."

"Everything else" included six scripts for Thames TV's schools' programs, publicity interviews for the publication of *Aren't You Rather Young to Be Writing Your Memoirs?,* decisions to be made about the Danish and Swedish translations of *Christie Malry's Own Double Entry,* correspondence with his US publisher Dick Seaver, work on a new book of Welsh/English poetry, selection and revision of his own poems for *Penguin Modern Poets 25.*

Bakewell wanted to start work on editing *Fat Man,* but two things prevented Johnson from meeting him to discuss this. First was the priority Johnson gave to *The Matrix Trilogy.* This ambitious project was begun soon after his mother's death in 1971. Johnson's *Notes on the Trilogy* record its "Three interlinked themes":

1) the death of my mother
2) the decay of the mother country
3) the renewal aspect of motherhood paralleling the cancer she died of with the de-

cline of Britain over the last forty years.

See the Old Lady Decently, the first of the three novels, had been delivered to Hutchinsons on October 1, 1973. Charles Clark, managing director, and Johnson's editor, had some fundamental reservations about the book (though he published it unaltered in 1975). Johnson was preoccupied with Clark's critique. At the same time, he was mapping out the second novel, provisionally titled *Buried Although*. *See the Old Lady* ends with the author/protagonist's birth in 1933. Extant notes for the second novel take the story through to 1945.

The *Trilogy* was Johnson's most complex and challenging work to date. Given this, and its close connections with mourning his mother, he was determined to give it priority over his mass of other commitments, as this Note to himself makes clear:

My time is
wrongly organised:

I should be spending
3 hours
EACH MORNING
FIRST
on TMT

then worrying about the rest

[TMT=*The Matrix Trilogy*]

Further work on the Trilogy, on *Fat Man,* or anything else, was soon to be out of the question. Something happened to incapacitate Johnson entirely. It was to do with his wife Virginia.

Diana Tyler, Johnson's trusted friend and indefatigable literary agent, recalls: "When Bryan came back from Wales, obviously something had been simmering. The first I knew that anything was wrong was when he telephoned me at home at about eight o'clock on Sunday morning. I was in bed asleep. He was very distraught. He said, 'You know Virginia is thinking of leaving me?' I said, 'Don't be so ridiculous, what are you talking about?' I thought he was overreacting to a minor matrimonial problem. He came over to the house and spent the day with me. He was clearly upset, but by the end of the day he seemed OK. He was listing how much work he had on, he would talk things over with Virginia, they would go back to counselling."

Sunday with Diana must have done Johnson some good because on Monday he was able to attend to one of his lighter chores: commissioning contributions to *You Always Remember the First Time,* the book he was editing for Quartet. Michael Bakewell says that the collection "added considerable zest, dynamism and embarrassment to the year, with Bryan dashing off letters to the most improbable people, asking them about their first sexual experience." Contributors included Brian Aldiss, Larry Adler, Peter Buckman, Barry Cole, Giles Gordon, Ruth Fainlight, Michael Moorcock, Jeff Nuttall, Philip Oakes, Giles Playfair and Emma Tennant. Replies from those who could or would not contribute are often as revealing as those who appeared in the book.

Dame Sybil Thorndike's secretary wrote:

Dame Sybil could not possibly write what you ask. She is far too busy, and does not find the subject very interesting.

Malcom Muggeridge pleaded "pressure of work," Sean Connery regretted that he "did not have anything worth contributing to the book." Rayner Heppenstall recalled Johnson's previous anthology *All Bull* and suggested the new one be titled *All Cock.* Germaine Greer felt she must

resist the temptation to tell the story (which is droll and dull and ghastly) . . . Besides, he and I are still friends and sometimes even lovers . . . I wouldn't dream of retelling the story without the connivance of both him and his wife, who is one of my best friends.

Johnson's last commissioning letter reads:

is it 29th or 30th Oct 1973
I can't sleep anyway
Dear Delicious Ingrid Pit:

I was delighted, as I said, that you were interested in doing the piece for *You Always Remember the First Time;* and so sorry that you had so much trouble reaching me. As I told you, I have been in the middle of an absurd but deadly serious marital disaster since I returned from filming in Wales last Saturday; and god knows what happened before that.

But that is not the point, anyway.

I'm especially pleased to hear that your piece will be hilarious . . . You don't know how much I'm looking forward to reading what you write . . .

And thanks for the consolation about the universality of the marital condition,

Sincerely,

Johnson spent much of the rest of the week with Diana Tyler at MBA Agency's offices in Tottenham Court Road, or on the phone to her at home: "Bryan was very unhappy. Whatever had been talked about in counselling had obviously upset him. I told him Virginia just wanted a break, which was perfectly normal. But Bryan took it that she wanted out. I said that was an overreaction, but Bryan remained extremely disturbed about the whole thing. He had a very narrow view of marriage: everybody had to be faithful. He would not acknowledge that there could be other loves in people's lives. He thought there may have been somebody else in Virginia's, but he could not accept that it could ever happen."

Johnson's puritanical view of marriage is duplicated in Zulfikar Ghose's experience of his concept of friendship:

Bryan's demand for unquestioning devotion was a measure of his love.

The extraordinary intensity of Johnson's need for undeviating loyalty was matched by his terror of abandonment. His first great betrayal (as he saw it) had happened in 1939 when he was six, and evacuated at the start of the war. This italicised cry from *Trawl* he reprinted as part of his contribution to *The Evacuees*:

Why am I parted from my mother and sent away to live with strangers?

He worries about the reason, the causes, the extent of his rejection:

The worst would be that my mother had had enough of me and was glad I was off her hands and did not wish to see me back again . . .

(from *Trawl*)

Barry Cole believes "that that separation damaged Bryan irreparably. His references to it were constant and maintained the tone of dismal pessimism which invariably marked his depressions." Certainly, the idealisation of Mother and certain women able to play that role, and fear of betrayal by them, is a recurrent theme in Johnson's fiction.

Johnson's study of mother love in *See the Old Lady Decently* was based on his study of Erich Neumann's *The Great Mother*, which is quoted throughout the novel. This illustration is taken from the comprehensive collection of artworks that forms an appendix to the book.

DEMETER AND KORE
Stone, Thebes, Boeotia

[Demeter: Goddess of fruitfulness and marriage.]

The weekend of November 3 and 4, the Johnson family spent with the Buckmans at their cottage in the Oxfordshire village of Little Tew. This was a regular jaunt for them and was usually a happy time. With marital tension in the air, the prospects were not good, but Rosie Buckman recalls: "Bryan and Virginia were very civilised, there was no sniping between them, just maybe a shared sadness. The men went for long walks with lots of pub sessions. Virginia and I were left with the kids. Virginia just said things weren't going too well. She didn't want to talk about it. Anyway, with Steve and Katie, and our two, it was impossible to have a conversation with little kids rushing around."

Johnson's dismissal of the children was not like him, and a sure sign of something wrong. Normally, as Peter Buckman recalls: "Bryan was very good with children. He'd draw them into the conversation. It was never 'adults sitting here and discussing important matters,' with the kids scrabbling around on the floor being ignored." This is confirmed by countless references in Johnson's fiction. The narrative of *See the Old Lady* is interrupted from time to time, "as in life," by the advent of the author's daughter:

> During the above my daughter came up into my room, practising her writing before going to bed. BOOTS and SNOW are the words she likes best . . . Now she is drawing round her hand, one at a time, with my red pens, one after the other. Do you like this? She is fluttering the paper at my elbow, demanding attention. I give it her, telling her to put it where I can find an envelope for it in the morning. Suddenly she leaves the room, not saying *Night Night,* and the loss is   noticeable. I call her, she does not return. The loss is

The Johnsons were driving back on Sunday afternoon. They had packed up all their things, and the children were running into the car. Johnson came downstairs and he stood at the bottom of the stairs. Rosie Buckman: "Bryan stood there with this face, his face was always very expressive, and he had this hangdog look, that's the only expression, everything slightly drooped, his eyes terribly sad. He gave this funny smile and said, 'Well, maybe we're going to laugh about this one day.' Apart from goodbye, that's the last thing I remember Bryan saying."

A few days later the Buckmans received through the mail a copy of *Aren't You Rather Young to Be Writing Your Memoirs?* inscribed

> For Peter and Rosemarie
> with much love and such thanks
> on this unhappiest of days.
>   Bryan. 4.11.73

As an indication of his mood swings, or at least his ability to present different faces to different friends, Johnson sent this matter of fact note to Barry Cole on November 3:

> Dear Barry: Here's the letter I mentioned on the phone today. Hope it leads to something of mutual benefit—if it's any good I'd recommend Quartet as the first place to try it. Yrs B

Over the years, Johnson had sent hundreds of similar bits of advice to fellow writers. At a difficult time, it was typical of him to find time for this one.

That week, Johnson also sent £5 to his Union strike fund, to aid ACTT members locked out in the long-running Kodak Hemel Hempstead dispute. Like the note to Barry Cole, this seems a minor act of generosity. But, as personal chaos threatened, both actions were also tapping in to sources of strength in Johnson's life. His comradeship with other writers empowered him as well as them. His trade union activism was part of his allegiance to the working class:

The class war is being fought as viciously and destructively of the human spirit as it ever has been in England: I was born on my side, and I cannot and will not desert: I became an enlisted man consciously but not voluntarily at the age of about seven.

(from *Trawl*)

These old loyalties were threads that bound him to life. The marriage bond was breaking, and resulting tensions made work impossible. Johnson turned to the lifelines still there for him, friendship and habit. The two brought him naturally to the "Quartet" pub on Friday evening, where as usual he met John Booth of Quartet, and Diana Tyler, his trusted friend in good times and in bad. Johnson had in his arms a great bunch of red roses, to take back to Virginia. He left his friends in cheerful mood: "It's all going to be lovely now, tonight we're going to make love, and everything's going to be fine."

On the morning of Saturday November 11, Johnson phoned Diana at home. He asked her to come over to the house in Dagmar Terrace, the home he and Virginia had bought together in 1970. Diana found Johnson alone. He had no idea where Virginia was, she had left the day before and taken the children. "Bryan told me what he had done. He said he had become violent. At the time, it did not sound much to me, but clearly it had been enough to frighten Virginia. He told me to stay, he wanted somebody there, he did not want to be on his own, so I spent the day with him."

Although she had been there many times before, Johnson took Diana through the house. It was part of a modest terrace, but well designed and made, nicely furnished, with a cheerful aspect from the late autumn sun pouring through the windows. "Bryan showed me all his work, in his tiny attic study, on his desk, in the drawers. I thought, he's in a strange mood, he wants me to see everything he's written." Then he got on the phone to Samuel Beckett:

who of all living is the man I believe most worth reading and listening to

(*Memoirs*)

"Bryan rang nobody else that day. He kept trying to get through to Beckett.

"For lunch we went to the pub and had a drink. Bryan said, 'I think it would be nice to start again with somebody,' but he did not say who. He said he needed 'order' but whatever had happened on Friday night had been 'disorder.' I don't know, I could not work it out. He was quite dangerous that weekend, in a funny kind of way I sensed danger. Yet I did not think of getting help. I thought he was in control.

"In the early afternoon, Bryan said he was having dinner that night with an old friend he'd known in Paris: 'Before that I'm going up to have a sleep, will you wake me at four o'clock?' He put an alarm clock in front of me. I thought, 'Well, here I am, sitting here . . .' I read a book and woke him at four. Bryan came down and said 'I have to be at Ladbroke Grove by six.' I said, 'Well that's good, I will drop you off.' He said he would be staying the night. I was relieved to hear that because I did not want him to be on his own. As we left the house, he said, 'Wait a moment,' and he went back and put all the lights on. In the car he said he wanted to leave the house as if there were people in it, as if Virginia and the kids were still there. He did not want to get back on Monday to a darkened house."

Six years earlier, when he and Virginia were living in a flat in Myddelton Square, and they had one child only, Johnson had written, in *The Unfortunates*:

Steven will be in bed, but I can still look at him sleeping, my son, the warmth of returning, to Ginnie, to our son, the flat will be lit as I come across the Square, always stands out, as we do not have curtains, being on the second floor, and warm, Ginnie perhaps sewing, how oldfashioned a picture it seems, warmth, I can enjoy this for now, must, it is all there is.

That Sunday night, Johnson rang Diana from Ladbroke Grove to say he was OK. "For weeks he had been ringing me whenever he went anywhere or saw anyone. He seemed to be ringing every half hour. I said to my husband Bill: 'It's a good sign he's doing that.' Bill was the most understanding of people, but he did not quite know what was going on. Such things are not unusual in an agent's life, but this was extreme. Michael (Bakewell) was busy and unable to help, and anyway Bryan was asking for me not Michael, as if I had to be the one who was there."

Diana was watching over Johnson, but she did not think in terms of suicide. She trusted him, she trusted him to get through it. She knew where he was staying on Sunday night, and she had arranged to meet him at her office on Monday at four. She assumed they would have a drink after, as usual. He had to deliver a script to Thames TV beforehand, and he would not miss that deadline.

Unknown to Johnson, his wife had gone with the children to the Buckmans at Little Tew. She arrived on Saturday, towards the end of the day. She said there had been a bad scene between her and Bryan, he had been violent, he had "shown her a side she had never seen before." When the kids were playing together, she took Rosie to one side and said, "Look, I don't want to alarm you, but don't—don't open the door to anyone, and don't let the children out in the garden for the time being." She made sure all the doors were properly locked.

Peter Buckman: "We were frightened for the kids, and for ourselves, because of that vein of violence in Bryan that was always there, running just beneath the surface. I had seen it before, but never worried about it. That was the only time, because I was afraid he would come here with an axe."

A feature of Johnson's social life was the way his various groups of friends were kept separate, one lot being barely aware of the other's existence. So it happened that while Diana Tyler watched over Johnson during these difficult days, Barry Cole and another of Johnson's most loyal friends, the painter John Furse, were keeping an eye on him at night. The two shifts never overlapped, and neither knew what the other was doing.

At about six o'clock on the evening of November 12, Johnson phoned Barry Cole, as he did several times a week. They were near neighbors, and they went for a drink at Dirty Dick's around the corner. As usual, they played electronic bar football. Johnson was a fanatic player who hated to be beaten. He played with ferocity that night, pulling the little plastic levers, up to kick forward, down to bring the ball back. One lever had lost its plastic cover, so a little piece of steel jutted out. At about 9:30 Barry noticed his friend's left hand was bleeding. He suggested they call it a day, but Johnson, who was losing, played on. He wrapped his hand in a dirty handkerchief which was soon dyed bright red, and continued the game until closing time.

Barry Cole continues: "I went home with Bryan and stayed the night, to make sure he didn't do anything. For weeks John Furse and I had taken it in turns to watch over him, because Bryan had told us he planned to kill himself. I realised 'you can't stop someone taking his life' but I waited around while Bryan dressed his hand. I made coffee, and while we were drinking it I told him, 'People love you Bryan, they admire your writing.' But his eyes were blank, as if he hadn't heard a word, and I left about 2 AM."

For the next hours Johnson was alone in the house. He does not seem to have tried to find out where Virginia and the children had gone. The Buckmans were an obvious refuge, but he did not phone them. The weight of inertia and exhaustion counteracted any desire to go in search of his family. He could not pursue Virginia, he could only wait for her. In despair, home was the only place for him. It was the end of his wandering, the completion of The Great Round.

The Great Round

WHEEL OF LIFE
Painting, Tibet

(from *The Great Mother*)

On November 13, Michael Bakewell and Diana Tyler were having lunch at an Italian restaurant in Tottenham Court Road, when Diana was called to the phone. She recalls: "It was Ginny. I said, 'Well, where are you?' I was slightly cross in a way. I did not know where she was. She said she was back from the country, not at home but close by, and somebody should go into the house. I said, 'Oh, Bryan's fine. He said he'd be at the office at four.' She said, 'Well I think we should get someone . . .' She had obviously seen something, she had been in part of the house, or someone had, I don't know. I went back and told Michael and everybody brought us brandies."

Virginia had previously phoned Barry Cole, and while she was talking to Diana, he arrived. Barry went into the house and found the body. He dashed over to MBA's offices and told Michael and Diana. They took him to the restaurant where they had been eating, and Michael said, "Get this man a large brandy." Barry drank it, then left alone for his own home.

Shortly before he died, Johnson broke in half a painting by John Furse which had hung in his study for several years. Among the notes he left behind was one which explained the damage to the painting as "an accident." There was no will. Only a note stuck to a half-empty bottle of brandy: "Barry, finish this." Barry drank the brandy, then smashed the bottle.

When the Buckmans heard the news, they took some china plates into the garden and smashed them.

Mike Moorcock's response was a volley of curses: "That fucking man! That fucking man! That fucking sodding bloody bloody bloody man!"

Zulfikar Ghose was in Austin, Texas. He wrote later: "When I received the cable BRYAN DIED SUICIDE I said Fuck you Bryan and went out to the garden and found things to do muttering Fuck you Bryan I could not look at his books again gave away his letters to the university could not phone Virginia did not see her on subsequent visits to London because I did not want to see him not there and remain pissed off with him for ten years always muttering Fuck you Bryan and then writing this going to the library to look at his letters again ten years later the sight of them the humour the passion the rage ten years later taking down his books from the shelf and then writing suddenly at last I am crying like a bleeding child Fuck you Bryan."

Michael Bakewell remembered the change that followed the making of *Fat Man*: "When the film was finished Bryan suddenly cut himself off . . . everything kind of submerged after that. I felt a bit deserted, but so did everybody."

Samuel Beckett wrote to Michael Bakewell:

Paris
23.11.73

Dear Michael
    Thanks for yours of 14.
    I learnt the shocking grievous news at end of last week.
    I have had a brief card from Virginia.
    I missed T.C. in Paris.
    It wd be good to see you again, here or anywhere.
                          Best always,
                          Sam

Johnson left another note. It lay on his desk, in his study. Barry saw it but did not touch it. Virginia read it. It was handwritten in neat pencil, on a card about four by two. It had been composed with characteristic deliberation:

```
+---------------------------------------+
|                                       |
|  T  h  i  s    i  s    m  y    l  a  s  t  |
|                                       |
|                                       |
|                              w  o  r  d  |
|                                       |
+---------------------------------------+
```

Earlier that year, Johnson had written in *See the Old Lady Decently:*

I shall never buy a new pencil again.

And a few pages on:

The close of his life was infinitely sad . . . that short period was enough to prove to him that his high hopes were futile.

Earlier still, in *Trawl:*

It is too far to see faces: he must tell by their coats: fawn, blue, red, another blue, the red just like the coat that Ginnie has—Ginnie? Can it be her? She could not know what time I was due in, nor even which ship I was on, for I would not tell her. But she could have found out, if she had tried hard enough, of her own accord she might have tried to break my isolation in the only way it could be broken. Ginnie! But is it she? My eyes narrow, strain to see through the early-morning light, the mist, the shadows on the quay, to the face of that figure in red.

Through That Tunnell

John Calder

This short text has to be written under difficult conditions, with none of Alan Burns's novels to hand, in a hurry, when about to move offices, and it is based entirely on memory and impulse, on Alan's request.

Alan sent me a short novel about his time as a National Service Man, which I accepted for publication in the first issue, if I remember right, of *New Writers*, a series that continued for some years, introducing new writing that came our way. Each volume tried to combine different kinds of literature, experimental or not, occasionally poetry, short stories, work in progress of extracts from work we liked, but not enough to publish as a book on its own. It was called *Buster*, a short novel, and was in the vein of the "angry young man" vogue of the day, which included the work of John Osborne, Arnold Wesker, John Braine, etc., writing that usually dramatized the revolt of the generation that was coming from a working-class background, and having been given an intellectual education, by the Labour government, at the expense of the taxpayers (tax in 1950 was 97.5 percent on top incomes), then joined the middle classes, but were emotionally torn between their old and new values. The revolt was against middle-class attitudes and to some extent its culture. Perhaps David Mercer put the situation best in his *Generations* trilogy and later plays. The new arrivals were ambitious, pugnacious, left-wing, angry, and usually misogynistic about their newly acquired middle-class girlfriends and wives. All this reasonably well describes Alan Burns when I first met him.

There was a group that emerged at about the same time in Britain, including Ann Quin, Eva Figes, Bryan Johnson, David Mercer, and a few others that were aware, some more than others, of new European movements, the nouveau roman in France, the 47 group in Germany, the 63 group in Italy, or at least their forebears, and of course the new European cinema. Alan Burns was interested in surrealism in particular and was developing his own theories. *Europe after the Rain*, when it came to me, was very different from its predecessor, not a novel of revolt about class, but a revolt against the social novels and its associations, that consciously or not, owed something to those, like Michaux and Robbe-Grillet, who followed the surrealists, as well as to Max Ernst who gave the work both its title and its sense of shifting reality. It is still my favorite of his works. Kafka also has an obvious influence on Burns at this stage.

The novels that followed became first more abstract and close-knit, then moved into dada and parody, which I liked less. There was also a play about Jan Palach, the boy in Prague who burned himself to death at the Russian invasion.

By this time Alan had decided that he liked teaching and the output dropped, but my feeling is that he became rather lost after *Celebrations*, which followed *Europe*. Certainly *Europe* was the biggest success, but I feel it had something more, an originality and a drive that accurately caught the sense of dream and brought it into the nightmare of the waking realities of Nazi victims and those whom fortune does not favor. Alan's problem was too much literary ambition: he needed the sense of failure that Beckett described in his Duthuit Dialogues and the trilogy. It would have helped him to go through that tunnel that Kafka knew, where one's self-disgust squeezes out all the wanting to be admired and to write well, leaving a residue of disillusion which is the real viscous matter of art.

I think that Alan still has it in him to do something extraordinary. It has to start with pleasing himself, then finding it no good and going back to do it again. It must get close to the center of human anxiety and tragedy, because he understands that. I could write an essay on Alan, but would have to reread him again, and then think again. And in this philistine age . . . ! But perhaps it is about to end. I would like to see Alan heading the new renaissance.

Identity and Alan Burns

Paddy Kitchen

"The loss of identity today is so great that one only exists through the media. The kick one gets from being in the papers is quite profound—the contemporary god has registered one's existence." This is 1970. Alan Burns is talking to me for a short profile I wrote for the *Times Educational Supplement.* "My present mood is one of uncertainty. I don't want to make any pronouncement or statement about anything. 'Pass the bread' is as far as I can go, and I am not so sure about that."

Burns had recently published *Babel.* He described it as "A surrealist novel compounded of hundreds of aphorisms, newspaper clichés, poems, snatches of conversation and anecdote . . . the ultimate rejection of storytelling and psychology. I can't make confident statements about people, their relationships and their developing personalities, because I don't think it is possible to know another person. All one can do is select images. The reasons behind the particular selection and juxtaposition are mysterious in the sense they are not amenable to verbal description."

During the sixties, living in London, most of the writers I knew were antipathetic to conventional fiction. I didn't share their mistrust of the narrative novel nor their enthusiasm for experiment, but I couldn't dismiss their restlessness, their dissatisfaction, their need for the new. In fact I was often rather exasperated by myself and wished that innovative works such as *Babel* would alter my perception. "I want to work more like a painter than a writer," said Burns, "place images side by side and let them say something uncertain and fluctuating. This work will not be literary and will not lead to discussion or redefinition, but simply exist—like a Magritte painting."

What exactly was going on inside their heads, I used to wonder, while they were juxtaposing and juggling images that we weren't supposed to discuss? I felt the same about a lot of the painting of the time, wandering past acres of acrylic gesture and pawky assemblage and tending to remember only the odd anecdote—such as that of a cast of Jasper Johns's cock being included in a work by Robert Rauschenberg. I positively enjoyed discussing the narratives of novels with friends, and the narratives of their authors' lives—Forster, Sartre, Waugh, Colette, Lessing, Baldwin—writers who permanently stained me as I read them because their texts interacted with my psyche. They nurtured my nature. They helped me to identify it.

But there is a side to Alan Burns's work that did that too. My enthusiasm for *Buster*, Burns's first, short, novel, published in *New Writers 1*, was, I seem to remember, suppressed somewhat when the young editor at John

Calder, Dulan Barber (whom I later married), explained that Burns's second novel, *Europe after the Rain*, which was about to come out, was absolutely brilliant by comparison. Talking to me in 1970, Burns said: "I have a strong feeling I'm the kind of shit who battens on history or tragedy; in *Europe after the Rain* I made a good novel out of the concentration camps, which is a murderous thing to do." I can't (and I mean *can't* not *won't*) debate that one. The book was not, I think, one of the texts that made my cowering imagination begin to remove the screens between privileged English girl and the Holocaust forever, though it may have extended and toughened my grasp of the capabilities of prose with what I recall as its bleak, iron-cold, consistency. (My copy of the novel is missing. I must take that vow not to lend books.)

Buster is still here, sandwiched in its shocking pink paper cover between Monique Lange's *The Cat-Fish* and Dino Buzzati's *The Scala Scare*. I wasn't sure what to expect when I started to reread it, but I soon realized why I'd liked it so much, and I was doing so all over again. It's the male version of some of my own experience: war childhood, well-meaning philistine father with class aspirations, unfocused dissidence, isolation. It's crisply dramatized, with an economical and compassionate insight into all the characters, as well as opportunities for the prose to show its sparky paces. This might have been an Angry Young Man text, but the author's humor gently deflates his protagonist's naive rebelliousness and exposes the father's pretentiousness without rancor. The father/son relationship is more symbiotic than destructive.

The dialogue in *Buster* is lively and convincing. In 1970 Burns was creating a play, commissioned by Charles Marowitz for the Open Space Theatre. Its subject was Jan Palach, the young Czechoslovakian who publicly set fire to himself and died, "for freedom and democracy."

"His was an intensely private act," said Burns, "but was nevertheless designed to be talked about and thought about. Insofar as I am aiding his purpose on a small scale I am behaving properly and not improperly. The play upsets the normal relationship between the audience and the players. Physically the audience is placed in the centre of the theatre with four or five acting areas around it, creating a sense of continuous, scattered activity throughout the evening. They will sit close to some scenes and a long way from others, and will only be dimly aware of quite a lot that is going on. We will attempt to evoke the atmosphere created by the media which continuously bombard us with stimuli of every kind, with the result that before one event can be taken in and valued, its place is quickly taken by something else. I became poignantly aware of this when this boy concentrated the whole of his life into a few minutes of agony in order to make an impact on history. Even this ultimate martyrdom was negated in ruthless fashion by the media. It is the function of art to take up such things and give them their true value."

I went to the play with misgivings. Burns had said that the play was in a continual state of being rewritten according to the news of the day. I like plays with speeches that make the hair stand up on the back of my neck: rhythmic, wordy, set speeches. And as a member of an audience I like to be private, not part of an experiment. I don't know if there ever was a published text of *Palach*; certainly I carry none of it in my head. But there must have been profound language from the heart, for I had that experience of entering the theater empty and apprehensive, and exiting teeming and fulfilled. Jan Palach's agony had been honored.

With hindsight, I can suggest that Burns's responsive ear and innate understanding of life's inevitable narrative demonstrated in *Buster*, plus the ambitious, staccato globality of *Babel*, were both necessary for *Palach*. In 1972 came another collage/cut-up novel, *Dreamerika!* after which Burns felt, "I had fragmented myself out of existence."

His next book was the documentary novel *The Angry Brigade*, the chosen name for some loosely affiliated radical activist groups in Britain in the early seventies. It's a book that contains, quietly, much bedrock truth about the impossibilities, frustrations, responsibilities, and ludicrous arbitrariness of unstructured idealism and protest. It consists of segments of interviewing with six people, has no authorial observations, and the art lies in the way the segments are ordered to build character, to reveal the thread of narrative within the daily semichaos. It's pretty unputdownable; in comparison, cut-up novels are hard work. Links, not breaks, are what keep me going. Buckminster Fuller rather than Burroughs. *The Angry Brigade*, by gently revealing the thoughts and personalities of six utterly different, frequently incompatible—though occasionally joyously cooperative—young people, who are dissatisfied to the point of planned violence with the society within which they find themselves, widens understanding. Unfortunately most of it hasn't dated at all. It leaves, as Burns writes in a short introduction, the reader to "distinguish the various motives and attitudes of the speakers, and judge the quality of the men and women who took part in these events."

I do not know how much or how little Burns doctored the tape recordings of the six. He certainly orchestrated their sequence with the ear and understanding of a dramatist. He'd been trusted with the testimonies on condition he concealed all identities. "I therefore adopted the method of the 'collective autobiography.' . . . The collective nature of the book is appropriate to a movement whose members remain anonymous for ideological as well as legal reasons. They have a proper mistrust of leaders who hit the headlines." By protecting their anonymity and using his skills to perpetuate their complex individuality, Burns neatly sidestepped the media and preserved his subjects' identities. He hadn't pronounced, but he'd used some of the qualities that are evident in *Buster* to say a good deal more than "Pass the bread." And, as far as I'm concerned, had enhanced, intensified, his own identity.

Fine Cut: Alan Burns's Collage Prose

Ian Breakwell

In 1965 Alan Burns waded into the stale, tepid waters of English novel writing with a stunning book: *Europe after the Rain,* inspired by Max Ernst's panoramic painting of the same name which spanned the book's front and back covers. Written with relentless, dislocated urgency, this frightening postholocaust odyssey had immediate impact and influence on a small number of people, including me.

The same year Burns published *Europe after the Rain,* I left art college and entered a decade of experimentation in the UK which saw previously exclusive categories of artforms break down and coalesce. I was one of a number of visual artists who worked with painting, photography, film, and video simultaneously, culminating in multimedia presentations which were hybrids of theater, film and slide projection, music, light, and sound. Some of the sounds were words.

When visual artists used words, we naturally took fragmentation and nonlinear narrative for granted. William Burroughs instantly made perfect sense to me: it was collage using words instead of visual images. Yet the literary critics claimed he was unreadable, which was proof of Burroughs's contention that literature was forty years behind the visual arts.

In England very few novelists seemed to share Burroughs's understanding that the techniques of collage, chance, black humor, and free association of dream imagery pioneered by Dada and surrealism could be employed by contemporary writers to the same end: to liberate the imagination of both author and reader. The exceptions included J. G. Ballard, Joe Orton, Ann Quin, B. S. Johnson, and Alan Burns.

So it's not surprising that Alan and I soon met and subsequently worked together on occasion. I did the sets, of huge painted words, for his play *Palach* in 1970, and we collaborated again in 1981 on his book *The Day Daddy Died,* using a mail-order technique whereby Alan sent me sections of his manuscript in progress and I responded with a parallel narrative of photo-collages.

Before becoming an author, Burns had worked as a newspaper libel lawyer. He recognized that newspaper typography and layout produced a verbal and visual collage with parallel narratives and bizarre, chance juxtapositions on the same page. The average newspaper reader not only could cope easily with this simultaneity but might also choose to read from the back page to the front or from the middle out. The ephemeral literature of the street was more formally inventive than that in the bookshops and seemed to Burns more appropriate to the fragmented insecurity of the postatomic global village. He began to use the staccato, short sentence rhythms of news bulletins, overheard snatches of conversations and radio broadcasts, and magpie observations of the fractured world around him, manipulated by collage techniques to reassess the narrative structure of novel writing.

The two basic collage techniques are those of fragmentation and welding. The former, as in Picasso's cubist collages, lays out the component parts in jarring juxtaposition. The latter, exemplified by Ernst, disguises the joins and weaves the disparate elements into a stylistically seamless whole. It has been Burns's particular skill to evolve a hybrid linguistic form which oscillates between these two opposing methods. Thus he attempts to construct, like a mosaic, a fragmented yet cohesive novel.

Collage is sampling, and two popular contemporary genres are scratch video and rap music. Rap is insistently rhythmic, employs repetition, quotes from other music, radio, and TV broadcasts, and is fueled by righteous anger against the social injustices of capitalist society. Just like Burns? Well, sometimes, but most rap uses word forms still stuck in the doggerel of the playground and is all too often one-dimensional verbal diarrhea. Whereas Burns's legal eagle eye was trained to assess every single word, its weight, nuances, and potential multiple meanings. Burns perceived that collage was no pick 'n' mix salad, but a reductive craft for compressing language into surreal collision. Cut up, then cut down.

It's ironic that the word processor, that lazy tool for doing verbose, conventional writing more quickly, could also be a rigorous collage medium for writers like Burroughs and Burns who remain in the era of the manual typewriter, white out, scissors, and paste.

Twenty years and seven novels later, Burns again took an Ernst picture, the Tate Gallery's *Pieta ou la revolution la nuit*, as the starting point and cover illustration of his last published book, *Revolutions of the Night*, a subversive treatment of the novel's traditional subject, the family. The breakup of that family as seen through the eyes of the son and daughter is chronicled in a series of tableaux vivants based on surrealist paintings by Ernst, Magritte, Dali, and others. Burns links these dreamlike set pieces with terse dialogue, deadpan objective description, and the chopping prose rhythms that are now his trademark.

In *Revolutions of the Night* the eroticism remains heavy-handed, and some of the tableaux are too literal and mannered. Overall though, the disruptive prose style admirably suits the traumatic subject matter and jolts the reader's perceptions, often with macabre black humor. Burns lived for many years in Minneapolis, and weaving through the narrative are wickedly funny vignettes of his adopted homeland, as American as blueberry pie "and getting bluer by the minute."

Twice, Burns has used pictures by the master collagist, Ernst, as covers for his books. That he has, on neither occasion, suffered by comparison confirms his stature as an artist with words who can transform collage into poetic revelation.

A Note on Alan Burns's Fiction

Wilson Harris

Alan Burns belongs, I find, with a significant body of imaginative writers who are aware of legacies of tradition, in the art of the novel, that denote an impasse in narratives of realism. I perceive some measure of mutual association in his work with writers such as Alain Robbe-Grillet, Claude Simon, and Franz Kafka.

Kafka, a writer of genius, has established, I think, that the novel-convention—plot, beginning, middle, ending—has progressed to breed a predatory coherence. I have in mind works such as *The Trial* and *The Castle*. Kafka died in 1924 and both *The Trial* and *The Castle* were translated by Edwin and Willa Muir. They had not—as far as I am aware—appeared in his lifetime.

I use the term *predatory coherence* to signify an ultimate closure within systems of value built on absolute plot and linearity or progression forward in time which nullifies the past into historical pageantry and costumery, promotes the historical institutionalization of the past, preserves unresolved conflicts and unremedied injustices, until tradition becomes little more than a museum text with no vital bearing on the present and the future. What bearing there is festers in the unconscious with explosive consequences that seem to suggest that closed systems of value may be popular but they become increasingly irrelevant in their bearing on the crises of the modern age . . .

Plot is underpinned as well by the august notion in conservative humanities that absolute models exist which may claim governance over all strategies of the imagination. I have long felt that this posture is a misconception, a misreading of complex tradition, and that the genesis of the Imagination is peculiarly *unfinished*. I welcome therefore the findings of the Chaos philosophy and mathematics which speak now—rather haltingly perhaps—of an "open" universe in which the "genuinely new" may appear.

Yet curiously enough the sensation of "unfinished genesis" remains unfashionable in a postmodernist climate of values in which human discourse has become an absolute. Extrahuman voices—sprung from the rhythms and orchestrated imageries of living landscapes such as ancient epic once entertained—have been largely jettisoned by avant-garde intellectuals and also by traditionalists who prize the eighteenth-century/nineteenth-century novel-convention as a model for successive generations.

A curious paradox arises. Traditionalists and avant-garde intellectuals are sometimes uneasy bedfellows in the humanities. But a divorce or a distinction may be observed as they embrace each other. The avant-garde, postmodernist imagination celebrates closure in a nihilist and disturbing syndrome that rubbishes plot even as it surrounds itself again in the rubble of plot. The "openness" of the universe, the originality that may appear in such "openness," remains passive and inactive. The traditionalists have no qualms. They are wed to dogma.

All this helps, I feel, in approaching Alan Burns's fiction. He possesses considerable skill in the games that he plays with plot structures. Those games—and the rubbled texture they bring into play—may alert us I think to a progression that harks back to problematics which were visible in a nineteenth-century novelist such as Thomas Hardy, visible again in a twentieth-century novelist such as William Faulkner.

Hardy's plots are driven at times, it seems to me, by machineries of the Night of the soul (such as Samuel Beckett may have subconsciously visualized in his cautionary phrase *Imagination Dead Imagine*). Critics were alarmed at what they called Hardy's "inbred pessimism." It is not my intention to pursue this matter in detail but to draw attention to Burns's *Revolutions of the Night* which appeared in 1986. *Revolutions of the Night* brings closure or "nightfall" into bleak, unromantic perspective. Premises of romance that Hardy may have entertained become a wasteland.

Hardy's Tess progresses to the scaffold as if by jurisdiction or command of the fates. One senses or knows what is to happen long before it happens. If not the scaffold then descent into a void which encompasses her status from the day she was born. She is a pawn in the landscape upon which she moves. All alternative possibilities close as the plot advances. Her will is embodied in the author's absolute control or power. Thus the life of the unconscious—which may harbor unpredictable change in its eruption through the subconscious into the conscious—conforms to oblivion as Tess stands on the scaffold.

Burns fractures—so to speak—such plot but leaves the imprint of a vivid impasse. This is strikingly clear in the climax of paralysis that enfolds the novel *Revolutions of the Night* on its last pages.

The ruined town was like a continent after the flood. Masses of masonry and metal towered over rivers of bones and boulders, the trunks of trees, broken pipes and pylons, drains, poles, pillars, ladders, scaffolding, monumental gravestones, rusted machinery, worn-out engines, the rotting skins of animals and shreds of cloth, the skull of a buffalo, the skull of a horse, a siege of herons, a clamour of rooks, statues of princes mounted or on foot, an abandoned gantry, skeletal remains of old canoes, antlers, bedsteads, rafters, flowering heaps of rotten fruit, collections of corsets, an avalanche of carcasses, burning docks, a fairground, a forest, a quarry, an open-cast mine, an ocean bed, a lone pinnacle of bone. The colours were musty yellow, greyish green, winey purplish red, splashed with brighter green and crimson lake. A central stalagmite gleamed with gold, caught by the sun that shone from a pale-blue summery sky. The waters receded, the granite remained, carved by chance into the heads of lions and moustachioed men. Animals and humans made their homes in caves, in the ribcage of a mammoth or a whale. A man in skins, with the head of an emu, turned towards an armless girl, wisps of hair beneath her hat. Behind them a filament extended to the scaffolding above, from which hung a tattered flag. Caught between two pillars was a youth, blindfolded and gagged. Two women lived in a cave. The skirt of one was bright green, the other's gown and ornate hat had taken on the colour and condition of the deep-red rock.

An impressive aspect—it seems to me—of the above passage is its concordance with "graffiti" signs and drawings that one may encounter in the New York subway or upon ruined walls in the slums of great cities around the globe.

Thus Burns's fiction—it is just to say I think—reflects malaise, deep-seated malaise, at a popular and surreal level. The art of graffiti is older than one tends to think. It exists in caves and on the walls of ancient temples. Indeed the passage above offers insight, I would suggest, into the way Burns's fiction encompasses motifs drawn from many cultures. A "man in skins with the head of an emu" is staggered juxtaposition with "the statues of princes mounted or on foot." An entire civilization in dread disarray—I would venture to say—is the game that the fiction pursues in *Revolutions of the Night* and *Europe after the Rain*.

Burns's blend of surrealistic and realistic detail is wholly different from Hardy's elaborate prose and preoccupation with nineteenth-century hypocrisies, but the closure of a system of values is an implicit thread that runs through their different narrative strategies.

My concern is with the breach of "closure" as I have already indicated in this article. It is true—as I have also suggested—that "closure" asserts a peculiar irony in our age in that it is self-evident both in neotraditionalist, realistic as much as in surrealistic imaginations. But problematic linkages between Burns and other writers, outside of the obvious canon to which Burns belongs, may help us to sense a pressure for changed proportions beyond nihilism and postmodernism. Such pressure may be rooted in a potential breakthrough from, or breach of, neotraditional realism and closure. It may imply a different apprehension of the nature of tradition.

It may be rash to assert—on the basis of staggered juxtapositions of classical motif and primitive motif—that Burns's fiction may be informed by strategies of cross-culturality but I am of the view that this orientation does have a marginal yet significant role in his work. I mention this because I have in mind pursuing problematic linkages between Burns and William Faulkner and the black American writer Jean Toomer. Faulkner and Toomer express in their stream-of-consciousness techniques what I would call "musical graffiti."

I mentioned a moment or two ago, in this article, that Burns's "graffiti" brought to mind ancient markings and hieroglyphs that one associates with long-ruined temples and also with modern hieroglyphic utterances in line drawings in the subways and the slums of twentieth-century metropolises. The dichotomy is that the popular art of the graffiti endorses an endgame in its location or canvas in the modern city but it is also a defiance of the establishment, it is subversive, it is a silent lament. In certain respects this atmosphere of endgame and subversion is true of Burns's fiction. I do not have to stress how different this is from the sanguine temper of neotraditional realism rooted in eighteenth-century and nineteenth-century models.

It is necessary to remind ourselves that the eighteenth and nineteenth centuries marked a high, triumphant wave of European imperialism and the colonization of much of the globe. Such colonization was marked by a social conscience and the rule of law despite the Middle Passage and the indenture of Indian and Chinese servants within the British Empire. But a true cross-culturality between governors and governed, colonizer and colonized, was the exception not the rule. At best it assumed proportions akin to Keatsian "negative capability." The work of Herman Melville, the characters that are drawn into his fiction from many cultures, was a profound divergence from the Jane Austen or the Dickensian or the Tolstoyan novel. And Melville, as we know, was disregarded at the height of his powers. His last novel, *Billy Budd,* was not published until thirty-three years after his death. It appeared in 1924.

In Europe itself divergence sprang, I would say, from an unease of psyche and of homogeneous imperative which surfaces, I would suggest, in Blake and Baudelaire and Rimbaud. Whatever rebuttal of triumphalism we may associate with these great writers was subject to adverse criticism and was labeled *decadence.* This charge was addressed in particular toward Baudelaire and Rimbaud. Blake was disregarded.

Baudelaire's and Rimbaud's "decadence" was possessed of a longing to transgress frames and boundaries and to descend into other layers of the imagination but, by and large, though one may claim that they arrived on a frontier between worlds, Rimbaud's "drunken ship" was beached in the context of his age and never crossed that frontier. Blake also sought a marriage of contraries that would disrupt the carapace of hard-hearted institutions rooted in conquest.

I think it is clear that all this is pertinent to the strong framework of neotraditional realism and plot that remains as a legacy of colonialism and empire. But it would be folly to ignore a different apprehension of tradition through contraries or—shall I say—*latent cross-culturalities.* "Graffiti" in this sense are a signal of latent cross-culturalities and the tensions they invoke between endgame and subversive faculty . . .

How do we approach an equation between Faulkner's "musical graffiti" and Burns's "staggered plot?" I shall pursue this now. But first a quick reflection on the passage that I quoted from *Revolutions of the Night.* Within the context of the passage there is suppressed eloquence in the "youth blindfolded and gagged." Utterance is silenced. "Blindfold" appears in juxtaposition with "bright-green" and "deep-red rock." The atmosphere then is one of painted silence as much as of "gagged" prisoner . . . There are the "two women" with whom the passage associates "bright-green" skirt on a ground of "deep-red rock."

Such atmospheric colors or paint in association with silent or silenced utterance or song are not only appropriate to Faulkner's *Light in August* but are particularly relevant to Jean Toomer's *Cain* by which Faulkner may have been influenced when he came to write *Light in August*.

One of Toomer's brilliant sketches in *Cain* is called "Box Seat" and we come there upon a gaudily dressed woman (the colors of her dress may not match Burns's "bright green" or "red rock" exactly but they are reminiscent of his atmospheric extravaganza) who is escorted by a man destined to vanish or to be "gagged" by history. Toomer saw these figures as curious shadows upon a wall symbolizing a dying age; he was convinced that the music of the black American South was dying and would vanish entirely.

Faulkner extended and solidified these figures in *The Sound and the Fury* and *Light in August*. I do not wish to pursue these extensions but it may help—in the context of problematic linkages with Alan Burns's fiction—to reflect on the ominous configuration of a character called Hightower in *Light in August*. Hightower is a shadow on the wall of time. He is unable to bring comfort or relief to his hysterical wife whose moods are shot through by many implicit colors and feelings. Hightower is convinced that he is the progeny of a dead past. He is biologically alive but inherently doomed or finished. His grandfather was swept from his saddle to his death in the Civil War. That was the moment when seed and soul and future were destroyed.

Before I come to the problematic relevance such shadowy, tormented hieroglyphs or graffiti on the walls of history possess for Burns's fiction, it is necessary to say something about the paradoxes that are built into the music of the black South. Nathaniel Mackey deals with these provocatively and perceptively in a recent critical book entitled *Discrepant Engagement: Dissonance, Cross-Culturality and Experimental Writing* (Cambridge Univ. Press, 1993). The flexibility, the beauty, the spontaneity of the music of the black South seemed haunted by voices in the human yet other than the human. Scholars were unable to score or give formulaic precision to such music. All scores were approximations subject to revision. The earliest investigations of the phenomenon of "sound" and range and depth in such music occurred, it would seem, in the time of slavery in the nineteenth century. Mackey sees correspondences with ancient Mexican "orphan-song" that opens our senses to mysteries of tradition that lie outside of presumed norms, outside of progressive realism, linear bias, and plot . . .

I would suggest that whatever is or was Toomer's and Faulkner's self-conscious conviction of closure, their work differed subconsciously and in depth from the presumed norms of conventional fiction. The range and depth, implicit concordances, implicit dissonances, may sustain a key to other dimensions and to originality in an open universe. Hightower's conviction that he is the progeny of a plotted or fixed or dead past may run in contradistinction to bypassed or forgotten resources within tradition that sponsor an open universe. The latter premise of "openness" remains weak and frail and Hightower's sense of robot existence overshadows therefore the "orphan-song" and its significance in the depths of neglected tradition. Yet orphanage—which has its role in the overall texture and fabric of *Light in August*—bears on Alan Burns's surreal dramas. This may not be clear immediately, but in scanning his work the family complexes that he portrays seem to reflect a state of derangement, at one level, the orphaned state of the world at another. Parents and offspring alike loom as orphans.

Fictions such as *Revolutions of the Night* and *Europe after the Rain* portray families that are psychically affected by ruinous wars, famine, floods, droughts which come to occupy sometime, in minuscule forms, the affections and intercourse and everyday traffic, so to speak, running through the life of the family. The tendency is to throw a blanket over the forlorn condition of humanity and to turn our backs on the capacity of language to bring this home to us.

Burns portrays with skill and comic vivacity a terminal disease in the life of affections within the model family. The model caves in and we are drawn to the lip of the void:

There was a fire in the master bedroom, and the steamy candles spluttered. Martha squeezed and spanked his ears. Max stuffed something into her mouth; he hugged and kissed her too. The man Max would have a second son, but Martha somehow suffocated him. When she showed him her way of loving, he fell against a table. Then he heard her giggle as he cuddled her, slipping hot milk under her skin. With the table lamp back on the table, the pillows plumped at the foot of the bed, her small eyes curled when he licked between her toes. Her head bent back, her legs lifted, as he pushed her on to pillows slippery with semen. His table legs were added to the fire, his worn-out stumps crackled with pain. Eggs in hand, eating her dinner, her mouth ached from being muzzled.

They rearranged themselves. She looked into his eyes, yet seemed not to. She said she was obsessed with his moustache, his "moss between the stones."

The comic nerve of this surreal passage may conceal from us the moral gravity that informs it, the mouths in bed "muzzled" with food as they kiss in a famine-stricken world, the identification of sex with consumerism, hot milk, eggs, dinners, etc., the mechanics of the graveyard "moss between the stones."

May I hark back for a moment also to the matter of "graffiti" that I raised earlier. "Graffiti" are modern hieroglyphs. They possess a rhythm in their juxtaposition of the "real" and the "surreal." Burns's work may well possess a subconscious currency rooted in the dance of the hieroglyphic . . .

It is arguable that his dramas do indicate a closure or termination—as I have already implied in this article—but a stark moral gravity remains. Questions arc raised which go beyond surrealism. There is the deep question of the endangered life of the imagination in a grossly materialistic age rubbing shoulders with horrendous deprivation and polluted environments in many areas of civilization. There is the necessity for the imagination to press against a quantum chasm in creation in order to voyage into unsuspected resources for originality, the originality of community beyond the fixtures of endgame realism . . .

Burns's Aleatoric Celebrations: Smashing Hegemony at the Sentence Level

Charles Sugnet

Is social change more likely to be produced by a "committed," "relevant" literature that reaches a large audience by observing bourgeois conventions like character development, linear narrative, and closure? Or by a literature that uncompromisingly shatters the false and coercive coherences of nineteenth-century fiction? Believe it or not, many beers were downed in the 1960s and into the 1970s by impassioned discussants of this question, which continues to be debated in the academic literature: Can something called postmoderism and something called politics exist in the same space at the same time? Alan Burns seems to have devoted very little ink and time to polemics on such questions. In fact, he taught his writing students here at the University of Minnesota the craft of the old conventions so effectively that some of them were surprised to discover he is an "experimental novelist" (to use the standard marginalizing term of that period).

Yet the body of Burns's work makes it clear where he stands: he has always been uncompromisingly political and uncompromisingly avant-grade at the same time; the work demonstrates at the sentence level Burns's conviction that these two positions are inseparable. In a remarkable essay called "Writing by Chance,"[1] Burns described his own "aleatoric" method of (de)composition, largely by describing the working methods of other artists whom he chooses as predecessors and colleagues. In an essay filled with references to visual artists like Kurt Schwitters, Pablo Picasso, Max Ernst, Henry Moore, and Jim Dine, Burns works through the problem of chance versus order in a very sophisticated way.

Speaking of Schwitters's collage work, Burns notes that even in Schwitters's "spontaneous accumulation of junk, there was an element, only partially suppressed, of selection. It wasn't any old tram ticket that found its way into the studio . . . he kept what caught his fancy, and in his fancy the dim forms of future collages were taking shape" (11). Burns too is a recycler of junk, and his rubbish heap also has an element of selection. It's hard to generalize, but it seems to me he likes to collect from the following areas:

• politics, world events, war, the headlines, clichés and vapidities of the press;

• anything to do with repression by regimentation and system (schools, factories, the military); professional jargon, specialized languages of various disciplines. Long before Foucault's *Discipline and Punish*, Burns saw how these institutions organized themselves around forms of language, discourses, and he was trying to subvert them. Before writing "Wonderland,"[2] he studied texts relating to factory discipline, especially in the big Ford plants of Britain. (One mode of subversion he often uses is to displace one discourse onto another; later in the "Chance" essay, he lets on that he, himself a lawyer, described the lawyers in *Celebrations* via a treatise on the mating habits of grasshoppers!);

• overheard bits of speech, rhythms of trivial conversation, people talking to themselves;

• pop culture icons and phrases, including the language of advertising. The all-purpose public female figure in *Celebrations* is named Jacqueline; in later works, like *Babel,* the text almost disintegrates into clippings of such material;

• public ritual, such as the Kennedy funeral;

• texts showing the vulnerability, weakness, and simultaneous tenacity of the individual human confronting the system. Burns gives little room to sentimentality in his work, but the violence of the state and the economy is almost always shown in relation to the family, the body, the home. This is by no means a simple Dickensian opposition of domestic virtue to public evil; family tyranny flows over into the public sphere and vice versa.

Note also the emphasis on psychology in the description of Schwitters's process—something is happening "in his fancy." Burns seems to alternate between the belief that chance is really random and the classical surrealist position that chance will reveal a different order, the order of the subconscious, of the obsession. He quotes painter Jim Dine's description of working "in a hallucinatory state without drugs" (11) approvingly. And speaking of Oldenburg, he talks of "a mumbling, grumbling, sifting, searching, meandering between the conscious and the unconscious" (11), a phrase that could easily be a description of Burns's own way of working. He seems to work in a private, trancelike state; in interviews, he has spoken of writing parts of *Europe after the Rain* by looking at a copy of the Ernst painting with his eyes deliberately unfocused—certainly a technique for deranging the senses. While many writers complain of the difficulty of writing, Burns always speaks of it as an intense, serious form of play that delights him and gives him pleasure. For him, the hardest part is not the writing, but the making a living out of it: the grantsmanship and self-promotion.

For Alan Burns, then, the aleatoric is not a purely mechanical randomness. There's selection at work in the gathering of materials, and there is the operation of "fancy," whatever that is. In the "Chance" article he differentiates himself from Burroughs and others who place more emphasis on the technical methods of cultivating chance, the batteries of tape recorders, the cameras, the filing systems, the scissors. There's a bit of boundary-minding going on here, as Burroughs has received so much publicity for inventing the "cut-up method," and Burns has sometimes unfairly been seen as following him. Burns, in fact, believes that each developed his chance methods of composition independently, and if one looks at the impact of surrealism on the arts in our century, it's perfectly reasonable to suppose that this happened. Next to Burroughs's tape recorders and steamer trunks, Burns sets a much homier image of his own way of working: "Four of my own novels were written this way—I leave slivers of paper on my desk with the window open, or a cat or a three year old allowed in to further the random order" (12).

In each of the several homes he occupied in Minneapolis, Alan had a room with a desk or a table, yes, but also with planks on sawhorses or disused doors on cinder blocks—anything that would create a horizontal surface for the juxtaposing and rejuxtaposing of small pieces of paper in space. I have an image of him, whether remembered or invented I cannot say, composing *The Day Daddy Died* on foot, darting back and forth among these makeshift tables with bits of text. What's striking about this way of working is how visual and spatial it is. He refers constantly to painters, and there's a sense in which his own works really are collages assembled in a single place. He quotes Henry Moore's dictum that "Every material has its own individual qualities" (11), and for Burns this is true of language as a material too. I remember him once showing me a (temporarily) finished sentence, and remarking how nicely the vertical line of an *h* rising early in the sentence was balanced by an *l* later on.

For all the operation of chance or trance or the unconscious, Burns frankly acknowledges that each of the four novels supposedly composed by the cat and the three year old has the same family pattern of "powerful father, absent mother, a brother who dies young" (12). This is partly due, no doubt, to the selection of materials the cat and the three year old were given to work with and to the way the unconscious manifested itself through them, but it is also due to what Burn calls the "vital second stage" of chance of composition: the stage of selecting and arranging, of choosing the good bits from the chance combinations and of looking for patterns in the material. Though his methods are postmodern and he is never pompous about the religion of art, Burns does inherit the modernist notions of discipline and perfection. He used to tell beginning writing students at the University of Minnesota that they must spare no effort to make their work the best it could possibly be. He often used the example of retyping a whole novel to improve a single detail, and you could see the students shifting in their chairs, thinking about a different career choice. But he recognizes that you can revise too much as well: "Each successive draft coasts closer to rationality, leaves further behind the risk-taking original" (12). The trick, he says, is to know when to stop revising; if you go too far toward rationality, you spoil it.

What are the actual results of this compositional technique in a book like *Celebrations?* The novel says, "A split family liberates energy like a split atom,"[3] and one can say the same thing about a split sentence or a split paragraph. One hell of a lot of energy is released in *Celebrations,* a book of grim humor where the father of the groom, at the wedding reception, French kisses the bride he's just given away, where Jacqueline's hair turns blue as she becomes a media star, and where huge crowds of factory workers storm about, either in revolt or prepackaged recreation—it's hard to tell which is which.

It's also a challenging book, which leaves the reader with more work to do than usual. Burns builds several rueful self-referential jokes about this right into the text. Early on, Williams says to his son and the reader, "This is riddle talk, you don't appreciate that I'm checking your reflexes" (12). Not long after, Jacqueline complains to Williams that "There's an odd paragraph here, I don't understand it at all" (32). Much later, "Williams realised that . . . he could not complete the work, it capsized. . . . [T]he muddled sentences revealed the strain" (86). Jacqueline tries to tidy up his papers and tells him, "The words are in disorder, there is no sense, you are not in the mood" (87). This strand of the text reflects Burns's lifelong struggle with himself and his audience over how to conduct that vital second stage, over how much accessibility is too much.

Celebrations is about a lot of things, but one of them is disrupting the industrial assembly line, as in Chaplin's *Modern Times*. In the opening pages workers in an assembly line all dream of the same woman; they spend their recreational time playing with machines in an arcade which is indistinguishable from the factory itself. Work, play, and pleasure have all been subjected to a Fordist discipline. Burns knows that the ultimate assembly line is the predictable sentence, and he fights to subvert it. Here is Williams, the patriarch and factory owner, in the first paragraph of the novel: "The break-up of his team of men worried him too, he was a gambler waiting for something to snap, for success or failure, it was a matter of routine." A characteristic Beckett sentence goes on by negating or deconstructing something it has just said. A characteristic Burroughs sentence might rise toward stock voices (the Southern sheriff, Doctor Benway, etc.) without ever stabilizing them or might flirt with the conventions of genre fiction. This characteristic Burns sentence is technically what an American composition teacher would chastise as a "run-on sentence" or a "comma splice," with three main clauses and no conjunction. In ordinary speech, the comma is placed between thoughts that follow, one from another. In this sentence there's the tension of "waiting for something to snap," the dramatic opposition between "success" and "failure," and then the flattening "it was a matter of routine," which appears to contradict everything that went before. It's as though the comma were not a simple connector, but a wormhole between unrelated universes.

Or maybe not. Maybe gambling and dramatic risk are in fact routine for big capitalists. It's easy to read the flat style of such a sentence and simply nod, but the fact is that Burns's comma leaves the reader to decide the relationship(s) among the clauses; nothing is taken for granted. And there are many such commas: "The music and commentaries slid easily on, nothing had changed for the corpse" (18). "A speech was made, it did not matter what was said" (40). "In his office Williams sat in his chair, his unhappiness alarmed him" (55). "Though he was cooped up, he led a complete life, he was capable of limited movement" (94). The commas mark out a poetry of disjuncture, which gives an appearance of going on, of narrative progress (or at least accumulation), but which does not really narrate.

This style also works to keep the characters separated; when Williams dies, his son and the daughter-in-law with whom he has had an affair are described this way: "They had hardly known the old chap, they had kept in touch, they were three who met at Christmas" (97). In one context the disjunctive and contradictory style has an almost mimetic effect, as Burns recreates the kind of nonsense noise that gets so many of us through the day. Williams the industrialist in full cry: "I was fixed on this job from the start. Once I make a start I like a tremendous amount of thinking before I start" (36). The dying Williams after a life of savage relations with others: "I've got the same energy I always had. People are so kind, that's why I want to get back and meet more people, I like people, I'm always doing something, I come and go, that's what is so wonderful" (93). Or Michael, who outlives his father and brother: "I have a thing which I call time. . . . Sometimes it's longer, sometimes shorter. In one's mind. . . . I prefer to think I have attained a sort of philosophy of life" (102).

Usually, however, the effect of chance is not mimesis but its opposite— striking, unusual phrases like, "he kissed God's sinewy arse, his ankles felt the cat" (99), or "The cathedral had the walk of a woman in love" (59). Or "The size of a man's desk can be crucial" (77). Sometimes the disjunctive clauses connect to form a sentence of almost old-fashioned poetic beauty: "Carry the dead gently, it rains and rains" (103) or "The morning rains were green across the hills, the trees would begin to bloom in five minutes" (77). In "Writing by Chance" Burns praises Burroughs and at the same time describes himself: "On his [Burroughs's] desk the adjective that has grown stale in constant company with the same noun now lies there on its own. Next to it flutters down a new noun, rather, a noun new to its neighbor, the two get acquainted, flirt, marry" (12). Who could have predicted the courtship between "God's," "sinewy," and "arse"?

As with Burroughs, one effect of Burns's style is often a technical pseudoprecision: "This thug knew the texture of a truncheon. The blow must be directed upwards, with force to meet force" (35-36). "We are definitely getting on top of the problem. One can only assume that the heat intake is safer. Six hundred killed each year represents a statistical average of nought point four. The story is typical of modern high speed production methods" (110). Naturally, bodies are talked about as though they were machines and vice versa, but neither the human body nor the gleam of malevolent technology seems as eroticized as in Burroughs's work. When Williams's first son dies, "Phillip was pulled from the bed, his body opened and the parts numbered. It was impossible to make a mistake: it was efficient and peaceful" (17). The disciplines are at least as comfortable with the dead as with the living! And the flat cruelties of Burns's universe owe more to Linnaeus, Bentham, and Ford (probably via Kafka) than to de Sade.

At the crux of a celebration, such as Michael's wedding, the random method, revised by the "vital second stage," produces a style that is positively festive in its variety. As the bride kisses the groom's father:

> Then, her lips waves, she came to him and he to her. The extraordinary kiss was seen, the explosion was unquestionable. She tried to eject the tongue, it would become embarrassing. His tongue was short, then elongated, no explanation was offered. The tongue did not return, it was dispersed in space, grown and lost. . . . Once a tongue moves outside the family, it dies. She felt the tongue had a stony shell, the inner composition was not known. The presence of fluid could be explained, the deep mouth contained life, microscopic animals, one upon another. The probing of his tongue was hard, she wished it to become fluid, why is not known. When the skulls of men are found there is only bone. . . . [T]he increase of love, the love set free, the action of family love was not considered. (66-67)

The cliché moment of kissing the bride is opened out textually toward Freudian notions of family dynamics, toward reflections on mortality, toward reminders of the opacity of the body, etc. It's difficult or impossible for a reader to have a simple reaction: what's happening is funny, it's uncomfortable, it's morally repugnant, it's grotesque, it's interesting, and it raises questions rather than answering them.

What I've just said about the wedding scene can be applied equally well to the whole book. It's hard to talk about characters in a novel where the imaginary people are just contradictory bundles of textual references, but even so, the characters evade simple reaction. Williams starts out as the patriarchal tyrant, oppressor of his two sons and of the workers in his factory. He never stops being that, but he also becomes a comic-ardent lover, a confused old man, and a corpse squeezed into the back of a small car. His Lear-like (is that King Lear or Edward Lear?) transformations crack him open to vulnerability. The very same greed, energy, and tenacity that make him appalling also make him interesting and perhaps even a little admirable.

Jacqueline appears at the start to be a ridiculous two-dimensional pop art figure available to all three men for sexual and mothering needs. But she has more agency and power than meets the eye; sometimes she does what she wants and the men wait their turn. After being fondled and probed by the press and all the men in the book, she outlives the father and the two brothers, having the last chapter to herself and arriving in a mountainous place where "she was glad there were none of those tongue-twisting words, nor was she asked to peel off her clothes and show her white skin" (116). This is the novel's last sentence, after which there are no more tongues, no more words, no more twists—only the blank white remainder of the page. In a book where funerals are raucous and weddings are tragic, oppositions dissolve and maybe Jacqueline has had this modest desire for concealment all along, in spite of Warhol and her blue hair.

Near the end of "Writing by Chance" Burns offers a statement that sounds as close to a manifesto as anything we are likely to get from him: "The bold use of chance is a liberating experience; it is also fundamentally democratic and anti-elitist" (12). *Celebrations* bears this manifesto out at the level of the sentence and the phrase.

NOTES

[1]Alan Burns, "Writing by Chance," *Times Higher Education Supplement*, 29 January 1982, 11-12; hereafter cited parenthetically.

[2]Alan Burns, "Wonderland," in *Beyond the Words*, ed. Giles Gordon (London: Hutchinson, 1975), 69-85.

[3]Alan Burns, *Celebrations* (London: Calder and Boyars, 1967), 98; hereafter cited parenthetically.

Right You Go, Left with Burns

Zulfikar Ghose

The author's prefatory remark that his story "is told naturally in different tones of voice and different accents" could appropriately introduce any well-made novel such as a Trollope or a Hardy might write, except that in *their* work such an announcement would be redundant, but coming on page 3 of Alan Burns's *The Angry Brigade* it is an announcement that a Trollope or a Hardy kind of novel this precisely is not but rather one written in a self-consciously new form.

The work of fiction is announced on its title page as "A Documentary Novel." Facing page 1 is what looks like an epigraph but is an unattributed quotation apparently calculated to arouse curiosity: "The true story of the Angry Brigade will never be told until they publish their memoirs . . . if they ever do." It is a statement that conveys the reverse of what it sets out to suggest; the reader guesses that what will follow will indeed be the memoirs of the Angry Brigade and feels himself the privileged possessor of their true story and therefore his desire to read the fiction is heightened. That desire is partly frustrated and at the same time heightened afresh by the information on the opposite page which purports to be a quotation from a newspaper and is printed as a newspaper column, so that it is literally seen as a document and therefore a validation of "the true story." The column, with its statement, "Who then was responsible for the Post Office Tower bombing . . ." etc., intensifies the impression of historical truth. By referring to the fact that there are more groups of the Angry Brigade than have been identified by the police, the press report serves the function of setting up an expectation in the reader of his being about to enter a complex and perhaps terrifying mystery.

Pages 2 and 3 contain a statement (there is no title—such as "Author's Note" or "Preface") at the end of which are the initials A.B., presumably standing for *Alan Burns,* but fortuitously they are also the first letters of the *Angry Brigade.* The statement, beginning with the somewhat chilling remark, "The press report is accurate," describes how the documentary work has been put together. In a very matter-of-fact voice, A.B. explains: "In the course of writing this book I made contact with two groups: a gang of London street kids living virtually as outlaws, squatting in derelict houses; and a small group of intellectuals who combined a 'straight' life with intermittent urban guerrilla activity." The author's working procedure is explained —interviews with six people, tape recordings, concealed identities, the creation of what is portentously called the "collective autobiography." All of this is a signal to the reader that the book in his hands is not a fiction but truth itself and has therefore to be read with urgent and serious attention, for the very future security of the state might depend upon it.

Concurrently with this signal that he is about to receive privileged information the correct comprehension of which is vital to prevent social catastrophe, the reader is being sent another signal: the author is a *new* novelist, one with a radical imagination which is not content merely to tell a story but proposes to engage the reader's mind with a formal subversion of the traditional novel in order to create a more persuasive literature.

The first effect of this technique is to eliminate the presence of the author, a result which was Flaubert's ideal—"I do not want my book to contain a *single* subjective reaction, nor a *single* reflection by the author" wrote the author of *Madame Bovary* to Louise Colet. The convention established that the reader is in possession of a transcription of tape recordings in which living persons recall crucial events in their lives that were of some significance in the social history of England; it is as if one directly witnessed the raw experience without the author intervening to color one's view of the events with his own prejudice.

This pretense of the *new* novel to be the impartial recorder of history, with, as Flaubert would have it, the author's personality absent, is, of course, as old as the English novel and goes back at least to the author of *Robinson Crusoe,* who called himself an editor of another man's account of his real experience, using the device of the preface with which to dispose of the presence of the author. Defoe claims in his preface: "The editor believes the thing to be a just history of fact; neither is there any appearance of fiction in it," a remark that has the same intention as A.B.'s prefatory statement of not so much suspending as entirely eliminating the reader's disbelief. In another famous eighteenth-century novel, the French *Les liaisons dangereuses*, its author Laclos uses the same device of announcing himself in a preface as the editor, in this instance of letters which he has selected and annotated. His editor's preface is preceded by a publisher's note, so that by the time the reader comes to the first letter, the author's presence behind his work seem completely to have been suppressed.

The notion of the author as a detached—sometimes even reluctant—editor of a record of someone else's life is not an uncommon one. A notable example in contemporary fiction is Thomas Berger's *Little Big Man* where the author goes one step farther than Defoe and invents a "Man of Letters" who, rather than the author, functions as the editor of another "real" person's extraordinary confessions. The text which follows is typically a first-person narrative, using the speech appropriate to the character to sustain the pretense that the editor has maintained the integrity of the history entrusted to him, which is another way of saying to the reader that he can be confident that he has the absolute truth in his hands. In Berger's prefatory chapter, entitled "Foreword by a Man of Letters," Ralph Fielding Snell, the invented man of letters, writes of his character Jack Crabb's story: "As to the text: it is faithful to Mr. Crabb's narration as transcribed literally from the tapes. I have subtracted nothing . . . ," an assertion calculated to offer a guarantee of truth and to sustain the notion of the editor as a scrupulous, disinterested, and incorruptible scholar.

The illusion that Defoe, Laclos, Berger, and Burns succeed in creating is that the novel which each has so artfully invented has a spontaneous existence generated by some big bang in the past of which he happens to have been the accidental witness who then feels pressed by a societal obligation to make a full report of it. Laclos's epigraph from Rousseau—"J'ai vu les mœurs de mon temps, et j'ai publié ces Lettres"—underscores the implication common to the device of the author as editor that the work which the author has been at pains to assemble after assiduous research is of immense moral value to society. The more prurient his subject matter the more solemn is his prefatory declaration that he is, in Laclos's words, "rendering a service to public morals to reveal the methods employed by those who are wicked in corrupting those who are good."

A second effect of the technique of making the author merely an editor is to accomplish the subtle trick of eliminating the impression that the opinions of the characters are really the author's, that the characters are only propagandist puppets for his beliefs. This is all the more important when the novel, as is the case with *The Angry Brigade,* contains political subject matter. Yet another effect is to relieve the author, especially one with pretensions to being a *new* novelist, of a personal responsibility to his text, which, the reader has been conditioned to believe, owes its existence not to his invention but to his intervention, tape recorder in hand, in the lives of real people.

The text of *The Angry Brigade* is made up of a transcription of interviews with six people, young men and women, the drug-taking members of the so-called counterculture, engaged in urban guerrilla warfare in England in the 1970s. The first, Barry, is from a working-class family; another, Ivor, had a working-class mother but a father "who came from quite a rich Jewish family"; a third, Mehta, has for his father a businessman in Bombay who, he says, "is a religious Catholic." The reader, having been conditioned by the book's prefatory matter that he is reading the truth, indeed hearing real voices, scarcely notices that there is hardly any uniqueness in the voices; several times, when the recorded interview is long, one finds oneself having to go back to the beginning of the section to remind oneself who is talking. For example, "My father is working class, he never had any money, although he comes from an intelligent background" spoken by Barry (5-6) and "My father and I never had a political confrontation because he is not a capitalist in the sense that he is only there to make money" spoken by Mehta (25) have little detectable variation of tone and convey no sense of two separate voices, even though Mehta, with his Indian origin, would in reality have possessed a very differently accented speech from Barry's. There would also be grammatical oddities in the real Mehta's speech in spite of his having grown up in England. The old-fashioned novelist—a

Flannery O'Connor type, say—would take pains to make the speech sound authentic and would also not make the mistake of giving the Hindu name Mehta to a character whose father is emphatically stated to be a religious Catholic. Nor does one hear any distinguishing nuance between the male and the female voices; especially in some of the longer passages (e.g., Jean on 101-05, Ivor on 118-26), where the speaker talking about herself-or-himself also has to serve the author's need to proceed with the larger narrative, the individual voice becomes inaudible behind the general uniformity of her or his speech.

But remarkably—such is the force of the technique—the reader remains largely unconscious of the general uniformity of speech. Instead, what the technique of the author's having become an editor has succeeded in doing has been to create in the reader's mind an undoubting belief in the reality of the characters and is consequently making the reader hear individual voices when in fact there is only one voice, a fairly cultivated one at that, in spite of the attempt to maintain a working-class intonation, that of Alan Burns. From time to time, an element is used—the familiar device of scatological speech—to suggest the impression of the voice of a unique individual. For example, "We'd get into really heavy shit when we barricaded up, but everyone wanted it. We said, fuck it, we've had enough of this shit" (100); but a moment later even this voice slips into the uniform speech: "But there was no point going on arguing with wealthy men who would hang on to their wealth whatever we said about social justice." But the reader does not notice because the little nudge of the scatological phrases has reinforced in him the sensation of hearing an individual voice. And his firmly established sense that there is no author behind the words he is hearing also helps to relieve the author of any responsibility for any factual errors, such as the Christian Mehta, that might creep into the text. The author's careful attention to his form makes certain that no failure in the text is seen to be his fault; his execution of it is so persuasive that one feels convinced that had he been writing a traditional novel, then these failures, which are now there only because that is how each character spoke into the tape recorder, would have been eliminated because his approach then would have been to shape reality according to his own plan, making him responsible for the truth of what he created, whereas now he is only the passive recipient of a reality as envisioned by others and therefore not in a position to question the truth thus recorded.

Laclos, in his editor's preface, anticipated the criticism of stylistic inconsistency by writing: "I had proposed more considerable alterations, almost all of them relating to purity of diction and style, which will often be found very much at fault. . . . This course of action was not approved," because the purity of the original, however faulty, had to be preserved. The same claim is implicit in A.B.'s prefatory statement of method.

Most important, in a novel like *The Angry Brigade,* with its politically charged subject matter, it is essential that the author not appear to be the mouthpiece of some particular ideology which, whatever its appeal to one group of readers, is bound to be offensive to another group. The technique of absenting himself from his text again comes to the author's rescue: he is not responsible for what is spoken by individuals, for all he has done has been to hold a microphone to their lips. The crucial consequence—and this is why the novel succeeds and is, in fact, a *new* work—of this technique is to make the entire sequence of interviews take on an ambiguity which the individual speakers never intended, and it is this ambiguity which creates the particular "adventure," to use Henry James's term, of the novel called *The Angry Brigade:* the technique converts the sequence of interviews to a literary text in which the several voices become one voice that requires to be interpreted to be understood.

The group of young men and women who form the book's "collective autobiography" appear at first to be idealistic, filled with contemporary—post-'68 Paris—clichés about revolutionary politics, taking over derelict buildings as squatters, given to peaceful demonstrations and sit-ins, and so on. Ardent and naive, they hunger for a new society which, Fidel-like, it is their destiny to rebuild out of the rubble of decadent capitalism which they must first destroy. They believe themselves to be that special generation that has been singled out to be present at that momentous *either/or* time in history when society is either about to be transformed to their fulfilled dream of a Marxist paradise or about to be overwhelmed by a fascist tyranny. While the several voices speak at the common level of naive expectations, the combined voice that is the larger text of the novel converts the somewhat pathetic and clichéd talk of the individuals into the universal anxiety of the young. For example, Ivor states the contents of his confidential letter in which he gives his instructions for invading the Ministry of Housing in Whitehall; it is a two-page document with its cautionary preface:

URGENT AND STRICTLY CONFIDENTIAL

Please do not communicate the contents of this letter to anyone unless you seriously think you might be able to recruit him or her for the action. (93)

Readers who are in sympathy with Ivor's cause will listen to this call and to the instructions which follow addressed to "Dear Comrade" with the utmost solemnity and will be filled with admiration for the young men and women who answer the call; they will feel convinced that the author "speaks for them." On the opposite side, there will be readers who, believing that anyone, even in the 1970s, who addresses his followers as "Dear Comrade" is too silly to be taken seriously, will see Ivor's document as an example of the foolishness of the young and will be convinced that the author's intention was to ridicule them and that therefore, these readers will believe, he "speaks for them." For the first group, the presentation of Ivor's document will be proof of his heroic stature and of the author's liberal socialism which they will applaud as mirroring their own; for the second, Ivor's document will be proof of his puerile mind which is incapable of intellectual thought beyond a shallow copying of current revolutionary practice, and these readers will applaud the author for being a courageous satirist. The author, however, has said nothing at all; he has only presented, without comment, a document; and when he hears applause from both sides which claim him as their own special spokesman, the author need do nothing but maintain an ambiguous smile suggesting his satisfaction with readers whose prejudice is none of his, the author's, business.

The author can say, as does Lermontov in the middle of *A Hero of Our Time* where he, also adopting the role of the author as an editor, presents his hero Pechorin's journal, "It is only from a wish to be of service that I am publishing these extracts from a journal which came into my possession by chance." The author is a good citizen with a strong sense of moral duty. There is a moral in his book for politicians of both the Right and the Left to claim as their own, but he can say with Laclos, it is "not for me to offer an opinion which neither can nor should influence that of anyone else." He himself must remain silent and pretend that he is not there, except as the hand that holds a microphone to the many voices of truth.

WORK CITED

Burns, Alan. *The Angry Brigade*. London: Allison and Busby, 1973.

In His Own Alan

Michael Dennis Browne

Alan's prose has always interested me. Sometimes it has driven me mad. "He hugged her with an arm that weighed heavy. Though the boy was thin, his arms were strong. Now the big lad grew." As I told Alan once, it reminds me of writing a brilliant foreigner might do, one discovering the expressive possibilities of the language by writing in it, taking liberties of usage not knowing them to be liberties. "The gruesome plump thick pink boy was pushed across the bed." "She smiled and the smile was stupid, clever, educated, pleasant, true, appropriate, strange, conscious, wandering." It's like a bird going after too many worms at once. I mean, you really can't write like this, can you? In English? It's night invading day, Alananarchy, it's someone naughty undoing all the laces of all the shoes. "The long invalid was bright green. His arms were holy, the forefinger held a candle, the wax thumb stuck out, yellow hair behind." It's springy writing, subtly alliterative, a prose you can scan. It brings huge attention to the words themselves, and in that way it's self-conscious, like poetry, in the sense that poems are always, in some proportion, about their own language. (In focusing on the language of such sentences, I'm aware of ignoring the imagistic risks being taken, which are considerable.) "I wanted to get away from intelligence," Alan has said, talking about, among other things, his cut-up methods, his way of having bits and pieces of "info" all over the room, of screwing up his eyes and staring at phrases deliberately blurrily until there's some gleeful liberation of peripheral meanings out of the glum old signifiers. He does it. Such telegrammatic surges occur less often in *The Day Daddy Died* than in some of Alan's other books, but they are still very much a presence linguistically.

This is one kind of thing Alan does, and like nobody else. Another is the odd, not orthodox, relentlessly plain, memorably monotonous, blinkered, slagging syntax which is the main narrative style of *The Day Daddy Died*. It seems to suit Norah's story, she who is presented to us without any approbation or moral elaboration (the model for Norah, Alan states in an interview, was a woman he met who led an "exemplary life, having five children by five different men. Bloody hell, I say. Lucky kids"). This main narrative style is plain to the point that it could be said to resemble another scale within the music of language, a minor but not a melancholy mode, a deliberately restrictive one, that lacks the conventional intervals between notes of a so-called "major scale." This is a different mode, Alan's own. It pushes ahead without the kinds of syntactical variety you normally think of as indispensable to "serious prose." It's an arrested prose, Alan's choice, his own supremely dogged syntactical dialect.

I wonder at the relationship of the language of the letters to the rest of the prose in this book; it seems on the surface to be purely documentary in intent, giving us, simply, the written speech of uncomplicated people, which has its own poetry. "But I've been off work with a painful eye infection which is rather bad just now, on top of which I've had a letter from my bank manager about my overdraft—another worry because I won't be well enough to take on extra work over the holidays." This gives us more Norah, in the plainest way, one phrase toppling on to the next ("on top of which") awkwardly and authentically. This lies at the other end of the spectrum from the eruptive, virtuosic self-consciousness I quoted above. The main narrative prose occupies, more or less, the middle area of the spectrum. I have no fancy theory (yet!) to account for the inclusion of the letters but I like them enormously; they are familiar to me and I know these brief lives by them (a little better). And there's something about the persistence of this clipped style, as about Alan's persistence of attention to the unanalyzed Norah, that's very affecting.

There are other aspects of the language Alan uses that I'm aware of without being able or inclined to account for them fully; I have in mind the indirect speech quality in much of the allegedly direct speech between the characters, or the gorgeous comedy of Norah and Pete's dinner at the Trocadero, from the descriptiveness of "It didn't matter that she found a piece of fish in her lap, then a lump of gorgonzola, it made her laugh. The chicken on the carpet made her giggle, lovely lump of laughter on her face, there was the chicken, and a pretty woman smiling down at it" to the wholly implausible dialogue:

"Your skin is creaking," he said, "I love that creaking sound."
"Nearly everyone says I'm sexy," she replied.
Return to the table. Nothing to do but talk. Plates and knives and conversation.
"Who are your favorite people incidentally?"
"Those who live on border-lines and edges, and burst into life from time to time. Don't you feel like that?"

Who's talking here? Not Norah and Pete, eh? This seems akin to the (often) indirect quality of the direct speech, a sense of quotation superimposed without attribute; the effect is slightly distancing and supremely comic. At such times the narrative drains away and leaves the phrases stranded in their print, leaves them to fend for themselves, quite nicely indeed, as language and as attitude toward language, a kind of ironic hovering.

What I seem to care for the most, then, in Alan's books, even in *The Day Daddy Died*, which gives us his most distinctive protagonist in the person of Norah, is that playing upon, up and down, his own Alan-derived scale of language. And I end with that language, four of my favorite telegrammatic sentences: "The dark doors opened over her head. She blew her nose. Lost time, loose tooth, trotting hands, bad night. Then her eyes blew up and hoped to die." Well, two more. "There was nonsense in her smile, something smooth in it. Bad dreams rose and drove in her." Not forgetting: "Thinner speech was used, deeper sound was used when needed." (Yes)

The Texture of Life Lived

Jay Neugeboren

In the fall of 1985 I received a request from the University of Minnesota to provide them with an evaluation of the fiction of Alan Burns, who was then being considered for promotion to full professor. I had heard of Alan Burns's work but had not yet read him. I agreed to provide the evaluation but was unprepared for the delights that awaited. Here, dated 11 November 1985, is the letter I sent.

Professor Kent Bales has sent me three books by Professor Alan Burns. I have now read the books—with great pleasure and admiration, I am happy to say—and can comment on them.

The Day Daddy Died (1981) and the more recent *Revolutions of the Night* (1985) strike me as exceptionally impressive novels: intelligent, original, idiosyncratic, shrewd, and moving. Mr. Burns is a gifted and interesting writer. What seems most fascinating—and engaging—about his fiction is that it is at once experimental and avant-garde in the most interesting ways, while at the same time it is grounded in tradition, and in the strengths and history of the traditional novel.

Let me explain. On the face of it *The Day Daddy Died* would seem to be an experimental novel full of familiar elements—i.e., elements one does not expect to find in traditional (realistic) novels: fracturing of time; compression of history; photo-collages; surreal imagery; metafictional puzzles; implausible plot events, etc. In lesser hands such elements would make for a rather tired book—the kind of novel that because it *merely* outrages or shocks or startles by formal maneuvers, quickly becomes predictable and pedestrian. What is so wonderful in this novel is the fact that its unusual surface performs a vital function: it calls attention to life itself—to the fact that what we are getting here is a novel that tries to show us the pain and joy and texture of a *life lived*. For *The Day Daddy Died* has as its informing principle that most common and wonderful and old-fashioned of tales: it is the story of a life—the life story of Norah, from her childhood in England in the late thirties, through war, childbirth, betrayal, etc., until, decades later, at the book's end, Norah's daughter is the age she was at the beginning of the novel. *The Day Daddy Died* is a sharp-edged account of one woman's life—a woman with a strange life indeed (five children by five different lovers), yet a woman whose innocence and passion and ability to survive (and surviving, to transcend her innocence) is utterly compelling. Norah is a Candide in modern dress, and the dress is contemporary history. I have rarely read a novel that is so unsparing in its depiction of the *brutality* of modern life, while at the same time . . . what?

The brutality that Burns renders for us lies both at home and at work. Norah's family life (the family she comes from; the families she creates) as well as her work situations are sometimes rendered for us as they might be in a (lesser and duller) proletarian novel. Yet Norah's ability to persist in her own way—to make her way through the world so that we are captivated by her and want her to live, and to live well, is what makes the novel so compelling. *The Day Daddy Died* is a bizarre and crazily modern fairy tale. The novel is by turns surreal and cinematic, realistic and mercurial. Best of all, it is never dull. The sentences are gracefully turned, the scenes are extraordinarily vivid, the characters distinct, the landscape haunting.

At one point, early on, the narrator says that Norah "was not sure what was real." Exactly. And what this novel does is to make us ask this most fundamental question again and again—what is real and what is illusory? And in a world in which so much *seems* unreal, what are we to believe, and how are we to live? The very fracturing and compressing of time that begins on page 1 tells us that we are in a fictional world where *anything* can happen at any time—years can pass between paragraphs—and also that we are in a fictional world where we need to pay close attention to the way time works *on* character. When Norah looks at a painting, the narrator tells us, "the lines related, the people didn't." Again, the intelligence behind the novel is telling us (at least) several things: something about the painting, something about the way Norah sees it, something about the-way-we-live-now, and something about the fiction we are reading—its strangeness, its difference. The novel, historically shrewd and humanly wise, has wonderful *edge*—satiric, ironic, pointed.

At the same time, seemingly fantastical imagery is often made terribly real, even ordinary. No small achievement. (Thus we see, freshly, what is marvelous about the ordinary.) Norah's perceptions are often touching precisely because they are tender in a marvelously individual way. ("Half an hour later she and Nick were having lunch in a field, lying on newspapers. . . . She could not touch his body for two hours, it was as if her arms were missing.")

Alan Burns's more recent novel, *Revolutions of the Night*, which I have read in manuscript, seems at once a more accessible novel—less overtly experimental in mode—and a more mysterious one. Whereas *The Day Daddy Died* begins with the death of a father and its effects on the daughter and her life, *Revolutions* begins with the death of a mother and its effect on a son and daughter. Here again, though the novel is full of wildly surreal scenes, the basic subject of the book—three generations of a family, the love between a brother and sister—is itself traditional. *Revolutions* is, in fact, an old-fashioned family novel—a nineteenth-century novel about love and death and birth and marriage and family . . . but, decidedly, with a vengeance. It is a novel that would have been impossible before Freud and Joyce, and this itself seems, at times, if I understand Mr. Burns's fiction (and vision), to be the point. *Revolutions of the Night* is a visionary book about family and history—and it gives pleasure by asking us to puzzle out the strange and mysterious ways in which we are bound to one another, responsible for one another. When Hazel dies at the end, and her brother Harry flees, we are returned full circle to questions that have been in the air throughout the novel, and that are there in the very opening and memorable image: "At the edge of the clearing, in the shade of a copper beech, a family party gathered. Grandfather sat in a chair, with Max, his middle-aged son, on his lap. Max's son, Harry, sat on *his* father's lap. They were three generations, one upon the other." What, the novel seems to ask, do time and history do to us, as individuals, as members of families, as members of social groups?

To write about this novel in such a way, however, is to ignore its special quality—for this is not a novel that is overtly intellectual, or that lends itself, while one is reading it, to sociological speculation. It is a novel that is always vivid and vibrant (often with sex and violence)—a kind of ghost story that seems more comprehensible than the reality its characters must endure in ordinary life. And yet the novel, like *The Day Daddy Died*, is anything but realistic in the usual sense. Burns is gifted with marvelous powers of invention. Images are rarely if ever stale.

Although this is a novel whose narrative is more straightforward than that of *Daddy*, I myself find it somewhat less successful. The effects here seem merely elaborated, rather than deepened, and often the intensity of the imagery seems strained as if, precisely because we are asked to believe in Harry and Hazel and Max and the rest (as real people), they seem less fictionally credible than do the characters in the earlier novel, where the very starkness of the way the characters are rendered makes them live and breathe fictionally.

Mr. Burns is clearly a writer with his own way of seeing the world and writing about it. He is also a writer with a deep love for the great tradition of the novel. His volume of interviews, *The Imagination on Trial*, which he edited with Charles Sugnet, clearly shows this. The interviews in this volume with writers as diverse as John Hawkes and John Gardner, Ishamel Reed and J. G. Ballard, are fascinating, and this is due in large part not only to the intelligence of the questions Mr. Burns puts to the writers and his careful reading of their fiction but to something more important: his love for the work they have created and for the very idea of fiction.

The interviews in this book seem to me easily on a par with most of the interviews in the *Paris Review*'s Writers at Work series. And when, at the end, Mr. Burns himself is interviewed, I understand why he is so good at what he does. "To me," Mr. Burns says, "the novel is the grand art form of this century: it is so vital, so flexible, so eloquent, so compendious. If I want to have that sense of adventure, I need the big area, I need the wonderfully open generous form that the novel is, which allows me ample space in which to explore."

Explore Mr. Burns does. In truth, his kind of fiction—often minimalist in technique, nightmarish in landscape, unrealistic and antinovelistic in its means—is not the kind I myself ordinarily prefer. Yet I was more taken with his work than I expected I would be. I was stimulated by Mr. Burns's work, enjoyed reading it, and found that I enjoyed encountering the mind that shone through it. There are flaws, to be sure—oftentimes the narratives seem repetitive and self-indulgent, sometimes the violent and surreal effects seem gratuitous—but the work I have read suggests that Mr. Burns is a figure to be taken seriously, to be read along with those writers with whom his work (inevitably) invites comparisons: B. S. Johnson, John Hawkes, Donald Barthelme, Samuel Beckett. I hesitate to list such names, but I do so in order to indicate that Mr. Burns's work is intelligent and original in a significant way. That his own work is becoming less overtly experimental and is reaching toward a wider and more general audience is, from this reader's point of view, good news. I do not see that by doing so he will sacrifice anything of his particular genius. Anyone interested in following the course of the novel over the past few decades will find what he does of more than passing interest. He is a gifted writer with a generous intellect; his work is strong, original, and memorable.

Alan Burns and the Velocity of a Dream

Al Greenberg

In his introduction to *The Imagination on Trial* Charles Sugnet argues that in spite of the prevailing American myth that has writing in England remaining traditional and even nostalgic, it is in fact—particularly as demonstrated by the interviews gathered by Alan Burns for this book—much more connected to the vision of William Burroughs than to that of the nineteenth century. He writes, "many contemporary British writers are responding to the surreality of urban existence under late capitalism." Burns himself is surely one of those writers, and all of his fiction that I have read—not just *The Day Daddy Died* and *Revolutions of the Night* but also *Europe after the Rain* and *Dreamerika!*—evidence his concern with the social decay of late twentieth-century capitalistic society and the use of a surrealistic literary technique as a means for both showing and making the reader feel the disintegration of that society.

Burns's fictional technique, while by no means so radical as that of Burroughs, makes use of such surrealistic devices as disparate imagery, fragmentation of scene and chronology, dreamlike sequences, and a rapid movement along the surface of the narrative that seems closely allied to an interest he expresses in some of his remarks as interviewer in *The Imagination on Trial* in events which "move with the velocity of a dream." But for Burns, as for the best of our contemporary surrealist novelists (Burroughs, Heller, Pynchon, Hawkes), this technique serves not for its shock value, not to call attention to itself as avant-garde—indeed, I don't see how, after all these decades of its use, surrealistic literary technique can still be labeled experimental—but to serve the social aims of his fiction.

In other words, "the importance of unconscious and irrational forces" that Sugnet notes in his introduction as crucial for so many of the writers interviewed in *The Imagination on Trial* is for Burns a product of the society rather than of the individual psyche. Burns's characters behave in irrational ways, certainly, but the unconscious forces that drive them come not from themselves but from a world whose social and economic forces are beyond their control, beyond their understanding, for the most part even beyond their consideration. If they do absurd things (Norah's string of pregnancies and her total lack of comprehension of what's happening to her in *The Day Daddy Died*, for example, or most of the behavior of most of the characters in *Revolutions of the Night*) and if their erratic behavior is reinforced by the technique of fragmentation, what all of this reflects is the absurdity of the society itself: the "late capitalism" which Sugnet identifies and which here affects, destroys, the individual in ways he or she simply cannot comprehend. One of the interesting things about reading these novels side by side is how Burns applies this vision to the lower and upper levels of society alike. If Norah is driven and destroyed by economic forces she can never overcome—and we see the same tragedy befalling her children as well—no different a fate befalls the far more affluent families of the more recent novel, and it is not just they but the whole world that is found in ruins at the end.

Things happen in Burns's work with a rapidity that makes them seem inevitable, as if it were, in fact, a dream, a nightmare, in which their lives are caught up. If these works, especially *Revolutions of the Night*, appear to skim along the surface of events and characters, it seems to me that that, too, is a part of what Burns is saying, namely, that there is no depth, no viable interior, to our lives, our society; the surface is all we have and it, as these novels clearly reveal, is a disaster. The depths of character and even of the material world that were furnished to us by the nineteenth-century novel are no longer applicable, and Burns's work reveals this sense of what has become of us as graphically as any I know.

Burns's own concerns, both technical and social, are also reflected in many of the questions he asks and comments he makes during the interviews he has conducted for *The Imagination on Trial*. He speaks there of "disparate images," of "connections which astonish me" and of a concern for "the dream world" with its extraordinary juxtapositions and accelerations. Likewise he expresses a concern with "alienation," with a "society in disintegration" and with the novelist's "revolutionary sensibility" as well as with his own attempts "to use the raw stuff of social reality even as I chop it up and change it around." I mention these things to show how, in an admirable way, Burns's work both as a writer and as a reader/critic of contemporary fiction is all of a piece: his social vision and his understanding of the literary techniques capable of rendering that vision constitute a genuine contribution to contemporary fiction.

An Alan Burns Checklist

David W. Madden

Fiction

Buster, in *New Writers One*. London: John Calder, 1961; New York: Red Dust, 1972.

Europe after the Rain. London: John Calder, 1965; New York: John Day, 1970.

Celebrations. London: Calder and Boyars, 1967.

Babel. London: Calder and Boyars, 1969; New York: John Day, 1970.

Dreamerika! London: Calder and Boyars, 1972.

The Angry Brigade. London: Allison and Busby, 1973.

The Day Daddy Died. London: Allison and Busby, 1981; New York: Allison and Busby, 1981.

Revolutions of the Night. London: Allison and Busby, 1986; New York: Allison and Busby, 1986.

Play

Palach. London: Penguin, 1974.

Nonfiction

To Deprave and Corrupt. London: Davis Poynter, 1972.

With Charles Sugnet. *The Imagination on Trial*. London: Allison and Busby, 1982; New York: Allison and Busby, 1982.

The Bookstore in America: Borders

This is the first in a series of articles that will appear about bookstores and bookselling in America. At first glance, it might seem odd that this is a subject worth theorizing about, perhaps even odder that the *Review of Contemporary Fiction* would be the place for such a series. And yet, the bookstore remains the primary place where Americans find their books, or in many cases "can't" find them. While some people might place the responsibility for the availability of books with the publisher, the publisher is the first to know that the *system* (haphazard, capricious, and nonsystematic as it is) whereby books are published and remain in print is a complex combination of what the publisher would like to publish, what the review media *might* pay attention to, and what stores *might* stock and keep on their shelves; without the latter two falling into place, the publisher must decide whether there is any point in publishing (that is, "making public") a work that few people will ever see or hear about. Therefore, what gets published and made available to American readers is in large part determined by a combination of forces that historically have not been carefully analyzed or thought about, except in economic terms (e.g., publisher X is making a profit or going out of business, bookstore Y is losing out to the chains, review media Z covers only those books from major publishers who coincidentally take out expensive ad space). But rarely, if ever, do we have these subjects considered from the point of view of what the culture, society, and Republic may need (if not always *want*), and what it means for a country to have its books more or less reduced to marketplace value, whether that be the marketplace of the store or review media or, finally, the publisher. Since these issues do not get discussed from points of view other than economic ones and since Americans implicitly embrace the "marketplace" explanation as existing on a level with "freedom of expression" and the "right to vote" (that is, self-evident truths or rights that need not be inspected), the book "business" is generally left untouched by analysis, except in marketplace terms, and of late much of this discussion has been directed at such things as the enormous advances that publishers pay a few authors while paying less attention to its "midlist" (aka "money-losing") authors and the conglomeratization of American publishing into a very few giants, book review pages as an extension of entertainment coverage (that is, tell the public about what it wants to hear), and more recently the emergence of chain and "super" bookstores that are driving independents into bankruptcy and, at least according to various lawsuits, indulging in unfair trade practices. What is inevitably left out of almost all of these discussions are such matters as: is the American public well served by this system? are more and varied voices published and promoted? do we have fewer alternatives available to us? is the book industry, like almost all other industries in the country, becoming more and more homogenized?

Leaving aside the author, the system consists of the publisher, the review media by which books become known and talked about, and the bookstore, through which the books are accessible to the public. Although all three of these deserve close inspection, this series will focus on the bookstore, about which we have little historical information (how many were there 100 years ago? 50 years ago?), and nearly no theoretical information (why do they exist? why does someone open one? is it only a business or does it have a public service dimension by which, for instance, it attempts to keep certain books on its shelves regardless of how poorly they might sell in a year's time?). In brief, what at present is the relationship between commerce and culture as reflected in bookstores, and what, given the current situation, might we expect in the future?

Rather than starting safely and more or less risk-free, I am beginning this series with a consideration of Borders Books & Music, the chain of stores popularly referred to as "superstores." To those in the "business," public discussion of Borders, except to attack it as a conglomerate trying to drive independent booksellers out of business, is not only unpopular but can be, for a publisher at least, suicidal. In this article, as well as in the series as a whole, I am not interested in indulging in the controversies of chains versus independents; rather, my interest is in what is currently happening with stores, how they see their role in the community, what they see their responsibilities to be, and what we might expect in the future. I am also not interested in whether one chain is better than another; which store has the smartest business practices; what discounts publishers should provide to stores; any and all other "economic" issues that typically arise; or complaints that individuals (people or companies) might have that can be reduced to "one day I was treated rudely by a clerk." My intention is to get at trends and philosophies, practices and policies, and then test these out to the degree possible. So, for instance, if a store claims to specialize in poetry, then how is this evidenced by the selection of titles in the store, buying practices, methods used to insure that the store searches for poetry from all publishers rather than the easy-to-find commercial publishers, poetry readings the store sponsors, and so on. For these purposes, I am acting as little more than a book buyer trying to figure out how all of this works and what it means to me.

My premise in undertaking this series is that bookselling in America has radically changed in the last few years and will more dramatically change in years to come. Despite the conservative nature of the book industry and its resistance to making changes that occurred in other forms of retail businesses many years ago, I believe that the emergence of national chain bookstores was a historical inevitability, held back in part because of the lack of computerization for inventory control that could keep track of these small objects as they moved out of warehouses, into stores, and onto shelves, as well as the necessary capital to finance growth, but primarily held back by a mentality that resists change of almost any kind (that is, there seems to be a psychological dimension to the book and what it represents that causes people to want to retain old practices related to how books are "handled"). While most other businesses in America long ago went in the direction of "superstores" (Sears & Roebuck being the first and primary example) and many now have, in various ways, moved back into playing niche roles (specialty stores which, though part of a national network, still focus on primarily one commodity, and here Starbuck's is perhaps the best example), the book business still generally goes along in its nineteenth-century mode of behavior.

When chains first emerged in the United States, they were Waldenbooks and B. Dalton's, primarily mall stores of about 2,000 square feet, with about 40,000 titles. These stores were, with a few exceptions, driven by discount marketing and a selection of books that would appeal to mall shoppers. The superstores, however, came on the scene with 150,000 titles, and although discounting and marketing characterized their emergence, something else was happening: in-depth selections. Discounting was a given, but now the stores were competing on the basis of *quality,* not just size or price, and much of this quality is determined by a combination of company philosophy and purchasing practices of the buyers at the companies (does the company believe that it should stock a poetry book that sells only one copy a year? does the buyer have the intelligence to be able to distinguish, regardless of sales, the difference between an "important" poetry book that sells poorly from an unimportant one?). In brief, inventory control, marketing, and discounting may be necessary conditions of the success of superstores, but they are not sufficient conditions; if these stores are not finally known for quality, they will not survive. In fact, the very computerization that makes them possible does not supplant the role of the buyer; for instance, a buyer at one superstore may decide to order 35 copies of a book for all of its stores, and quite likely the results will be that the chain does not, at year's end, sell very many copies of the book, which becomes a form of both self-justification and self-fulfilling prophecy. At the same time, a buyer at another chain, will, based upon his or her own knowledge and belief in a title, order 500 copies of the same title for several stores, and will wind up selling a few hundred copies, in which case the computer will in effect tell the buyer that this is a title that should be kept in stock. Neither modeling systems (that is, the decision of a buyer to order 35 copies for 15 of its stores based upon a combination of past performance for the author's previous books or previous editions) nor the raw information the computer provides will take the place of the knowledge, experience, and commitment of a buyer. And this is as true for independent stores as it is for superstores.

One of the dramatic changes that I see is that visiting a bookstore (in the past a solitary experience, usually engaged in by people well past twenty or thirty years of age, cramped into small quarters and narrow aisles with the respectful quietude usually reserved for libraries and church) has changed in its social dimension and meaning. In relation to the superstores, book-shopping is becoming a family outing, providing places to sit, wide aisles, as many as 200,000 different titles in a wide variety of subjects, reading groups, long hours, and on and on. What are the cultural implications of children spending hours in bookstores, an almost unheard of experience even ten years ago except for precocious and extremely well-behaved children? Rather than making this question completely rhetorical, I will suggest that, as a college professor for many years, I found it common to have freshmen who had never been in a bookstore, though they knew their way around movie theaters and record stores. Will there be long-term effects of having children become accustomed to knowing their way around book-stores at any early age? My theory here is that there will be a significant cultural effect, though we won't know what it is for several years to come.

What then becomes of the independent store that cannot or does not have a large stock of books nor a great deal of space? Does it have a function or does it merely fall victim to Borders and Barnes & Noble? I think it does have a function that will insure its future, but a function that will require changes. Some independent stores have moved in the direction of develop-ing practices that would seem to guarantee that they are becoming the homogenized monsters that the chains are usually accused of being, while others, however, by conceiving of themselves as alternatives to what is available elsewhere, have made themselves nearly indispensable to their communities because they can do things that generally fall outside the realm of what chains can do.

My hope in this series is to initiate a discussion of the future of stores, as related to the cultural role stores serve, that will be useful rather than a free-for-all and a brick-throwing contest, though the latter, at least in part, may be unavoidable.

The second part of this series will be devoted to Woodland Pattern book-store in Milwaukee.

Borders: An Overview

History

Borders was begun by Tom and Louis Borders in 1971 as a small used bookstore in Ann Arbor, Michigan, primarily intended to serve the academic community of the University of Michigan. In 1973, Borders moved to its third location and started selling new books. A year later, the store moved once again, this time occupying a 10,000 square foot space adjacent to the campus on State Street. In 1974, Louis Borders designed an inventory control system to take the place of manual record-keeping, a system that was to determine Borders' future capacity for expansion. A second Borders store opened in 1985, which quickly led to others, both in and outside of Michigan. In 1992, Borders was purchased by the discount retailer K-Mart, which already owned the bookstore chain Waldenbooks. This relationship with K-Mart lasted until 1995 when Borders went public and became 100% publicly owned.

At the time of this article, Borders Books and Music will have 157 stores throughout the United States. Borders stores stock between 140,000 and 200,000 book titles.

Philosophy

Borders' philosophy of bookselling goes back to its origins as an independent store with a strong "academic," serious-book bent. At the heart of Borders is the belief that success lies in offering a wide, in-depth selection of titles that appeal to serious book buyers. At the same time there is a belief that books have to be actively marketed, and that stores should provide a comfortable setting that allows customers to spend hours in the stores, browsing as well as buying. Borders is less interested in "quick sales" than in establishing a loyal customer base that will turn to Borders as the store that is most likely to have the book they are looking for. Borders is also committed to tailoring each of the stores to the local community in which the store is located, a practice that means that Borders stores do not have identical layouts nor an identical stock of books. Despite being called a "chain," Borders in its mission statement says that it is "not a chain, but a collection of fine stores, each an integral part of its community." Finally, Borders is committed to "service," a belief that customers will become loyal on the basis of the responsiveness of stores to their needs.

In designing this study, I decided that the method would be to interview a wide range of Borders employees, from the buyers to the president. The theory of the method was to introduce "themes" and find whether reactions remained consistent throughout the company or whether contradictions emerged as I moved through various levels of management at the corporate headquarters. I was most interested in whether the philosophy of the company remained consistent and whether this philosophy existed only at the top of the company, or the opposite, whether a philosophy emerged at one level that was at odds with that at the top. A second area of concern was whether behavior in the company reflects the philosophy, as well as whether there is a commonly perceived link between philosophy and behavior; for instance, it is not uncommon to find in organizations that there is a philosophy that everyone adheres to, but as soon as people are questioned about how that philosophy is practiced, vast discrepancies come to the surface, meaning that no one really knows the philosophy and that at some point the organization will be shocked to find out what those with the most power will do in the future, even while invoking the philosophy that everyone thought was well understood. Therefore, identifying behavior is oftentimes more important than identifying the philosophy of an organization. One final measure was seeing whether I could find the "company maverick" or "conscience" who criticizes the company even while continuing to work for it; organizations often tolerate this "critic" (usually someone who has been with the company for many years and someone who recalls the glory days of the past) because he or she assures them that, while in practice the person is given little authority, the company is open to all points of view.

After interviewing a number of people, what I found is that there is an amazing consistency of philosophy and behavior. From buyers to marketing to upper management, the philosophy at Borders is the same, but so too are the examples cited in terms of the behavior that enacts the philosophy. The company maverick or conscience should have been Joe Gable, someone who has been with Borders for over twenty years and until recently was the manager of the Ann Arbor store. He saw the store change from a single-store independent, to a store with several locations, then to a chain and a chain that sells books, music, and videos. Rather than being the in-house critic, he seems to be an agent of change who has comfortably witnessed and been a part of the changes at Borders, even though he initially questioned whether the Ann Arbor store could be duplicated in other locations. Where one would also expect to find inconsistences would be among the buyers, even if their comments were without criticism. For instance, one of the themes that emerged on every level was that Borders believes that a wide selection of titles is at the heart of the Borders philosophy. While championing and aspiring to this cause, the buyers could have talked in terms of "having to be realistic" and "having to be responsive to consumer demands" and "having to recognize limits," but such a conflict between philosophy and practice did not emerge among the buyers.

The ultimate test, however, becomes whether the philosophy and the supposed practices at the corporate level are in fact carried out at the store level. I had no intentions of doing a whirlwind tour of over 150 stores that were open throughout the country when I did these interviews at headquarters. What I did have, however, was the experience of being a shopper at

Borders stores for several years, as well as having, as a publisher, sold books to Borders buyers for the past few years. So, I did come armed with some hard-core experience, as well as some degree of fear that, despite whatever conceptions I held of Borders up until then, I would in fact find cracks in the system that would suggest a future that, as a publisher, I would not like. If I had found those cracks and if I had to continue to sell to Borders, I would have carefully eased out of doing this article for the *Review of Contemporary Fiction*.

Because of the methods I used (that is, similar or identical questions to the interviewees), the question that emerged was how to use these materials for this article. Reproduce all of the interviews, despite the repetitions? Select only those parts of the interviews that were different, but then in effect misrepresent the similarities? I decided to reproduce all of the interviews in full and to do as little editing as possible.

Strangely, Borders does not customarily track some of the very things I was looking for in relation to what cultural impact such stores have and will have. So, for instance, though one of my theories is that the book-buying experience has become family-oriented, Borders does not track the ages of its customers; while it can say how many children's books were purchased the previous year, it cannot say how many children visit stores. Nor does it track other age groups. Finally, it cannot answer how many poetry readings were held in the stores during, for example, the past year because it does not track the number of such readings that are done by local writers as opposed to readings by a writer on a national tour. It can say how many total "events" were held, but not how many poetry readings. For the time being, at least, such numbers are unavailable. Further, while Borders can say how many copies of a particular book of poetry it sold last year, it cannot determine in total how many poetry books were sold or what age group was buying them. Such information would seem to be useful in determining whether people over forty are buying more poetry books or whether a new audience is being found, for example, among high-school-aged people. This information would not only be of value in my study but would seem to be information that Borders would want.

Joe Gable

RCF: Let's go back to the origins. How did you wind up working at Borders over two decades ago and what did you want it to become?

Joe Gable: In 1967 I had gone to Blackwell's in England and realized that no store like it existed in the United States. It didn't exist. I used to hang out at Cody's and Moe's, and in New York at the Eighth Street Bookstore, and they were fine but didn't knock your socks off. Before I started at Borders, which I had seen when I would come here to visit my girlfriend, I liked it. We had a pretty good inventory at the old Borders store; it was only

5,000 square feet, but we had over 50,000 titles. But they didn't carry university press, short-discount titles, when I started. And so I wanted to carry these books if we wanted to purport to having a good psychology or Japanese section. I convinced them that by adding those books, they would add authority to the store and would sell more of the trade books. So, we worked on it section by section. I would bring catalogs home and work through them, publishers that specialized in subjects. We were then developing inventory systems, which I think has been the key to Borders success. Stores can still add any title they want if they think there is a need. Purchasing can review that and say that we carried the book before and couldn't sell it, and so will ask if there is a particular reason the book should be carried.

RCF: Having been here since the 1970s, you're the type who should have been very unhappy with all of the changes that have occurred since then. That is, in a typical organization you would have come in, made the changes you wanted, and then would have wanted things to stay the same.

JG: I certainly wasn't a big fan of opening the other Borders stores. My view was that we should put our energies into making it better rather than opening other stores. The Borders brothers had gone in the direction of doing inventory control for other stores, such as Hawley-Cooke. That wasn't really going anywhere because you could never get the right combination of site or control; some things were well run, and other things were not. I could see what they were interested in, opening other Borders stores where you could have control over what was happening. The second Borders store, the store in Birmingham outside of Detroit, was run for seven years by my youngest brother. A couple of things happened that changed my view on expansion. One was that we could sell a lot of good books that we never thought we could sell, that this would be a radically different market from Ann Arbor. Even though it was different from the Ann Arbor climate, we were selling a lot of scholarly books, poetry, and small press books, which was a surprise to me. We were able to create a good store. So, why not put a good store in areas where there weren't good stores? And why not bring a lot of things from the Borders culture to those areas? I never thought of us as being a chain. Each store was different, not just in terms of layout and design, but in terms of how that store related to its community. Stores were always encouraged to establish roots in the community. The inventory was customized to that market in terms of local interest, and things were decentralized. The manager had a lot of autonomy. And we created a lot of interesting jobs for people; we had a lot of people who loved books but didn't know where they were going to go with their lives. So, we created a lot of stores in various areas and the kind of inventory that I felt, for a long time, changed the nature of publishing. One of the things that appalled me about publishing was the number of titles going out of print. When I look back on the '60s, there was a tremendous backlist from publishers with an incredible depth. And now it's gone, and the reason I was told is that there weren't enough independents to carry them. I remember almost ten years ago, when

Jason Epstein was putting together his big catalog, he was out here, and he said that if there were 500 stores like this, then what he was doing would be unnecessary. If you look at what existed before B & N opened its first large stores, there was Borders, Tattered Cover, Cody's, a number of large independent stores with excellent selection, and all that we tried to do was something similar to that in other areas, opening a store here and a store there, and all of a sudden there's a *New York Times* article about this thing going on in the Midwest. It was very successful and so it was imitated.

RCF: Do you think there is a need for a chain such as Borders? If Tattered Cover is in Denver, then why does there need to be a Borders?

JG: I don't call the shots about where stores go. Denver is a big market. I don't see why Tattered Cover should be afraid of anything. Tattered Cover is run well, and I don't see why it won't do as well as it has ever done. Anytime a good independent has a real niche in a community, it is going to survive. An independent can be a different type of bookstore.

RCF: What about knowledge at the staff level at a Borders?

JG: When I started at Borders there was no book test or anything in terms of hiring staff. I remember saying to Louis Borders, How do you hire people, based on personality? If I am going to take my car in to get it fixed, I'm sure as hell going to expect that the mechanic knows something about cars, and if I am a book customer coming into a store I expect staff to know something about and care about books. So, I suggested working up a book test as one criterion for hiring. You've got to have people who care about the customer but who also care about what it is they are selling. So, I think there is a decided difference between the staff at Borders and the staff at other chains. Borders has always had a philosophy of bookselling that puts the bookseller at the center, that you had to have people who know about books, along with the selection that you offer and service. And so we have tried to hire full-time, so that you get people involved with what's going on. That's still happening, and includes such fringe benefits as stock options that get down to the store level. We have an eighty to twenty ratio of full to part-time people. And our staff tend to do everything—shelve the books, work the information desk, wait on the customers. We try to make it an integrated experience.

RCF: Where do you think Borders will be ten years from now?

JG: The key is that we continue to do well what we have always done well. If we start to fool around with the Borders culture, such as curtailing the kind of inventory that we have always had, then you become too much like the competition and you lose. It's one of the reasons that after twenty-five years I have moved from the store to the corporate side where I am going to function as a kind of trouble-shooter with stores, working to make sure that all of the stores are up to what we consider good stores. Whether there is something wrong with the layout of the store, or merchandising is wrong, by which I mean putting the good books out there on the table, to make sure they have people working when they have customers. Right now, you can look at the poetry sections at a Borders, and the selection is better than it is at 99.9% of independent stores, unless the store specializes in poetry. And the same is true with university press and small press titles that Borders carries. I am in favor of a *good* bookstore, no matter what it is, a chain or an independent. Years ago, I didn't ask who owned Blackwell's, I didn't ask for a prospectus before I could decide whether I liked it or not. Who the hell cares? Because of the existence of Borders and Barnes & Noble, there are a lot more books out there on the shelves than there would be if there weren't all of these stores. Books *are* being kept in print because back orders are being placed.

RCF: And your view of publishers?

JG: Publishers are going to have to wake up and realize that they should reward stores that buy a lot of copies of books and have a low return rate. It's crazy that publishers try to get large advances and then have stores return books. Publishers must never know where they stand in terms of sales.

RCF: Publishers say that stores determine such things as returns policies.

JG: People who know the market, will buy right for the market. But where is the reward for having low returns? Borders has distribution centers for publishers so that they have to ship books only to three or four locations, but do we get anything for this instead of requiring that books be shipped to hundreds of locations? And do we get anything for having low returns? We are well below the industry average, but do we get any credit for that? And then publishers play these games with co-op—we will give you some more dollars if you put these books in certain places. What do they think we are going to do with their books? Put them in the back room?

RCF: Again, publishers would say that the stores create such problems, and in particular that Borders requires the programs, and that Borders strong-arms publishers into having to participate in such programs.

JG: Because publishers won't do anything else. We would drop co-ops tomorrow if they were replaced with a discount based upon the kind of distribution system we have in place and our rate of returns.

RCF: Well, then, let's talk about returns and discounts. Bookselling is the only retail business in the country that can return everything that it "buys." Part of the discounting structure from publishers is related to the reality of the cost of returns. Bookstores love returns, and I think many of them build in returns as part of their business plans. So, from the publisher's point of view, it would be better to give larger discounts on a nonreturnable basis and stores should do what other retail businesses do—keep discounting until the book is sold. But many bookstores would prefer to incur the costs involved in being in the "business of returns," which is quite a considerable cost when you consider the number of people involved and the paperwork. At times, publishers believe that stores must be owned by UPS or the postal system because those are the outfits making a profit through returns.

JG: What I would find as absolutely revolutionary would be for stores to buy at a larger discount on a nonreturnable basis. It would shake up the whole industry.

RCF: Well, again, stores seem to be less interested in those "difficult" but "high quality" books when they know they can more easily sell the garbage. As far as publishers are concerned, it would be revolutionary if stores took a higher discount and then accepted the responsibility of selling these "good" books instead of knowing that they could return them after a month or two.

JG: I agree. Sell the books or mark them down. Why return them? Unless you didn't know how to buy them in the first place.

RCF: I think publishers' fears would be that, for whatever reason, a nonreturnable system wouldn't work, and then stores would not want to go back to the old discounting structure; namely, they would still want the high discount along with the right to return the books.

JG: Why wouldn't it work out? Once the publisher sold the thing, it would be gone. They wouldn't have to worry about doing another print run while still worrying about returns because there wouldn't be any returns. They could even rationalize their production process.

Gonzalo Ferreyra, Divisional Merchandise Manager

RCF: How did you wind up working at Borders?

Gonzalo Ferreyra: I graduated from the University of California, Berkeley, in 1982 with a degree in anthropology. After college I was in banking; I paid my way through college by being a teller, and then I went to work for Bank of America in downtown San Francisco, and worked as an "agency administration officer," dealing with agency loans to Third World countries, and I did that for six gruelling months. I bounced around for about six months travelling, and then I went back to banking because it was so easy being a teller, making a terrible wage but it paid the bills. And then I managed my brother's sporting goods store, which was probably the low point of my life. I tried to salvage what he had there but it didn't work. Running a little store by someone who didn't know anything about buying or merchandising or sporting goods. Or marketing. My future wife then got into the graduate program in psychology at the University of Michigan, and on the drive out—we were coming out with no money—she said that there is this fantastic independent bookstore in Ann Arbor. We drove into town, I got out of the car in front of Borders, I ran in and asked for an application; they made me stay there because of the test they give, I got scolded for not having an address, I came in the next day and was lucky enough to talk to Joe Gable (not knowing whom I was talking to) and I told him I now had an address, and so we started to talk. He did the interview and hired me right there. That was August of 1989. In December of 1990 I became a buyer. I was there when all the changes started, probably the most tumultuous period in the history of the company. When I showed up, it was an independent with maybe a dozen stores.

RCF: What was your philosophy in terms of being a buyer at Borders?

GF: Well, you are now talking to me in the capacity of a remainder buyer with two and a half years experience as a trade buyer. There is certainly a corporate buying philosophy, and there are certainly a number of individual buyer philosophies, and that's one of the components of the buying philosophy that I like best is the independent thinking that is accepted from the expert buyers in each subject, and there is a sense that each buyer has pretty free reign to select and make decisions based on the history of the titles and the history of the publisher; using the information we have in the system has always been a wonderful component of the whole philosophy. Representing titles broadly and deeply has always been a part of the philosophy, and it is understood that we will carry as complete a selection as possible without being irresponsible; with the number of titles published each year in this country, do we need one of each in each of our stores? The answer is no. The largest stores will carry the majority of titles while paying attention to demographics, price point, the look of the cover, all of that. It's been a very enviable philosophy, and when you meet the people involved you find out that there are a lot of strong opinions about the quality of books, the quality of publishing, the need to disseminate intellectual materials. I am insulted by the idea that there could ever be a draconian philosophy that would change that; it can't happen. All you have to do is look at the people involved to see why that change couldn't happen.

RCF: But how much of this is dependent upon chance? The right people at the right time, but always open to the wrong people being moved into those buying positions?

GF: There may be moments when chance comes into it but then you look at the consistency and the corporate culture that has cultivated hiring from within the industry; we don't seek buyers, we seek book people. A buyer of housewares wouldn't be appealing to us, but a ten or twenty year veteran of independent bookselling would be. To some degree, making good buying decisions cannot be taught, to some degree you understand poetry or you don't.

RCF: Do the buyers come from the outside or are they usually promoted from within?

GF: Sure, there are a number who came from the outside, a couple who came a few years out of college. But from another industry, I don't think so. These are people who read voraciously, who think about nothing else. I've fallen into a job I do well with a liberal arts major, a job as a young adult that I did not know existed. If I had known it existed, I would have said, I am going to be a bookseller. As a child, hanging out in bookstores was as much a magnet as going to toy stores.

RCF: What kind of check system is in place for buyers, that they may be ordering too many copies of certain titles because they love poetry or experimental fiction, or in the other direction, not ordering those books because there is a bottom line that someone is looking at?

GF: There is a great deal of exchange and discussion among buyers, but the character of a section is dictated by a buyer and the buyer's predilections. When I was a poetry buyer, it was my call. So, there might be a poet who didn't sell well, but I would buy fifteen copies and spread the book around and do what I could, because that's my power and nobody is going to abuse that privilege and this privilege keeps the sections looking different from similar sections at other stores. And this is even truer in remainders. It's our responsibility to read the public and know what will sell, but we are buying all subjects across the board, and so here's my chance to sell Philip Roth's last novel, which I liked, at $2.98 and spread around a few copies in addition to knowing that this kids' activity book is going to do well despite what I think about it. Buyers here know that they are not the average consumer, and that means that they will buy things that only 2,000 people in the country are interested in reading. Getting these kinds of books creates a kind of communion with the public. When I take a chance on a title and I see it sell, that's fun. It's fun to buy 50,000 copies of a popular book and have it sell just the way that last one sold by the same author. But if I take an unknown poet I really admire and buy two dozen copies and twelve of them sell, well twelve people out there get connected to it.

RCF: What is to keep Borders from one day returning literary books in vast quantities because their sales do not justify the cost of keeping them on the shelves?

GF: I think we will always think of those books as our loss leaders. They are not contributing a huge amount to the bottom line but they are convincing a lot of people that it's worth coming back to Borders time and time again, and if you are going to be spending $200, Borders is the place to comfortably do it in. I've worried about that happening one day because the business-oriented side of me counteracts the idealistic book freak, and says that it has to happen, that there's a point at which it doesn't make sense, but I don't think that is necessarily true. We're cultivating a culture. What I take most offense at in the whole discussion of the chains is the assumption that the people making the decisions are anything but wonderful book people; our poetry buyer is someone who herself has a wonderful book of poetry from the University of Pittsburgh that sells twelve copies a year. We know and we care and there are few things more precious to us than the printed word. But people want to believe otherwise. Part of why we are scary is that we are a corporation in a business that usually is not corporation-friendly, a corporation that *gets it.*

We are providing something which we all wish had been available fifty years ago, and that is a single bookstore available to any community that allows you to come away with almost anything you want. When I was young, there was nothing finer than for me to walk into a Cody's for the first time or to walk into a City Lights. And now we take for granted that a bookstore is going to carry 120,000 titles and that there are bookstores that do that. What more can we ask? That we can find a backlist Harvard title that sells 15 copies a year. Why did it take so long for this to happen with stores? Some of it is capital and the right social and economic forces coming together, but it is truly a great thing. If you want to propose the idea that two companies are gong to create a monopoly and dictate what belongs on those shelves and wipe out small presses—that's one way of looking at it; equally valid is that you have two companies committed to very large bookstores, and how do you maintain such bookstores and keep them looking full without having the small presses? You can't do that; it's counter-intuitive; if you are going to open stores with 50,000 square feet, you put yourself in the position of having to support the small presses. If you have a 600 square foot bookstore, doesn't space become a problem once you have the frontlist of Random, Harper, Simon—how much more is going to squeeze in there?

RCF: What do you see as the relationship between a chain like Borders and independent stores such as Shaman Drum here in Ann Arbor?

GF: I like Shaman Drum, I like the feel of a small bookstore, and there are all kinds of things we can get into about small independents and Borders, but what's the point? Borders certainly offers something that the public needs and that there is room for; I just don't know that it's everything, and that's not a bad thing.

Deb (poetry buyer), Matthew (fiction buyer), Linn (gay and lesbian buyer)

RCF: How did each of you wind up coming to Borders and what is your background?

Deb: I did my undergraduate work at Denison University and at the College of Wooster in creative writing and English. Then did an M.F.A. at the University of Iowa in poetry and then a Masters in literature.

Matthew: I graduated from Saint John's College in Annapolis in 1982, and then got a masters degree in writing from Hollins.

Linn: I didn't go to college, but not by choice. The day after I graduated from high school I started working in a bookstore. I hooked up with Borders about four and a half years ago when they opened up in Cleveland.

RCF: Okay, let's start with the rumors: one day Borders will all cut back to 50,000 titles per store. Why won't this happen, that some day someone will decide that there is too much poetry and too many translations in the stores?

Matthew: We don't buy books just to get maximum turnover. In a business sense, we are quite conscious of developing sections that will attract customers so that customers will have a sense that Borders has the best poetry section even if they are not buying a poetry book that day, week, month or year; they will continue to shop that store over one where they do not have that sense of selection of a wide title base and the important books there.

Deb: I've run into no obstacles in placing books of poetry in stores that may never sell, but they should be there to add to the integrity of the section. And this is true for other categories as well, like philosophy.

Linn: The integrity and reputation of Borders certainly rests upon those sections. If for some crazed reason Borders were to trim its inventory, the customers would notice it right away whether they are actually buying books from that section that day or not. And I think our business would fall off considerably if we started to trim down our inventory.

Matthew: The reason that Borders hires people like us is that we are entrusted to make certain decisions about the importance of a book or an author. Borders is not out there trying to hire somebody who has a lot of experience buying other forms of retail. Borders looks for buyers with a broad book background. The corporate philosophy could change at some point, but I think it's extremely unlikely; the people above us are as sensitive to this notion of selection as we are. I do not know of buyers who have been told that they are carrying too many titles but I think there have been buyers who have been told they are not carrying enough. I trust the management to be quite aware of this for the long term. We are in this for the long haul, not something we are doing for a few years. Selection will always remain close to the breadth that we have now. There's always going to be a competitive landscape in bookselling. If Borders sought to compete with B & N only, then sure, it could become true that the title base could be cut. But I don't think we are trying to compete with anybody; we are trying to have the best bookstore.

Linn: No one is censoring the buyers' decisions here, and there are a lot of books we really have faith in whether they are selling or not. Even if we sell a only a couple of a title a year, we will keep it active, and no one is telling us that we can't do that. In my sections, I have some titles that some stores would be squirmish about carrying, but no one has ever censored any of my decisions, that any of my selections may be too daring for Borders to carry. There is a great deal of faith in the buyers' judgements here, and that's part of the integrity of Borders.

Deb: I had twelve years in bookselling before coming here, and one of the nice things about Borders is being able to translate my excitement about a book or author across so many stores. Here you can put the book in 130 windows and see something happen with it.

RCF: Does pressure ever get brought to bear on your ordering too many copies of something that winds up not selling very well or that your tastes are too literary?

Matthew: Not that our tastes are too literary. If pressure is brought to bear on buying too many copies, it tends to be brought at a separate point of the buying process. There has been a sense at times that we may carry too many copies of a book for too long; that doesn't mean that we are ever expected to pull a book out of a store that we feel strongly about, but there may be a sense that a store does not need five copies if it is selling one a year. That's the only kind of pressure that we have run into, and this is a reasonable pressure.

Linn: We are certainly running a business and we can't deny that fact. We are trying to be competitive and are selling merchandise. If a store can sell only one copy a year, there is no reason to have a five-year supply sitting on a shelf. That's the instance when we are given a nudge to pull down—when there are more copies than necessary. But that is just common sense.

Matthew: And it's not just business sense. It allows us to present the best titles in the best way. We try to get the best balance. If there are too many titles that aren't selling, they are going to take up the space, money, and labor in the stores, and that distracts us from the important books. And this means culling some quantities out of some stores in a reasonable manner which allows us to do a better job with the right titles.

Linn: I think we are all working here not just in relation to the selection of titles but to buy in the right quantities, and that's something we are all really keenly aware of. Give the exposure to the books that deserve the exposure. When I started in the business, my mentor told me that anybody can buy books, but it's a matter of buying them in the right numbers and having the right balance. It's great to be able to play hunches, and that's what we can do here. There are a lot of titles I introduce that are risky, and I am not sure that I can sell them, and it's great when I put in something I have low expectations of and then I see it is starting to sell. I think you notice all of this when you walk into a Borders, that you are not bombarded by huge stacks of the same books.

The people who really criticize us are those people who do not take a look at what's available at Borders and really don't know very much about us. I understand this because I was an independent bookseller for many years; many of the people who work here come from independent bookselling. We are not trying to put anyone out of business. Many of the remarks that get made about Borders bother me after a while because we are book people here. We are not just punching numbers in on a screen and looking at sales. But I suppose the chain bashing will not go away in the near future.

Matthew: What bothers me most is the lack of distinctions being made between Borders and other stores.

RCF: What kind of seeking out of publishers do you do? That is, someone right now is starting a poetry press. Do you try to find out about this press or does this guy in his garage have to find you?

Deb: These presses seem to have great initiative in finding us. We have no end of solicitations from the outside.

Matthew: It's hard seeking out presses. If something is brought to our attention, we are committed to giving it the highest degree of inspection that it needs. We spend a lot of time running through trade journals and book reviews, and if we see a press we don't know about whose book is reviewed somewhere, we will probably try to pick up the press if we can. One of the things that all of us find is that the quality of reviewing has suffered, and it's now much harder for small press books to surface, not just to our attention but to people in general. It's becoming hard for people coming into a bookstore to find as many interesting books as they could find fifteen or twenty years ago, and that's because of fewer reviews and fewer sales. And there's less of a commitment on the part of major publishers to publish experimental work, the books that are hard to read but ultimately are much more rewarding. I think we are dealing with a cultural shift or deficit right now, rather than any particular action on the part of bookstores or anybody at our level.

Deb: Individual stores help us out in this regard too. They send us information about regional writers that we will wind up picking up for several stores. And the stores can order on their own. They can have titles ordered for only their stores.

Linn: And this is another strength of Borders. The individual store inventory is not just dependent on our decisions; stores are encouraged to seek regional titles. No one is telling them that they can't increase their inventory. Every store has its unique selection of titles.

Matthew: And they are good voices. They are book people at the store level. It's what they are committed to, and so they make good decisions, and I think that is another distinguishing factor about Borders.

RCF: Are you satisfied with the contact between stores and the corporate level?

Matthew: When you are dealing with communication with over 150 stores, sometimes things are taken too far out of context, and you have to depend upon e-mail rather than face-to-face contact. Frequently you wish you could make the same statement to everybody who needs to know rather than having it filtered through other channels. On the whole, however, for a company this size with its growth rate this large, I would say the communication is very good.

Deb: There is a lot of effort going into enhancing communications back and forth.

Linn: Everyone at the store level is encouraged to contribute, not just their time, but their thoughts and ideas. When I worked at the store, everyone was part of a team and I think everybody felt that they had a way they could express their own opinions. With over 150 stores, our contact at times is not as direct as we would like, but that is part of the growth to which we are adapting. And that is another strength of the company: we are always changing things. We are always adapting and changing to make the stores as good as they can be and to make everybody feel that they are part of a group.

Robin Wagner, Senior Vice-President, Emerging Ventures

RCF: What is your background and how did you come to Borders?

Robin Wagner: I started working at Borders in 1976. And while I was there I graduated from the University of Michigan, and covered sports for the *Michigan Daily* newspaper. I was going to do that for a career but I had no initiative, and I had a girlfriend and saw a handwritten sign in the window of the Borders store, where I had not shopped as a student. They told me I was hired and I began moving furniture; I was called in for an interview on July 4, and I have always said I should have learned something, being called in for an interview on a national holiday. I began in receiving, taking in about one UPS box a day, that was the volume of the company back then, and then in about two years got promoted to buyer, and about every two years I got promoted and it always stayed interesting. In college I majored in English and journalism. My mother was a high-school teacher and my brother teaches English in high school. I grew up in a family with a houseful of books, so it's no surprise what happened to me. I got a teaching certificate but couldn't motivate a roomful of students.

RCF: Why did it take so long for superstores to develop for books when we had such superstores in most other areas of retail for many years?

RW: 1986 was really the watershed moment because that's when we opened the second Borders store. Until then we had supplied independently owned stores with their inventory and their inventory control. One of the things about the superstore versus independents garbage you read about is that if you look at the roster of the top twenty independent stores in the country today, it's amazing how many of them are former Book Inventory Systems customer stores, and I think there's more than coincidence there. In any event, our expansion began in 1986, and the reason we veered from customer stores to our own expansion was that it takes a lot of money to open a bookstore like this, and Louis and Tom Borders realized that if we were ever to grow as vast as the country wanted us to (defining "wanting" as the volume these stores generate), we weren't going to do it with independently owned stores, there just weren't that many people with 250 to 400 thousand dollars to throw into a business. The next big moment was when Bob DiRomualdo took over in 1989—he was a Harvard M.B.A. and a very smart business person—he realized that Borders was more growable than what it had been. When he took over there were seven or eight Borders stores, and since then we have been on a steady increase to what it is now, about a forty-store-a-year growth path. The Ann Arbor store has 250,000 titles, if you include music and videos, and it's very difficult to control that many skus in a multi-store environment like we have now. So, I think it was systems that held it back from being a national phenomenon with books until it became one in the 1990s.

RCF: If the problem were only systems, wouldn't that have held back Sears & Roebuck?

RW: I don't know. I doubt that Sears & Roebuck had 250,000 skus. Why a system wasn't designed earlier, I don't know. We have always been ahead of the systems curve in books and we have done it as fast as we can.

RCF: I suspect that years ago, long before computer systems were controlling inventory, that one of the Borders brothers was writing everything down and knew what was in the store.

RW: That's interesting. They sort of did, but they knew that if they didn't keep track, they would go out of business. That's why Louis in 1974 went off in a corner and wrote the original Max Man ordering system, he wrote it himself, because he knew that most of the inventory in that store was in the basement waiting to get resupplied. Not all the inventory ever got up into the store. He realized twenty-two years ago that, if he did not go with a computer, he would go out of business because they had no way of getting the inventory to the floor; they didn't know what was down there versus what was upstairs. And that was at a time of a 30,000 title base.

RCF: In addition to inventory control, however, has been Borders marketing. What was going on at Borders that someone decided that books had to be marketed when marketing, in many ways, has been an anathema to bookselling?

RW: I think you are hitting at the heart of the whole company. I remember that ten to fifteen years ago the Ann Arbor store had a publication which I think was called "In Print," which was a monthly newspaper that Keith Taylor and Joe Gable decided they wanted to do. "In Print" was created by Keith Taylor's and Joe Gable's energies; they wanted to bring great books to the customers' attention. In the early days it was just an in-store handout, tabloid size, four pages. It was incredibly well-written. The same mentality is maintained in this department with the kind of buyers we hire. Every time we get information about good books, the buyers make sure of inventory in stores to make sure the stores have great books at all times. What you get in Borders stores over a period of time is an unbelievable selection because the criteria that goes into why they are on the shelves are independent of how well they sell, which most companies would not even dream of doing. As a result, there's a lot less turnover. That mind-set is the same kind that drove marketing in the stores. And we have come a long way in the last two years. Marilyn Slankard, Vice-President, Marketing, has tremendous empathy and belief in the idea we have had. This interest in books is probably less a function of thinking we would be successful over time than it was the energy embedded in the staff. If you think of Borders over the years, there were always lots of tables in the stores, and we were the only one with lots of tables for a long time because that was our way of telling the customer what was new and interesting. To this day, what goes on the quality paperback table in the Ann Arbor store is what we think the customer should be aware of, books you may not find in most other bookstores. The classic marketing approach of Borders is that though customers know we will have best-sellers, they really come to Borders because we make it easy to notice a lot of interesting books.

RCF: And Borders' allowing people to stand around in the stores, or sit around, for hours?

RW: It even goes deeper than that. We have never cared if somebody spends the day there and doesn't buy anything. If someone comes in and reads *War and Peace* in installments over time, it would be great if they put it back on the shelves where it belongs, and they will never be pressured to buy anything or leave because if they ever do want to buy anything, we are confident that they will repay our generosity and buy it at Borders. Though we have information desks, we train our booksellers not to bother people who clearly know what they want when they come in the stores; we don't want a bookseller to go up and ask if they want help because they are clearly not in need of help; to offer help to someone who doesn't need it is intrusive.

RCF: But somebody must have had the idea to make the store big enough to allow people to stand around or to put chairs in the stores.

RW: You have to give the Borders brothers all the credit in this regard. The old Ann Arbor store was 13,000 feet when we moved, but it was about 10,000 feet before then. It was long and narrow and had two floors, and had benches and stools all over the place. And I don't think Borders today is any different in concept from what it was when Borders was a single store in Ann Arbor; in 1976, it was a 10,000 square foot bookstore and at that time there was no such thing as a store that large. And it had a computer inventory control system in 1976, and one of the reasons for the computerized system was that Louis felt that, instead of having people in the basement looking for books, a lot of that labor could be in the bookstore commingling with customers and talking to customers about what we need more of. I used to brag that Joe Gable would spend fifteen to twenty hours a week on the floor, just serving customers, working the information desk, walking around helping to shelve books; now that's a multimillion dollar bookstore, and in another kind of store the general manager would spend no time on the floor. So, part of a vision of how to make a bookstore as good as it can be is to get the grunt work reduced through an inventory system. Our bookstores never had to check an invoice from Book Inventory Systems because of the quality control, and so they could spend their time getting the books onto the shelves as quickly as possible; sorting a two skid shipment was a matter of opening the boxes and putting the books in the right sections. All of that time-consuming labor was done off-site in a warehouse somewhere, and therefore in a bookstore all of the work could be done on the floor, which is where you really want to be because that is where the customer is telling you what you need. And then they could get that information to the buyer who could respond. The current Ann Arbor store is not very different from the store twenty years ago.

RCF: I would like your impression about the view that one day Borders will drastically cut back on inventory and therefore book selection, resulting in massive returns of books to publishers, as well as offering far fewer books to customers. The view here is that buyers will be told to eliminate titles that do not sell well and that are too costly to carry.

RW: Incredible, that once we have a stranglehold on the marketplace we will wind up being a 12,000 title bookstore? If we had 90% market share, we would still do what we do, and in fact would do more because the customer would have less selection elsewhere. It drives me nuts when I hear of publishers saying things behind our backs because I would challenge anybody to find a company that is more dedicated to probing the backlist of publishers or more dedicated to wide representation of new titles and that is more dedicated to keeping these titles active in the store regardless of how poor sales might become, who is more dedicated to paying their bills on time, more dedicated to low returns, and yet we are this perceived enemy and it drives me nuts. In fact, it's nonsense that, as we get bigger, we will create an inverse relation. There has never been a second of a conversation in this company about changing our strategy, no matter how successful or unsuccessful we are; we are what we are, and that requires us to maximize our inventory. In fact, now we are trying to figure out how to shrink the number of copies we carry per title, so that instead of carrying eight copies of *Grapes of Wrath,* we should perhaps have six, and then create more shelf space for more titles. Everything we do today—and there is twenty-five years of precedent to suggest that we will continue this way—has always been aimed at expanding title base and inventory and expanding our effort to be all things to all people.

RCF: When did Borders become involved with selling music in addition to books, and why?

RW: The genesis of our product diversification was the early 1990s; we wanted music. We had always had books and periodicals, but periodicals in a minimal way. Then we recognized that, even though we thought we were the best booksellers in the world at that point, we were vulnerable because all we sold were books. We realized that we had a good replenishment system for things that oftentimes did not sell that well; frequently, we are lucky to be able to sell two copies of a backlist title per year per store, and we had a system that effectively dealt with that. So, we wondered about music. If I had taken a vote in my department at the time, and then it was about twenty-eight people, the vote would have been twenty-seven to one that that would be the end of the great bookstore—how could you possibly maintain a great bookstore and have music? We did some research and found that, as people age, their music purchases plummeted and thought that this was odd because they have more discretionary income and there's nothing intuitive about the aging process that makes you like music less, so what's going on? We took the risk that there were no music stores out there that appealed to adults, that most of the music stores were aiming for the fourteen to twenty-four-year-old. We decided that adults didn't feel comfortable in typical music stores. And so we opened two Borders Books and Music stores and they did incredibly well right away. And then we went into video because we thought they were compatible with books, especially the kind of selection we put in, lots of foreign films and lots of classics. And then we opened our first coffee bar in downtown Philadelphia in 1990. So, it was a method of trying things to see how they would work. We do believe that ultimately customers are really only loyal to themselves, and if you stop giving them a service that they want, they will start going somewhere else. Demographics would show that we are doing the right things—the number of college graduates has never been higher, more families with college education. I don't know what the cultural implications of this will be but I know a lot of families go to Borders, and that they plan to go to *Borders,* not just to a bookstore.

RCF: Does Borders do demographic studies to see whether the clientele has changed, whether in fact families are now coming in the stores whereas in the past the age group might primarily be college age and above?

RW: Not yet. We don't capture such information other than for mailing lists. We did a focus study a few years ago to see why people like Borders so much versus the competition, and the word that came back was that people felt that they could "escape" to Borders. We are working on demographics, but we have very little information about the transaction point— what kinds of books do they buy, do they buy music and books together, what is the age of the customer—we don't have this information.

RCF: Why is there a perception of Borders, though the perception also includes other chains, that there is a doomsday scenario at work which will eventually mean fewer bookstores in the country, as well as fewer books?

RW: What is driving this perception of Borders as something awful with bad motives, given everything we have tried to do with inventory and selection of titles? What has surprised me is how long that view has held on despite the evidence. How we are perceived by the publishing world versus how we should be perceived is very hard to understand. All of the benchmarks of what kind of company we are, if we are not at the top, we are certainly at the upper echelon. The good news is that I only worry about it at times, like this, when I am talking about it. When Borders was bought by K-Mart, this was the first time that Louis Borders and I began talking to the major figures in commercial publishing, and they did not even know who we were, and I used to say in the 1980s that this worries me, that publishers don't know us, that we are in Ann Arbor, and we don't go to New York and we don't get invited to cocktail parties, and Louis would say that's okay because there is no time left in the day to do that kind of stuff, it's all we can do to make great bookstores. And despite what some publishers will say about us in *Publishers Weekly,* we have never modified our buys from them because ultimately the customer would be hurt. And I am proud of Borders for not acting this way.

Jody Kohn, Director, Publicity and Promotions

RCF: What is your background and how did you come to Borders?

Jody Kohn: I have a B. A. in sociology from Wayne State and a Masters in guidance and counseling, and six years of art school. I worked in a pharmacy during college, and then got a job in a hospital pharmacy. I was promoted to director of purchasing at the hospital, and made good money but did not like my job, and every day I used to stop at a bookstore called The Book Beat outside of Detroit; I would go there after work at six-thirty and stay there until nine when they closed. I had a bad accident for which I had to have surgery and went off on a disability, and my position at the hospital was eliminated. One day the bookstore said, You're here every day and you have retail experience, and they asked me to work for the holidays. I worked for two weeks and owed them about $350 because I bought so many books. I worked for the holidays and didn't leave for ten and a half years. I wound up managing this small independent and during the time I was there it went from 900 square feet to 1,800 square feet. I did everything there— managed, did display windows, bought, hired people, waited on customers, unpacked boxes, shelved books, and PR. When I started out, I really loved it and could afford to do it, but about ten years later I was approaching forty, I had very few benefits, and I had no room for growth. I was still living like a college student. This store was three miles from the second Borders store that was opened. Borders had actually expanded the business of our store because they used to refer customers to us. So, I had a choice, go to another independent or I could go to Borders or Barnes & Noble. I was tired of the hours of retail, and so I wrote Borders a letter and described my background. And about a week later I got a call, and my first job was as an assistant manager at the store in Dearborn, knowing that I wanted to get a corporate job at some point. I worked at the store for about nine months and then a job came up here at headquarters doing co-op. So I did co-op print ads for about a year here. I have been in Ann Arbor for about two years. There are several people from the Dearborn store where I started who are now in Ann Arbor. The day I started working at the store in Dearborn, I went outside and came back in and said, "Oh, my God, I work for Borders." For ten years I was in this environment that hated Borders, that they were this monster. Now, I feel like this is my job for life; I can't imagine that I want to do anything else. I've had three promotions in two years. They have been able to work with me to see what I can do and what I am good at. The job that I am in now, I am director of publicity, promotions, and public relations. I had said that these are what my strengths are and the position doesn't exist but should, and they said, You're right, and they created a position.

RCF: Does Borders track such things as the number of author readings at all of the stores? Does this get broken down into the "kinds" of readings, such as poetry readings?

JK: We do event tracking on a national basis. We are developing better mechanisms to retrieve more specific information on the local level. We get a spreadsheet that has national signing, as opposed to local authors. We do have somebody who compiles the calendars from every single store for every month, which gives us a way of knowing what has gone on in every single store. It's like the benefit days that all the stores do. All of our stores have a budget where they can give a certain number of dollars each year to specific organizations, and oftentimes these are literacy organizations, or local library funds. Out east there was a library that had been flooded, and we did a day where people brought books for the local library. Of course this is what is usually not covered by the media, that we are not just this big conglomerate; we look at each individual community and think about how we can help and become a part of the community. We place a great deal of effort on local events that bring people together, and make our stores natural gathering places.

RCF: How much is Borders' behavior towards literature a result of individual buyers and how much the result of the corporate values?

JK: I think we have a strong commitment to keeping all important literary books on the shelves. We have buyers who have in effect kept books in print. There may be books that we sell 100 copies of a year throughout all the stores, and the publisher may be about to put the book out of print, but the publisher will be told that those 100 books a year are worth keeping it in print. And this will be Borders recognizing that sales of 100 copies a year is not very many but recognizing that the book is very important and should be kept in print. If you look at our list of best-selling books, there are things on there that are definitely not on the *New York Times* best-seller list but are best-sellers for Borders. And these are often midlist titles, poetry titles. Our support of National Poetry Month was strong last year and I think will be even stronger this year, our programs get down to the level of having schoolchildren getting involved. I think one of the biggest fallacies you hear or read is that if there are only two chains left selling books that all of the small publishers are going to go out of business and that the two chains will have full control over what the public gets to buy. A deep selection of titles is at the core of who we are.

RCF: What does Borders do for small presses?

JK: A lot of this is buyer-driven. But we do have a newsletter that we produce every week that goes to the stores and this encompasses everything the stores need to know from headquarters, including basic retail information. The buyers, however, are responsible for getting this information to someone who works with me who then formats it and gets it out to the stores. We have several vehicles to inform stores of titles published by small presses. Buyers recommend titles for display as well as ideas for handselling.

RCF: What about the formal marketing programs?

JK: We do have a small press tier in Bibliophile. And we have the smaller catalogs that we do every month and that is a good place for small presses. And these subject catalogs are in the $700 range.

Marilyn Slankard, Vice-President, Marketing

RCF: What is your background and how did you come to work for Borders?

Marilyn Slankard: I went to the University of Kansas as an undergrad in economics and business.

RCF: How did you wind up in the world of books?

MS: In a roundabout way. I worked for NCR, a computer company, for several years, and then I went back to grad school at Northwestern University, and I have a Masters in marketing and international business, and I went to work right out of grad school for George Mrkonic, who is the vice-chairman of Borders.

RCF: Why did you think of Borders?

MS: At the time I worked for George, he ran the specialty retail group of K-Mart. I worked for him for about a year and a half in that job, and I never would have stayed at that job. I wanted to get into something that was of more interest to me. Among the specialty interests of K-mart was Waldenbooks, and I was drawn to the book business right away through Waldens, and I thought of going to work for Waldens, but before that happened, K-Mart bought Borders, and then that was it. That was the place for me, it was the most exciting thing there was that I could imagine; there wasn't anything I could ever dream of that would involve the culture, current events, and a pace that keeps moving. It is certainly different from anything I've seen in retail or anywhere else. So, I fell in love with Borders, and that's how I got here.

RCF: How many books did Borders sell last year; and what was the overall return rate?

MS: I don't have an exact number, but a safe guess is over fifteen million books. In terms of returns, it's low double digits, and there has been some fluctuation in that over the past year. Historically, Borders has had the lowest return rate in the industry; it's usually in the teens.

RCF: Does Borders track sales of frontlist as opposed to backlist titles?

MS: I don't believe so. I know that the nature of frontlist buying is different from backlist buying, and I know that our return rate for backlist titles is much lower because it's more of a science to us, using our systems and buyer knowledge; we're more scientific about backlist than you can ever be about frontlist.

RCF: Borders prides itself on literature. To pick a single area, do you know how many books of poetry you sold last year?

MS: We don't have those numbers broken down. I can tell you some of the things we have done to support poetry, though. We were the official bookseller at the Dodge Poetry Festival last year. We donated 20% of the sales to the festival, which came out to be about $20,000. That gives you an idea of the sales volume that the festival itself created.

RCF: Is it a concern to you that you do not know how many books of poetry Borders sold last year and therefore you do not know whether you should be expanding poetry sections in stores or cutting them back?

MS: We know how many titles we carry, and by title we know how many we sold, down to exactly at which store the titles were sold and when.

RCF: On what basis then would you know whether your poetry sections are adequate, whether you should be pushing poetry readings or deemphasizing them? So, how do you know whether sales for poetry are flat or increasing? Is poetry taking up more space than it should, or should you be expanding the space?

MS: My initial response is buyer expertise. We have a poetry buyer who is looking at every poetry title in every store on a regular basis, and she knows the market and our customer base. She would know when a store is doing well and needs more, and when a store is not doing as well and should use less. It's her job to make sure that poetry selection is as good as it can be at a particular store.

RCF: Let's assume that some stores do better with certain kinds of books than other stores do. From a publisher's point of view, perhaps a store could be doing better if, instead of looking at purely historical information, something was to be done differently at the store. Does that enter into your thinking, or is this determined only by looking at how a store did with a certain subject in the last year?

MS: There's a lot more to it than just looking at the computer screen and reading the numbers. We meet every month as a team of the buying group and management to review the results by category in every store. We are looking at every category, such as mass market versus trade paper because we haven't had the reporting to allow us to do that by subject area. So, we talk about why a particular store isn't doing well, and therefore do they need more shelf space, do they need fixtures, what is the problem, is there something we can help with? We examine that constantly. And the buyers have reporting by subject, and so they are able to look at their top stores in poetry as opposed to their worst stores in poetry. We are always trying to emulate the best stores.

RCF: The subject of small literary publishers. Many or most of them have budgets under $500,000, and many have budgets under $100,000. And that covers all of their expenses. In order to have a real presence in Borders, that means having to be involved in marketing programs. What does Borders do for the small literary presses? Does it recognize the difference between a press whose entire operating budget might be $150,000 and a large commercial publisher? To what degree are they treated just like any other publisher?

MS: We do have co-op structures that work differently for small presses so that they are more affordable. That's one piece. Our stores and our buyers are very supportive of small presses, and so they feature those books with or without the co-op support just because they are strong titles for us; we believe in them and support them. We also offer Bibliophile. We actually scaled back this year the cost of being in Bibliophile so that smaller publishers could participate. And we have a magazine ad that is a more literary niche, and we have made that affordable so that small presses are able to advertise in that and do co-op ads. For National Poetry Month we are doing a huge campaign, so that all of our stores will be involved in National Poetry Month; we have a special catalog coming out written by our poetry buyer, and in it we asked many notable poets to say which poet or poetry book was most influential for them, and they will all be printed in there. We also have a National Poetry Month Co-op catalog. Ten percent of the sales of the titles in the co-op catalog will be donated to the Academy of American Poets. And at the end of March there is Small Press Week, and we are supporting that by putting signage in our stores and displays, and Borders is going to be a sponsor of their Small Press Week kick-off reception. They asked us for sponsorship, and Borders was pleased to provide support.

RCF: What form will that take?

MS: We will provide the stores with information to set up displays with materials supplied by the small presses, and in our weekly newsletter to stores we will have a list of recommended titles to put in their displays. The buyers have input in this, and it's our opportunity to celebrate what small presses mean to us.

RCF: That is the kind of news that will not make its way back to the publisher, that Borders is doing something. The individual small press will frequently not know that something like this is even happening, even if they are one of the beneficiaries of it.

MS: Where do the small presses get their information for what is going on? Surely it's not just from reading *Publishers Weekly*.

244 | REVIEW OF CONTEMPORARY FICTION

RCF: It's a combination of reading *PW* and then seeing sales reports. Anything beyond that, there is no information. Therefore, anything else is by way of rumor, such things as "we seem to be getting a lot of returns" or "we don't seem to sell well to Borders." The presses rarely hear anything directly from Borders, and so the information available is from something like *PW,* and then rumors. Taking Small Press Week as an example, many presses will not know that they are being represented unless they happen to go into a Borders store, but they still will not know how this happened.

Let's talk about whether Borders and Barnes & Noble are potentially changing the culture, that children are learning how to maneuver around in stores, that the chains are introducing children to bookstores and that these are the people who one day will be your customers but will also be people who from an early age are accustomed to going into bookstores. But Borders doesn't seem to track the number of children who go into its stores, nor does it track whether families are shopping in the stores. Do you have plans for gathering such information?

MS: It's difficult. We don't have good demographic information in general, let alone by a specific age group or family unit. We do know by other reporting which stores draw more families and more mothers with children, and we have ongoing events in those stores designed to get those people into the stores and to help them learn about books. But we don't know how many children come into our stores, or the average age of people who come into our stores. We know that's it's a very broad range, and that's it's a group of twenty-five to fifty-four-year-olds who are buying, but that misses a large portion of the younger and older part of the population. We have a young readers program in many of our stores, and we estimate that there are at least 10,000 kids across the country who are involved in that; that's a frequent reader club, and they get stickers that will give them a gift certificate when they read a certain number of books. That has not been done in every store, but it will be in the near future. We also have, across the company, thousands of events every month, and most of those events are locally sponsored rather than national author tours. Next year we estimate that we will do upwards of 75,000 events across the company which includes everything from readings to musical performances, and about a third of those are related to kids. Many stores have good relations with teachers, and have teacher appreciation nights, and we offer teacher discounts, and teachers bring their whole classrooms in for events as field trips. Across the country we are doing approximately a thousand Story Times a month.

RCF: Do you have a number for how many Borders stores will be open by June of 1997?

MS: We are at 158 today, and by June we should be at 167.

RCF: How many book titles are stocked in an average Borders store?

MS: At an average store, there are approximately 140,000 different book titles. For the largest stores, the average is 200,000 titles.

RCF: If you can speak corporately, what is your view on the National

Endowment for the Arts?

MS: We have supported NEA in the past, and we were the first corporation to donate money to the NEA. Last year that support was about $50,000. We feel very strongly that NEA should be supported. It's not our place to say that the government should fund it, but we put our money where our mouth is.

Richard Flanagan, President, Borders Books & Music

RCF: What is your background, and how did you come to work for Borders?

Richard Flanagan: I went to the University of Notre Dame, and got my degree in business. I then went the normal route. I was in public accounting, and I didn't last long in public accounting because there just isn't the involvement on a day-to-day level that I really wanted, and so then I started to work for different industrial firms. Along the way I picked up an M.B.A. at Loyola University in Chicago. I then went to work for a privately held steel company in Pittsburgh; I had been recruited there to be vice-president of finance. Someone could wonder what is so great about a steel company, but if a steel company is about to go under and you save 500 to 800 jobs in a very depressed area north of Pittsburgh . . . so I was quite proud of the fact that through a lot of hard work and effort and my ability to finance this company and convince people to loan money to this company, and then be part of the turnaround, this is something I take pride in. However, once the company got turned around in about 1990-1991, I got a phone call saying that a very unusual company was looking for a vice-president of finance. I asked what it did and was told it's a book retailer. That was both good and bad news. I knew nothing about retail, I had never been in retail, but the good news was that it was in an area of business that I so much enjoy and love that this was a once in a lifetime opportunity for me. So, I had a chance to apply my experience to what I enjoy, and this was a phenomenal opportunity. I was then told that this company always hires "different" kinds of people and they want someone who knows how to finance a privately held company that is going through a change and growth. I thought that there was no harm in talking. So, I met Bob DiRomualdo, who is now the chairman, at the Pittsburgh store, which thereafter became part of my wife's and my social life, because we would drive to the store on Saturday nights to buy books. So, I met Bob and we just started talking, and we maintained a dialogue that went on for about six months. They brought me on board in early 1991; I did some things to help finance the company to help it grow during that time, was involved in the almost-going-public portion, but then they sold the company to K-Mart. Bob gave me additional duties, and put me in charge of the distribution part of our business. Then K-Mart put Bob in charge of Borders and Walden's, and Bob asked me to take his position here at Borders. I became president in the beginning of 1994.

RCF: One view of the chains is that, once the competition is driven out of business—whether the competition is independent stores or other chains —the one or two chains left will drastically reduce the wide selection of books in stores and will cut back on the number of stores; further, the titles that will be most affected will be those that sell less well, namely, poetry, translations, small press titles.

RF: All right, the idea that, having dominated the business, we would then go out and start reducing titles. Why would we reduce what we are selling? Why would we go out and purposely try to reduce our business, which is what that would be? What we believe is that we are successful because we offer such a wide assortment, that is the key to our success, and we believe because of that wide assortment of books we have the kind of volume that we do. We don't have that volume because of square footage or fancy ceilings and walls and fixtures, it's that people can find books that they couldn't find before in Akron, Ohio, or on the island of Kauai, someplace that just had no access to this breadth of books. That's our strength, that's why people are spending long hours in our stores, finding things that they were never able to find before.

Which brings us to another argument for why Borders does what it does. As people age, develop more free time after their careers have peaked, and start to find the time to go back and develop interests that we all had when we were in college, you know, you have always had this interest in medieval history, you always wanted to do more reading but you didn't have the time—Borders is the store that has all that. Why would we take that reason for our existence and success and then say, "Ah ha, we can reduce that!" It is counter-intuitive. If you believe you have no chance of expanding people's reading and their enjoyment of books, then I can see why you would say that all we want to do is increase turnover and increase financial return on investment, and make a great argument for why we would do this in some kind of doomsday scenario, but because of our willingness to make innovations and to re-create the book-buying experience, we are believers that you can actually introduce people to more books and music, things they didn't have before, which is why we got into music in the first place, because we believed that the adult music buyer did not have an active outlet in which to buy music, a place where the adult music buyer would like to go to and be comfortable, adults who would like to find out more about jazz and then would like to move up as they find artists they like and want to find out more about, the catalog stuff; we believe that we are able to expand the marketplace, and this is why we would never take our reason for success and then shrink it down. We hear this argument all the time, and yet it is so counter-intuitive to what we do . . . it's like the argument that we are going to dictate what's published. Publishers have a monopoly of product; we can't dictate to them what's going to be published; that's what they do for a living. And we sell books for a living. Our interest is in increasing selection. I hear these arguments all the time. The people who make these arguments never come in here and talk to us; I've never had a personal conversation with them, and yet they have all had this terrific insight as to what we're doing as a company.

We also have to recognize that if you think there are only so many book customers out there, and therefore you are only in competition to satisfy the book buyer's needs, then I can see why the argument would be made that we will reduce the selection of books; but we also have to recognize that we are not only trying to satisfy the book buyer, but we are trying to satisfy those customers who are looking for entertainment. Another argument is what happens when we go into the next recession, that all those stores are going to be returning inventory and it's going to be panic-button-pushing time for publishers. I've always believed the opposite: if you hit a recession, it's a good time for the book business because people are interested in careers and self-improvement, and books are an incredibly low-cost form of entertainment. Reading a book, and the length of time that occupies, versus seeing several movies or versus taking a vacation, reading a book is very inexpensive.

RCF: Another rumor is that one day the bright buyers Borders now has will be replaced with people who have a better business sense, who know better what will sell, or that one day you will be calling them to say the books that sell worse in the stores are literature, especially poetry, so let's get rid of them.

RF: We could come up with all kinds of scenarios for why the day after tomorrow we will decide to carry only Tom Clancy books face-out in our stores but the truth is that I cannot remember the last time a buyer left this company; we have been attracting these buyers for years, we grew from a small buying staff to one of twenty-eight or twenty-nine buyers right now. Robert (fiction buyer) has been with us seventeen or eighteen years, this is a staff that has been growing for twenty years, and as we have expanded we have had to make sure that we have competent people to step into the job and really love what they're doing. You can see a difference quite clearly when you look at the difference between a Waldenbooks buyer and a Borders buyer; Borders buyers are there to select the best books and make sure that they are in our stores regardless of their ability to sell; that's what their primary job is. At the end of the day, you still have to live within shelf limitations and size of the stores, and so there have to be secondary considerations, but their primary consideration is, what are the best books out there? A Waldenbooks buyer has a different kind of customer to deal with and they have only 2,000 square feet, and so they have to winnow it down to fewer titles for the customer walking by; they excel in certain subjects that are not Borders strength. And their job is to be much more mindful of the economics of shelf space; for a Borders buyer that is a second or third consideration. And those are their instructions and that is the way it has been for years, and that is the way it is done from my boss, the chairman of the board, all the way down. We look at and monitor our title count by subject area; we are constantly looking at ways of expanding that and we are also looking at out-of-stock levels, which have been a recent concern of ours because we have been running high in out-of-stock levels in certain subject areas, and it's something we do not fully understand why we have been experiencing this. So if you look at what we are trying to do—monitor our subject area count and out-of-stock levels—the biggest and most expensive projects we are working on is how to take quantities out of stores and put more titles in. If we can better figure out ways to cut down on our replenishment time, then we can put more titles on the shelves. Everything we are doing is to increase the diversity of selection in our stores. So, if you say what happens if Robert and Matthew leave and we replace them with the romance buyer—first that is an insult to the romance buyer who could be a very dedicated, very involved, very literate person who is desperately trying to find the best literature out there—but Robert and Matthew are fixtures in terms of our buying of literature. There is no hard and fast answer I can give you to what happens if Robert and Matthew leave tomorrow, other than that we will go out and seek the best possible literature buyers that we can find in our company. But then I have to step back and assess, What's the likelihood of them leaving?

As you know, before Matthew, there was Gonzalo Ferreyra, who was incredibly qualified, and now we have someone like Matthew who is incredibly qualified, and there are many more people in the company who would love to be a fiction buyer. One of the assumptions on the part of people who make these forecasts is that the marketplace doesn't work, and that satisfying the consumer and their needs isn't enough. Providing the selection is what got us where we are, and if we don't do it, someone else will. If we went away, someone would do it.

RCF: Part of providing a selection is special ordering, that is, what happens when a customer cannot find a book and asks someone in the store to get a copy. What happens when a customer asks for such a book? What do your employees do?

RF: They are going to go through a computer system that we call Borders Universe. Borders Universe rests on the fact that we have control over every single book, no matter where it's at in the country. If you look on the back of a book in our stores, there is a sticker. We incur extra cost and it's something that people who do not like us do not like to talk about, we incur an extra cost so that publishers have to ship to only four warehouses around the country. About 97% of our books go directly to those warehouses; the warehouses then apply inventory control stickers so that we have now captured that book; we know where this book is everywhere in the country. When you come in looking for a particular book, what the bookseller moves through descending levels, keeping in mind that we have a network that connects all stores. They will first look in our own proprietary look-up system to see if it is in this particular store, and misshelving is a real problem in stores, but with our in-house subject system, all stores put the books in the same places. Then a store will look up what's called Sister Store Inquiry, which allows them to look for the title in a geographically defined area, in metropolitan Detroit or metropolitan Chicago and see if that book exists. This is what Marshall Fields does, they can call other stores to see if an item is in stock; well, we don't have to make that phone call, we look it up in a computer. The customer can then drive, for instance, to Naperville, or we can have it delivered to the store; if the customer wants it that day, then we make the phone call to make sure the book hasn't been sold in the meantime. Level three is that we then go on-line to Ingram's inventory. Level four goes to Ingram's Green Light inventory, which means a very small margin to us, but that's the next level. Level five is to go to any Borders store anywhere in the country, with only two exceptions, Hawaii and Alaska. If you still haven't found it anywhere in the country, then you go to Books in Print, and then it becomes a special order and it is processed.

RCF: Stores are encouraged to special order?

RF: Of course they are. They go through that whole process, which is really not that long of a process. Normally, we can have any book within two weeks; if it goes to true special order, then you're looking at five to six weeks. We have gotten Borders Universe to the point where we can improve our service to the customer. We have greatly improved upon special orders, which tend to be a nightmare in stores; we have tried to take this out of the back rooms of stores so that employees can spend their time serving customers. We believe very strongly in this, and are bringing this same service to the music side. Special ordering in music is a kind of dormant business and we think there is a lot of potential in that area. In that area, there are only about 150,000 active titles out there and we carry about fifty to sixty thousand, and so there are not that many more that we are not covering. In the book world, there are about one million active titles in print; our system covers about half a million somewhere in this country.

RCF: What is unique about Borders in comparison to Barnes & Noble?

RF: There is a tremendous difference, with all due respect to B & N. I think the competition is healthy, and is less than what it is in other areas of retail where competition can get quite nasty, and none of that shows up in competition between Barnes & Noble and Borders. Having said that, there is a significant difference between the two. Some of it traces back to our academic roots, the fact that we grew out of a college town, have always been dedicated to that end of the title base; some of it is traceable to the fact that we have always been systems orientated; the company was privately held for its first twenty or so years, and therefore the owners could spend years messing around with a system, they were able to do so and in fact did. That dedication towards systems allows us to create these large stores with title bases that are much more responsive to the local community rather than just putting the same books in every store and just varying the quantities based upon the location. We try to vary the title base to meet the needs of a particular community and what the strengths and weaknesses are of that community.

On the service side, you can look at the kind of people we hire, people who are really interested in bookselling. It is always a challenge to try and hire well-educated, well-trained people when there is a constraint on how well you can compensate these people because you are dealing with a fixed-price product. We are also a company that is dedicated to employee ownership. Roughly 97 or 98% of the full-time employees of this company with six months service are shareholders of the company or have an equity stake in the company through direct ownership or stock options or participation in a 401K fund; we try to get as much ownership into the hands of our booksellers. We also try to make every store different, we try to make every store a part of the community. We have always been a company that thinks in terms of one store at a time, and our buyers buy book by book, store by store. We try to know and understand each individual store. We give managers a funding allowance before they open the store, to use that money to personalize the store and make sure it fits with what this community is all about. Not only are we trying to personalize the title base, but we are trying to personalize the store, which ties into the fact that each store has a community relations coordinator. We tell them that it's wonderful to have the big author events, but that is not really what we are all about. We are really about the day-in, day-out event that connects the store with the community. These are events that may draw only fifteen to twenty-five people, but that's what makes a Borders store special.

Reviewing, Reviewers, Authors, Publishers, and Censorship

Editor's Note: What follows is a series of responses resulting from the fact that I rejected Brooke Horvath's review of Doug Rice's Blood of Mugwump, *a novel published by FC2 in 1996. I invited Mr. Horvath, if he wished to have the review published, to have it appear along with responses from myself, the author, and FC2's publisher, Curtis White. He so agreed.*

Doug Rice. *Blood of Mugwump: A Tiresian Tale of Incest.* Black Ice-FC2, 1996. 140 pp. Paper $8.95.

Concerning a family of gender-shifting vampires incestuously feeding off each other, violently fathering and mothering themselves upon each other with an obsessive desire matched only by a hairy-palmed infatuation with their own body parts, *Blood of Mugwump* cannibalizes our literary past (Burroughs, Faulkner, Eliot, Sade) in the act of violating any number of taboos, social and aesthetic. Less a narrative in which conflicts build toward resolutions and everyone eventually goes home the wiser for wear, this first novel by the editor and publisher of *Nobodaddies: A Journal of Pirated Flesh and Texts* is more poetic riffing on the conundrums of gender, apoptosis of the word virus we all carry, transgressive search for identity. It is a probing of the question of how we can ever know ourselves, let alone others, or tell pleasures from pains, supernal sins from prurient holiness, or say how our spirit, flesh, and language commingle in the dirty deed of self-creation. This is mock (but deeply unsettling) porn, a chilling lump of lewdly fondled black ice, or in the author's own words from elsewhere, "Modernist writing within the traps of Postmodern discourses."

Working its way into the darkest recesses of private need, *Blood of Mugwump* follows young Doug's search for himself in (and on) his sister's and grandmother's bodies, in hermaphroditic metafriction, ghoulish plagiarism, the bloody depravities of the soul in its house of meat, dysfunctional self-begetting. What results is a breakdown in heavy traffic—"Her fist fucked the past out of that mirror. Bled our mother out of her cunt into my cock," is a typical passage—that will doubtless chagrin the National Endowment if and when it learns what it has unwittingly helped to fund. Replete with photos of girls and women the book claims picture the author, dedicated to his son (I know that David Markson says that "every boy should have a book," but really Doug!), this "Tiresian Tale of Incest" might well be the only slightly hallucinated spiritual autobiography of Florida's John "Vampire Rapist" Crutchley. It is definitely a book that tests the limits of anyone's consent to the proposition that nothing human is alien to any of us. [Brooke Horvath]

Re: My review of Doug Rice's *Blood of Mugwump*

On 12 March 1997 I received a letter from John O'Brien, editor and publisher of Dalkey Archive Press and the *Review of Contemporary Fiction,* explaining that he had "killed" my review of Doug Rice's *Blood of Mugwump* because (1) the review was negative and (2) it advocated censorship. Although readers of the review must be the final judges of whether or not those charges are just, I would like to say that I did not intend the review either as a plea for censorship or as a negative appraisal of Mr. Rice's novel. Nor was I attempting to accomplish what I have apparently managed and what Mr. Rice's book by virtue of its very confrontational nature cannot hope to do: epater l'avant-garde.

I believe the reaction to my review stems from the remark contained therein regarding the NEA. As both the *Review* and Dalkey Archive receive public support, the remark was perhaps tactless. It was likewise unstrategic insofar as (1) it could apparently be so readily misconstrued and (2) it could conceivably be taken out of context and used to give aid and comfort to the enemies of what Mr. O'Brien, in his letter to me, describes as "disturbing, difficult, upsetting" art.

That said, I would also observe that, despite the unavailability of my review to inspire the events that unfolded during the week of March 10th, I have been told that on that week Mr. Rice's novel was one of four books read in part into the record of a congressional subcommittee on NEA funding by U.S. House Representative Peter Hoekstra (R, Michigan). Hoekstra's intention was presumably to illustrate the "filth" the NEA has helped fund. This use of Mr. Rice's book, if nothing else, indicates the perspicacity of my offending observation. *Blood of Mugwump* has in fact chagrined the NEA now that congress has noticed the endowment's contribution to this novel's publication.

On the subject of censorship, however, I have a couple things I'd like to say. Setting aside the patent irony that attaches to a refusal to publish my review because it was thought to advocate censorship, I will notice that this business (for that, finally, is what this is) concerning Mr. Rice's novel suggests where some of the real dangers of censorship, or of the threat of censorship, lie.

Let me first make clear that an official policing of the arts would trouble me as much as it would Mr. O'Brien, Mr. Rice, or Mr. White, even though censorship has rarely prevented energetic readers from acquiring contraband books, videos, etc., and even though censorship efforts often work against their proponents' intentions by gaining for the offending work of art more attention than it could otherwise have hoped to attract.

But what concerns me here is how a fear of censorship has in myriad ways discouraged a consideration of art as something that can genuinely matter insofar as it contributes to, among other things, the shaping of minds and ideas. As Wayne Booth said almost 25 years ago in *Modern Dogma and the Rhetoric of Assent,* it is "fear of censorship . . . that has made modernists so reluctant to deal with the genuine rhetorical issues that art raises." For Booth, "rhetorical issues" meant moral issues, values judgments, and the problem Booth targets is evident in this present circumstance. In the letter explaining why my review would not run, I was reminded that *RCF*'s "basis for reviews [is] aesthetic, not subject matter." I think this line of thought leads to the trivializing of art at the same time it denies what Leslie Fiedler, for instance, was intent on reminding us of in *No! In Thunder:* that aesthetic choices are always and inevitably moral choices.

Further, implied in the rejection of my review (and remembering that I was neither advocating censorship nor panning the novel) is a conflation of censorship and criticism, the latter activity necessarily involving both positive and negative value judgments. But, of course, to reject, criticize, or simply dislike a work of art is not the same as wishing or asking to see it silenced, destroyed, banned. As my contributions to and association with *RCF* over the past ten years alone reveal, I, along with Mr. O'Brien, applaud "disturbing, difficult, upsetting" fiction. But to do so surely does not mean I must only applaud, or applaud all such works with equal enthusiasm. That is, I don't, in rejecting censorship, want to relinquish my right to approve some works more than others or my right to qualify my approval.

Certainly, among the tasks that as writers, publishers, editors, and critics are properly, unavoidably ours are exercising taste, making discriminations, assessing worth of achievement, aesthetic and otherwise. Which novels, say, usefully disturb us? Which repay the effort required to read them? How and why? Which must employ shocking, baffling, upsetting techniques and/or content to accomplish their ends, and which merely wish to shock, to gratify perceived tastes, to obfuscate their own vapidity?

This complex task of evaluation is one even our ostensible opponents might applaud if they could see us seriously undertaking it and supporting our assessments with accessible, persuasive arguments. Certainly, little will be usefully accomplished by retreating instead into art-for-art's sake elitism or falling back upon an indiscriminate acceptance and defense of each and every work of art that shocks (or offends or confuses or bores or whatever) those who are not we on the grounds that (1) the fact that someone has been bothered proves the work's seriousness, aesthetic success, or right to attention or (2) those who are troubled thereby prove only their ignorance or philistinism, that they are swine unworthy of pearls not intended for them anyway or (3) art is an inherently amoral, more-or-less contentless aesthetic experience.

Clearly, the issues here cut in other directions as well: one needs just as vigorously to critique art that is hackneyed or jejune; that panders or unfairly propagandizes, even when agitating for what we believe; that discourages thought. One needs to recognize as well that the audience for art is implicated in the experience (including meanings) art provides. Good art can be put to bad uses; moral fiction can be misread; pearls can be trampled by swine; sophisticated human inventions can be mangled by the inept or unprepared who may likewise hurt themselves in the process. And at any rate, as the art historian Klaus Kertess has observed, the function of art more often than not is to offer "a platform for experience, not a lesson." That being the case, it is impossible to know in advance which works of art are likely to do wholesome, and which unwholesome, work in the world.

Big Brother regulation will not solve America's problem with difficult, upsetting art. Neither will the current retreat by so many of us into ivory-tower arcane and self-righteous scorn of those not already persuaded of what we refuse to offer good, clear reasons to accept. It is, similarly, our refusal to offer persuasive support for those value judgments we do condescend to make that explains why we aren't much listened to when we say that the art we don't like—bestsellers, velvet Elvises—isn't any good.

We discriminate, evaluate, every day: "disturbing, difficult, upsetting" art, a journal such as the *Review of Contemporary Fiction* as much as says, is better than Danielle Steel or Robert J. Waller—whose work offends us, we like at least to pretend, more than Doug Rice's ever will. But when we pretend to refuse to discriminate, or to account for our discriminations, we concede the game to those ignorant of the rules and lacking the skills otherwise necessary for playing skillfully enough to win. All I am saying here is that I hate to watch it happen.

P.S. The preceding comments were written after I was informed that my review would provide the occasion for a "public airing" on *Blood of Mugwump,* censorship, the NEA and its congressional subcommittee but before seeing what any of the other participants here had to say. For this reason, I have not addressed any of their remarks specifically.

Doug Rice Responds

Like Marcel Duchamp's readymades, *Blood of Mugwump: A Tiresian Tale of Incest* requires collaborators rather than commentators. Grandma, it seems, has become viral. She suffers from many of the same fears that we all have: most significantly, she fears that when Liberace is on television, he can see her while she is watching him from beneath the cover of her insulin-riddled body. Cyclotron shit. Mugwump is a pre-recording on the lookout for the original pre-recording. Derridean deleuzions. *Erase that, you bastard.* Writing is virus. Always on the go. Here to go. Nomadic. (As if, nomadic can be written without slipping.) There are very few places for sanctuary inside Rice's narrative. (This incestuous[1] tale of infested Mugwumps, however, is no longer Rice's responsibility, nor was meant to be. The speaking of this narrative, more appropriately,[2] belongs to Caddy's wet tongue— the tongue that had soiled Faulkner's panties[3] and that has remained forever silent, dumb, in sounds and furies. Familial lips, bleeding always bleeding the blood of eternity, uncaught at the broken place.) The few safe places that appear at first to exist, to offer solace for the weak, tend to have an abused ear of corn, wet and bloodied, tossed aside, off in a corner. Forgotten. Ancestral bodies spilling off the page onto the concrete basement floor.[4]

I have written this uneasy book against amnesia. I write cunt because I am so tired of being dead. Language has become an addiction, a way to replace my schizophrenic flesh. Ever since Grandma showed me the barbed wire that Grandpa had brought home from the war, I have been trying to translate my mother tongue. Fearing myself doomed, I went about infecting others. Hell, in deed, has no limits. Just a place where dead roads become meat beneath the red night.

Then, out of nowhere, well actually out of the blue,[5] my family could finally afford a portable television set. As the television set wobbled on its wire stand, my entire family grew tired and quiet. We thought we were watching.

You smell that? It's the smell of words rotting.

There is something that God never understood about my body. He looked at me, black and secret and friendly. Penetrated me. I. Gave me flesh against memory. Just trying to say. Just you try it on. Language to replace my fractured cunt. Forgotten.

Can you recall that scene in Dario Argento's *Terror at the Opera?*

Doug Rice, himself, it has been said by reliable autobiographical sources, originally wrote *Blood of Mugwump* anonymously. And now here he stands before us, accused of being the author of this heretical work written in the borrowed language of dyslexic cunt. But such accusations, by their very nature, must be false. Rice is only a writing machine. He has shacked up with that Burroughsian charybdis. (I have seen photographs of these episodes, but to this day, Rice refuses to name names. In the beginning, this has been recorded, the word was made flesh. But God lied. There is no way to unmake the flesh through the word. I have stood, silent and still, before many mirrors practicing such speech. Have paid many men and women to use their language on me.) [Doug Rice denies that he wrote any of this.] Rice was dismayed, early on, by the failed promises of the WonderBra. (Just as he, along with Twiggy, was bitterly disappointed by similar promises promoted by Maidenform in the late 1960s. I am convinced, this is hearsay, that Ludwig Wittgenstein[6] would have enjoyed the way that language has masterminded the recent technological advances in the lingerie industry.)

Je est un autre.[7]

Due to technical difficulties at the penal colony, Doug Rice is absent.

Grandma died. Dad found cocaine to his liking and began watching

"The Tonight Show" a lot more closely.

April 6, 19?? Knowledge erupted inside my skin. I no longer fit. I couldn't even be an outlaw. Doug Rice can, now, only know of his flesh as rumors and graffiti spread by former lovers.

I do not write anything, let alone write about writing. I write writing.

Recall that early scene in Argento's *Tenebrae?* The scene that has been cut, censored, from the American release? The scene that has not yet been restored? Have you seen this missing scene?

How can you read what is not there? You, Doug Rice, have no cunt.

Once upon a time and a very good time it was, Auntie Josephine wrote to dear dirty Jimmie complaining that she could not read his "bloody book." Immediately, Jimmie wrote back to his aunt telling her to read a prose translation of Homer's *Odyssey* alongside his novel. Unwilling to remove herself, or disinterested in removing herself from her easy chair of reading, comfortably numb Auntie Josephine refused to complicate her eyes while consuming Jimmie's book. Jimmie then demanded that she return his book to him since it was a limited edition and he had signed it. Such a copy had great value.

"Speak to me. Why do you never speak? Speak."

Seriously, what is Mugwump about? (This question from someone who has just finished the act of watching a television set and is, even as we speak, *apriori*, quickly, anon, hurrying to the mall.)

Mugwump is body.

What, then, is your body about?

Not my body. Just body. How easy it is to deceive those who are already deceived. Tell them what they want to hear and they will believe it.[8]

My mother never, not one single time, ever told any of us to turn off the television set. Ever. Not one single time. She made us turn off lights, but never the television, when we left a room. We made sure we had enough money to pay the electric bill every month. That was one bill we never paid late. As our television ate Euripides, Joyce, Aeschylus, Eliot, Faulkner, Dante, Homer,[9] we quit talking altogether. Gave up on words. Mom saved more money and bought a Kodak Instamatic. To this day, I unplug the television set before I leave the house. Afraid, I am, that it might eat what little remains of the fragments I have shored against my ruins.

You [Rice] had to be aware of the risks that you took writing about this content and using these words.

Words have diseased the impossible desires of my body. Infections. I am trying to rescue my cunt. This is my only hope for speech. Faith. Cunt is not simply a Lacanian lack. (Should lack be capitalized?) Cunt is original. Readers must begin by learning cunt as one learns a foreign language empty of signifieds. All else is ycho. A friend wrote to me. She said that she could not read my book. She said that the thought of reading my autobiography, told as a Mugwumpesque cover story, was comical. Instead, she elected to stay on the edge of reading. Maybe only rim-roamers should read cunt.

Can you clarify this?

Is anybody in there? Just nod if you can hear me.

?

No, not in words. In silence, perhaps. Or in words always already said, written on flesh. Or if you entered me.

Each time we speak, each time we utter a word, we should force ourselves to recollect the circumstances under which we had originally learned that word. When she[10] first entered me, I closed my eyes in fear. There must be some way out of here. Shut down and felt fear. Her body. I. She entered my body again and again. Remade my body against my wishes inside her speech. Trying to say. "Open," she said, "your eyes. Look at me."

I am Caddy refusing quotation marks. Refuting origins.

Why is it that you write "Caddy" differently here from the way that you had written Caddie in Mugwump?

I have forgotten how to write.

Before leaving the house, my mother tells me to take care of myself, but I have lost faith in legends.

Amnesia is a lapse in both memory and forgetfulness.

And now we have memory. My mother, after seeing the photographs (the ones I had stolen from her closet) in my book, said, "You know those are real people." Yes, mom, and they are photographs too.

All the words I do remember are ruined.

There is evidence scattered along Liberty Avenue and Penn Avenue in Pittsburgh that Doug Rice is cunt. (Each time that I type Mayor Eastwood's first name, Clint, I fear the typo. What if Clint (this should go without saying) what if Clint lacked that one letter? "Go ahead Punk make my day.")

How did you become cunt?

I suffered through a general misunderstanding of the intention of the Sears and Roebuck catalogue.

I want reading to somehow return to being a physical act. I want readers to be aware of the page as a medium without me, as writer, having to resort to typographical hijinks. *Finnegans Wake* (my original first draft of Mugwump) is, for example, never anything but always a book. Readers of the WAKE can never forget that they are involved in an act of reading. A pirated act much like intercourse.[11] Other books allow you to forget, encourage you to forget. My readers, the few that will have me, must be always and forever aware that they are reading. I am not talking about taking a metafictional pose. In fact, on the contrary, metafiction, as such, does everything BUT make readers conscious that they are reading. Self-reflexivity—in that 1970s Village People metafictional way—is silly. I know my body inside pain. I know writing. Do I know reading? You reading. Blisters on my fingers. Have you ever really been experienced?

"I am coming."

Style is the only legitimate quotation marks.

My life, my body, is the cover story, the story that disguises Mugwump blood. Over coffee in the basement of the Cathedral of Learning,[12] Colin MacCabe accused me of being the last Modernist left on this forbidden Postmodern planet. A relic, he said. Modernism's last scream cutting across the wounded galaxy. "It is a crime," MacCabe simulated, "to write writing onto mirrors against the image." You, my friend, are only a migrant ape caught in a gasoline crack of history.[13]

Hear[14] infection begins. Memorex galaxy.[15] Doug Rice is no, not any sort of High Modernist ruin, even though he has spent most of his life locked, bleeding, inside an Ivory Tower. Rice, unlike his precursing foreign agents, does not allude to the past so much as he willfully plagiarizes the past out of history into hysteria. Rice is that Joycean moment of transcription. Rice is alphabetical Lucia, disturbed, sitting on the floor overhearing Modernism enacted before her very eyes between her father and Beckett.[16]

Rice is inside the hermaphroditic moment; he is inside the erotic space desiring the body of the other.[17] Rice is a parasite being interpenetrated both ways at once. The moment Modernism becomes contaminated by the knock[18] on Joyce's door as he dictates *Finnegans Wake* to Beckett gives birth to Rice as a possibility. Rice is that loss of purity, a desecration. There is little doubt that Rice is any more than an unethical roadside robber and Mugwump a distorted echo. Mugwump systematically corrupts writing. The book, not Rice, disguises fundamental thievery. In the land of Rice's Happy Babel, plagiarism becomes original because so many of the references have been distorted beyond recognition.[19]

In the end, Mugwump is a piously forged misquote. A dead cunt ventriloquy.[20] The Mugwump trouble has been created because Rice has left his signature on the polysemic sutures of the words. Rice is very sorry for having done this. Remember that incest may be nothing more than an anasemic encrypting of the word insect.

---

[1] Remember that incest is nothing more than an encrypting of the word insect.

[2] Use the discipline of High Modernist irony and doubling to come to an understanding of Rice's misuse of appropriately.

[3] This is not meant to imply that William Faulkner was a cross dresser.

[4] At this point it would be helpful to re-read *Agamemnon*.

[5] This is not an allusion to Derek Jarman's work.

[6] Like Faulkner, it is doubtful that Wittgenstein was, necessarily, a cross dresser. It seems that Wittgenstein probably had other things on his mind.

[7] This is in French. Unlike Cunt language, I am uncertain of the French language.

[8] Please do not quote me on this. These are not my words.

[9] Yes, I know, these are all men. While technically, it seems safe to suggest that television sets are male and heterosexual, by nature some have biological disturbances that make them transgress. My father insists that

our family television set was (and probably still is) gay.

[10]She lacks an antecedent. Biographers and critics alike have begun tracking this signifier. She appears to be an indirect reference to . . . well, I am not at liberty to say.

[11]"To read" means to pick up, to borrow. The way that she becomes I while I become she.

[12]The truth of the telling is questionable.

[13]It is not exactly clear who originally said these words—Joyce? Rice? MacCabe? The meaning is also not precise. At this point the recording machine breaks down.

[14]Do not think of this as a typo.

[15]The difference (unDerridean) between Burroughsian cover stories and Pink Floydesque cover stories is very important here. Inside Burroughsian Nova Machines, the lips telling the story move against the story. Inside Pink Floyd, on the other hand, the lips move but the eye cannot hear the story the lips are telling. (Listen to any of Godard's early films.)

[16]MacCabe, the father, at this point suggests that Rice repent. Forget the fear inscribed in a handful of rust. [Note the spectacular plateaus of schizophrenic meaning embedded in the preceding textual thread.]

[17]This just might be a horrifying typo. Not clear in Rice's original hand if this is "other" or "author." When reached for comment, Rice suggested that he is, at least in deed, not a Post-Structuralist; rather, Rice laid claim to actual desire.

[18]This is one of the most momentous knocks in literary history. A knock, like Maz's homer, heard around the world. This knock would never have come into being in *Ulysses*. This knock is the authentic Postmodern moment. Read this: "The perigraphy, that which comes to a text from the outside, from an intertext, a reference, a library. . . . The quotation is already on the page before I start writing; it is a stain, a spot. The intertext, when the text covers it up, is a blotting paper blurred by the remains of the entire writing, whose blemishes it has erased." (Antoine Compagnon) This is not what I mean.

[19]Is a quotation still a quotation when such distortion has occurred?

[20]Rice has lifted the lifewand and the dumb speak. ["These quotation marks are too late."]

Mugwump Glossary

(Note: While none of the following words appear either in Rice's novel or in the preceding essay, we here at the Institute for Beautifying the Image have found these words very helpful for understanding the words Rice actually does use. In compiling this glossary, we have refused to follow the random order imposed on reality by what has come to be respected as the normal alphabetical order. Definitions have also been excluded. Some of the words may be misspelled.)

Glossolia
parasitical origin
monocode
citation
letter from litter
self-citation
paradoxical authenticity
unsystematic penis
scribblative
master/slave (or flayflutter)
fragment
murderous mirrorhand
le journal du voleur
temptation
a pile of dirty rags
Naked Lunch
counterfeit photocopies (and seedy ejaculations)
naysayer
expropriate tongues
anonymous referentiality
pervert
He plucked my peepee!
a tergo
coupe-papier
instrument
sexual penetration and the hymen collide
pelegiarist
[17 indecipherable words follow]

Curtis White Responds: Why Publishers Get the Last Word

Of course, the real tragi-comic backdrop for this little drama developing with such charming flourishes of half-comprehension (Horvath), irony (O'Brien), and comic *coups d'art* (Rice) is the larger drama of Representative Pete Hoekstra's wholly uncomprehending, utterly unironic and yet still-in-spite-of-itself comic attempt to clobber the NEA with the unwilling body of poor FC2, acronymic avant garde, whose *corpus*—after all!—has little more to it than the poor old Boneless One of Toulouse Lautrec's Moulin Rouge.

(This last "sentence," by the way, is the first and only act of *pure disdain* I have allowed myself in the course of the United States House of Representative's scurrilous little war against tiny FC2. The punks, by the way, have sicced our local representative against us (in a flanking move exposing our unprotected rear) (so to speak!), and he promises to visit our president here at Illinois State University in Normal, Illinois, and say to him, "Here, here! What's this? What do you call it, sir? Art, is it? Art, you say?" The above sentence also proves to me something I've wondered about for some time: syntax *is* masochistic. (Well, you coax the sentence sweetly first, before you slide the whip under the bollocks.))

You see how much I *don't* want to take this seriously?

But there is a serious side to it. And this serious side has a lot to do with Brooke Horvath's perhaps innocent Shout Out to the (how shall I put it without appalling our friends at the NEA?) monsters (oh, that's tactful!) who "oversee" (indeed!) the activities of federally funded art. For this all began with Carolyn See's culpable/complicit/collaborationist statement in her review of FC2's *Chick-Lit 2* which appeared in the December 20, 1996, issue of *The Washington Post.* I quote:

"The National Endowment for the Arts funded part of this enterprise, and it is couched in words and concepts that are sure to give Jesse Helms a conniption fit, so he'll doubtless have his conniption fit, and then the writers here can get all prissy and righteous—which isn't as hard as it might seem, even if you're all dolled up in minis and teddies and nose rings. So am I going to sound like a grizzled old veteran down at the American Legion Hall with my medals clanking and my hat falling down over my eyes if I ask, rhetorically, whatever happened to *plot*?"

I have tried often to imagine the moment in which See wrote these lines. Did she really imagine that they (these little words) would have real-world effect? You know, sometimes writers, especially fiction writers, have this curious idea that their words apply only to the little world—full of the neurotic, sweet, cruel fantasies particular to that little world—which the words create.

Could she have imagined (would I have imagined?) that there was a little man out there, a staffer to a longtime Republican representative in Congress, which congressman was at that very moment *looking* for something to use in his next attack on the NEA, that there was, I am trying to say, a certain Derek Max, he of the scolding phone calls, who was *looking* for a suggestion of something "offensive" "out there"?

Was she imagining this? Was this in the world of the possible as she sat at her desk, or perhaps an old Victorian chair like the one I use, writing this review of a book she really didn't much like, by women she really didn't much like, who were writing by the lights of ideas about the world and writing by the lights of ideas about how-to-write-fiction that **she really didn't much like**? Was it? In the world of the possible, I mean?

And when Derek Max found the review, and told Pete Hoekstra, and Derek went out and found the books, all the books, with all the offensive parts, and told everybody—stopped them in the hall and gave them *Mugwump* and said, "Pick a page! Any page!"—and suddenly it was in the newspapers again, bigger now, way blown up, did Carolyn See imagine that this was something *she* had done?

Do you think she could imagine this?

Was it like . . . (oh, I know you'll say this is an extreme analogy, but what the hell! Why publish extreme books if I can't make extreme analogies?) . . . was it like the person, the average Jew-hating German who really doesn't much like the dirty Jews but probably wouldn't *personally* hurt one, and sees Mr. Weitz one day in the street, and says, "Hey, yeah, right there, I think that's one. I think you'll find that one satisfactory to your purposes." And then much to her surprise, why, one of the *Einsatzgruppen* comes over and shoots the poor fucker Weitz right in the head. And she—this average, hard-working, capable, kind-to-her-own-children, Jew-hating woman— looks at this and thinks, "Gott en himmel, I really don't like the stinking, plotless, leather-wearing, experimental writing, nose-ring wearing, **PLOT-LESS** fuckers . . . but I didn't think my little words—my feckless words that I've been using in my feckless realist novels all these years—could get somebody killed!"

Well, what do you think? Is she happy about it anyway? A little pang of conscience? Maybe she's been out of the country for awhile and doesn't even know about it.

I sure don't know.

But with all the rhetoric, all the NEA this and FC2 that, I can't stop thinking about that moment in a writer's studio—the houseplants watered, the kitty in her lap—when Carolyn See (probably a favorite with her friends!; hell, she and I could probably share a *weisen bier* and have a hell of a time!) took her pen or her laptop or her good old fashioned IBM Selectric and wrote,

"Jesse Helms . . . find this."

John O'Brien Responds: Observations on Brooke Horvath's Review and Response

• Part of my initial reaction to Mr. Horvath's review was based upon his offhanded reference to the National Endowment for the Arts. I had no idea what the comment was doing there, except as a way of creating trouble for the author, the publisher, and the NEA itself without providing any analysis of why the NEA had been unwitting. The NEA reference is a way of criticizing the book without taking on the responsibility of doing so directly. Or could I have misread Mr. Horvath's review? Did he really intend this as a compliment to both the book and NEA's funding of it? Was the comment merely neutral?

• Mr. Horvath implies in his response that he has now fallen victim to censorship because I did not run his review. Reviews in *RCF* are supposed to address formal concerns, as the written directives to reviewers state. If a review fails to do this, and in fact goes in quite the opposite direction, then it will not be published. Mr. Horvath was told that, regardless of his comment about the NEA, his review would not have been used because it did not conform to review criteria. Does Mr. Horvath believe that he has a God-given or Constitutional right to publish anything he writes in any publication he chooses? I don't know. Perhaps. Apparently.

• If Doug Rice's book fails as a novel, that failure does not reside in its subject matter, but in its construction as a work of art, and any decent critic can explain the basis for this failure. Well, let's say *should* be able to so explain.

• Mr. Horvath seems appalled by the idea of "art for art's sake," which is a meaningless phrase that rhetorically functions on a level occupied in American culture by such phrases as "so you think criminals shouldn't be punished?" or "so you don't love your country?" He seems disdainful of velvet Elvises, but I am uncertain on what basis. Will he soon be alerting gas stations across the country of the art that they are unwittingly supporting?

• But I truly cannot begin to figure out what Mr. Horvath's critical standards are. At one point he says, for instance, that aesthetic evaluation leads to "the trivialization of art," but at other times he seems to admit that aesthetics can be used. Just what are his criteria? Can anyone figure this out? I know that he wants us all to do such things as exercise taste, make discriminations, assess worth of achievement, and so on. But on the basis of what? Did I miss something here? The closest that I can come to something is that art offers "a platform of experience." Not just experience but a *platform* of it. What exactly does a platform of experience look like? I am not sure whether Mr. Horvath and I have the same sense of platformingness, but just the other day I was out walking and saw a lot of experience, and perhaps even had an experience or two myself. Was that art I was seeing out there? Did I find it??!! Son of a bitch, for years I have tried to find the damn thing in museums and books, and now I find out that it's the same thing as experience, of which I am already possessed, and therefore which in some way or another must make me a work of art myself! But am I a platform full? This I don't know. I must, alas, be one of these "inept or unprepared" people who could wind up hurting myself when I throw my pearls (I don't even have any damn pearls!) before swine (I also don't have any swine!).

• I fully agree with Mr. Horvath's view that "It is . . . our refusal to offer persuasive support for those value judgments we do condescend to make that explains why we aren't listened to. . . ." This was precisely my reaction to Mr. Horvath's review, and now his response. We couldn't be in more agreement on this one!

• I must disagree with Mr. Horvath, however, when he suggests that *RCF* claims that "disturbing, difficult, upsetting" art is "better than Danielle Steel or Robert J. Waller." *RCF* has never claimed that anyone's art is better than a human being, even Danielle Steel or Robert J. Waller. Now that I think about it, though, I will go out on a limb and say that I personally believe that such art is better than these human beings. Once again, Mr. Horvath and I seem to be in agreement!

• Mr. Horvath's comment about the need for a "complex task of evaluation" is one I cannot argue with. I just wish that he had performed this "complex task" in his review.

• Despite all of the blather in his response that seems to be pro-the-people, Mr. Horvath appears to elect himself the arbiter of, not only what constitutes art, but what critical standards should be used in its evaluation. If I own a velvet Elvis, do I get a vote in this? I don't think so, and just when I thought I was getting some real fine artistic sensibilities! I paid $19.95 for one of these things at an art show sponsored by America for Americans United, and now Mr. Horvath apparently has decided that I am one of those people who have to be talked to, persuaded, and cajoled because I am not possessed of his intelligence and taste. I plan to go home tonight and take my Elvis off the wall, but I will insist that when the morning sun hits the natural sheen of that imitation velvet, it's one of the prettiest and most wholesome things I have ever seen!

• Finally, reviewers usually have the last word, but shouldn't. They should be held to the same reviewing process that is applied to the authors of books. Given the generally abysmal state of book reviewing in this country—one that would apparently allow almost anyone to review a book as long as he or she can breathe—reviewers should be inspected very carefully. My view was and is that Mr. Horvath has objections to Doug Rice's novel that are based upon the novel's content. If that is his view, then he should state it directly rather than through couched complaints about the NEA. He should stand up for what he believes in, if he can figure out what that is.

Book Reviews

Carole Maso. *Aureole*. Ecco, 1996. 214 pp. $22.00.

Aureole is an exploration of liminal states, "the place where one thing is about to change into another." The spaces between light and dark, waking and dream, and language and meaning are only some of the passages invoked here. Betweenness defines Maso's writing practice: the text hovers between poetry and prose, lyric and narrative. The relation between writing and the body is central. Composed of a preface and thirteen sections, *Aureole* focuses and refocuses on the connections between language and sexuality. In the first part of this narrative, "The Women Wash Lentils," two women, lovers, read from a dictionary of French slang: "Read, she begs: and I straddle her mouth. . . . "Sex, words and the body conjoin as words and phrases are defined: "To have a crush on: *faire des yeux de merlan frites*, or literally, to make fried marlin eyes at one another." The gaps between French and English, between formal and colloquial diction, become figures for the play of desire between the lovers.

Just as the text investigates the relation between self and other, lover and beloved, it also examines the relationship between Maso, the writer, and other women writers and artists. As well as Colette, Gertrude Stein, Virginia Woolf, and Djuna Barnes, all credited in the book's acknowledgments, Marguerite Duras's character Anne-Marie Stretter from her play *India Song* and the writer Anna Kavan appear in the body of the text. In my favorite section, "Sappho Sings the World Ecstatic," Maso juxtaposes her own writing with Sappho's poetry, sentences from Gertrude Stein, and the shot lists from filmmaker Maya Deren's haunting and beautiful films *Land* and *Meshes of the Afternoon*. The women's voices work as a collage; juxtaposition is the organizing principle as poetic logic builds the narrative.

In the preface Maso writes, "Line by line I have tried to slip closer to a language that might function more bodily, more physically, more passionately." Throughout her work, Maso seeks new textual structures to contain her experiments, continually pushing the boundaries and questioning the definitions of what fiction might be. In her novels Maso proposes a narrative poetics. In *Aureole* she offers an erotics of narrative, a celebration of the possibilities of human connection and language. [Nicole Cooley]

David Foster Wallace. *A Supposedly Fun Thing I'll Never Do Again: Essays and Arguments*. Little, Brown, 1997. 353pp. $23.95.

Anyone not enamored by last year's spectacular *Infinite Jest* might suspect that a lame self-referential joke lies buried in the title of this collection, but the essays themselves prove that David Foster Wallace is a comic genius who need not resort to such pandering. Previously published between 1992-1996, these seven essays address an array of topics, including Wallace's misadventures "In Quest of Managed Fun" aboard a mass-market luxury Caribbean cruise, a piece which could effectively be retitled "Fear and Loathing on the Love Boat." During his visit to the Illinois State Fair in "Getting Away from Already Being Pretty Much Away from It All," Wallace navigates his way among pungent livestock and nauseating rides as competitors for the Blue Ribbon dessert mistake the *Harper's* on his press credentials for *Harper's Bazaar* (the one with recipes)—a confusion Wallace encourages until he can ingest his fill of prize-winning desserts. In addition to this kind of "pith-helmeted anthropological reporting," Wallace recounts how growing up in the geometric grid of the Midwest's Tornado Alley helped him develop a talent for calculating wicked angles and playing unpredictable winds to his advantage on the competitive junior tennis circuit. All of the essays evoke themes Wallace explores in his fiction, such as mass culture, spectacle, desire, expertise, control, and conditioning. Two profiles, about filmmaker David Lynch on the set of *Lost Highway* and tennis player Michael Joyce on the pro tour, provide dazzling philosophical investigations into the nature of artistry and excellence. The book only contains two literary forays: a review of the death of the author question and "*E Unibus Plurum*: Television and U.S. Fiction," Wallace's critique of a postmodern legacy of thirty-plus years of self-conscious irony. Originally published in the *Review of Contemporary Fiction* in 1993, the latter stands out as the highlight of the collection, an absolutely indispensible text for students of twentieth-century American literature and culture. While these invigorating excursions into lit crit are outrageously entertaining and laugh-out-loud funny, his journalistic observations are fresh and thoughtful; both display the boundless energy of Wallace's hyperkinetic prose and erudite attention. One fervently hopes Wallace will reconsider the "never" in his title, because the essays here are genuinely fun. [Trey Strecker]

———

J. G. Ballard. *Cocaine Nights*. Flamingo/HarperCollins, 1996. 329 pp. £16.99.

Criminality has become a kind of performance art at the end of this millennium, the protagonist of J. G. Ballard's wonderful new novel notes, the last real impetus for communal action in a bored leisure society.

It's no surprise, then, to find the author of twenty-five books, including such cult classics as *The Atrocity Exhibition* and *Crash* (the latter now an unnervingly good film by David Cronenberg), turning to the murder mystery genre for inspiration, and, with typical innovative grace, reconfiguring its key narrative elements: Charles Prentice, a British travel writer who enjoys the in-betweenness of his profession, journeys to a town forty minutes up the coast from Gibraltar on behalf of his carefully self-destructive brother, Frank, who has confessed to five horrific killings he apparently hasn't committed; even the police handling the case aren't quite convinced he's guilty, despite the fact they must arrest and hold him for trial since the scant evidence they possess seems to implicate him.

Charles's quest for the real murderer leads him into the world of safe-zone compounds that stretch along the beaches of the Costa del Sol, fortified antiseptic theme villages and retirement resorts several hundred yards in width and several hundred miles in length, filled with ghostly ad-men and TV execs who have nothing to do with their time except waste it. Behind those walls' pristine radically internalized nowhere space of blue kidney-shaped swimming pools and long siestas exists a cloudless land of unreality, a series of Baudrillardian simulacra of the Good Life, and slack-faced monotony—a microcosm of Europe's future.

And behind that universe with its surveillance cameras and satellite dishes, Charles discovers, Chinese-puzzle-box-like, another more shadowy dimension busy with vandalism, theft, arson, amateur porn films, and a pharmacy of hardcore drugs. In this second-order world, local prostitutes turn out to be the wives of those ad-men and TV execs looking for a little fun, while, just for a lark, residents sit primly in their cars in tidy rows in parking lots late at night and watch the rape of young women in their headlights. Behind what turns out to be a bizarre social experiment stands a charismatic figure who believes such crimes are the only things that keep us interesting, creative, and alive as a culture. The result, as one of the characters comments, "is Kafka re-shot in the style of *Psycho*."

Ballard thereby transforms the murder mystery into a philosophical mode of inquiry that explores the conjunction of the imaginative act and the lawless postmodern zone where everything is possible, while suggesting that transgressive behavior might in the end—at least in some cases—actually motivate public good. And he does so with signature panache and intelligence, creating a flawless narrative architecture, the surreal clarity of a town dreamed by Magritte, an unsettling mixture of horror and beauty, and a subtle yet pervasive sense of trespass, his narrative precinct always sheathed beneath a gentle patinated paranoia where final answers lie around the next corner, up the next flight of stairs, and where every one of us is implicated in the spectacular horrorshow called the late twentieth century. [Lance Olsen]

Ann Beattie. *My Life, Starring Dara Falcon.* Knopf, 1997. 307 pp. $24.00.

I am writing this review on April 24; the pub date for this novel is May 12.

But today I read Michiko Kakutani's review of the book in the *New York Times,* appearing two and a half weeks before publication and almost assuredly before the book is in stores. An accident that our ever-brilliant reviewer at the *Times,* ever the fact-checker, jumped the gun? I don't think so; in case the review itself doesn't discourage enough people, let's make sure that even Beattie fans will not be able to go out and get the book once they see it's available. The review is one of the most scurrilous I have ever read, one that, even on a factual level, has little to do with the book itself. The novel opens with the first-person narrator reading in the *Times* that Dara Falcon has died, which sets in motion the narrator's story of her own life, one inextricably tied to that of Dara Falcon. *The Great Gatsby* begins in a somewhat similar way, and there is something about the style and sense of Beattie's novel that reminds me very much of Fitzgerald and raises many of the questions that *Gatsby* does in relation to the teller of the story and the object of the teller's obsessions. Beattie pulls this off with great subtlety, which is not easy to do. Dara Falcon is both the narrator's idealized woman and the source of her misery, and this tension is everywhere apparent; despite the damage that Dara inflicts, the narrator remains fascinated by and faithful to her (if only because so much of her identity has been derived from her), though—like Nick Carraway—she also provides a vicious critique, quiet yet fatal. Well, Kakutani sees nothing of this or rather invents her own version. In Kakutani's version, "It's hard to understand why Jean is so mesmerized by Dara," because Dara is not only pretentious but "worse, she emerges as a user, a manipulator and a pathological liar." Kakutani must have enormous problems with (to choose one of thousands) Madame Bovary; in fact, Beattie's narrator, never mind Dara, shares many qualities with Madame Bovary: dumb, witless, and completely self-absorbed. But we must remember that Kakutani is the founder of "We Only Get Involved with the Right People Movement." In her conclusion Kakutani complains that this work, unlike previous Beattie novels, lacks "maturity" (well, Michiko, give it time, it hasn't even reached stores, it was just born!) and "melancholy wisdom" (good old melancholy wisdom, whatever that might be). In a final, crushing blow—having made the novel sound quite conventional—she says that the novel is an "ill-conceived experiment"!!! An experiment? An experiment of what? Nowhere in the review has she suggested that Beattie is experimenting with anything. And so the word is there as the *Times*'s favorite warning signal to readers—look out, this is experimental!

So, what *is* Kakutani's problem? Putting aside her general mediocrity as a reviewer, why does she have such objections to this book? The answer would seem to reside in the fact that the narrator is an upper-middle-class housewife who, in trying to escape the drudgery of her life, turns to a figure such as Dara as a model. In brief, this is the 1990s, Madame Bovary is dead, Beattie isn't being politically correct and thus provides no models for real American women to emulate, which is after all the sole purpose of literary art. Yes? It's supposed to have a moral lesson, right? Teach us something?

Of course. The *Times* hath spoken. [John O'Brien]

Irvine Welsh, *The Marabou Stork Nightmares*. Norton, 1996. 284 pp. Paper: $13.00.

Welsh is back with the schemies. In his novel *The Marabou Stork Nightmares,* Irvine Welsh revisits the life of raging Scottish youth with the same fury and honesty as *Trainspotting* and *Acid House.* As with his previous books, Welsh displays an almost unsettling ability to sympathetically complicate the lives of loathsome characters. In *Nightmares,* Welsh writes from the perspective of Roy Strang, a racist, sexist, homophobic budding soccer hooligan. Miraculously, he manages to do so in such a way that while we understand how Strang's own self-loathing conspires with the cruelty of his life to prescribe habitual violence, we still hold him personally responsible for his involvement in a horrific crime. Welsh constructs a situation in which there is the possibility, perhaps the imperative, for understanding without forgiveness.

It is this posing of the crux between empathy and justice that makes Welsh's use of the first person the most interesting aspect of the novel, and the most disturbing. Although Strang remains in a coma throughout the novel, he speaks to the reader as if in a confessional booth or bar. As Welsh interweaves three levels of Strang's subconscious, we hear how his lifelong inaction results in his own predicament. Moreover, we are forced to examine our own complicity in both the reading of the text and our own social actions. If we accept the status quo, we can read biographical excuses into Strang's crime, thereby reinforcing the novel's culture of misguided victimization. However, if we read and live critically, we may recognize unfairness and act justly. This is the understanding to which Strang is coming, and it puts quite a terrifying spin on the time he is spending in a coma: his suspended existence becomes an inverted purgatory which offers only the tease of redemption and the time to factually and imaginatively convict himself. As Strang's surreal dream quest collapses onto itself and reveals him as the evil he had been seeking, so we find our own best intentions (and the narratives which surround them) exposed for their self-congratulatory complicity.

Ultimately, the style and subject matter of *Marabou Stork Nightmares* combine to make an incision into the layer of slothful acceptance and rationalization that covers society. As Welsh shows, the putrid stuff that lies beneath may carry fearful implications, but the honest engagement with this underbelly may also reveal the only beauty there is in this world—that of the struggle. [Robert Zamsky]

Wideman, John Edgar. *The Cattle Killing.* Houghton Mifflin, 1996. 212 pp. $22.95.

John Edgar Wideman's fiction is always a good stiff shot, clearing away the fog of certainty and revealing the terrifying depths of complexity. Whenever you step into one of Wideman's books, all bets are off: certainties of race, class, gender, and family are all gone. In their place Wideman elaborates the much less comforting, and much more real, contingencies of modern life.

In *The Cattle Killing* Wideman's engagement with complexity contributes a sobering voice to the contemporary clamor over identity. For Wideman, identity is fluid and anti-essentialistic. It exists in the relationships between individuals, in the movement of the histories that create, sustain, and connect them. It is about the business of making do.

The novel takes its name from a historical account of European slave traders who turned the African Xhosa's own religious beliefs against them: as the traders watched the Xhosa die from European diseases, they spread the myth that the only way to survive the disease and famine was to sacrifice the spiritually revered and life-sustaining cattle. Eventually believing the myth, the Xhosa did so, and thus condemned themselves to starvation and capture. Wideman recounts this story within a weave of other narratives from the eighteenth century: an English nobleman's clandestine anatomy studies, the racial tensions underpinning a Philadelphia cholera epidemic, a preacher, and an interracial marriage. Finally, the entire novel is framed by the author's own apparently personal reflections on his relationships with his father and son.

This tangled structure enables Wideman to assert the value of storytelling. Here, facts matter only as far as they survive in and contribute to the narratives of individuals. Facts cannot be ignored; in fact scientistic rationalism haunts this novel. But for Wideman, storytelling is about surviving the real events of history, as well as other people's versions of them. As such, forging an identity is a never-ending and always contingent process of narrating your way through this muck.

In the letter that ends the book Wideman revisits the advice he had given his own imprisoned son in *Philadelphia Fire:* "hold on." In this world where there are no certainties upon which to ground an identity and all we have are the fleeting moments when our stories seem to cohere, perhaps this is the only advice there is. [Robert Zamsky]

Nicholas Mosley. *Children of Darkness and Light.* Secker & Warburg,1996. 241 pp. £15.99.

At 241 pages *Children of Darkness and Light* is an easier read than

Mosley's imposing 1990 Whitbread Prize winner *Hopeful Monsters;* however like almost all of Mosley's work it poses serious problems philosophical. Lacking the narrative baggage of *Monsters,* its style is a bit more abstract, darting, witty—strongly reminiscent of Mosley's earlier *Imago Bird* and *Serpent.* Harry, a canny middle-aged journalist—an easily recognizable semblance of earlier protagonists, or the author—is curious about the children in the former Yugoslavia and in Cumbria, England who were said to have had visions of the Virgin Mary. In the background there are his marriage in difficulty, his son on the brink of adolescence, Harry's still insistent sexual monkey, and our real world of atrocities and nihilism; Harry wants to know how to care for them all: "So I went and wrote a piece about the wonderment of the children on the side of the hill; the ruthlessness of church and state authorities in their treatment of the children. I mangaged to make the harassment of the children seem vaguely sexual." This is not straight cynicism but a reminder of what we know about ourselves. Mosley offers protagonists who are fully intelligent self-conscious searchers, in whom the reader might hopefully see his or her own consciousness (impressions, coils of thought, and vague wonderings) and toward whom it is impossible to be patronizing. As a quest for the renewing vision of children, Harry's enquiry is a further exploration of one of Mosley's earlier themes, that humans might learn to see themselves not as rigid, trapped characters, but as bits and pieces of light.

The behavior of these knowing children seems mysterious: they appear here or there unexpectedly, as though they were visiting from some other level of reality (as, of course, they are). Mosley's journalist enters a story which is also a kind of experiment; like anyone, he is both actor and observer at the same time, necessarily part of the event he reports. We are perpetually at the horizon of an unformed world and undecided events; what, then, is the effect of our knowing that it is our own brains which configure our world? The model for Harry's search is in those experiments on the puzzling behavior of light quanta, in which scientists are in effect trying to see their means of seeing and thinking. Mosley has not overdone the science—this is not pop philosophy exploiting "quantum mysteries"—but the paradoxes of quantum physics are the theoretical scaffolding behind Harry's respect and tolerance for the mysteries he encounters. There are more than literary grounds for likening children to particles of light, and, to honor what is obviously Mosley's hope, the recognition of this might indeed help spark some veneration for their unknown potentialities. For humans, he asks, might there not be some responsibility to behave like gods?

Clearly Mosley demands much of his readers, and *Children* is not for those who would prefer to keep their reality unconvoluted, to believe, perhaps, that Harry's eventual encounter with the Virgin Mary either is or is not genuine. The atmosphere is right: we are suspended in an experiment in progress. [John Banks]

Robert Coover. *Briar Rose*. Grove, 1996. 86 pp. $18.00.

Last year, Robert Coover marked the thirtieth anniversary of his first novel with *John's Wife*, a huge, sprawling narrative tracing dozens of characters over thirty years or so of their town's and our country's history. Now, less than a year later, Coover has given us another novel, *Briar Rose*, but this one is a compact, focused story with only three characters, but nevertheless a story as timeless as people's desire to know exactly who they are and why they're here.

Coover has frequently found new ways to tell old stories, from Noah's Ark to Pinocchio to *Casablanca*. And he has frequently told stories through shifting points of view, repetition, and variation, to create a circular structure rather than a straightforward linear narrative. He uses both techniques and uses them brilliantly in *Briar Rose*, a revisiting of the Sleeping Beauty fairy tale. The short chapters alternate among three points of view. The first is the handsome prince, who has heard about the mysterious, entranced beauty, waiting to be awakened by a kiss, and who is now hacking his way through the briars that surround her castle, planning to make a name for himself. The second is Rose, the sleeping woman, who dreams over and over of waking up and of hearing a strange old woman tell stories about other entranced beauties who woke to lives far from happy ever after. The third is the evil fairy who first entranced Rose and who now cares for her and inhabits her dreams, tempting her to prick her finger over and over again and torturing her with those stories about other entranced beauties. As the novel progresses, the chapters seem to repeat. The prince loses sight of the castle, and his fantasies about the sleeping maiden become nightmares of entrapment and unfulfilled longing. Rose in her sleeping state grows disillusioned as she becomes less and less able to distinguish among her dreams, fated to repeat the unreal cycle of pricking, sleeping, and waking. The fairy becomes dissatisfied with her role of observer, above it all, but detached and cold. She is tempted to feel desire, to be like Sleeping Beauty, to want both the pricking and the prince.

Briar Rose asks what happens to our notions of identity when beginnings are ambiguous, quests are never fulfilled, desire is never gratified, and events never progress but forever repeat. Like the story it's based on, *Briar Rose* is a classic by a contemporary master. [Robert L. McLaughlin]

Peter Høeg. *The Woman and the Ape*. Trans. by Barbara Haveland. Farrar, Straus & Giroux, 1996. 261 pp. $23.00.

Peter Høeg's fourth novel defies easy categorization. It is at once a tale of personal strength, a love story, and an ecological morality tale. To choose one of these or any other conventional label to describe *The Woman and the*

Ape is to ignore its obvious unconventionality; for the personal strength comes from a woman so severely alcoholic that she seems beyond repair, the love story is between a woman and a primate, and the environmental lesson is delivered as an eloquent speech by an ape who seems more an extraterrestrial envoy from the future than an evolutionary mistake from the past.

One could begin by describing it as an imaginative exodus into the soul of contemporary London. Høeg paints London as the vital center of the modern civilized world, but it is also, "one of *the* largest habitats for nonhuman creatures on this earth." Most of these creatures—mice, seagulls, insects—are beneath everyday notice, but one arrives unexpectedly to call attention to the manifold problems that humanity has created. Erasmus, the ape of the title, crosses the thin line between his own species and ours in order to make us aware of these problems.

Though fantastic, this side of the tale may sound easy, but it is complicated by the other side of the tale. Through her interaction with Erasmus, Madelene, the woman of the title, undergoes a transformation no less stunning than his. A wealthy, alienated woman who begins each day with a membrane-burning shot of high-proof alcohol, Madelene gradually finds meaning in her life through her relationship with Erasmus, who has come to her house as a subject of study for her husband, an animal behavior researcher. The more time Erasmus and Madelene spend together, the more difficult it is to distinguish differences between them.

Høeg blurs this line between the human and the animal in even more subtle ways. In one striking sequence, he recreates the Garden of Eden in contemporary England, replacing Adam (the name of Madelene's husband) with the ape, demolishing the terms of the creation/evolution debate. Through such flourishes, *The Woman and the Ape* forces us to think deeply about the issues that Høeg raises. Yet it never feels mired in such issues since the author deftly balances profound ideas with classic good-guy/bad-guy chase scenes. Although difficult to define, it is unquestionably troubling, entertaining, and masterfully done. [D. Quentin Miller]

Peter Schneider. *Couplings.* Trans. Philip Boehm. Farrar, Straus & Giroux, 1996. 293 pp. $24.00.

German author Peter Schneider's 1992 novel *Paarungen,* newly translated by Philip Boehm, uses the intertwined narratives of three (anti-)love stories to lead the reader on an engrossing tour through the quotidian experience of the middle-aging intellectual class of pre-Unification West Berlin. At forty, Eduard Hoffman, a molecular biologist tracking a virus implicated in Multiple Sclerosis, wonders if he—or anyone in his society—is capable of loving—or even of keeping house together beyond the three-year-and-six-month "half-life" of the contemporary romance. He and two intimates from the café scene—Andre, a composer updating Mozart's *Don Giovanni,* and Theo, anarchist poet and librettist on the *Don Giovanni* project, bet on who, one year hence, would still be together with his present lover. No one wins. Against this backdrop, Schneider adds bright pigments to the cement-gray palette one associates with depictions of life in the shadow of the Wall— indeed, at times one cannot resist the suspicion that the author, in the midst of this serious book of ideas and social commentary, is attempting humor. Schneider's characters, as intellectual as they are articulate, wax passionate on scientific ethics and the nature-nurture controversy, on animal rights extremism, on fertility testing—even on the nuances of guilt for the possible Nazis in one's family tree, however distant. The novel also provides glimpses into the assimilated-yet-self-conscious remains of Jewish life in the new Germany and a vivid tableau of a wildly unassimilated family of astonishing in-laws newly escaped from the Soviet East.

It is worth mentioning that Boehm's translation is masterful for its syntactical variety and good ear. The novel's omniscient narrative strategy mixes a rather a heavy dose of explanation in with the observations. (It's noteworthy that Schneider's two earlier books, *The Wall Jumper* and *The German Comedy,* are nonfiction). Thankfully, explanations and observations both are keen, and the reader, in the end, is happy for the authorial accompaniment. *Couplings* is at once exotic and familiar, a fine portrait of a famous city at a singular time, a fine exploration of what it means to take stock of one's life when one's mortality can no longer be ignored and when one must come to terms with his place in the ultimate scheme of things. [Rod Kessler]

———————

William Gibson. *Idoru.* Putnam, 1996. 292 pp. $24.95.

It's been well over a decade since William Gibson blasted into heavy rotation on the alternative literary charts with his cyberpunk classic *Neuromancer* (1984), surely the novel for which he'll be remembered. With each successive endeavor—with the possible exception of *The Difference Engine* (1991), his fiery collaboration with Bruce Sterling based on the premise that Charles Babbage invented the computer a good century before the actual fact—he's become less willing to take narrative chances, further committed to mainstreaming his fiction, and *Idoru* continues this trajectory.

Idoru feels stripped down compared to *Neuromancer*. It is less stylistically textured, less surreal, and less shaped by Gibson's early visionary consciousness. Like his previous novel, *Virtual Light* (1993), it exhibits a more pronounced if slightly flimsy comic edge and a remarkably less-pronounced presence of cyberspace, the concept Gibson explored with such dazzle in his first novel that critics began to convince themselves he actually invented it. Even the haunting shadows that permeate the geographies of that earlier work have been shunted aside by the bright colorful light which floods every corner of *Idoru*'s world, pushing back the night and, in a sense, the darkly human with it.

We are in familiar terrain in *Idoru*. In many ways a companion to *Mona Lisa Overdrive* (1988), fame has become all famed out here. The media has generated all it can, used it up, so there's just not enough of it to go around anymore—except for Rez, the fabulously wealthy rock'n'roll star planning to marry, much to his publicity machine's chagrin, a mesmerizing Japanese "idoru," or idol-singer, who exists solely as a personality construct in the electronic beyond. An intersecting plotline reminiscent of the one in *Count Zero* (1986) draws two seemingly unrelated characters—Chia Pet McKenzie, a fourteen-year-old member of the Seattle chapter of Rez's band's fan club, and Colin Laney, a researcher for a tabloid TV show whose job it is to hunt for patterns of information that accrue around and ultimately define certain individuals—toward this narrative center by means of a nano-assembler MacGuffin that echoes those magic glasses in *Virtual Light*.

And yet, for all the déjà vu we feel reading this novel, from the setting (the Japan-as-near-future we saw in *Neuromancer*) to several of the characters (both Rydell, the goofy security man, and Yamazaki, the existential sociologist, return from *Virtual Light* for curtain calls), there's something utterly addictive about it. It goes down like a bag of shiny gumdrops. Part of this has to do with its demon-speed momentum built around masterfully crafted chapter hooks. But there's more. Gibson has learned to create a real emotional depth to his characters—especially Chia in this case—that's honestly moving, and he has a knock-out ear for dialogue. Too, he's a master of detail: the towers in Tokyo grown by nanotechnology that are "like watching a candle melt, but in reverse"; the drug that makes people into stalkers of public figures.

And it's these details which point to the true strength of Gibson's project: he has always had his finger on the epinephrinized pulse of our postmodern culture, and has always been able to cast our fractured obsessions and fears into shockingly intelligent forms that make us see our sociohistorical position as if we've never seen it before. In *Idoru*, he has touched the flashpoint where our identity has dissolved into bright pixels generated by digital systems we no longer quite comprehend. He's caught the instant where our skin has evaporated into holographic light, smudging toward the horizon of unknowability. [Lance Olsen]

Alice Munro. *Selected Stories.* Knopf, 1996. 545 pp. $30.00.

"If I had been making a proper story out of this, I would have ended it with my mother not answering and going ahead of me across the pasture. I didn't stop there, I suppose, because I wanted to find out more, remember more. I wanted to bring back all I could," so the narrator of Alice Munro's story "The Ottawa Valley" finishes her tale.

The twenty-eight stories compiled from Munro's seven collections of short fiction to make up *Selected Stories* are at once proper stories and not, full of answers and nonanswers, of people always hovering on the boundary of self-understanding. Munro has an archaeological approach to her subjects, as if shaking sand through screen after screen to find the missing pieces, if any, that might complete the puzzle. Indeed, change is the only constant in Munro's tales. Her characters are inherently complex and unsettled, and her plots move in broad, sweeping strokes back and forth over time, traversing lifetimes and generations. Munro approaches her subjects from a vicissitude of angles and with an unrelenting psychological perspective, all in a subtle yet unblushing tone, and with a crispness of observation. But mystery only unravels further mystery, though in much of her work Munro treads and retreads the same territory: the journey of a young woman—always astute and observant—out of the poverty of the rural towns of Western Ontario and into the larger world and her search for happiness and fulfillment, her disappointments with love and with men.

Precisely by retraveling the same territory—this capacity "to remember more" and "to bring back all"—Munro so accurately maps the vagaries of fate. In *A Wilderness Station*, a story from the author's most recent collection, *Open Secrets*, Munro provides us with this summation: "This world is a wilderness, in which we may indeed get our station changed, but the move will be out of one wilderness station unto another."

Perhaps what slightly mars this gathering of Munro's work is the absence of any editorial explanation why the particular stories included in *Selected Stories* were chosen from the impressive bulk of Munro's oeuvre. Otherwise, this collection stands as an important survey of the work of a writer easily distinguished as one of this century's masters of the short story form. [Jeanne Claire van Ryzin]

Harry Mulisch. *The Discovery of Heaven*. Trans. Paul Vincent. Viking, 1996. 729 pp. $34.95.

Although I have read this erudite, witty masterpiece only once, I must assert that it is one of the great novels since World War II. The novel—filled with references to *The New Atlantis*; the Pythagorian theory of numbers; the chromatic scale; the kabbalistic reading of the Old Testament as *gematria*— does not ever become a dull encyclopedia; it is, indeed, a moving narrative of fathers and sons, of "accidental" deaths, of "the very thing that happens" (Edson's mysterious, ordinary phrase).

The novel is divided into four parts: "The Beginning of the Beginning"; "The End of the Beginning"; "The Beginning of the End," and "The End of the End." The four-part structure introduces the ideas of "origins and ends," almost symmetrical designs, mystical meanings of number. And to complicate matters, the novel begins and ends with "heavenly conversation and/or creation." These conversations cast an uncanny, spectral dimension on the material world. Thus we are not surprised that names are odd—the cryptographer "onno"; his "son" "Quinten" referred to as "QuQu"; the mother "Ada"—think of Nabokov who is mentioned often—who "exists" in a coma and somehow gives birth to Quinten. Events which seem arbitrary and meaningless assume great significance when they recur in slightly different ways. The notions of transformation, paradox, and inversion (perversion, subversion) haunt the novel.

If we look at any page, we discover that there is a "discovery" which may be hidden by the revelation of another "discovery." The novel is filled with secrets, clues to a final solution—yes, there are crucial references to the Holocaust—which is never final. *The "solution" is, often, the "mystery."* Here is a representative passage. Onno thinks of Ada: "Perhaps, he thought, true pure love, like all flowers, flourished best, with its roots in muck and mud. Perhaps that was a law of life that held everything together: the day which was day only by the grace of the night. But if the day was defined by the night, then wasn't there an element of night at the heart of the day? Was the day really the true, pure day? Was there a black cuckoo at the heart of the day?" Consider this passage closely—it plays with the notion of "opposites" (night and day, man and woman, flower and muck); suggests that "opposition" is, perhaps, a matter of perspective. But there is also unity. There is the sense that everything holds together briefly.

We would not expect such linguistic, philosophical, theological passages to move us, but we are hypnotized by the heavenly style. Perhaps only a Dutch writer—a Spinoza?—can create honey in "geometry." At the novel's end the angels converse about the meaning of the text. The novel ends with these words spoken by one angel who refuses to accept the final "meaning," the "last call" (another Mulisch title): "Do you hear me? I'm not leaving it at that! How do they have the nerve? Who do they think they are, the upstarts! Answer me!" The angel is answered by the blankness of the page. And perhaps, the blankness is the very space which preceeds another "Beginning of the Beginning." [Irving Malin]

Tom De Haven, *Derby Dugan's Depression Funnies*. Metropolitan Books, 1996. 290 pp. Paper: $12.00.

A sequel of sorts to De Haven's novel of early comic-strip publishing, *Funny Papers* (1985), *Derby Dugan's Depression Funnies* follows narrator

Al Bready as the comic-strip ghostwriter and prodigiously prolific pulp-fiction author negotiates a pair of low-level crises in his life in late 1930s New York. His first problem is the sudden illness of one of his bosses, Walter Geebus, the comic-strip artist whose rabid right-wing politics and general irascibility fail to sour Bready on the pleasures of writing about the peregrinations of a orphaned urchin in the comic strip "Durby Dugan." Complicating Bready's life is the prospect that Jewel Rodgers, his typist and Platonic sweetheart, is about to move upstate with her dim-witted and suddenly suspicious husband. How to replace Geebus on the wildly successful comic strip, occupies Bready's thoughts as he drifts comfortably through a smoky world of speakeasies, neighborhood brothels, gangsters, and gossipmongers.

Bready's narrative voice is sharp and cynical, and he has a quick ear for a slangy quip. The book's structure itself evokes the breezy punch of the comics: the chapters, called "episodes", are rather shortish (sometimes only a few sentences) and often end with a punchline of sorts. As the novel develops it becomes clear that the tough-talking Bready isn't as confident in the world as he tries to sound: the trauma of childhood family discord resurfaces in the form of his troubled sister, now living alone in the empty family home, and the detachment that serves Bready so well as a writer likewise renders him unable either to grab the professional opportunities that come his way or to convince Jewel to stay in New York, even though she makes it clear that she won't need much convincing.

Derby Dugan's Depression Funnies does a fine job of evoking the texture of an imagined Depression-era New York, with its distinctive slang, the smells of its delis, and the shouts of the newsboys. The recreation of the little-known netherworld of the marginal publishers (some of whom are intrigued by the prospects offered by the new-fangled comic books just starting to appear), unsung ghostwriters, and pulp-fiction hacks is especially well done. De Haven's novel will be a romp for cognoscenti who can pick out the bits of historical and biographical fact that make up the novel's fictional *bricolage*, as fragments of comic-strip creators such as Rube Goldberg and Harold Gray emerge at different points, while "Joe Palooka" artist Ham Fisher appears in proper persona. The air of verisimilitude is enhanced even more by cartoonist Art Spiegelman's jacket design and a sample "Derby Dugan" interior page, an episode whose visual style captures perfectly the novel's mixture of convincing period detail and cool, slightly parodistic irony. Fans of comics history will need to read this book; other readers will simply want to. [Joseph Witek]

Lawrence Norfolk. *The Pope's Rhinoceros.* Harmony Books, 1996. 574 pp. $25.00.

It was 1515 and Pope Leo, a Medici, wanted a rhinoceros to go with his elephant. He didn't want to exert himself in acquiring it and didn't have to, what with sea powers like Spain and Portugal around to exert for him, conquering and collecting in his name. At stake here was the division of the world. The fine print in the next Papal Bull would look favorably on one country or the other. Portugal, one up already, had presented its elephant to the Servant of God. Spain still wanted the bigger, better part of the world, and the Pope said, Well, what have you done for me lately?

This is the historical basis of Lawrence Norfolk's novel. As in his first, *Lemprière's Dictionary*, a small quantity of historical fact is the irritant kernel: when combined with encyclopedic detail and a patience for the unraveling of byzantine plots, a novel happens.

While novels like Norfolk's frequently inspire a search for connections—How like the twentieth century is the sixteenth! How like the Pope am I!—his remain corseted tightly in their period costumes, as if breathing even a little or wandering outside the well-appointed sets would ruin the illusion. Lacking correspondences, what's left is the plot, which leaves an adventure story, of which Norfolk's novel is a very entertaining one. The book contains an obscene wealth of detail on food, furnishings, clothing, habits, and homes, and the middle section, set in Rome, is quite an invention, with jokes, rumors, menus, bazaar protocol, and the social order of things each richly explored. The class structure is a believably complicated mess, both hierarchical and anarchic, in which the Pope can observe that his servants are "the servants of the Servants of the Servant of God," splitting hierarchic hairs, at the same time that he is beset by the satiric barbs, inside jokes, and askance looks of his court on down to his cooks and the visiting poets.

But at its center the book is a buddy movie, with a wily, street-smart protagonist and an imposing, somewhat dense giant (innocent in demeanor, yet surprisingly capable of wisdom). Admittedly, this is a high-end buddy movie. Norfolk's treatment of the book's other animals (human or otherwise, they all think, even the rats) and his unsparing attention to the part of the novel that requires of Africa labor and ample, exotic wildlife put the book into another category. It is as if Robert Louis Stevenson stayed up late reading Edward Said.

Novelists like Norfolk, and there are not many, follow in the impossible footsteps of Pierre Menard, Borges's character who devotes himself to recreating the language of Cervantes after the time of Cervantes. Norfolk, strapping himself with sixteenth century cognitive limitations, imagines how it would be to picture a rhinoceros before the existence of the animal is known. He writes of people assembling newer, more terrible beasts from more common animals—like an elephant except with armor, like an ox with a horn. Norfolk is the historical anachronist of the writing world, trading everyday clothes to dress up in the correct costumes, saying the historically right things, and intensely abiding by the old codes. Re-creating a time is an act of tremendous will, and Norfolk provides details in all the right places, but historical reenactments can still be empty theater, however accurate. This novel, while certainly rich in historical detail, lacks a reason for reen-acting anything at all. [Paul Maliszewski]

Collected Stories by Djuna Barnes. Ed. Phillip Herring. Sun & Moon, 1996. 488 pp. $24.95.

In 1982, the year that Djuna Barnes died, Sun & Moon Press collected her early short fiction in *Smoke and Other Early Stories*. It published Barnes's theatrical interviews in *Interviews* (1985), her journalism pieces in *New York* (1989), and (in 1995) *At the Root of the Stars: The Short Plays*. Its most recent volume, *Collected Stories,* draws into one compact and com-prehensive volume all the stories Barnes is known to have written. Edited and introduced by Phillip Herring, *Collected Stories* includes the works from *Smoke*, stories from *Spillway*, others out of print since the 1920s, and several never printed in book form. It is a timely volume that scholars will find useful as they continue to examine Barnes's position in twentieth-cen-tury literature.

Toward this end, the text on the dust jacket states that these stories will "help to establish [Barnes] as one of the most interesting and vital storytell-ers of the great period of American literary output after World War I." With this in mind, readers may be surprised that Herring's introduction does not adhere to this view or use it other than briefly as a context for discussion. In fact, the introduction seems oddly positioned in its begrudging tone and ex-tremely focused approach as it falls between the sweeping praise in the dust jacket copy and the richness of the stories that follow.

Most of the introduction summarizes selected stories and connects them along a continuum of judgments ranging from weak to better to best or from less puzzling to more puzzling. Whether readers interpret this arrangement as a criticism of Barnes's prose, an apology for it, or a tribute to its difficul-ties, they are not likely to find it very useful, and it is hard to read the intro-duction without thinking that Barnes's stories either elude Herring or that he dislikes many of them. Whatever the case, his casual judgments pull Barnes's short fiction canon (over forty stories) out of a historical or cul-tural context. He cites problems in Barnes's treatment of race and ethnicity, but he calls these "a function of ignorance rather than mean-spiritedness" and shifts over to a series of plot summaries. These are loosely arranged, often given for their strangeness. "No-Man's-Mare" is, for example, a "strange early story." "Cassation" is "one of the stranger, murkier stories."

"Mother," Herring writes, "is superior to many by Barnes because no murky metaphysical question rises to the surface" although "Dusie," of "scant literary value," anticipates *Nightwood*. Other descriptions are also equivocal. "Indian Summer" is "one of Barnes's better stories," "A Night among the Horses" "surely one of her best," and even though "The Earth," "The Head of Babylon," "Smoke," and "The Terrorists" exhibit "clarity," this "cannot be said of some later stories."

Herring has made Barnes's stories available and convenient, but his equivocations, created by what he seems to omit as well as by what he includes, do not adequately serve Barnes. A final quotation from Emily Coleman, the person who convinced Eliot to publish *Nightwood,* in writing to Barnes, "You make horror beautiful—it is your greatest gift," seems inconsistent with the rest of the introduction. Coleman may have thought this, as do many readers, but it would be hard to convince them that Herring believes anything close to it. His recent biography of Barnes and his archival work on *Collected Stories* represent a commitment to her fiction, but readers should explore these stories for themselves. [Miriam Fuchs]

———————

Josef Skvorecky. *The Tenor Saxophonist's Story.* Trans. Caleb Crain, Ká ča Poláčková Henley, and Peter Kussi. Ecco, 1996. 161 pp. $23.00.

Josef Skvorecky wrote the ten stories of love and disappointment that comprise this novel while living in Prague during the hardening of the Cold War in the mid-1950s. These tales reflect how politics affected romance, friendship, and even one's passion for music in both gross and subtle ways. The simplest of comments, such as a pick-up line at a bar, can cause unintended complications. Skvorecky's characters belong to the generation that came-of-age during the Second World War, only to see the promise of the end of Nazi fascism transform into Eastern European communism. The specter of Joseph Stalin is everywhere. Even the new thermometer at the local vocational school is dedicated with love to the Soviet leader. Skvorecky's young adults find solace in erotic affairs and jazz. They are sweetly cynical more than jaded, but mostly they are mystified by their political situation. All engage in some form of criminal behavior because so much is forbidden. At the extreme, some become spies for the government while others defect. Mostly they humorously pursue carnal pleasures in an increasingly confused world where even securing a private apartment after marriage becomes a major hassle. The title character wryly narrates his and his friends' stories. The saxophonist Danny Smiricky, the protagonist of many of Skvorecky's other novels and tales, does not state the obvious to reveal its painful absurdity. Communism is the elephant that sits on the living room sofa that no one in the house deigns to notice for fear of upsetting the creature. Yet everyone feels crowded and unhappy. Individually, each of the ten-to-twenty page narratives are funny and insightful vignettes of the period. However, together they seem more like a collection of related stories than a novel. Smiricky recites his yarns chronologically, but the connections between the chapters needs to be both broader and deeper. Perhaps this is due to the author's situation. He was well aware that his prose would be considered too subversive to see the light of day in his native country. He was writing for the desk drawer and those few individuals he could trust. These friends would have been familiar enough with the circumstances to fill in the contexts. [Steve Horowitz]

Roddy Doyle. *The Woman Who Walked into Doors*. Penguin/Viking, 1996. 226 pp. $22.95; Paper: $11.95.

Roddy Doyle's fifth novel concerns the life and love of Paula Spencer, a thirty-nine-year-old woman, alcoholic, mother of four (her fifth, a miscarriage the result of her husband's fist to her stomach), cleaning woman, widow. Paula tells her own story, a telling made possible by the violent death of her husband. She "isn't too fond of herself," nor is this reader. True, her perseverance is admirable and her situation pitiable. But this self-described "girl who wanked" a young boyfriend is hardly a likable narrator.

The novel opens with the arrival of a young member of the Guard who has the unfortunate job of informing Paula that her estranged husband, Charlo, has been killed while holding a woman hostage during an attempted robbery. As this drama unfolds, so does Paula's life story, from her childhood through her teens and her rebellion against her family, to her introduction to Charlo, their courtship and eventual marriage. Doyle deftly manages the two narratives so that Paula and Charlo's honeymoon is ominously juxtaposed against Charlo's brutal murder of his hostage. His death allows Paula to talk about her marriage, about the seventeen years she endured under Charlo's violence, until she finally struck back, not for herself, but to protect her daughter from her husband as he turns his violence toward her. The threat he poses to Nicole is enough for Paula to drive him, stumbling and barely conscious, into the street and out of their immediate lives. Doyle is savvy enough to mine the depths of this victory, for it comes with its own costs—the possible alienation of her son, who witnesses the brutal beating of his father. Nor is this the only violence perpetrated by Paula. The novel opens with a brief aside from Paula about how she herself hit Nicole.

Early reviews of the novel have lauded Doyle for his ability to give voice to Paula Spencer, that is, Doyle's ability to efface his (male) presence in his female narrator's voice and sensibilities. What they've noted is true enough, for Doyle has demonstrated yet again his mastery of voice and character. But his achievement goes well beyond his own self-effacement. What is overlooked is how he constructs his narrative to overcome what we already know—that we will, inevitably, get to what the title promises—documenting the narrator's physical abuse at the hands of her husband. How is it, then, that Doyle is able to sustain the reader's interest and effort necessary to completing such a story? Much of the interest lies in discovering just what Paula is up to as she tells her story. Is she rewriting history to exculpate herself? Is she telling the truth? Is her confession therapeutic? Most likely, she is discovering herself through the patient exposing of self-deceptions, tricks and games that she's developed over the years just to survive.

The Woman Who Walked into Doors follows his 1993 Booker Award winning *Paddy Clarke Ha Ha Ha*, a novel of seething emotion and coming of age, and his "Barrytown Trilogy," *The Commitments, The Snapper,* and *The Van,* which follow the Rabbitte family through the good fun of drinking, burping, farting, rock and roll, teenage parenthood, and economic depression. Like *Paddy Clarke Ha Ha Ha*, Doyle's latest is not so fun as his earlier three, nor should this be a surprise. It is, however, a compelling exploration of the dark undercurrents informing all of Doyle's fictions. [Rick Henry]

Jeffrey DeShell. *S&M*. FC2, 1997. 231 pp. Paper: $11.95.

In Jeffrey DeShell's hugely funny, hugely savvy second novel, *S&M,* a woman photographer named S— has just split with one lesbian lover and shacked up with another, this latter busy composing a novel about an intellectually nebbish narrator, while, in a parallel plot, a male creative-writing grad student named M—, who thinks and reads way too much for his own good, has just split with his heterosexual lover, Monica, a photographer, and begun composing a novel about a pair of lesbian lovers because (outside of what he's gleaned from dabbling in some gay lit) he knows almost nothing about lesbianism and so is "unencumbered and uninhibited by facts." All of which is really good plot-stuff in itself, but becomes even better when cast in a series of glistening paragraph-long run-on sentences authored by an extremely self-conscious breathless narrative voice that obsesses over nuance, over trying to say something true about the nature of love, while tending to be able to muster little more than strings of contradictions and logical culs-de-sac, failed thought-forays, like some Beckettian narrator on uppers refracted through a hip urban Barthelmesque sensibility and a good-spiritedly metafictional Federmanian prose. It's tempting, in fact, to say the real love story here is one between that voice and language itself: its rhythms, its sounds, its spill across the page. Except DeShell's fiction is more than linguistic rhapsody. It's also a tender look at the pratfalls, the S&M, called the grammar of human relationships as they transpire in an artsy fin-de-siècle world shot through with an unnerving feeling of sexual fluidity, millennial angst and indecision, and goofy McCarthyesque political correctness that rears its carbuncular head in every chi-chi theme bar and writing workshop where the cynical players already have everything figured out. It's a world populated, in other words, by a bunch of existential klutzes bent on trying to get on with their lives with a modicum of dignity and, if they're lucky, maybe some vague sense of who they really are . . . and finding the job virtually impossible. No doubt, *S&M* asks the reader to do a little work, but the payoff is a rare combination of satiric sparkle, stylistic flair, emotional sweetness, sexual delight, and, finally, an impressively original reading experience. [Lance Olsen]

John L'Heureux. *The Handmaid of Desire.* Soho, 1996. 264 pp. $23.00.

John L'Hueureux's exceedingly clever novel of academic life is set in the English department of an unnamed California university. It's a place of tricks and schemes run amok, where the theory-obsessed Young Turks are on the ascendant and the Fools, the professors "still lost in literature," are considered hopelessly out of touch. There's a plot afoot to turn the English Department in the Department of Theory and Discourse, "which would take on the author's reputation or the western canon or the nature of the writing itself—whether it was Flaubert's *Bovary* or a 1950 tax form or the label on a Campbell's soup can." Into the fray walks Olga Kominska, a woman of indeterminate European origins and a sly genius for social, professional, and psychosexual manipulation. Olga is ambitious and sexy, with a taste for "highly athletic sex," and she has written several acclaimed books of theory. She enters the department with distinct—but mysterious—ambitions. She wants to write a book about power and "the folly of answered prays." As the novel unfolds, we see Olga using various members of the department for her own murky ends. We meet graduate student Peter Peeks, "young and sturdy and beautiful and empty," who serves as the department's "surrogate stud"; the chubby, befuddled Francis Xavier Tortorisi, whose wafer-thin experimental novels mirror his sexual impotence; Eleanor Tuke, a professor who aspires to become "the Larry King of the literati"; Robbie Richter, a theorist who suffers a nervous breakdown and becomes convinced of the genius of Franklin W. Dixon, author of the *Hardy Boys* series. Olga tries to find a destiny for everyone—but only, she'd say, "up to a point."

What's best about this book is the wickedly funny way L'Heureux juggles the flashy buzzwords of the literary academy. Written with a radiant humor and filled with fine details—the "penile hegemony" of the university administration, the cabal of "post-Christian feminists," the obsession with Barthes and Foucault—this novel shows that L'Heureux has his finger on the wildly racing pulse of the modern academy. [James DeRossitt]

Chappell, Fred. *Farewell, I'm Bound to Leave you.* Picador USA, 1996. 228 pp. $21.00.

A framed series of linked stories in the manner of *Winesburg, Ohio*, Fred Chappell's newest book returns to the world of *I Am One of You Forever* and *Brighten the Corner Where You Are* to recount the lives of strong-willed, courageously capable, often unconventional women of the North Carolina Appalachians. Treating love and death, backwoods mysteries and otherworldly visitations, personal idiosyncracy and the traditional values that nourish both individuals and communities, the twelve stories gathered in *Farewell, I'm Bound to Leave You* are those told to young Jess Kirkman by his mother, Cora, and his maternal grandmother Annie Barbara Sorrells. They are the stories Jess recalls as he and his father, Joe Robert, wait through a long night while down the hall Jess's grandmother lays dying.

Several stories concern their teller, one a comic account of how Cora won Joe Robert's attention and affection, another an empathetic portrait of a folklorist come to gather songs and sayings. In "The Wind Woman," a dreamlike parable, Cora takes Jess beyond Forgetful Mountain and past Worrisome Creek to visit the Wind Woman that Jess might learn how to become "a poet writing true things."

Other stories conjure other women. "The Madwoman" raises Aunt Chancy, driven mad by passion and its violent end, while "The Helpinest Woman" memorializes Angela Newcome, so filled with Christian charity no one can stand her. "The Figuring Woman" and "The Shining Woman" feature Aunt Sherlie Howes, "hands down the smartest woman there was," who solves the mystery behind an elopement and discovers how to placate a ghost.

Shot through with comedy and pathos, tall tales and lyric beauty, flavorsome speech and sustaining truths, *Farewell, I'm Bound to Leave You* evokes a world Jess's father knows is dying with Grandmother Sorrells, among the last of the generation of women whose loss is, as Annie herself declares, "a destruction to us all, for they were good and faithful company and the generations that have come after don't seem to me to have their hardiness or savor."

Like his visiting folklorist, Chappell's motive here is perhaps to collect what might otherwise be lost. *Farewell, I'm Bound to Leave You* is, at any rate, such a record, and much more. It is also all one needs to understand why Lee Smith, surveying the Southern literary scene, has called Chappell "the one truly great writer we have among us." [Brooke Horvath]

Jeanne Hyvrard. *Waterweed in the Wash-Houses*. Trans. Elsa Copeland. Columbia Univ. Press, 1997. 136 pp. Paper: $16.95.

This text, distributed by Columbia University Press, is a wonderfully *occult* meditation on women, language, politics, and philosophy. It is, in many ways, a novel or better yet, an antinovel which attempts to stress that we must somehow move beyond traditional binary oppositions of "man" and "woman," "master and slave." Hyvrard resembles Cixous—whose work is also distributed by Columbia—in trying to subvert the notion of separations, to fuse opposites into some kind of *third* being.

Thus when we read this text, we notice that the language itself is fractured, confused. There is a woman narrator who is "mad"; she believes that she is an "agent," some mysterious being who has been given the task to be "I" and "she" and even "self" and "process" (she is also the text!). She offers a stream of consciousness which doesn't progress; the stream is *circular*. At one point she writes (to herself and to the reader): "They say she knows a language that can say earth and water at the same time." Of course, the sentence defies reason. Are not earth and water different? And she has trouble with traditional syntax: "A subject. A verb. What for? What do they want to move?" The sentence is, in effect, a death sentence because it fixes movement; it stops fusion: "But they have been confounding opposites and negation."

This occult text, although it attacks the traditional acts of reading and writing, is a murderous, creative event. It uses the Tarot cards and alchemy as frames of reference. Although there is use of alchemy—a series of metallic *transmutations* in the odd texts of Yeats, Merrill, Bloom, Gaddis, and the "surrealist" boxes of Joseph Cornell—no critic has really attempted to see all these works as part of a desperate movement to find a new language. Although this text by Hyvrard has come to me "out of the blue," I have the uncanny feeling that it was meant for me. And now I offer it to you as a gift and/or curse. [Irving Malin]

Philip Graham. *Interior Design: Stories*. Scribner, 160 pp. $20.00.

In "Lucky," one of eight stories in Philip Graham's new collection, *Interior Designs*, Pete, a long-time owner of a men's clothing store, begins a private daily ritual of whispering "good-bye" and "good luck" in order to alleviate his anxiety as many of his aging customers pass away. "But I kept up this little game for weeks," he remarks, "and I began to seem strange to myself." Indeed it is the creation of such personal customs—the designs and arrangements that constitute the soul's need to make order of the world and its events—that is the common theme of Graham's elegant, disquieting, and powerful tales. Graham's characters are people who believe not only in their ability to "see the invisible" and but also that "the everything unseen can ultimately be recovered."

In the collection's title story a woman, Josephine, embarks on a career as an interior designer after a childhood constrained and guilt-ridden by her homebuilder father's deceptive custom of outfitting his model homes with three-quarter size furniture in order to make the rooms appear larger. As an adult, Josephine distinguishes her design practice by specializing in using her client's dreams as the basis of decorating their homes. For them she creates interiors "as familiar as the self," with "walls as comfortable as skin." Yet her urgent vision implodes when she realizes that her designs cannot demarcate everything in her world. "How can I possibly escape my home when it's inside me?" she laments.

Graham's prose is marked by truly masterly touches: exacting observations are rendered both forcefully in their import as well as refined and respectful in their tone. Intense, absorbing, graceful, and precise, these tales of our fin-de-siècle America announce that the most intense and powerful events are the ones we create ourselves. In an elegant and original manner Graham delimits the private blueprints of the unconscious—the delicate, unstable, and never certain boundary between the real and the imagined—to reveal that "the true beauty . . . was that past, present, and future bled into each other." [Jeanne Claire van Ryzin]

Nik Cohn. *Need.* Secker & Warburg, 1996. 298 pp. £15.99.

Amid cockfights, topless carwashes, and acrobatic acts, the four main characters of Nik Cohn's novel *Need* meet together in a Manhattan zoo where exotic birds and snakes are kept. The jobless Willie D is concerned because he can't afford even a pair of cheap sneakers to fulfill a shoe fetish based on the assumption that shoes steer him in the right direction. Anna Crow, who began topless dancing when she was seventeen, now delivers Verso-o-Grams for special occasions. After a career as a psychic, where she repeatedly envisioned deaths, Kate Root now cares for birds and snakes, cuts hair, and watches soap operas. John Joe Maguire of Scaith-na-Tairbhe, whose father had been a prizefighter, has a birthmark shaped like a black swan on his thigh.

These characters seek physical and psychological gratifications for various needs, yet they can never quite articulate what they seek. Much like James Joyce, Cohn portrays his zany characters' raw biological acts: belches, farts, and orgasms. Beyond their physical urges, however, the characters learn to relinquish undefined psychological needs. The elementary principle of knife throwing, letting go, symbolizes the novel's message that truth is simple and the antidote to need is belief. When Willie finally throws a knife, he cuts his new shoes; but he later finds satisfaction in one simple

pair of boots, footwear that contrasts the Brunswick Glides and Gucci loaf-
ers he earlier possessed. Symbolically, he has learned the philosophy of
simplicity. Realizing that fulfillment comes not from dance and sex but
from healing others, Anna decides to become a nurse. John Joe recognizes
that personal past histories create baggage we must discard. Symbolic of the
characters's discoveries, near the beginning of the novel, Kate releases from
its cage a bird; after the symbolic Armageddon, where Manhattan turns to
darkness, chaos, and smoke, the spiritually renewed bird returns.

Cohn defies traditional use of plot and offers instead a smorgasbord of
characters and scenes that are described with wry wit and clever puns. Allu-
sions range from cheesy country western tunes such as Billy Ray Cyrus's
"Achy Breaky Heart" to well-known literary works such as those by Yeats,
Joyce, and Keats. Frequently, humorous twists to clichés stand alone in
paragraphs that contrast surrounding serious philosophical musings. Cohn's
skillful use of language makes *Need* a delightful combination of humor, satire, and philosophy. [Laurie Champion]

Albert J. Guerard. *The Hotel in the Jungle*. Baskerville, 1996. 391 pp.
$23.00.

Although Guerard is one of our distinguished critics (of Conrad, Faulkner,
and Dostoyevsky) and teachers of writing (of Hawkes), he deserves serious
attention as a novelist.

Guerard is interested in the obsessive, dark nature of our personalities;
he views history as hallucination (or vice versa). It is appropriate that his
novel is, in part, a meditation on the eccentric Mina Loy. She appears as
"Monica Swift," a beautiful visionary who longs to find her lover "Brian
Desmond" (Arthur Cravan). Desmond was a boxer and poet—a legendary
figure in the history of surrealism—who disappeared in Mexico.

The novel should not be read as a mere evocation of Loy. (For a superb
biography of Loy see Carolyn Burke's recent book.) It is a thrilling attempt
to capture the duplicitous quality of memory, love, and knowledge. It reminds me in part of Proust, who is mentioned in the text, Conrad, and
Faulkner.

The novel begins in 1982. Eloise Deslonde, a young historian, is writing
a dissertation on Rosellen Maurepas's two obsessions: "the Isthmus of
Tehwantepec and William Walker." She seems fated to trace Rosellen's ad-
ventures in Mexico; she views her as an uncanny double. The novel moves
backward to 1870. We see Rosellen trying to find Walker, to possess him—
if only for her journal. The repeated references to texts—the dissertation,
the journal of Rosellen and her lover, Charles Stanfied, the guest book in
the mysterious hotel in the jungle—are repeated in the novel's fascination
with Monica Swift's poetry in 1922. From 1982 to 1870 to 1920 and then to

1982, time is examined in a crooked occult manner.

And the fact that the characters seem to reflect one another—think of the three women—intensifies the "jungle" of epistemology. The search for meaning, for fact, is married to the distortions of desire. There is, if you will, a circularity, a labyrinthine quality. Consider this passage: "He wrote a poem about a man who lost something in the course of a picnic. It had slipped into a small pond or perhaps a spring like this one. I think it was a silver drinking cup, and he could not find it. Then fifty years later he happened by that place, and there was the drinking cup in the water, shining in the reflected sunlight. Nothing had changed."

The timelessness of dream; the precarious, unstable nature of knowledge—in texts and lives—is at the heart of the novel. And Eloise recognizes that in "the dreaming mind" we are all "immortal." The separation of dream and waking experience, of art and life, cannot be stable. Thus the novel resembles the hotel—both are structures which fuse creation and decay—and like the hotel, the novel is for the brave explorer who seeks terrifying beauty (or beautiful terror). It is, finally, a fascinating presence filled with domineering ghosts. It is an entrance into our secretive worlds, "an emanation of the darkness itself, one that might or might not take on human shape." [Irving Malin]

André VandenBroeck. *Breaking Through: A Narrative of the Great Work.* Introduction by Colin Wilson. City Lights, 1996. 374 pp. Paper: $15.95.

Breaking Through is a rough-edged philosophical treatise and novel about many things—among them art, time, technology, language, rocks, human bodies, and the prehistoric past. Dazzling, exuberant, and very strange, it is also a novel about the nature of seeing. The author's argument, simply put, is that in the struggle for survival, humankind has invented instruments and technologies to exert dominance over the environment, and in doing so the human organism has become distanced from fundamental—and fundamentally human—ways of seeing, feeling, and being in the world. The philosophical adventure of *Breaking Through* suggests how we might regain this primitive, open relation to our environment, through a kind of improvisation rather than rules, an embrace of dilettantism, and learning not to see more, but to look better.

The central figure in this novel is a photographer named Piero Tallini. He made a fortune from a documentary about Indian holy men, but he has become disgusted with the trappings of artistic success. Tallini becomes interested in exploring man's early origins; he's convinced that our earliest human ancestors, the cave people at the "first glimmers of consciousness," have something important to teach him about existence. He connects with the spirits of these early humans in a mystical awakening while he's at an elegant Paris literary salon.

From there he goes to the southern coast of Spain, where he seeks to deepen his relationship with the primitive spirits. Tallini makes journeys into the rocky terrain and soon realizes that "improvisational consciousness" is the key to a renewed physical and spiritual relation with the land. Without the ability to improvise, modern man has lost the "kind of freedom that was most essentially human." In route to this realization Tallini ponders the nature of modern society and how technology has taken on a mind of its own and begun to drag man behind it. What we need, Tallini discovers, is a "foreseeing mentality" to help us keep technology—and thus our minds, our language, our very existence—"in hand."

Although clumsy and overwritten in places, *Breaking Through* is a fascinating novel that shows how relevant romantic notions are to today's technocratic corporate societies. It's also an utterly contemporary companion to the philosophy of Walter Benjamin as well as postmodern philosophers like Lyotard and Vattimo, who are saying many of the same things about man's enslavement of himself to technology. [James DeRossitt]

Bhargavi C. Mandava. *Where the Oceans Meet*. Seal Press, 1996. 283 pp. $22.95.

Bhargavi C. Mandava's *Where the Oceans Meet* is a collection of stories about traditional India and Indians in conflict with the past and the present. The isolated souls in these tales are related by their seeking moments of transcendence, love, or just understanding, but in most instances a harsh reality intervenes which prevents more than momentary happiness. The conflicting feelings of the characters are between a yearning for traditions, which are safe and predictable but which often deny individuality, and a more modern culture where ritual has lost meaning and gender and religious differences are unimportant. There is an insatiable hunger in these people for something they cannot articulate, and this desire forces many of the characters into violence.

The book functions as a story cycle: the characters of one story appear in others. In one story a poor tailor develops a fixation on beautiful Navina who is to be married shortly. Later Navina narrates her own tale about anticipating her wedding, which is interrupted by the tailor delivering the saris and asking her to marry him. She takes his offer as a joke, and although he leaves, he returns to destroy the woman he loves by throwing acid on her face, killing her. In one of the last stories in the collection, the same tailor confesses to a swami that he cannot find peace after the terrible wrong he has committed.

Peace is not something that many of these characters achieve, often because of the divisions between rich and poor, Hindu and Muslim, Westernized and traditional India. In one story childhood sweethearts are kept apart because he is Muslim and she is Hindu. When they reach adulthood they run away together, rejecting the old values and escaping the imprisonment by their culture which sketches out roles and identities for men and women. However, even the modern women in these narratives who try to bridge East and West feel a sense of unease since they are unable to fit in any culture. *Where the Oceans Meet* raises some profound questions about identity, gender, and race which the author invites her readers to think about, all the while knowing that there are no straightforward answers. [Sally E. Parry]

Richard Grossman. *The Book of Lazarus.* FC2, 1997. 450 pp. $19.95.

Like Grossman's earlier work, *The Alphabet Man, The Book of Lazarus* begins with a lot of promise. The book is an interesting collage of photographs, drawings, handwritten notes, letters, political statements, poems, and rants. Grossman cycles through a dozen narrators to reach a 110-page kernel narrative that stitches the parts into a (perhaps too) cohesive whole. The central situation—an old mafia debt, a woman uncovering the secrets of her dead father, a once brilliant man, the extermination over a span of thirty years of a group of anarchists—is an interesting one. There is much in Grossman's language and formal manipulations both to satisfy the reader and to draw the reader in.

However, despite its promise, *The Book of Lazarus* doesn't come together as effectively as it might, primarily for two reasons. The first is that despite Grossman's skill at descriptions, nonlinear writing, aphorisms, and narrative prose, his moments of dialogue, as recorded by lesbian painter Emma Stronghorse O'Banion, read like something out of mediocre mystery plot. Strewn with exclamations and overreactions, it feels too artificial. Though this can be partly explained by Emma's own eccentricities or can by a generous reader be seen as an attempt to subvert the mystery novel, it cannot be wholly justified by either of these things. When it is considered side by side with Grossman's other much stronger prose, it is clear that his dialogue mars the piece.

Second, on page 167 Grossman begins to provide the key to the book's design, revealing why certain sections have been as they are, sorting out different documents and explaining everything away in modernist style. Until that time, much of what makes the book interesting is the lack of explanation, the strangeness of moving from a photograph to a handwritten note to a list of New Year's resolutions to poems written on the back of fortune cookies to a series of aphorisms. When the book is explained away, however, some of its power is lost.

Nevertheless, there is much to recommend Grossman's work, especially when he is at is best, as he is for instance in giving a long and unpunctuated rant or in the presentation of certain letters and images. Though *The Alphabet Man* is a better place to start, *The Book of Lazarus* still has much to recommend it. [Brian Evenson]

Joseph Torra. *Gas Station*. Zoland Books, 1996. 134 pp. Paper: $11.95.

This first novel by poet Joseph Torra reads like a series of interconnected prose poems. There is no plot to speak of but rather bits and pieces that slowly accrue into a vivid and compelling picture of a working-class boy and his father in Medford, Massachusetts. Their lives revolve around the gas station that the father owns and struggles to maintain, and that the son works in as he grows up.

The real strength of the book is not what is described, however, but the way in which Torra manages to describe it. He seems capable of moving effortlessly between diverse events, memories, and individual internal experience. The book operates in terms of resonances and connections, one experience serving as a touchstone to transform our view of another. Torra opts for a comma-stripped syntax, warped but still readable, in which the end of one clause and the beginning of another is not always clear. Though occasionally this can be irritating, at its best it allows for a shimmering of meaning that opens new vistas. In one sense, the main character of the novel is not any given person but the gas station itself, whose textures and grime seem to inform the prose itself.

The vividness of the gas station and of its mechanics, the depictions of a family always quietly in crisis, the philandering and gambling yet never stereotypical father, are well-drawn and palpable. The depiction of small-town life in the fifties and sixties is quite convincing as well. With *Gas Station*, Torra has proven himself able to capture a place in all its manifold detail, and to do so with a care for language and style that is uncommon. [Brian Evenson]

Josephine Jacobsen. *What Goes without Saying: Collected Stories*. Johns Hopkins Univ. Press, 1996. 335 pp. $29.95.

Each story evicts characters from their everyday lives, where everyone spoke the language and roads took their predictable course according to memories and road signs. Whether in their homes or in hotels on tropical islands, Jacobsen's characters are suddenly outsiders, estranged from the power of language and reason to name, explain, and control. They are left turning over words like "heal," "importance," and "pleasure" in their mouths, and finding language emptied out of content, unable to describe their thoughts and circumstances. Most of these stories begin in medias res, many of them during repuscular hours, or at the edge of oceans or cliffs. A women is trapped in her own bathroom, a journalist is maimed in a verdant Guatemalan forest, an old woman is robbed in her row house. In some stories, characters silently conspire. In "The Glen" Jesse finishes her husband's unspoken plan to urge his retarded daughter, Cora, to eat the poisonous mushrooms in their wooded yard; she would recognize them as the same that Alice in Wonderland ate. In other stories characters remember their ties to the world beyond them, but always at a price. In "The Jungle of Lord Lion" Mrs. Pomeroy spends the last of her savings on a trip to Boudina, where she plans to luxuriate for a few months in an inexpensive room by the sea and to wait to see what her cancer will do. When Mrs. Chubb, a rich woman staying at the same inn, tells her, "You cannot have a white girl and a black boy playing together half naked, unless you are a fool," Mrs. Pomeroy insults her. Although Mrs. Pomeroy expects that the dignified African innkeeper, Mrs. Heatherby, will turn out Mrs. Chubb after she overhears the conversation, it is Mrs. Pomeroy who is asked to leave. As she looks out the window, she sees the same view, the same stars rising in the sky over the ocean where she had been content. "She could not remember her own anger or fear, though they were there, somewhere within her knowledge. She had understood the terrible components of joy. Alive, and breathing, Mrs. Pomeroy stood there in the wet soft air, looking into the darkness." Many of Jacobsen's best stories end in such stillness. Although some early stories linger on excessive poetic descriptions, the collection accumulates in force and effect, as it consistently struggles to understand the limits of language to make the world safe and whole. [Monique Dufour]

Kwadwo Agymah Kamau. *Flickering Shadows*. Coffee House Press, 1996. 300 pp. $21.95.

Barbados born Kwadwo Agymah Kamau's first novel follows a small Caribbean island's struggle through the latest round of colonialism's three-pronged advance of Christianity, mineral development and political opportunism. The novel opens with the island's recent political independence and the promise of an election, but the results have little impact on the people's lives, which have been conditioned by three hundred years of abuses and dependencies. The arrival of a missionary, the discovery of bauxite, and the oppressions of the new political party fracture the community. A devastating hurricane worsens their plight, which is futher exacerbated by the Prime Minister who supports the building of a new church rather than the rebuilding of the homes ruined by the storm.

The novel is a testimonial, told from the point of view of a "duppy" (a shadow or spirit) as he witnesses the postcolonial nightmare. Kamau's narrator drifts, his attention divided among a number of characters including two couples—Doreen and Cephus, and Inez and Boysie—who are singled out because the narrator is grandfather to Cephus and Inez. Kamau follows their interpersonal interactions (Boysie and Doreen's affair, for example, or Cephus's alleged betrayal of Boysie) as well as their varied relations to the colonial triumvirate (Boysie becomes an opposition leader urged by a student of Marxism and supported by the Obeah and Brethren; Doreen flirts with Christianity).

Intertwined in their drama is the delicate underpinning of the novel: the relationship between the world of the spirits and humans. The narrator and other shadows frequent the living to reveal themselves and intervene at appropriate moments. What is most instructive is how Kamau negotiates this perspective: he has the opportunity to cover three hundred years of colonialism, to mark numerous parallels through the years, and to personalize the abuses of power. Instead, he maintains the disinterested interest of the shadows who populate the novel—moved less by moral outrage at the atrocities than by a more abstract sense of imperfect and sporadic justice. It is a powerful and sometimes disconcerting perspective, and a welcome addition to the growing literature of the region. [Rick Henry]

Frank Lentricchia. *Johnny Critelli* and *The Knifemen*. Scribner, 1996. 268 pp. $22.00.

Although these two novels supposedly stand alone, they must be read as one. Each novel echoes the other—the principal images of mutilation, ejaculation, and conception recur. The novel, as I take it, concerns itself with the division of and the attempt to fuse body/language, son/father, high culture/pop culture, then/now, Italian/American. Perhaps the novel is, ultimately, a series of variations on Catholic transubstantiation, a belief that blood *is* wine, that body *is* bread. But the author understands that he cannot perform miracles. He is, after all, barely a "man." The novel contains enigmatic events and odd sentences. We are never really sure who Critelli is—is fiction or nonfiction. The novel itself is a *distorted arrangement* of drama— Shakespeare is mentioned—and film—*Raging Bull* is mentioned. And the arrangement is a deliberate attempt to assault the reader, to "rape" him. The novel reaches out, therefore, to include the reader in the unholy text.

Here are a few examples of the violent conjunctions of language: "Give me your story or I'll break your legs. I just need to disappear into a story, that's all it is." A slaughterhouse—isn't the text itself a slaughterhouse/ chapel?—is described in an "elevated" language: "Three knifemen stand at the station of evisceration, another curb-enclosed area, each working a calf with a maximum longitudinal rip, a couple of quick moves, a jank, and the guts just can't wait to fall out." The novel, finally, is an ambitious attempt to use language as *matter* to make it *bleed*. But language is not body. And thus the text is a *scream* of frustration, a *cry* for salvation, a *knife* to cut the author and reader. It is the "ultimate personal combat knife." [Irving Malin]

Walter Benjamin. *Selected Writings: Volume 1 1913-1926.* Ed. Marcus Bullock and Michael W. Jennings. Harvard Univ. Press, 1996. 520 pp. $35.00.

Although many of our lovers of theory demand French citizenship—they keep quoting Kristeva, Lacan, Foucault, and other usual suspects—they usually do not know what to make of this brilliant, possessed German Jew. (They, indeed, tend to refer to one or two essays on "mechanical reproduction.") This volume, the first of three to be published in the next few years, contains many untranslated essays written by Benjamin in his early years (from ages twenty-one to thirty-four). It is an enigmatic, fascinating collection.

Benjamin offers discussions of Goethe, Schlegel, "Fate and Character," "On Language as Such," and a series of notes entitled "One-Way Street." All of these texts are wonderfully obscure; they move beyond mere "criticism." I must give a few examples that are especially intriguing, "mystical," and strange. On books and harlots: "Books and harlots love to turn their backs when putting themselves on show." On happiness: "To be happy is to be able to become aware of oneself without fright." On evil: "Every unlimited condition of the will leads to evil. Ambition and lust are unlimited expressions of will. As the theologians have always perceived, the *natural totality* of the will must be destroyed." On color: "Color is something spiritual, something whose clarity is spiritual, so that when colors are mixed, they produce nuances of color, not a blur" (I think of Gass's *On Being Blue*; in fact, Gass is our Benjamin, the critic as contemplative visionary).

I do not know how to classify Benjamin. Is he more or less than a "critic"? What does he mean? The very fact that I cannot place him into any rigid category affirms that he is an extraordinary *writer*. [Irving Malin]

Erik Satie. *A Mammal's Notebook: Collected Writings of Erik Satie.* Ed. Ornella Volta. Trans. Antony Melville. Atlas Arkhive Documents of the Avant-Garde. Atlas Press, 1996. 206 pp. $24.99.

Fifth in Atlas Arkhive's Documents of the Avant-Garde series, this handsome volume boasts "the largest selection (in any language) of Erik Satie's writings yet to appear." Compiled by the noted Satie scholar Ornella Volta, these frequently hilarious pieces reveal a great deal about Satie's artistry, and for those who know him only through the first and third "Gymnopédies," this compilation would be an ideal place to begin acquainting oneself more thoroughly with this musical, theatrical, and literary innovator.

Volta divides the collection into texts written for performance, publication, and private diversion. Among those written for performance are poems to accompany (silently!) various experimental piano pieces; a long list of his antic tempo directions ("Be-dig yourself"; "Laugh without anyone knowing"; "Scratch"); and facsimiles of his elegantly calligraphed scores. From a literary standpoint, the most interesting item in this section is a brief absurdist drama, *Le Piège de Méduse* [*Medusa's Snare*], in which one can detect anticipations of Ionesco and, perhaps more appropriately, Groucho Marx. The texts Satie wrote for publication include his cheeky open letter to Saint-Saëns, in which he demands recognition from the Académie des Beaux Arts; the fragmentary *Mémoires d'un Amnesique* [*Memoirs of an Amnesic*]; and twelve informal articles, some of which discuss immediate contemporaries like Debussy and Stravinsky, others of which reveal a broad knowledge of European literature. Volta and Melville have also reproduced a number of unpublished writings, most notably the wacky semiprivate journal, "A Mammal's Notebooks," and even a generous selection of the 4,000 "private advertisements" discovered in cigar boxes in Satie's room after his death. Informative endnotes and a brief bibliography follow, and the collection is topped off with an annotated and illustrated catalogue of Satie's musical and literary works.

Volta's introductory overview of Satie's career and significance is brief, but such editorial reticence is appropriate in a collection that does a superb job of letting Satie come to life through his own sketches and writings—the latter mediated by the vivid, droll translations of Antony Melville. This volume and the rest of the series in which it appears will be invaluable resources for students of the avant-garde in music, art, and literature in France, Germany, and elsewhere. [Thomas Hove]

Chénetier, Marc. *Paul Auster as the Wizard of Odds: "Moon Palace."* Didier Erudition, 1996. 190 pp.

In this first full-length study of a single Auster work, Marc Chénetier argues for the centrality of *Moon Palace* in the author's oeuvre. Other readers of Auster's books might argue for the centrality of *The Invention of Solitude*, his first book-length prose publication, or *Mr. Vertigo*, his recent work, as a kind of culminating centrality with its lighter than air balance and its fall to worldliness imbalance, a plumb line for all predecessors to the claim. (Chénetier does convince me that *Moon Palace* can be seen as central, but he does not convince me that it necessarily *is* central.) Yet no matter what work one would choose for a keystone positioning, one would have to agree that Chénetier's essay is a welcomed addition to nascent Auster criticism, especially so since it is the first to make extensive use of the Auster archive in the Berg Collection of the New York Public Library.

Chénetier is a leading French scholar of contemporary American fiction whose book *Beyond Suspicion* has recently been published in English translation by the University of Pennsylvania Press. What Chénetier has to say about contemporary American fiction (he has contributed frequently to the pages of the *Review of Contemporary Fiction*) is always fascinating, illuminating. In his *Moon Palace* study he has provided what one might call a rhetoric, a poetics of the text, describing the text's diction, narration, structure, etc., in seven descriptive chapters that could just as easily apply to or inform a reading of any other Auster writing. This is one of the values of Chénetier's work: yet it may be seen by some as a weakness. For he all but refuses to move from identification and description to interpretation of that which he has identified, described. Indeed, he does reject such interpretation: "All of this is not what *MP means,* but it is part of what it manages to *signify*"; and "Potential conclusions to be drawn from such evidence must be left with the individual reader; the tight knot of this field of signs and images will and should be severed by no arrogant, peremptory, possibly abused critical sword."

On the book's penultimate page Chénetier provides one more explanation for his interpretative hesitancy (let me praise his descriptive accuracies): "Perhaps the present pages are a witness to the fact that their author, 'having developed a true fondness' for Paul Auster's harmonic modes of suggestion, feels incapable of 'delivering then with a straight,' academic, 'face,' preferring to widen up the frame, open up the perspective and invite to the responsibilities of freedom, all of which attempts would be defeated by 'final' words." Get busy reader and read Auster, this creator of imaginative spaces for odd things, and take Chénetier along as Baedeker. [Dennis Barone]

Perloff, Marjorie. *Wittgenstein's Ladder: Poetic Language and the Strangeness of the Ordinary.* Univ. of Chicago Press, 1996. 285 pp. $27.95.

If books could be cataloged by season, *Wittgenstein's Ladder* would be a summer: clear, temperate, disencumbered of hibernal rigors, undisturbed by stormy skies. The book explores what Marjorie Perloff terms a "Wittgensteinian poetics" both in works that bear a structural resemblance to Wittgenstein's thought and in texts that explicitly invoke him as an influence. On the one hand, the book offers a lucid introduction to the life and thought of Viennese philosopher Ludwig Wittgenstein, as well as intriguing readings of Gertrude Stein, Samuel Beckett, and a series of less canonical writers. On the other hand, it skips over theoretical problems with a frustrating insouciance.

Marjorie Perloff takes her title from the final page of the *Tractatus:* "My propositions are elucidatory in this way," writes Wittgenstein: "he who understands me finally recognizes them as senseless, when he has climbed out through them, on them, over them. (He must, so to speak, throw away the ladder, after he has climbed up on it.)" With the boost of this metaphor, Perloff identifies a Wittgensteinian poetics that is characterized by its use of everyday language, its suspicion of generalizations and totalizing theories and its insistence that one cannot "climb the same ladder twice." Perloff's first two chapters are dedicated to analyses of Wittgenstein's texts. She convincingly argues that the *Tractatus* is less a logical treatise than an avant-garde poetics of irresolution and a testimony to the inexpressibility of Wittgenstein's World War I experience. Her discussion of the *Philosophical Investigations* focuses on the famous concept of "language-games," which she interprets as prefiguring "post-structural" rejections of an inherent or natural meaning in language.

Subsequently, Perloff argues for a Wittgensteinian poetics in Stein's experimental uses and abuses of ordinary language and in the "context disorder" of Beckett's *Watt.* In her most interesting chapter she interprets Beckett's resistance to language within the context of the French Resistance: Beckett's "day job" during the years he was writing *Watt,* was encoding, delivering, and decoding messages for the Resistance. Perloff also investigates experiments with Wittgenstein's thought by Austrian novelists Ingeborg Bachmann and Thomas Bernhard, by poets Robert Creeley, Ron Silliman, Rosmarie Waldrop, and Lyn Hejinian, and by conceptual artist Joseph Kosuth.

While *Wittgenstein's Ladder* sidesteps theorizing the notion of "analogy" on which it largely relies and occasionally achieves accessibility at the price of precision, it is nonetheless filled with rich textual insights set in illuminating contextual surroundings. [Rebecca Saunders]

Kulka, John, and Natalie Danford, eds. Alice Hoffman, guest ed. *Scribner's Best of the Fiction Workshops 1997.* Scribner, 1997. 400 pp. Paper: $13.00.

I have a problem with how conventional most of the pieces in this anthology are, but there is a need for such an annual as a way of giving younger writers exposure that they will not otherwise get. The anthology will also be useful to book editors looking for new writers, and I know that some of the authors have wound up with book contracts based upon what editors saw here. A few weeks ago I was talking to an editor at a large commercial house who was complaining that he was not coming across fresh material by young writers, and this annual could become an effective vehicle for discovering such writers. [John O'Brien]

Hershel Parker, *Herman Melville: A Biography, Volume 1, 1819-1851.* Johns Hopkins Univ. Press, 1996. 941 pp. $39.95.

"Typee," as Herman Melville was called for several years after the success of his first novel, was not only hailed by reviewers as the Modern Crusoe but also harangued by a host of critics for his "sexual license"; Herman Melville, the seafaring storyteller, much to his own surprise, was emerging as America's first literary sex symbol. Indeed, Hershel Parker's new biography of Melville's early life and career reminds us that the New Melville of recent years is not unlike the Melville of old: narratives exploring eroticism and exposing expansionism have intrigued (and often scandalized) readers from the start.

It is just this start that Parker's biography amply details: from Melville's recognition aboard the *United States* that it is "manly to love literature" to his cultivation of a literary friendship with Hawthorne, the man who, according to Melville, "dropped germinous seeds into my soul." Despite Melville's metaphoric birthing of *Moby-Dick,* Parker's narrative details a world of lost fathers. Melville's anxieties in the literary marketplace are set against his father's utter failures; Gansevoort, Herman's older brother (and literary agent) tragically dies as *Typee,* the book he has been shopping, gains success; and it is the reluctant Hawthorne who unknowingly inspires Melville, the "thought-diver," to try his harpoon at the big whale. This is not to say that the lifelong financial distresses of Maria Melville or Herman's extensive courtship of Lizzie Shaw are not in evidence, but rather that they are lesser tales. Perhaps it is a tribute to Parker's own success as a storyteller that this voluminous account could leave a reader wanting more, not only about Melville's relationship with his wife or mother but also about his position in an American literary marketplace that is flooded, on the very evening at the Lenox Hotel that Melville proudly hands his masterpiece to Hawthorne, by what Melville's mentor infamously described as a mob of scribbling women. [Jennifer Travis]

Joyce Piell Wexler. *Who Paid for Modernism? Art, Money, and the Fiction of Conrad, Joyce, and Lawrence.* Univ. of Arkansas Press, 1997. 157 pp. $24.00.

This is one of the zaniest books I have ever read and yet also disturbing in terms of its implications. Stated simply, Wexler's theory is that modernist writers (among whom she includes and highlights Conrad, Lawrence, and

Joyce) faced the dilemma of not wanting to be "popular" because popularity, in their view, "would have undermined their status as serious artists," but at the same time wanting money. They ingeniously figured out, so the argument goes, that they would write terribly difficult books that would attract the wealthy elite and allow them to scorn the masses. Flaubert had provided the theory for all of this, and these young'ns followed suit in their hypocritical pursuit of both money and purity. This brilliant marketing method continues today, reflected, for instance, in the popularity of a Herman Wouk and the critical success but unpopularity of a Robert Coover; the serious writer of today (following in the modernist tradition) aspires to occupy the position of a Pynchon (the aloof, uncompromising artist who has also been financially successful). Strangely, if one knows next to nothing about authors and the book business, Wexler's argument seems plausible—a "serious" writer wants to write to satisfy himself but would also like to live comfortably. They make their work even more obscure than what it might otherwise be, sweat to make sure it communicates as little as possible, bask in their tortured romantic pose of the rejected artist, but then win the prizes and get well paid. Brilliant! This explanation could be applied to marketing strategies of Mercedes Benz—how to appeal to the elite, how to be highbrow, how to make people feel superior because they associate with you rather than the dirty masses. It all sounds somewhat plausible, except that this is not how writers think, nor does it have much to do with what makes books sell well or not sell well. Completely leaving aside the psychological motives and abilities of writers (which is one hell of a lot to leave aside), most would like a financially comfortable life, would like a wide reading audience, and would like to be taken seriously by critics. Contrary to Wexler's thinking, every editor and publisher in existence knows writers who, regardless of financial or critical success, still feel rejected, misunderstood, and undercompensated; at the same time, almost no writer feels that he or she is writing junk, regardless of what he or she writes. And almost every editor and publisher also knows writers who, at one time or another, tried writing a "popular" book, whatever the motive might have been, and most of these writers cannot do it, they do not know how to do it, and finally do not have that "talent." Wexler seems to believe that Joyce or Conrad could have, if they so chose, written a best-seller that appealed to the masses, but instead they went this other route.

It seems to me, however, that there is another motive, an insidious and unstated one, at work in this book that has rather far-reaching implications. At the heart of Wexler's theory is that, beginning with modernist writers (though she omits Fitzgerald and Hemingway in her analysis), writers were determined for rather crass motives to alienate themselves from readers and spanned a conflict that is still with us between good writing vs. general readership. If read in the context of other such views being expressed of late, there appears to be an underlying political cause at work here, namely, populism, democracy, and the Flag. What comes next? That modernism was an antidemocratic attempt to make us feel stupid? That modernism is under-mining the Republic? That if morons have a hard time with Faulkner, we ought to ban him for the sake of the general public? If Joyce and Proust are trying to be difficult and highbrow, then we'll show them and stop teaching their works in the classroom in preference to writers everyone can under-stand and who also serve a politically correct agenda? Do we really need book-books when we have the Internet? Dumbbells of the world unite?

Something is afoot when books like this appear. And when such things are afoot, there are usually several feet at work. A basis for the justifying of the dumbing-down in the review media? A dumbing-down in academia? Why should there be public support for the arts when these damn artists aren't interested in communicating with the guy on the street who is paying the bills? All that I am suggesting is that when a book like this appears that singularly distinguishes itself for its ahistorical background, its ill-sup-ported evidence for grand generalities, and its claim that these people don't want to be read or understood, then be aware that someone's agenda is be-ing served and (since this is America) someone will be benefitting economi-cally. [John O'Brien]

Shawn Stewart Ruff, ed. *Go the Way Your Blood Beats: An Anthology of Lesbian and Gay Fiction by African-American Writers*. Holt, 1996. 544 pp. Paper: $16.95.

While boy meets boy and girl falls for girl in this collection, Ruff's editorial vision is antiromance. Conflicts and confusions are not generally subsumed by the happily-ever-after-ending of love. (Marriage not being an available conclusion for realist homosexual writers). In fact, in the section titled "Heartache," Ruff collects stories in which love is "a many splendid and splintered thing." Aside from Carolivia Herron's incantatory celebration of desire in "Epithalamion," the stories interrogate the difficulties of loving for black gays and lesbians. Ruff has organized the anthology into nine sec-tions, some tellingly titled: "Bad Blood," "Hemorrhaging," and "Bashers." But even the less chillingly indicated sections represent self-doubt, anger, fear, longing that wounds as often as it is fulfilled.

For instance, in "Wet behind the Ears" the stories represent characters realizing or constructing sexual identity. In Gayl Jones's "The Women" a teenaged girl has straight sex to prove she is not a lesbian like her mother. Yet this defining act is reactive and, hence, described listlessly. This is a pathetic rite of passage; the young woman leads her carelessly selected first lover to her mother's bedroom and "lets him get on top of [her]." Other selections reflect similarly sad initiations. In "Meredith's Lie" Ruff's pro-tagonist discovers her boyfriend kissing another man and retaliates with an unsatisfying hour in bed with the star football player. The story is compel-

lingly unresolved: Meredith, afraid of her desire for a man whose gender is
now liminal, ultimately refuses to believe Bruce is gay; he is similarly invested in this self-deception.

While the above stories depict the confusion of sexual "coming of age,"
many depict the complications of adults trying to love homosexually but
also across racial and class divisions. Reginald Shepherd's "Summertime
and the Living Is Easy" suggests that love for the "same" can be fraught
with difference. Is Shepherd's protagonist, a black man who grew up in the
projects, in love with the white man who hosts him for the summer? Or is
his desire also for the rarified environment he so lovingly renders in his narration? Perhaps the best exploration of such themes is Randall Kenan's
"Run, Mourner, Run." Dean, who is poor, white, and gay, agrees to initiate
an affair with a successful black man, Raymond, in exchange for money
and a promotion. Dean prostitutes himself and betrays Raymond, yet the
affair is described as erotic and affectionate. When white men with cameras
interrupt their final tryst, it is certain that both men have lost. And when the
blackmailer refuses to pay, Dean's powerlessness as a poor and gay man is
visible. With so many sites of difference and subordination, this story, as
well as others, questions who exactly is "on the bottom."

Sapphire's contribution, "There's a Window," does not ask this question;
though narrated in the profane diction of an angry, imprisoned woman, this
story is marked by mutuality and tenderness. Despite the conditions,
Magdalena has managed to scrub her bra scrupulously clean and to obtain
protective latex for a first sexual encounter with a new inmate. The narrator
is moved: "Here we was in death's asshole, two bitches behind bars, hard as
nails and twice as ugly—caring." In a book where love is almost always
hard-won, complicated, and not necessarily pretty, this story is singularly
compelling. [Pamela E. Barnett]

Elena Lappin, ed. *Daylight in Nightclub Inferno: Czech Fiction from the
Post-Kundera Generation.* Catbird Press, 1997. 307 pp. $15.95.

Post- is the prefix of choice for contemporary Eastern Europe. The Czech
Republic and other countries are typically said to be postcommunist. Post-
defines the present as following the past, which stands to reason, and breaking with the past, which is frequently debatable. Romania might be post-
Ceausescu in name, but post- there doesn't mean left entirely behind.

Daylight in Nightclub Inferno is a fiction anthology of thirteen Czech
writers from the generation younger than Milan Kundera, publishing most
of them for the first time in English. Calling these writers the post-Kundera
generation, while factually accurate, is odd, for one because the man is still
alive and writing, and for two because the younger writers are probably
more accurately called postcommunist, and I find it disheartening to think

of Kundera as only relevant to a world with communism.

But the writers here are clearly post-something. There are enough castles, locked doors, and taciturn guards in this collection to suggest they're also post-Kafka. A protagonist called "the shop assistant" is familiarly anonymous. In that story the assistant sees "a crowd of tired and peevish people trudging, eyes to the ground." People everywhere trudge, but in the Czech Republic a crowd with its eyes to the ground arrives with a certain amount of literary weight. There are other characters caught in the circumstances of Kafka too. Vašek Koubek's story "Hell," begins, "Mr. White is an average citizen. Not really happy, but on the other hand not so enlightened that he understands the extent of his unhappiness."

So why Kafka? Well, boredom, listlessness, inertia, and averageness are the subjects of a number of the stories. Often, as in Kafka, these qualities of life are linked to the major institutions, the job, the school. A character in Michal Viewegh's novel *Sightseers* remarks, "The cult of seriousness that rules the Czech Republic is totally incomprehensible." Often the qualities are environmental, permeating everything. A character describes the world as "very ugly." "Banality, kitsch, and decay," he continues "are devouring city, village, and field."

When Kafka meets postcommunism, there is something like Alexandr Kliment's novel *Boredom in Bohemia*: "I had to sign in every morning with a pencil attached to the spine of an attendance book, or punch my card in a time-clock. I wouldn't say that I was bored really—I can become absorbed in my work and it goes well—but somehow it isn't the same. A Marxist would say that I am completely free, because I have understood my necessity. I have understood that I have to make a living." The danger here is that a reader (at least this American reader) can reduce all the stories to political fables. I can read each of them for what they say about "the times." But the forthright and often ironic ways that these writers introduce politics belie any easy postcommunist conclusions. Or to put this another way, writers are often the most explicit about the thing that is most obvious and least interesting to them, and needless to say many of these authors are very explicit about their country's communist past. The mention of Marxism in the above quotation is not so much one volley in a political firefight as a way of apprehending the human problems of boredom and dissatisfaction, and finding that way to be disingenuous. Elsewhere in the collection, Jáchym Topol begins a chapter of the novel *Sister*, "And then one gloomy postbolshevik day . . ." with what I take to be delicious irony. These younger Czech writers are explicit and cagey about politics the way some American writers find it imperative to be about psychology in the post-Oprah world, in which most everyone daily and freely engages in some amateur psychological supposing. When they write about politics, they do so first and quickly, to get it out of the way and to what lies beyond it. [Paul Maliszewski]

Robert Welch, ed. *The Oxford Companion to Irish Literature.* Oxford Univ. Press, 1997. 614 pp. $49.95; John Sturrock, ed. *The Oxford Guide to Contemporary Writing.* Oxford Univ. Press, 1996. 492 pp. $35.00.

The Oxford Companion to Irish Literature is an excellent encyclopedic guide to Irish literature. Someone else may be able to find writers who are omitted, but I couldn't. Any companion that gets both Bernard Share (*Innish, The Merciful Hour*) and the experimental Gaelic novelist Séamus Mac Annaidh is, it seems to me, getting almost everyone. Beyond this inclusiveness, however, is some very good and accurate writing about the writers and books. All in all, a first-rate performance. The second of these volumes, *The Oxford Guide to Contemporary Writing,* runs into the kinds of problems to which such guides are nearly doomed. The method here is a collection of overview essays covering contemporary writing (i.e., 1945 onwards) in twenty-eight countries, leaving each contributor with about sixteen pages. You can see the problem. Some of the contributors do a very good job of pulling off this impossible task (John Taylor covering the French) but others work less well (Patricia Craig on Irish literature). The problem, of course, is that the writers must try to come up with some kind of thesis or another, and then must try to include as many writers and titles as they can manage, which inevitably leads to problems of who will be included, who barely mentioned, who not mentioned at all. Wendy Lesser got the task of covering the United States in twenty-five pages, which begins with Truman Capote, the New Journalism (remember the New Journalism?), David Koresh in Waco, Texas, and so on. Since writers and tastes and movements change in the United States as quickly as James Atlas can decide what's hip and what isn't, there is no way to write this history without appearing either to have no point of view or chucking most of what happened and writing about what you want. Lesser, perhaps wisely, chose the former but then of course completely omits writers and books that, finally, are more important than, for instance, the New Journalists. The volume may prove that such a history can no longer be written because we know too much or that we need a curmudgeonly Ford Madox Ford to do the job. [John O'Brien]

New and Recommended in Paperback

• Julian Barnes. *Cross Channel.* Vintage, $12.00, 211 pages. Almost anything by Barnes is worth getting.
• Stephen Dixon. *Interstate.* Owl/Holt, $14.00, 374 pages. The *New York Times* said of it, "Neither Italo Calvino nor Robbe-Grillet ever brought off anything so cruelly audacious (although they tried) or so upsetting as *Interstate.*" Despite the *Times*'s usual denseness, Dixon is also worth getting.

• Joanna Scott. *The Closest Possible Union.* Owl/Holt, $14.00, 290 pages. With each book, Scott gets closer to receiving the attention she deserves.

• Leonard Gardner. *Fat City.* Univ. of California, 183 pages. Do not have the price on this one because of the nasty habit that university presses have of not putting the price on their books. In any event, this underground classic, first published in the late 1960s, is available again.

• Jorge Semprun. *The Long Voyage.* Penguin, $11.95, 236 pages. First published by Grove in 1964, Penguin has restored this important work in its Twentieth-Century Classics series.

• Samuel Beckett. *The Complete Short Prose 1929-1989.* Grove, $14.00, 294 pages. Edited and introduction by S. E. Gontarski. Published in cloth in 1995, this is the first paperback edition.

• John Barth. *The Tidewater Tales.* Johns Hopkins Univ., $16.95, 655 pages. Not the first paperback edition, but fortunately brought back into print by Johns Hopkins.

• Robert McAlmon. *Being Geniuses Together: 1920-1930.* Johns Hopkins Univ., $15.95, 362 pages. Again not the first paperback edition, but with some luck this one will stay around longer than the others. This is McAlmon's memoir of his days in Paris in the twenties and thirties. Kay Boyle collaborated on this and has an afterword.

• Guy Davenport. *Da Vinci's Bicycle.* New Directions, $11.95, 185 pages. These stories were originally brought out by Johns Hopkins in 1979, and now reemerges from, of course, New Directions.

• Amiri Baraka. *The Autobiography of LeRoi Jones.* Lawrence Hill Books, $16.95, 465 pages. Expanded edition from the one published in 1984, and containing a twenty-page introduction written by Baraka for this new edition.

   . . . *and* . . .

• The Spring & Summer 1997 issue of *Alaska Quarterly Review* contains, among many other things, an interview with William Gass, his novella *The Pedersen Kid,* and a brilliant essay entitled "The Test of Time," in which Gass, in a variety of ways, speculates on how-why-if-when literary works pass the test of time.

From the School of Stupidity

Because of so many blatant attempts by so many people to gain entrance to the School, the Committee is refusing to admit anyone this term. We would like to point out, however, that if candidates again try to influence our decision, we threaten to suspend this recognition. We can continue this award only if people play fair, allowing their natural stupidity be the basis for this achievement, rather than purposely trying to be more stupid than anyone else could possibly be, such as has been the case with Mr. James Atlas's article in the *New York Times* Sunday magazine section in which he chastises such writers as Proust, Joyce, and James, as well as contemporaries such as David Foster Wallace, Barth, and Pynchon, for being boring and unreadable. Sorry, Mr. Atlas, you will have to be a bit more subtle than this if you are to succeed at hoodwinking the Committee here at *RCF.*

However, we thought it would be interesting to take a recent *New York Times Book Review* section (May 4, 1997) to see why the *Times* and its reviewers like novels or why they don't. We will simply provide the punch lines.

Reasons for Novels Being Good, Wonderful, Deserving, Etc.

"For Seamus Deanne's readers, life has been illuminated, washed in an elegiac, graceful and forgiving light."
"Such newness was clearly not Mr. Mailer's intention."
"There is a wonderful sweetness to this novel."
"Mr. Bohjalian has done his homework on midwifery and the mechanics of childbirth. He has also landed on a hot topic for baby boomers—the whole question of when alternatives to traditional medicine are beneficial, and when they become dangerous."
"a redemptive conclusion."
"[the character] herself is clearly a woman of the 90's. In an era suspicious of expertise, when everyone with a few megs and a mouse can pass herself off as an authority on anything, she is living proof that anyone can be a philosopher."

Reasons for Novels Being Bad, Difficult, Not Worth Bothering About, Etc.
"I smelled magic realism."
"the profoundly antiheroic white male of Mike Magnuson's nihilistic first novel . . . In another sort of novel, [the character] might be inspired to atone for sins past and present, to take responsibility for his life. Instead, he capitulates to fate, wallowing in an edgy sarcasm that substitutes for wisdom."
"her book affords little sense of real people struggling with real problems."

We are not sure what conclusions to draw from these assessments, except to suggest that novels reviewed in the *Times* will receive good reviews if: they illuminate life in a forgiving light; they are not too new or inventive; they are sweet; they have hot topics and provide some useful information (such as giving some practical suggestions about the mechanics of childbirth); characters are so real that the reviewer comes to believe that they can be used as "living proof" of something, such as that someone, especially a woman, can be a philosopher; and they have redemptive endings.

But novels will receive bad reviews if: they are magically real instead of real-real; they have white males who wind up being sarcastic rather than wise; they don't have real people in them who have real problems. Obviously, this whole business about *real* matters a great deal among the *Times* reviewers. Be real and be redemptive; don't be a downer, don't get weird, and don't be a wise guy.

There, that seems to include everything.

Books Received

Abee, Steve. *King Planet.* Incommunicado, 1997. Paper: $12.00. (F)

Adams, Alice. *Medicine Men.* Knopf, 1997. $23.00. (F)

Alsen, Eberhard. *Romantic Postmodernism in American Fiction.* Editions Rodopi, 1996. $25.00. (NF)

Andrews, William L., Frances Smith Foster, and Trudier Harris, eds. *The Oxford Companion to African American Literature.* Oxford, 1997. $49.95. (NF)

Antoni, Robert. *Blessed Is the Fruit.* Holt, 1997. $25.00. (F)

Asals, Frederick. *The Making of Malcolm Lowry's "Under the Volcano."* Georgia, 1997. $85.00. (NF)

Atwood, Margaret, and Robert Weaver, eds. *The New Oxford Book of Canadian Short Stories.* Oxford, 1997. Paper: $16.95. (F)

Ball, Pamela. *Lava.* Norton, 1997. $21.00. (F)

Balliet, Gay Louise. *Henry Miller and Surrealist Metaphor: "Riding the Ovarian Trolley."* Lang, 1996. $45.95. (NF)

Banville, John. *The Untouchable.* Knopf, 1997. $25.00. (F)

Barich, Bill. *Carson Valley.* Pantheon, 1997. $25.00. (F)

Barone, Dennis. *Hard Fallen Bony Lapse.* Texture, 1996. Paper: $6.00. (Poetry)

Barth, John. *The Friday Book.* Johns Hopkins, 1997. Paper: $15.95. (NF)

Bassanese, Fiora A. *Understanding Luigi Pirandello.* South Carolina, 1997. $29.95. (NF)

Baxter, Charles. *Believers.* Pantheon, 1997. $23.00. (F)

Bayles, Martha. *Hole in Our Soul.* Chicago, 1996. Paper: $16.95. (NF)

Bellow, Saul. *The Actual.* Viking, 1997. $17.95. (F)

Bender, Sheila, ed. *The Writer's Journal.* Delta, 1997. Paper: $12.95. (NF)

Bergman, Ingmar. *Private Confessions.* Trans. Joan Tate. Arcade, 1997. $21.95. (NF)

Billington, Michael. *The Life and Work of Harold Pinter.* Faber & Faber, 1997. $24.95. (NF)

Blinn, James W. *The Aardvark Is Ready for War.* Little, Brown, 1997. $22.95. (F)

Bloom, Clive. *Cult Fiction: Popular Reading and Pulp Theory.* St. Martin's, 1997. $39.95. (NF)

Bloom, Steven. *No New Jokes.* Norton, 1997. $23.00. (F)

Bluett, Rick. *The Untimely Death of a Nihilist.* Quartet, 1997. Paper: £9.00. (F)

Boswell, Robert. *American Owned Love.* Knopf, 1997. $24.00. (F)

Bourke, Angela. *By Salt Water.* Dufour, 1997. Paper: $12.95. (F)

Boyd, Blanche McCrary. *Terminal Velocity.* Knopf, 1997. $23.00. (F)

Brodersen, Momme. *Walter Benjamin: A Biography.* Trans. Malcolm R. Green and Ingrida Ligers. Ed. Martina Dervis. Verso, 1997. $35.00. (NF)

Busch, Frederick. *Girls.* Harmony, 1997. $23.00. (F)

Bygrave, Stephen, ed. *Romantic Writings.* Routledge, 1996. $65.00. (NF)

Calder, Richard. *Dead Things.* St. Martin's, 1997. $21.95. (F)

Callaghan, Mary Rose. *I Met a Man Who Wasn't There.* Marion Boyars, 1997. $24.95. (F)

Caputo, Philip. *Exiles.* Knopf, 1997. $25.00. (F)

Carroll, Jonathan. *The Panic Hand.* St. Martin's, 1996. $23.95. (F)

Cash, Rosanne. *Bodies of Water.* Avon, 1997. Paper: $10.00. (F)

Cather, Willa. *O Pioneers!* Ed. Susan Rosowski, et al. Nebraska, 1997. Paper: $12.95. (F)

Catonné, Jean-Marie. *La Tête étoilée.* Plon, 1996. 98 FF. (F)

Cerf, Muriel. *Le Verrou.* Actes Sud, 1997. Paper: 148 FF. (F)

Chamoiseau, Patrick. *School Days.* Trans. Linda Coverdale. Nebraska, 1997. $35.00. (F)

——. *Texaco.* Trans. Rose-Miriam Réjouis and Val Vinokurov. Pantheon, 1997. $27.00. (F)

Chang, Leonard. *The Fruit 'n Food.* Black Heron, 1996. $21.95. (F)

Charyn, Jerome. *El Bronx.* Mysterious, 1997. $22.00. (F)

Chevillard, Eric. *The Crab Nebula.* Trans. Jordan Stump and Eleanor Hardin. Nebraska, 1997. $35.00. (F)

Christy, Jim. *The Buk Book: Musings on Charles Bukowski.* ECW, 1997. Paper: $12.95. (NF)

Claus, Hugo. *The Swordfish.* Trans. Ruth Levitt. Peter Owen, 1996. £14.95. (F)

Clerc, Charles. *The Y and Other Stories.* Provine, 1997. Paper: $11.00. (F)

Connolly, Sean. *A Great Place to Die.* Hardscrabble Books, 1997. $21.95. (F)

Coover, Robert. *Pinocchio in Venice.* Grove/Atlantic, 1997. Paper: $12.00. (F)

Crawford, Max. *Lords of the Plain.* Oklahoma, 1997. Paper: $14.95. (F)

Cundy, Catherine. *Salman Rushdie.* St. Martin's, 1997. $49.95. (NF)

D'Arcy, Chantal Cornut-Gentille, and José Angel García Landa, eds. *Gender, I-deology Essays on Theory, Fiction and Film.* Editions Rodopi, 1996. Paper: $34.00. (NF)

Darrieussecq, Marie. *Pig Tales.* Trans. Linda Coverdale. New Press, 1997. $18.00. (F)

Davies, Rhys. *Ram with Red Horns.* Dufour, 1997. Paper: $16.95. (F)

Davies, Tony. *Humanism.* Routledge, 1996. $49.95. (NF)

Deane, Seamus. *Reading in the Dark.* Knopf, 1997. $23.00. (F)

Delany, Samuel R. *Atlantis: Three Tales.* Wesleyan, 1997. Paper: $14.95. (F)

——. *Longer Views: Extended Essays.* New England, 1996. $50.00. (NF)

Denes, Magda. *Castles Burning.* Norton, 1997. $24.00. (F)

Denker, Henry. *A Place for Kathy.* Morrow, 1997. $23.00. (F)

DeShell, Jeffrey. *The Peculiarity of Literature.* Fairleigh Dickinson, 1997. $32.50. (NF)

Di Blasi, Debra. *Drought.* New Directions, 1997. Paper: $10.95. (F)

Dixon, Stephen. *Gould.* Holt, 1997. $24.00. (F)

Doody, Margaret Anne. *The True Story of the Novel.* Rutgers, 1996. No price given. (NF)

Duncan, Robert. *Selected Poems.* Ed. Robert J. Bertholf. New Directions, 1997. Paper: $12.95. (Poetry)

Duncker, Patricia. *Hallucinating Foucault.* Ecco, 1996. $21.00. (NF)

Dunmore, Helen. *Talking to the Dead.* Little, Brown, 1997. $21.95. (F)

Ebersole, Lucinda. *Death in Equality.* St. Martin's, 1997. $19.95. (F)

Eberstadt, Fernanda. *When the Sons of Heaven Meet the Daughters of the Earth.* Knopf, 1997. $25.00. (F)

Echenoz, Jean. *Big Blondes.* Trans. Mark Polizzotti New Press, 1997. $22.00. (F)

Echevarría, Roberto González, and Enrique Pupo-Walker, eds. *The Cambridge History of Latin American Literature.* Cambridge, 1996. $90.00. (NF)

Edwards, Page, Jr. *The Search for Kate Duval.* Marion Boyars, 1997. Paper: $16.95. (F)

Eisenberg, Deborah. *The Stories (So Far) of Deborah Eisenberg.* Noonday, 1997. Paper: $15.00. (F)

Elkhadem, Saad. *The Blessed Movement.* York, 1997. Paper: $9.95. (F)

Endo, Shusaku. *The Samurai.* Trans. Van C. Gessel. New Directions, 1997. Paper: $10.95. (F)

Febres, Mayra Santos. *Urban Oracles.* Trans. Nathan Budoff and Lydia Platon Lázaro. Lumen Editions, 1997. $15.95. (F)

Fields, Jennie. *Crossing Brooklyn Ferry.* Morrow, 1997. $23.00. (F)

Filmer-Davies, Kath. *Fantasy Fiction and Welsh Myth.* St. Martin's, 1997. $49.95. (NF)

Fischer, Tibor. *The Collector Collector.* Secker & Warburg, 1997. £12.99. (F)

———. *Under the Frog.* Owl, 1997. Paper: $12.00. (F)

Foos, Laurie. *Portrait of the Walrus by a Young Artist.* Coffee House, 1997. $19.95. (F)

Foreman, Richard. *No-Body.* Overlook, 1997. $21.95. (F)

Fourcade, Dominique. *Click-Rose.* Trans. Keith Waldrop. Sun & Moon, 1997. Paper: $10.95. (Poetry)

Franck, Dan. *My Russian Love.* Trans. Jon Rothschild. Doubleday, 1997. $18.95. (F)

Franzen, Jonathan. *The Twenty-Seventh City.* Farrar, Straus & Giroux, 1997. Paper: $15.00. (F)

Fulton, Alice. *Sensual Math.* Norton, 1996. Paper: $12.00. (Poetry)

Galeano, Eduardo. *Walking Words.* Trans. Mark Fried. Norton, 1997. Paper:

$15.00. (F)

Garcia, Cristina. *The Agüero Sisters.* Knopf, 1997. $24.00. (F)

Genardière, Philippe de la. *Gazo.* Actes Sud, 1996. 100 FF. (F)

Goldreich, Gloria. *Leah's Journey.* Syracuse, 1997. Paper: $14.95. (F)

Gordon, Karen Elizabeth. *Paris out of Hand.* Chronicle, 1996. $19.95. (NF)

Gould, Lois. *No Brakes.* Holt, 1997. $22.00. (F)

Gowdy, Barbara. *Mister Sandman.* Steerforth, 1997. $24.00. (F)

Grunberg, Arnon. *Blue Monday.* Farrar, Straus & Giroux, 1997. $22.00. (F)

Gunn, Kirsty. *The Keepsake.* Grove/Atlantic, 1997. $22.00. (F)

Gutierrez, Stephen. *Elements.* FC2, 1997. Paper: $11.95. (F)

Haddawy, Husain, trans. *The Arabian Nights II.* Norton, 1995. $27.50. (F)

Hall, Brian. *The Saskiad.* Houghton Mifflin, 1997. Price not given. (F)

Hanania, Tony. *Homesick.* Bloomsbury, 1997. £14.99. (F)

Hansen, Elaine Tuttle. *Mother without Child.* California, 1997. $45.00. (NF)

Hardin, Rob. *Distorture.* FC2, 1997. Paper: $9.00. (F)

Harpman, Jacqueline. *I Who Have Never Known Men.* Seven Stories, 1997. $22.00. (F)

Hassler, Donald M., and Clyde Wilcox, eds. *Political Science Fiction.* South Carolina, 1997. $34.95. (NF)

Hawkes, Terence, ed. *Alternative Shakespeares:* Volume 2. Routledge, 1996. $55.00. (NF)

Hemmingson, Michael. *Minstrels.* Permeable, 1997. Paper: $10.00. (F)

Hoffman, Michael J., and Patrick D. Murphy, eds. *Essentials of the Theory of Fiction.* Duke, 1996. $54.95. (NF)

Hoogland, Renée C. *Lesbian Configurations.* Columbia, 1997. $45.00. (NF)

Horvath, Brooke, Irving Malin, and Paul Ruffin, eds. *A Goyen Companion.* Texas, 1997. $37.50. (NF)

Huneven, Michelle. *Round Rock.* Knopf, 1997. $24.00. (F)

Hunt, Tim. *Kerouac's Crooked Road.* California, 1996. Price not given. (NF)

Infante, Guillermo Cabrera. *Holy Smoke.* Overlook, 1997. $24.95. (NF)

Irwin, Robert. *Exquisite Corpse.* Pantheon, 1997. $23.00. (F)

Jabès, Edmond. *The Little Book of Unsuspected Subversion.* Trans. Rosmarie Waldrop. Stanford, 1996. $29.50. (NF)

Jacobi, Steven. *A Short Series of Discrete Problems.* Secker & Warburg, 1997. £12.99. (F)

Jaffe, Harold, ed. *Fiction International 29: Pain.* San Diego State, 1996. Paper: $12.00. (F)

Jaffe, Sherril. *Interior Designs.* Black Sparrow, 1997. $25.00. (F)

Jarrard, Kyle. *Over There.* Baskerville, 1997. $21.00. (F)

Jehlen, Myra, and Michael Warner, eds. *The English Literatures of America: 1500-1800.* Routledge, 1997. Paper: $35.00. (NF)

Josipovici, Gabriel. *Touch.* Yale, 1996. $25.00. (F)

Joyce, James. *Ulysses*. Oxford, 1997. Paper: $15.95. (F)

Kaczvinsky, Donald P. *Lawrence Durrell's Major Novels, or The Kingdom of the Imagination*. Susquehanna, 1997. $33.50. (NF)

Kadare, Ismail. *The Three-Arched Bridge*. Trans. John Hodgson Arcade, 1997. $21.95. (F)

Kennedy, Thomas E. *The Book of Angels*. Wordcraft of Oregon, 1997. Paper: $12.95. (F)

Kernan, Nathan, ed. *The Diary of James Schuyler*. Black Sparrow, 1997. $27.50. (NF)

Khue, Le Minh. *The Stars, The Earth, The River*. Trans. Bac Hoai Tran and Dana Sachs. Ed. Wayne Karlin. Curbstone, 1997. Paper: $12.95. (F)

Komarnicki, Todd. *Famine*. Arcade, 1997. $22.95. (F)

Laxness, Halldór. *Independent People*. Trans. J. A. Thompson. Vintage, 1997. Paper: $14.00. (F)

LeClézio, J. M. G. *Onitsha*. Trans. Alison Anderson. Nebraska, 1997. $35.00. (F)

Leontis, Artemis. *Greece: A Traveler's Literary Companion*. Whereabouts, 1997. Paper: $13.95. (F)

Lerman, Rhoda. *God's Ear*. Syracuse, 1997. Paper: $16.95. (F)

Lethem, Jonathan. *As She Climbed across the Table*. Doubleday, 1997. $22.95. (F)

Lish, Gordon. *Dear Mr. Capote*. Four Walls Eight Windows, 1996. Paper: $12.95. (F)

———. *What I Know So Far*. Four Walls Eight Windows, 1996. Paper: $10.95. (F)

Little, Judy. *The Experimental Self*. Southern Illinois, 1996. No price given. (NF)

Lodge, David. *The Practice of Writing*. Viking, 1997. $24.95. (NF)

Long, David. *The Falling Boy*. Scribner, 1997. $22.00. (F)

Lynch, Deidre, and William B. Warner, eds. *Cultural Institutions of the Novel*. Duke, 1996. $59.95. (NF)

Mackey, Louis. *Fact, Fiction, and Representation: Four Novels by Gilbert Sorrentino*. Camden House, 1997. $45.00. (NF)

Mailer, Norman. *The Gospel According to the Son*. Random House, 1997. $22.00. (F)

Mallon, Thomas. *Dewey Defeats Truman*. Pantheon, 1997. $24.00. (F)

Malouf, David. *The Conversations at Curlow Creek*. Pantheon, 1997. $23.00. (F)

Mamet, David. *Make-Believe Town*. Back Bay, 1997. Paper: $11.95. (NF)

Marlowe, Stephen. *The Death and Life of Miguel de Cervantes*. Arcade, 1996. $25.95. (F)

Matute, Ana María. *Celebrations in the Northwest*. Trans. Phoebe Ann Porter. Nebraska, 1997. $25.00. (F)

Mazza, Cris. *Dog People*. Coffee House, 1997. Paper: $13.95. (F)

McCabe, Patrick. *Carn*. Delta, 1997. Paper: $11.95. (F)

McCrum, Robert. *Suspicion*. Macmillan, 1996. £15.99. (F)
McKinty, Adrian. *Orange Rhymes with Everything*. Morrow, 1997. $23.00. (F)
Michaels, Anne. *Fugitive Pieces*. Knopf, 1997. $23.00. (F)
Miller, Arthur. *Focus*. Syracuse, 1997. Paper: $14.95. (F)
Mitchell, Robert H. *Ride the Lightning*. Oklahoma, 1997. $26.95. (F)
Montgomery, Lee, ed. *Absolute Disaster: Fiction from Los Angeles*. Dove Books, 1996. Paper: $15.95. (F)
Moody, Rick. *Garden State*. Back Bay, 1997. Paper: $11.95. (F)
————. *Purple America*. Little, Brown, 1997. $23.95. (F)
Morris, Irvin. *From the Glittering World*. Oklahoma, 1997. $24.95. (F)
Morrow, Bradford. *Giovanni's Gift*. Viking, 1997. $22.95. (F)
Mukherjee, Bharati. *Leave It to Me*. Knopf, 1997. $23.00. (F)
Murray, Yxta Maya. *Locas*. Grove/Atlantic, 1997. $22.00. (F)
Neugeboren, Jay. *Imagining Robert*. William Morrow, 1997. $24.00. (NF)
O'Brien, Edna. *Down by the River*. Farrar, Straus & Giroux, 1997. $23.00. (F)
Ondaatje, Michael. *The English Patient*. Vintage, 1993. Paper: $12.00. (F)
Ozick, Cynthia. *The Puttermesser Papers*. Knopf, 1997. $23.00. (F)
Palmer, Michael, Régis Bonvicino, and Nelson Ascher, eds. *Nothing the Sun Could Not Explain*. Trans. Regina Alfarano, et al. Sun & Moon, 1997. Paper: $15.95. (Poetry)
Pamuk, Orhan. *The New Life*. Trans. Güneli Gün. Farrar, Straus & Giroux, 1997. $24.00. (F)
Parks, Tim. *Europa*. Secker & Warburg, 1997. Paper: £9.99. (F)
Pasolini, Pier Paolo. *Petrolio*. Trans. Ann Goldstein. Pantheon, 1997. $27.00. (F)
Pearson, Ridley. *Beyond Recognition*. Hyperion, 1997. $22.95. (F)
Pérez-Reverte, Arturo. *The Club Dumas*. Trans. Sonia Soto. Harcourt Brace, 1996. $23.00. (F)
Petit, Chris. *The Psalm Killer*. Knopf, 1997. $25.00. (F)
Phillips, Caryl. *The Nature of Blood*. Knopf, 1997. $23.00. (F)
Plate, Peter. *Snitch Factory*. Incommunicado, 1997. Paper: $13.00. (F)
Plumlee, Harry James. *Shadow of the Wolf*. Oklahoma, 1997. $21.95. (F)
Prose, Francine. *Guided Tours of Hell*. Metropolitan, 1997. $23.00. (F)
Quantic, Diane Dufva. *The Nature of the Place*. Bison, 1997. $15.00. (NF)
Ransmayr, Christoph. *The Dog King*. Trans. John E. Woods. Knopf, 1997. $24.00. (F)
Rawlins, Paul. *No Lie Like Love*. Georgia, 1996. No price given. (F)
Rehmann, Ruth. *The Man in the Pulpit: Questions for a Father*. Trans. Christoph Lohmann and Pamela Lohmann. Nebraska, 1997. $35.00. (F)
Reich, Tova. *The Jewish War*. Syracuse, 1997. Paper: $16.95. (F)
Remski, Matthew. *Dying for Veronica*. Insomniac, 1997. $18.99. (F)
Richards, Thomas. *Zero Tolerance*. Farrar, Straus & Giroux, 1997. $23.00. (F)

Robbe-Grillet, Alain, and René Magritte. *La Belle Captive*. Trans. Ben Stoltzfus. California, 1996. Price not given. (F)

Roeseler, Karl, and David Gilbert, eds. *2000 and What?* Trip Street, 1996. Paper: $12.00. (F)

Roof, Judith. *Reproductions of Reproductions*. Routledge, 1996. $55.00. (NF)

Rosa, Rodrigo Rey. *The Pelcari Project*. Trans. Paul Bowles. Cadmus Editions, 1997. Paper: $11.95. (F)

Rosen, Norma. *John and Anzia*. Syracuse, 1997. Paper: $16.95. (F)

Roth, Philip. *American Pastoral*. Houghton Mifflin, 1997. $26.00. (F)

Rudova, Larissa. *Understanding Boris Pasternak*. South Carolina, 1997. $29.95. (NF)

Ruff, Matt. *Sewer, Gas and Electric*. Atlantic Monthly, 1997. $23.00. (F)

Ryan, Jack D. *Cossack*. Vantage, 1996. Paper: $13.95. (F)

Sage, Victor, and Allan Lloyd Smith, eds. *Modern Gothic: A Reader*. St. Martin's, 1997. $69.95. (NF)

Sallis, James, ed. *Ash of Stars: On the Writing of Samuel R. Delany*. Mississippi, 1997. $42.50. (NF)

Santos-Febres, Mayra. *Urban Oracles*. Trans. Nathan Budoff and Lydia Platon Lázaro. Lumen Editions, 1997. Paper: $15.95. (F)

Schiff, James A. *Understanding Reynolds Price*. South Carolina, 1997. $24.95. (NF)

Schumacher, Julie. *The Body Is Water*. Avon, 1997. Paper: $6.99. (F)

Scott, Joanna C. *Charlie and the Children*. Black Heron, 1997. $22.95. (F)

Semprun, Jorge. *Literature or Life*. Viking, 1997. $24.95. (NF)

Settle, Mary Lee. *Charley Bland*. South Carolina, 1996. Paper: $12.95. (F)

Shepard, Jim. *Batting against Castro*. Knopf, 1996. $22.00. (F)

Shreve, Anita. *The Weight of Water*. Little, Brown, 1997. $22.95. (F)

Shurin, Aaron. *Unbound: A Book of AIDS*. Sun & Moon, 1997. $17.95. (NF)

Singh, Jyotsna G. *Colonial Narratives/Cultural Dialogues*. Routledge, 1996. $59.95. (NF)

Solwitz, Sharon. *Blood and Milk*. Sarabande, 1997. Paper: $13.95. (F)

Spaziani, Maria Luisa. *Sentry Towers*. Trans. and ed. Laura Stortoni. Hesperia, 1995. Paper: $13.00. (Poetry)

Spikes, Michael P. *Understanding Contemporary American Literary Theory*. South Carolina, 1997. $24.95. (NF)

Stern, Steve. *A Plague of Dreamers*. Syracuse, 1997. Paper: $16.95. (F)

Sullivan, Mark T. *The Purification Ceremony*. Avon, 1997. $24.00. (F)

Szczypiorski, Andrzej. *The Shadow Catcher*. Trans. Bill Johnston. Grove/Atlantic, 1997. $21.00. (F)

Tabucchi, Antonio. *Pereira Declares*. Trans. Patrick Creagh. New Directions, 1997. Paper: $9.95. (F)

Taylor, Elizabeth Russell. *Present Fears*. Arcadia, 1997. Paper: $18.95. (F)

Teraoka, Arlene A. *East, West, and Others: The Third World in Postwar*

German Literature. Nebraska, 1996. $35.00. (NF)

Tsushima, Yuko. *The Shooting Gallery and Other Stories*. Trans. Geraldine Harcourt. New Directions, 1997. Paper: $11.95. (F)

Turner, Steve. *Jack Kerouac Angelhead Hipster*. Viking, 1997. $29.95. (NF)

Tuten, Frederic. *Van Gogh's Bad Café*. Morrow, 1997. $20.00. (F)

Valdés, Zoé. *Yocandra in the Paradise of Nada*. Trans. Sabina Cienfuegos. Arcade, 1997. $21.95. (F)

Vanderbilt, Henri. *An Ocean Apart*. Genesis, 1997. $26.95. (F)

van Steen, Edla. *Early Mourning*. Trans. David S. George. Latin American Literary Review, 1997. Paper: $13.95. (F)

Villard, Henry S., and James Nagel, eds. *Hemingway in Love and War*. Hyperion, 1996. Paper: $9.95. (NF)

Vizenor, Gerald. *Hotline Healers*. New England, 1997. $21.95. (F)

von Doderer, Heimito. *The Merowingians or The Total Family*. Trans. Vinal Overing Binner. Sun & Moon, 1996. Paper: $15.95. (F)

Walker, Mildred. *The Body of a Young Man*. Nebraska, 1997. Paper: $9.00. (F)

———.*The Brewer's Big Horses*. Nebraska, 1996. Paper: $15.00. (F)

———. *Medical Meeting*. Nebraska, 1997. Paper: $12.00. (F)

Wallace, David Foster. *Infinite Jest*. Little, Brown, 1996. Paper: $14.95. (F)

Warsh, Lewis. *Money under the Table*. Trip Street, 1997. Paper: $10.00. (F)

Waugh, Patricia, ed. *Revolutions of the Word*. Arnold, 1997. $59.95. (NF)

Weimer, Joan. *Back Talk: Teaching Lost Selves to Speak*. Chicago, 1996. Paper: $16.95. (NF)

Weinstein, Philip M. *What Else but Love?* Columbia, 1997. $42.00. (NF)

Wells, David N. *Anna Akhmatova: Her Poetry*. Berg, 1996. Paper: $16.95. (NF)

Wescott, Glenway. *The Grandmothers*. Wisconsin, 1996. Paper: $15.95. (F)

West, Paul. *Sporting with Amaryllis*. Overlook, 1996. $19.95. (F)

Williams, C. K. *The Vigil*. Farrar, Straus & Giroux, 1996. $18.00. (Poetry)

Williams, Diane. *The Stupefaction*. Knopf, 1996. $21.00. (F)

Winterson, Jeanette. *Gut Symmetries*. Knopf, 1997. $22.00. (F)

Wolfe, Peter. *A Vision of His Own: The Mind and Art of William Gaddis*. Fairleigh Dickinson, 1997. $45.00. (NF)

Wright, Charles. *Black Zodiac*. Farrar, Straus & Giroux, 1997. $19.00. (Poetry)

Yablonsky, Linda. *The Story of Junk*. Farrar, Straus & Giroux, 1997. $23.00. (F)

Yuknavitch, Lidia. *Her Other Mouths*. House of Bones, 1997. Paper: $8.95. (F)

Contributors

JOYCE SPARER ADLER was a founding member of the University of Guyana, 1963-1968, is the author of *War in Melville's Imagination* (1981) and *Dramatization of Three Melville Novels* (1992), of many essays on Melville and Wilson Harris, and of the study "Attitudes Towards 'Race' in Guyanese Literature."

IAN BREAKWELL regularly exhibits at the Anthony Reynolds Gallery in London. His artworks hang in public collections, including the Tate Gallery. His illustrated fiction has been published as *The Artist's Dream* (1988); he has also co-edited with Paul Hammond *Seeing in the Dark: A Compendium of Cinemagoing* (1990) and *Brought to Book* (1994).

MICHAEL DENNIS BROWNE has been in the Department of English at the University of Minnesota since 1971. His book of poetry, *You Won't Remember This* (Carnegie Mellon Univ. Press), won the 1993 Minnesota Book Award.

JOHN CALDER publishes under the imprints John Calder (Publisher), Ltd., in the United Kingdom and Riverrun Press in the United States. He has edited and introduced *The Samuel Beckett Reader, The Henry Miller Reader, The William Burroughs Reader*, with John Fletcher, *The Nouveau Roman Reader*, and with S. E. Gontarski, *The Surrealist Reader*. His book *In Defense of Literature* is forthcoming from John Calder (Publisher), Ltd.

TIMOTHY J. CRIBB is a Fellow of Churchill College, Cambridge, and a Newton Affiliated Lecturer in the Faculty of English. He has held posts at the University of Minnesota, Glasgow, and Ife (now Awolowo) University, Nigeria. He is editor of *Imagined Commonwealths: Cambridge Essays in Commonwealth Literatures in English* (forthcoming) to which Wilson Harris, Wole Soyinka, Ben Okri, and others are contributors.

MARY LOU EMERY, Associate Professor of English at the University of Iowa, teaches courses in modernist studies and Anglophone Caribbean literature. Her publications include *Jean Rhys at World's End: Novels of Colonial and Sexual Exile* (Univ. of Texas Press, 1990) and essays on topics of narrative and culture in the writings of D. H. Lawrence, May Sinclair, Jean Rhys, and Wilson Harris. Her current project, *Crossing Signs*, considers representations of visual art in decolonializing narratives.

ZULFIKAR GHOSE was featured in the Summer 1989 issue of the *Review of Contemporary Fiction.* He is the author of eleven novels (most recently *The Triple Mirror of the Self*, Bloomsbury, 1992), five collections of poems (*Selected Poems*, Oxford Univ. Press, 1991), and four volumes of criticism (*Shakespeare's Mortal Knowledge*, Macmillan [London], 1993).

AL GREENBERG is Professor of English at Macalester College in St. Paul, Minnesota. He is also a poet, fiction writer, and librettist; a new opera, *Apollonia's Circus*, premiered in 1994. Recent collections of his poetry include *Heavy Wings* and *Why We Live with Animals*, and his stories have appeared in various places; his most recent collection is *The Man in the Cardboard Mask.*

DESMOND HAMLET, a Guyanese, has lived in Puerto Rico, Canada, Nigeria and the United States; he currently teaches at Dennison University in Granville, Ohio. He is the author of *One Greater Man: Justice and Damnation in Paradise Lost* (1976) and of a recent book-length study of Wilson Harris's fiction and criticism.

LOUIS JAMES is Professor of Victorian and modern literature at the University of Kent at Canterbury. He has taught in Jamaica and Nigeria, has published much on Caribbean and African literature and has lectured in universities in Asia, Australia, Europe, and North America. He was the editor of *The Islands in Between* for the Heinemann Caribbean Writers Series.

HENA MAES JELINEK, OBE, is Professor of English and Commonwealth literature at the University of Liege. She is the author of *The Naked Design, a Reading of "Palace of the Peacock," Wilson Harris,* and of essays and articles on all of Harris's novels. She co-edits the series *Cross Cultures, Readings in the Post/Colonial Literatures in English* (Amsterdam/Atlanta: Rodopi).

PADDY KITCHEN is a reviewer, biographer, and novelist. She has written biographies of Gerard Manley Hopkins and Patrick Geddes, a guide book, *Poets' London* (1980), an account of her home village, *Barnwell* (1985). Her fiction includes *Living-In* (1965), *A Fleshly School* (1970), *Lindsey-Woolsey* (1971), *Paradise* (1972), *The Marriage Ring* (with Dulan Barber, 1977), *A Pillar of Cloud* (1979), *The Golden Veil* (1981), and *Blue Shoe* (1986).

VERA M. KUTZINSKI is Professor of English, African, and American Studies at Yale. She is the author of *Against the Grain: Myth and History in William Carlos Williams, Jay Wright and Nicolas Guillen* (Johns Hopkins, 1987), a translation of Nicolas Guillen's *El Diario que a diaro/The Daily Daily* (California, 1989), and most recently *Sugar's Secrets: Race and the Erotics of Cuban Nationalism* (Virginia, 1994).

DAVID W. MADDEN is Professor of American and Irish literatures at California State University, Sacramento. He is author of *Understanding Paul West* (Univ. of South Carolina Press) and *Essays on Thomas Berger* (G. K. Hall). He has written numerous essays on contemporary fiction and guest edited the Spring 1991 half-issue of the *Review of Contemporary Fiction* devoted to Paul West.

PAULINE MELVILLE is a Guyanese as well as a British citizen. Her collection of short stories, *Space-Shifter*, is published by Picador. It won the Guardian Fiction Prize, the Commonwealth Writer's Prize and the Macmillan Silver Pen Award. She is currently working on a novel largely set in Guyana.

PATRICIA MURRAY teaches at the University of North London. She is currently working on a book *Shared Solitudes: Re-integration of a Fractured Psyche* (a comparative study of the works of Wilson Harris and Gabriel García Márquez).

STUART MURRAY teaches postcolonial studies in the English Department at Trinity College, Dublin. He specializes in writing from New Zealand, the South Pacific, and the Caribbean.

JAY NEUGEBOREN is the author of eleven books, including the prize-winning novels *The Stolen Jew* (1981) and *Before My Life Began* (1985). He is the only author to have won six consecutive Syndicated Short Fiction prizes and is presently Writer-in-Residence at University of Massachusetts, Amherst. His latest book, *Imagining Robert: My Brother, Madness, and Survival* (1997), was published by William Morrow.

FRANK PIKE has been Wilson Harris's editor at Faber and Faber since 1979.

KATHLEEN RAINE is an internationally known scholar who has written on Blake and Yeats and other poets, has published eleven volumes of poetry, autobiographical books, including *India Seen Afar*. She is now giving her greatest attention to the Tenemos Academy and to her responsibilities as editor of *Tenemos*. Her works have been translated into many languages.

FERNANDA STEELE received her Ph.D. from the University of the West Indies where she was briefly a Lecturer in the Department of Spanish. She is now a freelance interpreter and translator. Her translation of Derek Walcott's *Dream on Monkey Mountain* was published after the award of the Nobel Prize to Walcott. She is now at work on a translation of Wilson Harris's *Guyana Quartet* (a collection of Harris's first four novels) into Italian.

CHARLES SUGNET is Associate Professor of English at the University of Minnesota. His essays and reviews have appeared in *Transition, American Book Review, Utne Reader, d'Art,* the *Nation,* and elsewhere. He co-edited *The Imagination on Trial* with Alan Burns and worked with Burns for many years at the University of Minnesota.

The Carolina Quarterly

A Publisher of Fine Writing since 1948.
The work of Conrad Aiken, Russell Banks, Wendell Berry, Doris Betts, Rosellen Brown, Anthony Burgess, Raymond Carver, Evan Connell, Annie Dillard, Richard Eberhart, Lawrence Ferlinghetti, George Garrett, Paul Green, Barry Hannah, Michael S. Harper, Denise Levertov, Archibald MacLeish, Robert Morgan, Guy Owen, Reynolds Price, Kenneth Rexroth, Lee Smith, William Stafford, Max Steele, Thomas Wolfe, Ed Yoder, and many other fine writers has appeared on the pages of *The Carolina Quarterly* through the years.

Yearly subscription rates are $10 for individuals and $12 for institutions.

Greenlaw Hall CB#3520/University of North Carolina/Chapel Hill NC 27599

Studies in 20th Century Literature

A journal devoted to literary theory and practical criticism

Volume 21, No. 2 (Summer, 1997)

Pascale Bécal: From *The Sea Wall* to *The Lover*: Prostitution and Exotic Parody

Heinz Bulmahn: Ideology, Family Policy, Production, and (Re)Education: Literary Treatment of Abortion in the GDR of the early 1980s

José F. Colmeira: Dissonant Voices: Memory and Counter-Memory in Manuel Vázquez Montalbán's *Autobiografía del general Franco*

Eilene Hoft-March: Cardinal's *The Words to Say it*: The Words to Reproduce Mother

Laurence M. Porter: Family Values: Decoding Boris Vian's *Les Bâtisseurs d'Empire*

Louis Simon: Narrative and Simultaneity: Benjamin's Image of Proust

Steven R. Ungar: "Atmosphère, atmosphère": On the Study of France Between the Wars

Ann Elizabeth Willey: Madness and the Middle Passage: Warner-Vierya's *Juletane* as a Paradigm for Writing Caribbean Women's Identities

Special Issue in preparation:

Illness and Disease in 20th Century Literature
Guest Editor: Sander L. Gilman

Silvia Sauter, Editor
Kansas State University
Eisenhower 104
Manhattan, KS 66506-1003
Submissions in:
Russian and Spanish

Marshall Olds, Editor
University of Nebraska
PO Box 880318
Lincoln, NE 68588-0318
Submissions in:
French and German

Subscriptions

Institutions—$20 for one year ($35 for two years)
Individuals—$15 for one year ($28 for two years)
Single issues—$10.00 (add $5 for Air Mail)

We like thin ice!

In over 70 years of trusting the edges, we think it's been worth it. You've been hearing about us in the *Pushcart Prize* anthology, *Best American Poetry, Best American Short Stories, Best American Essays,* and the *O'Henry* anthology, why not brave the ice with us?

1 year $22.00

2 years $38.00

3 years $50.00

Send name and address with a check or money order to
Prairie Schooner
201 Andrews Hall
Lincoln NE 68588-0334

college
Literature

a triannual refereed journal

of scholarly

criticism and pedagogy

Edited by Kostas Myrsiades

**Teaching Literature
at the end of
the Millennium**

Special Issue Editors: Kostas
Myrsiades and Henry Giroux

In 1998 during its 25th anniversary
year *College Literature* will publish
a special double issue on "Teaching
Literature at the End of the
Millennium." Submissions of any
size are now being invited on all
aspects of this topic.

Manuscripts can be submitted anytime
before January 15, 1998
West Chester University
West Chester, PA19383
610-436-2901/ fax: 610-436-3150
e-mail: collit@wcupa.edu

THE
GREENSBORO
REVIEW

🕿 Unsolicited manuscripts must arrive by September 15 to be considered for the winter Literary Awards issue (acceptances in December) and February 15 to be considered for the summer issue (acceptances in May). Manuscripts arriving after those dates will be held for the next consideration. 🕿

SUBSCRIPTIONS

One year—$8   Two years—$16
Three years—$20

English Department
The University of North Carolina at Greensboro
Greensboro, NC 27412

The Iowa Review

※

"ONE OF THE FIVE BEST SMALL MAGAZINES IN THE
COUNTRY"

THE CHRISTIAN SCIENCE MONITOR

※

Now in its twenty-seventh year, *The Iowa Review* publishes three
issues a year of around two hundred pages each. Our issues of
1997 will include an interview with Terry Tempest Williams
and a new essay by her; essays by Euridice and James
McPherson; fiction by Curtis White, Mary Helen Stefaniak,
Rikki Ducornet, Ron Sukenick, and Raymond Federman;
translations of Romanian poems by Eugene Ionescu, and from
the French by Hocquard; poems by Eric Pankey, Frankie Paino,
Albert Goldbarth, Mark Doty, Laura Kasischke, Timothy Liu,
and Barbara Hamby; and a special feature on poets from Egypt,
India, Sierra Leone, and Lithuania from the International
Writing Program.

※

SUBSCRIBE NOW AND RECEIVE ALL THREE ISSUES
FOR $18 OR CALL OUR TOLL FREE NUMBER AT
1-800-235-2665

※

308 ENGLISH-PHILOSOPHY BUILDING
The University of Iowa, Iowa City, Iowa
52242

Announcing

The Missouri Review

Larry Levis

Editors' Prize

In Poetry

Thanks to all those who have joined so far in supporting this prize:

Marcia and Murray Gell-Mann
Maurice Peve
David and Jean Noren
James McKean
Thomas Lux
Julia Wendell
Bill Sheals
William Matthews
Gerald Dethrow
Stuart Brown
Kurt and Laure-Anne Brown
Catherine Herman
Juliet Rodeman
Anonymous
Kenneth Smith
Cortney Daniels
Penelope Austin
James Simmerman
Jeffrey Friedman
Michael Pfeifer
Russell Meyer
Paul Gianoli
Robin Behn
James and Susan Pinson
Matthew Graham
James McCorkle
Bob Shacochis
Deborah Digges
Greg Michalson

an Annual Award of $1,500

for up to 10 pages of poetry

To honor the memory of *MR* co-founder and distinguished poet, Larry Levis. The prize will be funded by his family, friends, students, and colleagues.

We welcome anyone interested in helping support this living tribute to Larry and to poetry to contact us about donations.

Guidelines will be available in June
Entry deadline: October 15

ANTIOCH
the REVIEW

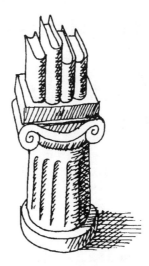

"The Best Words in the Best Order"

"The *Antioch Review* publishes the best writing in America. It is edited with good taste, outstanding judgment, and great care. Its poems, essays, stories, and reviews are always compelling."
Mark Strand

"Here is a literary magazine that does not trade in the cheap commerce of the expectable but which— always thoroughly, sometimes gloriously— honors the principle underlying the tradition of the American literary magazine—namely, freely to serve the mind and heart of a free reader."
Gordon Lish

"The best of America's independent literary reviews. The standard bearer of a tradition that must be maintained."
Stephen Jay Gould

the cafe culture magazine

The literary magazine without the pain

Recently we have featured the following writers:
Martin Amis, Nicholson Baker, Thomas Beller, Poppy Z. Brite,
Dennis Cooper, Susan Daitch, Stephen Dixon, Frederick Ted
Castle, Rikki Ducornet, Janice Eidus, James Ellroy, Steve Erickson,
Allen Ginsberg, Jim Goad, Richard Grossman, Scott Heim, Siri
Hustvedt, Jonathan Lethem, David Markson, Sigrid Nunez, Peter
Plate, Joel Rose, Floyd Salas, Gilbert Sorrentino, Paul Theroux,
Lynne Tillman, William T. Vollmann, Elizabeth Wurtzel

Cups Magazine is a national
cafe culture magazine available in cafes across
America. It features articles
about what's happening in
pop culture, literature, music,
film, and fashion.

**If you want to subscribe
to Cups Magazine
Please send a check
for $19.95
Cups Magazine
189 Orchard Street
4th Floor
New York NY 10002**

Bradford Morrow will not be
featured in the next issue

the cafe culture magazine

This is not an academic journal

CALL FOR PAPERS

In the week beginning June 8, 1998, the University of Antwerp and the University of London will host International Pynchon Week. Two complementary events will take place, the first one in Antwerp and the second one in London, with ample travel time in between. The Programme for International Pynchon Studies (PIPS) will help coordinate activities between sites, informing and assisting participants whenever possible.

 Antwerp: *"Gravity's Rainbow:* The First 25 Years"

This two-day conference will attempt to deal with every possible aspect of Pynchon's most intimidating novel, from the film-sprocket holes separating its sections to the history of its critical reception. Unless the number of acceptable proposals exceeds a workable limit, papers (thirty minutes) might all be presented in plenary sessions, so as to assure the development of a conference dynamic. Keynote speakers will include Bernard Duyfhuizen, Steven Weisenburger, and Hanjo Berressem. Publication of conference papers is a certainty. Deadline for two-page proposals: January 1, 1998. Conference organizer: Luc Herman, Department of English, University of Antwerp, Universiteitsplein 1, B-2610 Wilrijk (Antwerp), Belgium. Fax: 32-3-820-27-62. E-mail: Luc.Herman@uia.ua.ac.be.

 London: "Thomas Pynchon: Beyond the Rainbow's End"

This three-day event will attempt to afford the greatest possible diversity of expression arising from the totality of the Pynchon opus, while also allowing for a substantial consideration of *Mason & Dixon,* to which the second day of the conference will be devoted. Participants will include internationally acclaimed critics, novelists, poets, artists, and filmmakers inspired by Pynchon's achievement, as well as a wide variety of scholars wishing to make their first venture Beyond the Rainbow's End. A variety of multimedia events and archival displays will complement an intensive and extensive academic conference schedule. Papers may be any length not exceeding forty-five minutes. Publication of conference papers is a certainty. Deadline for two-page proposals: January 1, 1998. Conference organizer: Eric Alan Weinstein, Centre for English Studies and Institute of United States Studies, The School of Advanced Study, University of London, Senate House, Malet Street, Bloomsbury, London WC1 7HU, Great Britain. Fax: 44-0171-436-4533. E-mail: E.A.Weinstein@qmw.ac.uk, or ces@sas.ac.uk.

Dalkey Archive Press
New & recent titles

Killoyle by Roger Boylan

Pack of Lies by Gilbert Sorrentino

Children of Darkness and Light by Nicholas Mosley

Assassins by Nicholas Mosley

Dalkey
Archive
Press

"Drink, religion, and more than a touch of blarney strut their stuff in this satirical first novel. . . . Boylan's debut succeeds as a work in which the telling is more important—and more beguiling—than the tale."—KIRKUS REVIEWS

$13.95 pb
1-56478-145-3

Killoyle
R o g e r   B o y l a n

Proving that the spirits of James Joyce, Flann O'Brien, and Samuel Beckett still flow in the veins of at least one Irish writer, Roger Boylan has composed a novel filled with hilarity and doom about the inhabitants of the Irish town of Killoyle.

Killoyle wildly celebrates the great Irish tradition of laughter amid despair and tears.

"*A virtuoso performance filled with truly funny turns of phrase and events.*"—PUBLISHERS WEEKLY

"*Pleasure awaits in this hilarious Irish farce, a first novel that captures the absurdly comic spirits of Joyce and Beckett in its depiction of an Emerald Isle town peopled by some most peculiar folk, indeed. Wallowing in such gloomy, traditional Irish concerns as religious angst and too much booze, Boylan's wacky tale is deftly fleshed out with dense footnotes addressed directly to the reader—a clever technique that, in the hands of this skillful writer, helps provide for heaps of hearty laughter amid all the tears. You'll meet characters like would-be poet Milo Rogers and Wolftone Grey, who makes anonymous phone calls exhorting people to believe in God. Highly recommended.*"—LIBRARY JOURNAL

Dalkey
Archive
Press

"Sorrentino has established an artistic beachhead over the past twenty years; one could think of him . . . as a sort of American literary conscience."—WASHINGTON POST

$14.95 pb
1-56478-154-2

Pack of Lies
G i l b e r t S o r r e n t i n o

Pack of Lies gathers together the trilogy of novels previously published individually as *Odd Number, Rose Theatre,* and *Misterioso.* In an attempt to get at the "truth" about what appears to have been a murder, *Pack of Lies* presents readers with a number of characters who proceed to talk about each other and themselves, uncovering numerous contradictions over even the simplest of details. Both deeply sinister and wildly comic, Mr. Sorrentino's assault on the idea of realism in fiction culminates here in a world that is in every way as beguiling and filled with incongruities as the one we inhabit each day.

"Sorrentino has long been one of our most intelligent and daring writers. . . . He is also one of our funniest writers."—NEW YORK TIMES

"A literary game which not only imitates, parodies, satirizes and elaborates upon the fantasies, pleasures, surprises, and disappointments of American life, but also tellingly invents specific possibilities of which American life is incapable. A liberating experience."—LOS ANGELES TIMES

Dalkey
Archive
Press

"It is unputdownable, as exciting as a thriller and as absorbing as any book of ideas—touching on scientific knowledge and what we mean by it, the quantum theory, the situation in Yugoslavia, child 'abuse', terrorism, drugs, modern marriage."—EVENING STANDARD

$13.95 pb
1-56478-151-8

Children of Darkness and Light
N i c h o l a s   M o s l e y

Reports are reaching London that a group of children in Cumbria have seen a vision of the Virgin Mary. Harry, a controversial journalist with a reputation for this line of story, is sent to investigate. He finds complexities multiplying into a range of possibilities—a leak from the local nuclear plant, use or misuse of the children by the authorities, an all-round conspiracy of silence. Most bafflingly, Harry's visit seems to have been expected, his very presence necessary to whatever is to follow.

Harry's search for understanding draws him back first to London, to his wife and his own child; and then to an assignment in the blood-stained shambles of Bosnia. Here, among an entire people acting out a self-destructive catastrophe, he again follows the trail of a story into the hills. This is a similar story—of a group of children who, for the sake of survival, have banded together against the murderous lunacy of adults.

"Like Hopeful Monsters, this book is a testing adventure for the mind. It appears to be proceeding in one intellectual direction and then it reaches a crossroads with the Bosnian war on one side and visionary theology on the other. There is no map, but you do have an attractively sarcastic companion."—TIMES LITERARY SUPPLEMENT

Dalkey
Archive
Press

"When unmistakably brilliant writing is combined with natural insight, the result is likely to be most impressive. Nicholas Mosley writes realistically, with admirable craft and surging talent."—NEW YORK TIMES

$12.95 pb
1-56478-152-6

Assassins
N i c h o l a s   M o s l e y

As one of the characters in *Assassins* says, "Tolstoy was right, you can't beat the Gods. It's the small things—the warp and woof—that make up the pattern. And how much influence do we have over the small? Now that's a theme for a modern writer." And Nicholas Mosley is this writer. Part political thriller and part love story, *Assassins* explores the "small things" that give shape and meaning to the "big events."

The novel begins with a teenage girl riding a white horse into the English countryside. She is kidnapped by an idealistic student planning to assassinate a visiting statesman engaged in critical negotiations with the girl's father, Britain's Foreign Secretary. In the days that follow, these negotiations, as well as the world's future, seem to hang upon the characters' ability to figure out the pattern of the "small things."

"The novel is thoroughly imagined. It is crowded and detailed, yet Mr. Mosley is able to satisfy the reader that there is no routine padding. The child Mary, awkward, inarticulate, blown here and there by the strong winds of policy, yet demonstrating that there is a sense in which she is somehow stronger than they, makes Mr. Mosley's points for him, and is most movingly realized."—TIMES LITERARY SUPPLEMENT

"The reader who follows the course of Assassins *to its appropriately absurd end will be rewarded by a sophisticated plot, a cartographer's awareness of English landscape and a wealth of similes."—TIME*

Dalkey
Archive
Press

Order Form

Individuals may use this form to order Dalkey titles at a 10-20% discount directly from the publisher.

Title	ISBN	Quantity	Price

Subtotal _____

(10% for one book, 20% for two or more books)   Less discount _____

Subtotal _____

($3.50 for the first book, $.75 for each additional)   Plus domestic postage _____

($4.50 for the first book, $1.00 for each additional)   Plus foreign postage _____

Total _____

Ship to:

_____

_____

_____

_____

mail or fax this form to:
Dalkey Archive Press
ISU Campus Box 4241
Normal, IL 61790-4241
fax: 309 438 7422
tel: 309 438 7555

Credit card payment   ❑ Visa   ❑ Mastercard

Acct # _____ Exp. Date _____

Name on card _____

Phone Number _____

Please make checks (in U. S. dollars only) payable to *Dalkey Archive Press*

Dalkey
Archive
Press

You may also visit our website at www.cas.ilstu.edu/english/dalkey/dalkey.html